A HISTORY OF IRISH THOUGHT

Thomas Duddy

London and New York

First published 2002
by Routledge
11 New Fetter Lane, London EC4P 4EE

Simultaneously published in the USA and Canada
by Routledge
29 West 35th Street, New York, NY 10001

Routledge is an imprint of the Taylor & Francis Group

© 2002 Thomas Duddy

Typeset in Garamond by BC Typesetting, Bristol
Printed and bound in Great Britain by
TJ International, Padstow, Cornwall

British Library Cataloguing in Publication Data
A catalogue record for this book is available from the British Library

Library of Congress Cataloging in Publication Data
Duddy, Thomas.
A history of Irish thought / Thomas Duddy.
p.   cm.
Includes bibliographical references and index.
1. Ireland–Intellectual life. 2. Philosophy–Ireland. I. Title.
DA925.D78 2001
941.5′009′9–dc21   2001048674

ISBN 0–415–20692–8 (hbk)
ISBN 0–415–20693–6 (pbk)

A HISTORY OF IRISH THOUGHT

'strikingly original and sorely needed. There is an engaged, illuminating intelligence at work here, reflected in the crisp, remarkably lucid style.'
Terry Eagleton, author of *The Truth about the Irish*

'an admirable job . . . a solid contribution to Irish studies and the history of ideas.'
David Berman, Trinity College, Dublin

'a delight to read.'
Noel Ignatiev, Harvard University

'an important contribution of considerable merit. It is comprehensive, challenging and clearly written, a model of clarity . . . I am very enthusiastic about the book.'
John Newsinger, Bath Spa University College

Thomas Duddy teaches in the Department of Philosophy at the National University of Ireland, Galway.

For my father
and in memory of my mother

CONTENTS

CONTENTS

CONTENTS

CONTENTS

PREFACE

'A history of Irish thought? But surely there isn't such a thing as Irish thought – at least not in the sense in which there is, say, English, French, or German thought!' Since I began a few years ago to work on this book and to tell people, perhaps unadvisedly, about the nature of my undertaking, this is the kind of objection that has most frequently come my way. The assumption behind the objection is that Ireland, given the ebb and flow of its colonial history, has not been in a position to sustain the continuities of culture, institution, and civic life that are the prerequisite for a national, ethnically distinctive intellectual history. Whenever I point out that there is a good deal less continuity in English, French, or German thought than is generally assumed, I am quickly told that there is nonetheless a distinctive clustering of concerns in each case, a distinctive vocabulary, a distinctive ethos or style of thought, and that these marks of distinction are most evident among the great or most important thinkers. When I point out that most great thinkers are highly individual in their thinking and that this fact should weigh against their being easily 'nationalized', I am then told that even genius has roots, that these roots are always grounded in culture, and that culture is always in some sense national. It is usually conceded by these objectors that Ireland has indeed produced a few fine individual thinkers but that these have been isolated figures, that they do not constitute a national tradition of thought, and that their influences were not particularly Irish anyway. So, the objectors reiterate firmly, if with a touch of sympathy, there *really* is no such thing as Irish thought, at least not in the sense in which there is English, French, or German thought.

The clue to the serious error in the objector's position lies in that phrase 'at least not in the sense in which there is English, French, or German thought'. Imperial history is taken as a standard for all national history, as if nations that have been the target of invasion, conquest, and colonization cannot have histories appropriate to themselves – histories that tell a story of disruption, displacement, and discontinuity. The truth is that the intellectual history of Ireland cannot be written if it is assumed that the country must first find itself a past replete with lengthy periods of expansive power, a past created out of the resources of wealth and economic independence, a past held securely in place by weighty continuities of language and culture. But this requirement – the requirement that Ireland find itself an imperial past in order to meet imperial standards of identity and continuity – is a profoundly unjust one, a requirement that adds new insult to old injury. There is, of course, such a thing as Irish thought, but it cannot be characterized in imperially nationalistic terms, or in any terms that presuppose privileged identities or privileged periods of social and cultural evolution. Non-imperial or colonized nations will have a different story to tell. Instead of a history of shared vocabularies and shared frameworks continually exploited by like-minded individuals of talent and genius, there will be a history of conflicting vocabularies and shattered frameworks, sporadically and irregularly exploited by gifted individuals. Influences on these individuals of talent and genius may come from anywhere, and are most likely to come from the direction of powerfully impressive neighbouring cultures. Instead of contributing to evolving native traditions they are more likely to find themselves contributing to traditions evolving elsewhere. Instead of finding patronage at home, these individual thinkers are more likely to find patronage and stimulation in exile. In a cultural and political environment of shifting allegiances and shifting vectors of power and patronage, there will be constant uncertainty about identity and provenance. Each thinker's most defining relationship will not be with a relatively stable internal 'native' culture but with the particular circumstances that obtain at a particular historical time. Irish thinkers, if you like, are not going to be at home as much as thinkers from imperial nations.

'But surely this could be put another way. Some of your Irish thinkers are not as much at home in Ireland as you might like to think. Some of them are only accidentally Irish. Many of them are people of Irish birth but English blood – people like Molyneux, Berkeley, Swift. Are these really Irish thinkers?' This represents the second kind of objection that I've most frequently encountered, and it is prompted, like the first, by a blithely imperial sense of history. The assumption in this case is that the 'accidental' is somehow less real than the supposedly more substantial continuities of nature and race. But the histories of dependent, colonized nations are for the most part histories of 'accidents' – accidental births of history-making individuals, accidental implications of the outcomes of war, accidental shifts in political allegiances, accidental catastrophes at home and abroad. The more vulnerable a nation is to events occurring abroad, the more prone it is to the momentous accidents of history. For accidental, then, read historical. When Jonathan Swift protested that he was an accidental Irishman, we should accept that this was in fact true. But we should accept it only on condition that 'accidental' is taken to mean something like 'historical' – historical in that deep and defining sense in which we want to use the term here. Swift is accidentally Irish in the sense that anyone born in Ireland is, in some sense, accidentally Irish. In a country with a history of settlement, displacement, and emigration, it is to some significant degree a matter of accident whether even those with the longest Irish roots are born in Ireland or elsewhere. To say that Swift is Irish in this context is to say that he is Irish, like everyone else, by dint of history. We will find that Swift's historical Irishness is confirmed and deepened by his own distinctive contribution to Protestant or Hibernian patriotism, itself an 'accidental' but pivotal development in modern Irish political thought.

Even an earlier thinker like Robert Boyle, who was far from being a Hibernian patriot, is Irish by force of history and also, like many members of the Anglo-Irish ascendancy, Irish by privilege. This concept of 'Irishness by privilege' will be used from time to time throughout this book, but it is particularly useful in confirming Boyle's Irishness. Boyle's wealth, which enabled him to become a self-supporting scientist and experimenter, came from the vast estate that his opportunistic father had carved out of the Irish landscape.

He therefore had a powerfully vested interest in the land of Ireland, even if his orientation was towards English life and culture. This conscious orientation is not very relevant. What is far more relevant is Boyle's defining relationship with the historical and material conditions that lay at the foundation of his intellectual life. This relationship has Irish history inscribed all over it. Consciousness and orientation aside, Boyle is for the best of reasons – that is, material and historical reasons – indisputably an Irish thinker, and no apology will be made for his inclusion here.

What is presented in this book, then, is the intellectual history of a country with a particular kind of past – a past marked by periods of invasion, plantation, and social upheaval alternating with periods of assimilation, recovery, and reconfiguration. The intellectual history of Ireland is the history of a country that finds itself hosting some thinkers, while sending others into exile, a country that finds different kinds of thinkers on its shores, either coming or going, all of them touched by intellectual and cultural traditions that may have originated anywhere but locally. The history of Irish thought has its own peculiarity and uniqueness, but it is a peculiarity and uniqueness that must not be analysed in terms of blood and race, or even in terms of native genius, but in terms of the contingencies of history and of the fruitful interactions of accidental individuals with those contingencies. Such a history will be characterized most of all by its inclusiveness – a degree of inclusiveness that may indeed trouble those who are committed to narrowly exclusive senses of ethnic or national identity. Historically, Irish cultural nationalists have been pleased to accept Matthew Arnold's notion that the Celts are distinguished by a sensuous nature and a determination to reject 'the despotism of fact'. These cultural nationalists have been inclined therefore to sing the praises of Ireland's imaginative, especially its literary, achievements at the expense of the country's contribution in other areas of cultural activity. The Irish contribution to the history of thought has been marginalized, partly because thought has been too narrowly understood, partly because much of the best 'thinking' was done by individuals whose Irishness was in question, and partly because an emphasis on thought would be an effective refusal of that backhanded Arnoldian compliment with its emphasis on imagination and sentiment rather than on reason and intellect. It may also be the case that, during a period of urgent nationalist reclamation and redefinition, both imagination and sensibility lend themselves more easily to racial or ethnic characterization than do reason and intellect. After all, intellect travels, goes abroad, spreads its wings, tends to be unpredictable and eclectic in its range of interests, and therefore less easy to 'nationalize' or domesticate than imagination or sensibility.

The period of reclamation and redefinition may not be past, but the time is surely ripe for the development of modes of reclamation and redefinition that are confident enough and generous enough to embrace Ireland's neglected intellectual history. Apart from Richard Kearney's ground-breaking anthology *The Irish Mind* (1985), no attempt has hitherto been made to write a comprehensive and up-to-date account of Irish thought. Of course, there have been fine publications on individual thinkers or individual works, including the recent book by Philip McGuinness, Alan Harrison, and Richard Kearney on John Toland's *Christianity not Mysterious*. And there have been some excellent contributions on particular aspects or areas of Irish thought, such as David Berman's work on eighteenth-century Irish thinkers or John Wilson Foster's work on Irish scientific culture, of which his *Nature in Ireland* (1997) is the most significant and most visible product. The aim of *A History of Irish Thought* is to build on, extend, and complement the work of Kearney, Berman, Foster, and others by offering for the first time a synoptic, wide-ranging, inclusive survey of the varieties of Irish thought, beginning with the thought of the anonymous seventh-century monk, the Irish Augustine, concluding with the thought of the contemporary Irish political philosopher, Philip Pettit, and taking into account along the way the ideas of political economists and social reformers as well as of moralists, metaphysicians, and satirists. A small number of these thinkers have been assumed already into the 'Western' intellectual canon, while many others are neglected minor thinkers who engaged intelligently and earnestly with the controversies of their time and who still merit respectful attention. I cannot claim, of course, to have attempted an exhaustive study of all the minor thinkers of any period, or of the thought of all the poets, scientists, or clerics who made some contribution to intellectual history. I can only hope that the particular assortment of minor and marginal thinkers who succeeded in interesting and impressing me will also succeed in interesting and impressing others.

Traditionally, histories of thought have been histories of particular forms or levels of thought — that is, fairly speculative, fairly worked out, fairly original, fairly accessible forms of thought. This is a generous conception but it is not an unduly nebulous one, and it is the one that I will work with throughout this book. It will enable me to cover the kinds of ideas that we find in philosophy, theology, and science, in political and cultural theory, in the best polemical and satirical writing (such as the writing of Jonathan Swift), and in certain kinds of 'visionary' writing (such as the prose essays of W.B. Yeats). The main difficulty arises with highly technical, specialized writing, such as one finds in contemporary scientific journals. That sort of material is simply not accessible to the public and cannot be made accessible to a reader who has not had a lengthy process of technical education. In any case, such material is often neither very speculative nor very original — it is part of the technical puzzle-solving activity of a professional group of academic workers, and as such is no more communicable to a general readership than the technical reports of engineers in some branch of industry. Very useful and necessary work, to be sure, but having no more to do with the history of thought than the records of decisions made by engineers. Material of such a technical and specialized nature is not discussed here, but the more accessible — and quite revolutionary — ideas of the early scientific thinker Robert Boyle are discussed in Chapter 3, while the relatively plain-spoken, conscientious responses of Irish thinkers to the theories of Charles Darwin are discussed in Chapter 8.

ACKNOWLEDGEMENTS

I must begin by expressing my indebtedness to a number of scholars whose intensive studies in their specialized fields have made this book possible. In the first chapter I rely on Francis P. MacGinty's careful translation and scholarly annotation of the Latin texts of the Irish Augustine, while in the second chapter I am indebted to the Sheldon-Williams and O'Meara translations of John Scottus Eriugena. I am grateful to Liam Chambers for drawing my attention to, and permitting me to read his work in progress on, Michael Moore. In the case of the chapters on eighteenth-century thinkers I owe a particular debt to the original historical and interpretive work of David Berman. For the chapters on the nineteenth century, I am indebted to the researches and counsels of faculty colleague, Tadhg Foley, who is a connoisseur of little-known or forgotten nineteenth-century Irish thinkers. Some of the less celebrated figures from this period owe their inclusion to Dr Foley's unflagging advocacy.

I am indebted also to those who read and corrected early drafts of the various chapters, and to those who answered queries, or provided me with solicited and unsolicited materials, or simply gave encouragement along the way. These put-upon readers, patient responders, long-suffering encouragers, and magnanimous providers of materials include Tom Boylan, Dan Carey, Liam Chambers, Dolores Dooley, Steve Ellis, John Foley, Adrian Frasier, Luke Gibbons, Colm Luibhéid, Niall Ó Cíosáin, Dáibhí Ó Cróinín, Paschal O'Gorman, Rosaleen O'Neill, Bill Starr, and Markus Wörner. Thanks of a more formal and more general nature are owed to the members of the Arts Faculty of the National University of Ireland, Galway, for a research grant awarded from the university's Millennium Research Fund.

Finally, a special word of thanks to individual members of two different library staffs – to Margaret Hughes in the Special Collections reading room of the James Hardiman Library at the National University of Ireland, Galway, for her patience, helpfulness, and courtesy; and to Bart Hollingsworth of the library staff at Brown University, Rhode Island, for making it possible for me to consult a rare and fragile item from their eighteenth-century holdings.

1

INTERPRETING MARVELS

The Irish Augustine

If the predominantly oral culture of pre-Christian Celtic Ireland contained much in the way of philosophical, speculative, or abstract thought there is no evidence for it. Significantly, the rich heritage of myths, legends, and sagas transcribed by the early monastic scribes in Ireland does not contain even fragments of philosophical specu-lation. Despite the claims made by Herbert Moore Pim (1920) that an Irish idealist tradition originated with the druidic belief system, there is really no serious evidence of a druidic Socrates whose wise say-ings might have been recorded by the same scribes who were happy to record the Celtic mythological tales. The most we can say is that the pre-Christian Celtic philosophies were 'sacral, not Socratic', that they were part of a tradition of knowledge that was 'ceremonial rather than critical' (Rankin 1996: 297). Regardless then of how impressed we are by the artistic and imaginative achievements of the pre-historic period in Ireland (as recorded in the archaeological evidence and in the transcribed literature), there is no denying that the properly historical period begins in the fifth century with the introduction of Christianity – that is, with the arrival of 'the religion of the book' (Richter 1995: 219). Christianity brought literacy, writing, documents – the makings of history, including intellectual history – to the island of Ireland. A history of Irish thought cannot therefore begin earlier than the intro-duction of Christianity and Christian literacy.

The early writings of a culture, however, are rarely philosophical or speculative. The earliest writings in Ireland were predominantly

1

connected with the day-to-day preaching and teaching of the new Christian belief. These writings included gospel-texts, psalm-books, biblical commentaries, lives of the saints, penitentials (handbooks of penance), Latin grammars, and computistical manuals (attempts to reckon the correct date of Easter). Although biblical exegesis and commentary would in due course develop into theological analysis and speculation, most of the Irish writings from the early Christian monastic period are not the product of individual speculative genius. One of the earliest documented references to an 'Irish' thinker is both uncomplimentary and of doubtful accuracy, despite the fact that it was made by no less a figure than St Jerome (c. AD 370–420), best known for his Latin translation of the Bible, namely, the Vulgate. In the prologue to his *Commentary on Jeremiah*, written early in the fifth century, Jerome refers to 'an ignorant calumniator', a most stupid fellow 'heavy with Irish porridge', who had the temerity to criticize the good saint's earlier commentary on the Epistles of Paul to the Ephesians. The offending party is Pelagius. Though he is not named in these recriminatory remarks, it is known that Jerome was then engaged in controversy with Pelagius, as were other leading lights of the church, including St Augustine. The name of Pelagius is associated with a heresy that ran counter to the teaching of the church fathers on original sin, baptism, freedom of the will, and the nature of divine grace. Pelagius had emphasized the freedom of the human will, the ability of human reason to know God implicitly and to act in accordance with the divinely instituted laws of nature that are inscribed in the human heart. In particular, he had argued that human beings had the ability to be without sin. This struck at the notion of original sin and also threatened the importance of divine grace. Instead of accepting the notion of the congenital sinfulness of human beings, Pelagius regarded sinfulness as a habit developed historically rather than as a necessary inheritance of fallen human nature.

Most scholars no longer accept that Pelagius was Irish. The brief allusion by Jerome to his 'Irish' adversary is not confirmed by other anti-Pelagian commentators, who refer to their heretical antagonist as a Briton. James Kenney thinks that Jerome's reference to his adversary's Irishness is not so much a mistake as a way of expressing opprobrium. There is little doubt that Jerome had a poor opinion of the Irish (or *Scotti*, as the Irish were then called). In one of his treatises

Jerome reports having seen Irish people feeding on human flesh. He also observes that the Irish are sexually promiscuous and 'take their pleasure like the beasts of the field' (Kenney 1993: 138). Given this antipathy towards both the Irish in general and Pelagius in particular, it is perhaps no surprise that, as Kenney puts it, 'that opprobrious term *Scottus* had that freedom from ethnological accuracy which characterized vituperative literature then as now' (162). Kenney raises the possibility that Pelagius was Irish only in the sense that he belonged to one of the Irish settlements in Britain. One Pelagian scholar has concluded that all we can now say with conviction about the origins and early life of Pelagius is that he was in fact a Briton, that he was born some time in the early part of the second half of the fourth century, that he emigrated to Rome in the early eighties and was neither a monk nor a priest. The rest, he adds, is buried in the quicksand of the 'pre-history' of the once-maligned heresiarch (Rees 1988: xiv). This, for the purposes of this history, is how the matter stands. It is worth noting, however, that the work of Pelagius was known to the early Irish church. It has been claimed that one of his few remaining works, his *Commentaries on the Epistles of St Paul*, has survived only because it was preserved in the Irish schools (Kenney 1993: 163).

ENTER, THE IRISH AUGUSTINE

The first extant work by an Irish hand to have an explicitly interpretative, argumentative, and modestly philosophical content is *De mirabilibus sacrae scripturae* (*On the Marvels of Sacred Scripture*), a Hiberno-Latin treatise which has been dated, on the basis of internal evidence, to 655. The anonymous author is thought to be Irish because of direct references to Ireland in the text and because of other references – to tidal data, for example – which are consistent with Irish topography (see MacGinty 1985). He is called the Irish *Augustine* because his treatise was for some time believed to be part of the corpus of St Augustine of Hippo and was even included in early printed editions of St Augustine's writings. The reason for the erroneous attribution lies in the prologue to the treatise itself, in the opening sentence of which the author represents himself as *Augustinus* and proceeds to dedicate his treatise to the bishops and priests of Carthage. While some scholars suggest a deliberate attempt at forgery, possibly by a third party (Esposito 1919), others suggest that the use of the name Augustinus is a playful and harmless *jeu d'esprit* (Grosjean 1955), while yet others go so far as to argue for a Hiberno-Latin tradition of pseudonymous authorship that 'had as much to do with erudite games as the concealment of identity or the enhancement of authority' (Herren 1996: 131). The most generous scholars simply take the name Augustinus to be a patristic pen name and leave it at that (Richter 1988; Ó Cróinín 1995). Perhaps the wisest conclusion to come to at this distance from the original events is to say with Kenney: 'Either the author adopted the Latin form "Augustinus" or some later scribe, with or without intent to deceive, modified the name into that of the famous Father of the Church' (1993: 276).

While it can be read as a contribution to biblical exegesis and commentary, with particular reference to the miracles described in both the Old and New Testaments, the *De mirabilibus* also contains an attempt to make sense of the miracles in the light of a more or less naturalistic conception of divine creation. This in itself is a surprising feature of the text. Why should the anonymous author – almost certainly a monk – have a difficulty with the miracles, especially those recounted in the Bible? After all, other early writers, especially the hagiographers, did not hesitate to attribute miracles to their saintly subjects. If the early Christians generally did not have a difficulty with miracles why should the Irish Augustine wish to make an issue of them? We are not surprised that later philosophers, such as the empiricists and rationalists of the eighteenth century, should have a difficulty with the very idea of a miracle. Hume's essay 'Of Miracles', contained in his *Enquiry concerning Human Understanding* (1748), is essentially an essay in applied empiricism, and is, moreover, a sophisticated piece of reasoning that has behind it a millennium of philosophical analysis and exploration. But why should a member of an early monastic Christian community wish to rationalize miracles and seek to make them fit in with a naturalistic understanding of creation?

One possible answer is that the Irish Augustine saw miracles as too close to the magical elements in the pagan beliefs which the early Christians were striving to supplant. In this regard, he may be registering the influence of his mentor, St Augustine of Hippo, who remonstrated at length with the pagan beliefs of his contemporaries. In other words, he may be responding to the strong undercurrents of pagan belief prevalent in early Christian Ireland. While it is true that the early Irish missionaries sometimes accommodated themselves to existing pagan practices – by, for example, turning pagan sacred sites into Christian holy places – they nevertheless needed to put down clear markers in key areas of belief and doctrine. The pagan magicians were reputed to be able to control nature by appealing to the pantheon of gods and spirits who inhabited the natural world. The Christians, on the other hand, wished to show that their belief system was a substantively different one, that there was only one magician or wonder-worker, namely, God, and that he worked miracles that were in harmony with nature – that were in harmony, that is, with his own original creation. It is arguable that the Irish Augustine was anxious to make a fundamental distinction between a magical pagan conception of nature and a monotheistic Christian conception. His aim was not to deny the possibility of Christian miracles but to show that these miracles, when they occur, are always consistent with the laws of nature – laws of nature that are, first and foremost, God's own laws. The Irish Augustine is not a precursor of the rationalist or humanist seeking to square revelation with reason. He does not have a difficulty with revelation, or with arguments from authority. Neither does he question the veracity of the Bible as far as the reporting of miracles is concerned. At the same time, however, he possesses an independent, questioning mind, and is slow to defer to existing authorities. His reasoning may be securely bounded by the parameters of his religious faith but it is nonetheless reasoning of a sufficiently critical and reflective kind to be considered theological or philosophical.

The key intuition of the Irish Augustine, reiterated throughout his treatise, is that God governs the world without substantively adding to it or amending it, or doing anything that is inconsistent with the completeness of his original act of creation. This intuition turns on a distinction between creation (*creatio*) and governance or government (*gubernatio*). As far as creation is concerned, there is nothing new under the sun. All of nature was created over the six-day period described in the first chapters of the first book of the Bible. On the sixth day God perfected his creation of the diversity of natures and

species, and on the seventh day he rested from this work of creation —
but he did not rest from the work of government or 'management'.
While Genesis highlights the original foundational work of divine
creativity, it may be assumed that God did not abandon his creation
but has continued to oversee and govern it, sometimes directly inter-
vening to uncover or develop its hidden potentials. God should be
understood therefore as governor as well as creator, but acts of governance should not be confused with acts of creation. Even if we should see
something new or exceptional appear before us, we should not assume
that this is a new creation or an addition to creation. The sorts of
marvels reported in the Bible may give the impression that God
continues to create new natures or realities but this is a mistaken
impression. What the creator does is to bring forth from nature
what was contained or hidden within it since the beginning of created
time. Although terms like potency or potentiality are not used by the
Irish Augustine, the concept is implicit in his thinking.

THE THEOLOGY OF THE FLOOD

In some of the early chapters of the first book of his treatise, the Irish
Augustine discusses a number of problems that seem to arise around
the biblical account of the flood (Gen. 6–8). There is, first, the question
of why only land animals were destroyed in the flood. If God wished to
destroy all living creatures, with the exception of those brought by
Noah within the safety of the ark, why were the aquatic creatures
spared from divine retribution? Why did God not also curse the
waters when he cursed Adam and all earthly species? The Irish
Augustine's solution is that when Adam sinned by eating the for-
bidden fruit he did so by eating the fruit of the earth, not the fruit
of the sea. The earth and its fruits, therefore, are condemned by association with the original sin of Adam, while the sea and its species remain
innocent. The divine privileging of water is also indicated by the fact
that water is used sacramentally in baptism; the privileging of aquatic
life itself is suggested by the fact that the Lord 'did not eat the flesh of
land but of aquatic animals, when, to confirm his resurrection in the
presence of his disciples, he took and ate a piece of broiled fish and a

comb of honey' (1971: 21; all references to *De mirabilibus* are to the 1971 MacGinty translation).

A more specific – and more difficult – conundrum is posed by the amphibian creatures. Since the amphibians can live neither on land alone nor in the water alone, how did *they* escape the flood? If they were shut up in the ark, they would have been unable to live without the aid of water, and so would not have survived; but if they had remained outside the ark they would have had no place to rest, sleep, or breed, and so would not have survived. But at least some amphibian creatures are still with us, so they must have survived somehow. The Irish Augustine will not allow a miraculous solution. It will not do to say that God used his miraculous power to alter either side of the already God-given nature of the amphibians – not because God couldn't work such a miracle but because attributing such a miracle to him in this case would mean attributing an inconsistency or an imperfection to him. For, 'how could he wish to keep these by miraculous power, who did not wish to preserve Noe and his household by miracle, but by the ark?' (22). To avoid attributing an ad-hoc miracle to the creator, the Irish Augustine suggests that some resting place may have been available to the amphibian creatures on the roof of the ark itself. The roof of the ark could have provided the equivalent of a 'dry land' space to enable them to move safely to and from the waters of the flood (23).

Many other biblical marvels are accommodated in a similar manner, though not always conclusively. The onset and retreat of the great flood itself present the Irish Augustine with a particular problem, leading him to discuss several different accounts of the matter without giving greater authority to one over another. We are, he says, 'held back by the littleness of our knowledge from resolving the difficulty of this matter with a definite opinion' (23). The particular difficulty here is caused by the exceptional and unprecedented nature of the flood. If the flood is not a wholly new phenomenon – either a new creation or an ad-hoc addition to creation – then how can such an exceptional event be explained in terms consistent with the completion of creation at the end of the six days? Where did so much water come from, and where did it go? What capacities of nature made such an unprecedented event possible? The Bible account identifies the two obvious sources for the waters that constituted the flood, namely, the 'springs of the great abyss' and 'the floodgates of heaven'. The Irish Augustine finds that the experts or 'masters' disagree on the precise nature of the springs of the abyss (or the deep) and also on the location of the floodgates. They do not agree on whether the springs existed from creation, or were brought into being on the occasion of the flood. Nor do they agree on whether the increase of water from the abyss is to be understood as 'unwonted flooding' – an unusually massive swelling or expansion of the volume of water – or simply a redistribution of an already existing and constant body of water. If the water burst forth from the springs as a result of expansion, then the receding of the same could be explained as shrinkage, while also allowing for a certain amount of absorption by the soil. On the other hand, if the deluge was effected by redistribution, then its retreat from the land can be explained quite mechanically, as the return of the water to whatever spaces or cavities it vacated when it flowed up out of the abyss. There is disagreement too over the nature of the heavenly floodgates. For some authorities the floodgates are understood to have been located in the clouds – the same clouds from which we receive normal rainfall – but for others they were situated in the highest firmament, 'which God made in the beginning to divide the waters from the waters' (26). Rather than choose between these competing theories, the Irish Augustine remains undecided, even emphasizing the mystery that still surrounds the everyday ebbing and flowing of the ocean tides. Given the mystery of the ordinary tidal movements, it follows that an even greater mystery must continue to surround the extraordinary ebbing and flowing that was the great flood. We have some knowledge in these matters, he concedes – and goes on to make observations about the relationship between the moon and the tides, including the neap tides and spring tides – but there is always so much more to be known that we cannot hope to achieve complete wisdom until we arrive at the everlasting kingdom where there is no ignorance.

Before he concludes his speculative musings about the flood the Irish Augustine reiterates his point – which is the only point he wants to make – that this particular marvel was not, despite its apparent uniqueness, contrary to nature. We do not need to understand fully how it was done in order to appreciate *that* it was done, and that it was done, moreover, within the limits of the first creation. Regardless of which theory one might opt for, each theory is consistent with the natural order of the original creation. The expansion or 'swelling-forth' of the waters in the abyss might look like a more marvellous eventuality than mere mechanical upsurge, but in fact there is a precedent for such expansiveness in nature, 'for it is not contrary to custom that we see even small things grow into greater' (31). The seas themselves give witness to this reality when they rise beyond their ancient boundaries, thereby creating new islands. He makes the interesting scientific observation that the wild animals which inhabit islands 'are proven to have been found there at the time of the separation of the islands from the neighbouring land and not brought there by human effort' (32). He adds that this was how such animals as wolves, deer, foxes, badgers, hares, and squirrels came to be in Ireland in the aftermath of the flood, implicitly rejecting St Augustine's hypothesis (briefly stated in his *City of God*, 1998: XVI, 7) that animals on remote islands might have sprung up from the earth itself as they sprang up in the beginning when God said: 'Let the earth bring forth the living creature'. An explanation of the kind suggested by the Irish Augustine or by St Augustine himself was necessary in order to account for the reappearance of wild animals on islands so far from the mainland that they could not have swum there from the mainland, given the assumption that the ark would have released its menagerie of saved animals on to some part of the mainland.

THE THEOLOGY OF MARVELS

While it is difficult to extrapolate clear principles of explanation from the Irish Augustine's answers to his opening questions about land animals and amphibians, it could be argued that his approach to the problem of the receding flood is based on what might be dubbed 'a principle of accelerated increase'. On this putative principle, the biblical flood can be understood as an example of the abnormal (but not unnatural) enlargement of an already existing natural phenomenon, even if the mechanism involved remains unknown to us. The same principle of accelerated increase is implicitly used to explain the transformation of Lot's wife into a pillar of salt (Gen. 19: 26) and the multiplication of the loaves and fishes (Luke 9: 12–17). There is evidence that small amounts of salt are already present in the human body. All that happens in the case of Lot's unfortunate wife when she turns to take a last backward glance at the city of corruption is that her whole body is rapidly converted into the substance of a small part it. While it remains true that what happened was marvellous and required the intervention of 'the powerful Governor', nevertheless no new substance or principle is needed to explain what happened. In the case of the multiplication of loaves and fishes there is also a principle of increase at work, albeit in a different sense. All natural, living things have been commanded to increase and multiply, and this they do in the normal course of events over a period of time. God, through his creation of a fruitful earth, has been feeding multitudes of human beings since the beginning of time – a relatively marvellous process in itself. All that happens in the case of the multitudes in the New Testament story is that the process of divine sustenance is speeded up, and some of the intermediate stages have been bypassed. God can, as it were, expedite the processes of food-provision and make happen in an instant what would normally take a period of time. The Irish Augustine introduces a useful distinction here between a higher and a lower method of divine governance. The lower method is at work in the daily processes of increasing and multiplying, while the higher method is evident in the more marvellous instances. In both cases, however, it is the same original activity of increasing and multiplying that is at work, and it is the same natural substances that are worked upon.

Other explanatory concepts used by the Irish Augustine include natural reversal, natural parallels (or precedents), natural versatility, angelic ministry, and illusion. The notion of natural reversal is used to explain what happens when Moses strikes the rock at Horeb, causing water to pour from it (Exod. 17: 6). The Irish Augustine accepts without question the popular belief of his time that rocks and other hard substances, such as crystals, were made from densely compacted snow or water that has remained unthawed. While the normal process is from water to rock, it is still within the bounds of nature that in certain circumstances God could simply cause the process to be reversed. Such reversals are not unnatural or essentially mysterious since they occur in natural substances anyway and are merely a temporary unravelling of a normal process, rather on a par with the thawing of ice or the decay of a plant or other matter. There may be supernatural agency behind the flowing of the water at Horeb, but the event involves natural substances – rock, water – and has some precedent in natural processes.

The Irish Augustine has recourse to natural parallels in order to make even the incarnation and virgin birth of Christ intelligible in terms of created nature. It may look as if this event is rather uniquely outside nature and therefore something truly new and inexplicable. But it is not as unique or as 'unnatural' as it looks. In the first place, the substance of Christ's flesh is taken from a woman's womb, which suggests that at least part of a natural process is involved in the incarnation. In the second place, the process of fatherless generation can be seen in other species. In the Irish Augustine's unreconstructed folk biology, bees are generated without fathers 'by the warming of their mother's body only, and all flying things of that kind conceive their offspring in such wise' (1971: 154). In what is perhaps the most risky, most potentially profane piece of reasoning in the treatise, the Irish Augustine suggests a parallel between the virgin birth and the fatherless self-replication of the worm, adding obscurely that the Lord himself did not disdain to say 'by the prophet' that his incarnation resembled this lowly process. The point of the strained parallel, however, is not to belittle Christ's birth in any sense or to glorify, in a pantheistic sense, the life of the worm, but simply to extend the 'logic' of a familiar natural process to a very special event in human history, the better to bring it within the bounds of originally created nature.

The natural versatility of some substances is used to explain the transformation of water into blood in the Egypt of the recalcitrant Pharaoh (Exod. 7: 17–20). Water is present in all liquids and is daily and routinely absorbed by all sorts of substance as part of the natural process of sustenance and refreshment. In the vine tree, for example, water is converted in the natural course of events into the colour and taste of wine; in the olive tree the same water is converted into a form of oil; when it is digested by bees it ends up as honey. The same water, then, when passed through three different processes, yields three different substances with different properties. Water also takes the form of milk, blood, bile, tears, and numerous other liquescent substances, all of which are essential to life. It is no wonder then that God should be able to exploit the natural versatility of this commonly protean substance and simply accomplish in a moment what a natural process can accomplish over the longer span. The changing of water to blood is not contrary to nature but is, once again, a fast-forwarding or expediting of an otherwise common event.

Exodus presents the Irish Augustine with many of the marvels that he needs to 'naturalize'. This is to be expected, since God, before he commands Moses to return to Egypt to help the afflicted children of Israel, gives him the power to 'do signs' before the Pharaoh (Exod. 4: 17). Before giving him this power, God first demonstrates to Moses the kinds of signs he will be able to do. He begins by changing the rod held by Moses into a serpent and then back into a rod again (Exod. 4: 2–4). The Irish Augustine is unable to find a precedent in nature for this too-magical transformation. It will not do to say that, since all things are made of earth, therefore the nature of the rod is convertible in principle into a living serpent. If that were the case, then anything can change into anything else and we will be obliged to give our consent 'to the ridiculous fables of the magicians who say that their ancestors wandered through the ages as birds' (1971: 52). We will be obliged moreover to concede that God has not created fixed natures after all, that there is anarchy in nature. The Irish Augustine agrees with those authorities who prefer to say that the rod in Moses' hand was only changed into the likeness of a serpent in the imagination of Moses. Later, Aaron's casting down of a rod to change it into a serpent before the Pharaoh – only to have the Pharaoh's magicians conjure up their own serpents, which are duly swallowed up by Aaron's rod – is just a more elaborate version of the earlier illusion. The Irish Augustine suggests that since only the doing or showing of a *sign* was necessary, this function could be served as much by an illusion as by a really magical or miraculous transformation. It is more reasonable to opt here for an explanation in terms of illusion, because illusions are more in accordance with what happens in the normal course of events than are magical transformations of one kind of thing into another: 'For nothing is found in the nature of wood which could make a serpent, and accordingly, save at the time of the sign, that which was naturally a rod, always seemed to look like a rod' (53). The raising of Samuel from the dead is also interpreted as an illusion conjured up by the pagan priestess of En-dor to whom Saul appealed when he failed to receive a response from God (1 Sam. 28: 14–19). There is a strong hint here of the general maxim on which Hume, writing a millennium later, would base his essay on miracles, namely, the maxim that 'no testimony is sufficient to establish a miracle, unless the testimony be of such a kind, that its falsehood would be more miraculous, than the fact, which it endeavours to establish' (Hume 1975: 116). Significantly, Hume uses an example that involves not only illusion and deception but also the idea of restoration from death:

> When anyone tells me, that he saw a dead man restored to life, I immediately consider with myself, whether it be more probable, that this person should either deceive or be deceived, or that the fact which he relates, should really have happened. I weigh the one miracle against the other; and according to the superiority, which I discover, I pronounce my decision, and always reject the greater miracle.
>
> (116)

Like the Irish Augustine, albeit on the basis of more elaborate and transparent reasoning, Hume opts for the lesser or more probable marvel – in this case, an exceptionally cogent illusion rather than an unnatural event as reported.

THE THEOLOGY OF ANGELIC MINISTRY

One of the explanatory concepts used by the Irish Augustine – the concept of angelic intervention – would not have met with the approval of the sceptical Hume. Several marvels, including the descent of manna from heaven (Exod. 16: 15–18) and the star moving before the Magi (Matt. 2: 9–11), are explained in terms of secret intervention by angels. Since angels are considered part of creation along with visible, palpable, corporeal things, it causes the Irish Augustine no difficulty to interpolate them into his explanations. His conception of nature or creation is broader and more essentially biblical than that of latter-day rationalists or naturalists. It may seem odd that he should have a difficulty about manna or the moving star but not about the existence of angels. There is, however, no oddness if we understand the framework within which the Irish Augustine is reasoning. Angels are presumed to have been created and to have existed before the creation of the physical world, as described in Genesis, but there is no reference in Genesis to bread that can rain from heaven or to stars that can depart from their natural positions in the firmament. Hence the need to explain these seemingly worldly marvels. The Irish Augustine insists that the manna, though described as heavenly food and as the bread of angels, was in fact solid in nature and earthly in origin, otherwise it would not have served as sustenance for human beings. The manna originated in that upper part of the earth – the 'heavens' in a worldly sense – where hail and snow are produced, and may be described as the bread of angels only to the extent that it was 'administered' by angels. Its origin was as natural as the origin of hailstones. Once again, God did not produce food from outside created nature but from the earth itself. Of course, he *could* have furnished the people with ordinary bread but chose a more marvellous way in order to remind the people that they do not live by bread alone but by every word which proceeds from the mouth of God (1971: 68–9).

Angels are granted an even more active role, at least hypothetically, in explaining the movements of the star that guided the Magi to the birthplace of Christ at Bethlehem. The Irish Augustine does not accept that a star can have actually moved from its established position in the firmament. Although he could have argued from a geocentric point of view that there is some movement in the heavens – such as the rising and setting of the sun and the waxing and waning of the moon – he prefers to think that the heavens are fixed and are the same now as they were at the time of their creation. He does not think that the gospel account can gainsay the Genesis account, but admits two possibilities, both involving heavenly shape-shifters. Either an angel assumed the appearance of a star in order to serve as a guide for the Magi (who were astrologers in any case); or, alternatively, the Holy Spirit – already noted in scripture for his transformation into doves and tongues of fire – did so instead.

THE IRISH AUGUSTINE AND THE
AFRICAN DOCTOR

Assessments of the Irish Augustine, mostly by historians and mediev-alists, have ranged from disparagement to qualified praise. Certainly, if his single extant treatise is placed against the voluminous and mas-sively influential work of his intellectual mentor, St Augustine of Hippo (353–430), then the Irish treatise is diminished in the com-parison. The comparison is, however, an unfair one. Apart from con-siderations of individual genius, there is a world of difference between the intellectual culture of St Augustine and that of his later pseudonymous namesake. Born in a Roman province of Africa to a Christian mother and pagan father, St Augustine had access to classical literature and learning, and while still a young man was sent by a wealthy benefactor to study rhetoric in the African city of Carthage. Before his baptism into 'Catholic Christianity' at the age of thirty-two he would live a full cultural and intellectual life. He would, for example, fall seriously under the influence of Manicheism, dally awhile with philosophical scepticism, and fully experience the intellec-tual attractions of Neoplatonism. Professionally, he would hold impor-tant teaching positions in the discipline of rhetoric in Carthage and Milan. Out of this rich and varied cultural mix his individual genius would eventually produce a voluminous literature on religious, theo-logical, political, and philosophical questions. No such heady cultural mix was available to the Irish Augustine. Though the monasteries of seventh-century Ireland were indeed centres of learning, the learning was not, for the most part, classical learning. The monastic culture of the early centuries of Irish Christianity was largely responsible for Ireland's reputation as an island of saints and scholars, but the scholars in question were more concerned with the promulgation of the Christian message than with classical learning. They were concerned with matters of faith, penance, and ritual rather than with the more thought-provoking matters of theology and philosophy. The pagan culture with which they had to come to terms was very different from the pagan culture with which St Augustine remonstrated at length in his *City of God*. Whereas St Augustine's pagan protagonists were themselves formidably cultured and literate, well-versed in Greek thought and literature, those whom the early Irish monks

encountered belonged to a culture that had been predominantly 'bar-
baric' and oral during the classical era. Instead of sharpening their
wits in the course of critical engagement with the texts of established
schools of pre-Christian philosophers, the early Irish scholars were
themselves the main bearers, producers, and transmitters of a wholly
new text-based culture, a culture that would be devotional to begin
with. Given the great differences between the cultural contexts of
the two 'Augustines', it is as much to be wondered at that the Irish
Augustine should produce his treatise, minor as it is, as that St Augustine of Hippo – 'the African Doctor' – should have produced his greater
body of vastly more influential work.

This is not to say that we should be unduly charitable in our assessment of the lesser text, merely that we should be willing to value what
is thoughtful and original in it. There is no doubt that the Irish
Augustine was influenced by his African mentor. The central idea for
his treatise can be traced to St Augustine's *De genesi ad litteram* (*The
Literal Meaning of Genesis*). The concept of divine governance is clearly
stated in *De genesi ad litteram*, Book IV, Chapter 12, § 22:

> It could . . . be said that God rested from creating because He
> did not create henceforward any new kinds of creatures, and
> that even until now and beyond He works by governing the
> kinds that He then made. None the less, even on the seventh
> day His power ceased not from ruling heaven and earth and all
> that He had made, for otherwise they would have perished
> immediately. For the power and might of the Creator, who
> rules and embraces all, makes every creature abide; and if
> this power ever ceased to govern creatures, their essences
> would pass away and all nature would perish.
>
> (Augustine 1982: 117)

St Augustine, however, was primarily concerned with what is
implied by the idea of God's 'resting' on the seventh day. He was
anxious to point out that God did not rest because he was exhausted
– that God did not rest at all in the human or creaturely sense of resting
but only in the very special sense that he did not continue to create any
new natures. Nor does God's resting mean that he stopped caring for,
or exercising an active influence over, his creation. It is at this point

that St Augustine introduces his version of the distinction between creation and governance. Despite resting on the seventh day God continued to 'work' in the sense that he went on governing the universe he had created. The originality of the Irish Augustine consists in his taking St Augustine's concept of governance and using it quite differently – first, to resolve certain questions about the nature of miracles, and, secondly, to reconcile a religious conception of creation with a more mundane understanding of the natural order of the world. The power of the creator is not at all constrained by the Irish Augustine's notion of an established natural order. Rather, the very law-like stability and regularity of the natural world is acknowledged and attributed to God's original handiwork. Carol Susan Anderson has noted that while earlier writers had provided occasional naturalistic or even rationalistic explanations of individual miracles, the author of the *De mirabilibus* went much further and 'systematically applied a relatively coherent cosmology to solve scriptural problems which that cosmology had itself raised' (1982: xi). She subsequently explains the popularity of the Irish Augustine's treatise during the medieval period in terms of its cosmological assumptions, assumptions that were turning out, moreover, to be consistent with the increasingly popular Aristotelian conceptions of the natural order. Anderson notes that from the twelfth century onwards the treatise was frequently copied – that in fact more than sixty-five manuscripts, containing versions of the text, have survived from the period between the beginning of the twelfth century and the close of the fifteenth. Significantly, this was also the period when something like an early medieval 'science', under the auspices of an Aristotelian philosophy of nature, was being developed by scholars (Anderson 1982: 187–8). It is worth noting in conclusion that one of the earliest uses of the *De mirabilibus* is to be found in an early eighth-century text, a cosmological treatise – an account of the descending order of creation – called *Liber de ordine creaturarum*, now also understood to be by an Irish hand (see Smyth 1996).

2

THE PHILOSOPHY
OF CREATION

John Scottus Eriugena

It is not known when Ireland's greatest pre-modern thinker was born, though it was probably during the first or second decade of the ninth century. This was also the period during which the Scandinavian adventurers, the Vikings (or Norsemen), had begun to sail up Ireland's estuaries and waterways to plunder monasteries and schools for their stores of food and valuables. By the time that John Scottus Eriugena makes his first appearance in the historical record he has left his increasingly terrorized native country and made his way to the Continent, to the more secure and supportive surroundings of the court of Charles the Bald, grandson of the great eighth-century Frankish emperor, Charlemagne. Eriugena certainly lived in northern France, at one or other of the royal palaces, between 845 and 877. Confirmation of Eriugena's Irish nationality comes from no less an authority than Pardulus, the bishop of Laon, who, when presenting Eriugena to the clergy of Lyons, referred to him as 'the famous Irishman at the court' (Wohlman 1998: xvi). It was not a matter of chance that a scholar and prospective philosopher such as Eriugena should have found himself on the Continent at the court of Charles the Bald. Charles had chosen to continue the programme of reform and revival that his grandfather had initiated in the final quarter of the eighth century and which is known to historians as the Carolingian renaissance or *renovatio*. Just as Charlemagne had attracted scholars to his palace from all over Europe, so his grandson proceeded to do the same. And just as Irish scholars, such as the geographer Dicuil, had been among

Charlemagne's learned retinue, so Irishmen like the poet Sedulius Scottus and the scholar Eriugena were among those welcomed and patronized by his grandson.

By 850 Eriugena had already established his reputation as a teacher of the liberal arts at the cathedral school of Laon, one of the principal educational centres in Charles's kingdom. In that year his career as a scholar and thinker began in earnest when he received an invitation from Hincmar, archbishop of Rheims, to reply to the arguments of a troublesome theologian called Gottschalk. In his contribution to an ongoing debate about predestination, Gottschalk, a Saxon monk, had argued in favour of a double or twofold predestination, claiming moreover that his position was no more than an explication of the views of St Augustine. Gottschalk's basic point was that human beings are predestined to either hell or heaven, and that there is nothing that they can do to alter their fates. Hincmar was among those who considered this to be a heretical interpretation of St Augustine; and it is a measure of Eriugena's reputation that he is the one who is called on to expose the supposed error of the interpretation. Eriugena's main argument is that double predestination undermines belief in divine judgement, free will, and grace. First, given that there will be a day of judgement, it follows that human beings must be possessed of free will, since the idea of a final judgement only makes sense if people are free to choose between good and evil in the course of their lives. If double predestination were true, then there would be no need for a final day of judgement. Secondly, human beings are made in the image and likeness of God, and since God is possessed of both will and reason, it follows that human beings are also possessed of a free and rational will appropriate to their finite nature. Thirdly, since evil cannot come from God and since God cannot be said to 'know' evil, it follows that he cannot be said to predestine or foreknow it. The only mode of predestination or foreknowledge that could be attributed to God in this context would be a mode consistent with God's perfect and eternal nature. Eriugena concludes that, given these considerations and clarifications, the theory of double predestination is heretical, and that there cannot be predestination towards sin or evil. In the epilogue to his *Treatise on Divine Predestination* he declares it impermissible 'to believe that the highest good, which is the source of every good thing, has predestined any wickedness for anyone, or that the highest life, from which, and in which, and through which all things live, has pre-destined ruin or punishment for anyone' (1998: 129).

Eriugena's critique of Gottschalk did not end the controversy over predestination. On the contrary, Eriugena found himself under suspicion, himself accused of heresy, including Pelagianism. Archbishop Hincmar was so unhappy with Eriugena's treatise and with the controversial response to it that he took it upon himself to write a treatise of his own in which he attacked the heresy of Gottschalk while at the same time rejecting Eriugena's position. After it was rumoured that Pope Nicholas I was sympathetic to the doctrine of double predestination, Hincmar began to withdraw from the controversy, eventually composing a synodal letter in which he adopted a diplomatically conciliatory stance on the debate (Wohlman 1998: xxvi). Despite his difficulties with Hincmar and other ecclesiastical worthies, Eriugena did not lose favour with Charles. Between 860 and 862 he undertook, at the invitation of the king, the translation from Greek into Latin of the works of the sixth-century Neoplatonist and mystical theologian, the Pseudo-Dionysius. (The Pseudo-Dionysius is so called because the author of the texts in question was believed for a long time to be the original Dionysius the Areopagite who was converted to Christianity by St Paul at Athens, an event that is recorded in Acts 17: 34: 'Howbeit certain men clave unto him, and believed: among which *was* Dionysius the Areopagite, and a woman named Damaris, and others with them.') The sixth-century author of these texts is not known, but continues to be identified as the Pseudo-Dionysius or Dionysius the Pseudo-Areopagite, in keeping with a scholarly convention of pseudonymous attribution. Because of the esteem in which his work was held prior to the findings of later scholarship, the unknown author succeeded in contributing substantially to a tradition of theological and mystical thinking within the Christian churches. His reflections on negative theology (or the *via negativa*) – that is, on the unknowability or 'darkness' of God – had a profound influence on Eriugena, whose own great work, the *Periphyseon* (*On Nature*), later entitled *De divisione naturae* (*On the Division of Nature*), was written during the 860s. All references to this work in the following sections, unless otherwise indicated, will be to the Sheldon-Williams and O'Meara translations of the *Periphyseon*, published by the Dublin Institute of Advanced Studies between 1968 and 1995.

THE FIVE MODES OF INTERPRETATION

The *Periphyseon* takes the form of a dialogue between a master (Nutritor) and a pupil (Alumnus), an arrangement that is sometimes used to good effect by Eriugena. The pupil is more than a passive receiver of the wisdom of the teacher – he is persistent at times, asking for clarifications of obscure terms, harking back to earlier points, sometimes reminding the teacher of the extent of his digressions. At other times he rehearses the teacher's views and explanations, the better to ensure that he has understood them fully, and this habit of trying out things 'in other words' is a useful service to the reader. There are several occasions when even the most attentive reader will feel that Alumnus has not asked enough questions. One such occasion occurs at the very beginning of Book I when the teacher declares that the first and most fundamental division of all things is the division into 'those that are and those that are not' (1968: 37), adding that the term 'nature' embraces this distinction. When Nutritor asks Alumnus if he thinks otherwise, Alumnus replies that he does not. The pupil seems to be getting the sense of things rather more quickly than the reader. Nutritor, thus unduly encouraged, is then pleased to repeat, rather unhelpfully, that nature is indeed the name for all things, 'for those that are and those that are not' (37).

This is not a promising start for the modern reader, who will find it odd that 'things that are not' are included in the definition of nature. Modern science and common sense concur in assuming that if something does not exist – e.g., the unicorn, the abominable snowman, the Loch Ness monster – then it does not belong to 'nature', no matter how inclusively one might wish to define it. It seems incoherent to declare that something is a nonentity and yet maintain that it nonetheless belongs to nature. This discouraging start is not mitigated by what immediately follows Nutritor's definition of nature. Nutritor now introduces four further divisions into his scheme of things – *that which creates and is not created*, *that which is created and also creates*, *that which is created and does not create*, and *that which neither creates nor is created*. This series of divisions or distinctions – which will be progressively discussed throughout the five books of the *Periphyseon* – is somewhat less obscure than the first and more fundamental one but it does not help us out of our initial bemusement. Eriugena is in serious danger of losing our attention rather early in the day. Luckily for us, Alumnus, too agreeable in the very opening stages, now at last expresses second thoughts about the earlier all-and-nothing definition of nature. Indeed, it occurs to Nutritor himself to say 'a few words' about his original definition, and Alumnus is happy to encourage him to do just that, adding on our behalf that this distinction 'both in appearance and in fact is more obscure than the others' (39). This is the first of many digressive 'flashbacks' that will occur throughout the *Periphyseon*. Such flashbacks are among the dialectical strategies used with ingenuity by an author who seems to be aware of the question-begging difficulties of his material.

After the scene-setting obscurities of the opening exchanges we get our first attempt at a clarification – a clarification of the claim that nature consists of both what exists and what does not exist. The main thrust of the clarification is that existence can be interpreted in five different modes, such that what counts as unreal or non-existent according to one mode may be found to be perfectly real according to another. The first mode of interpretation is one that is articulated from the point of view of the bodily senses. When we consider things from the lowly perspective of the bodily senses, only sensible or physically perceivable things seem to really exist. All other kinds or modes of reality, 'because of the excellence of their nature', seem to be unreal or non-existent. Things not perceivable by the senses – invisible, intangible, spiritual things – 'rightly seem not to be' (39). From this physical-sense perspective, God is unreal, non-existent. The fact that God's existence does not register in the bodily-sense mode has a positive significance for Eriugena. Rather than merely confirming the inadequacy of the bodily senses, this fact about the limitations of the sense-mode confirms instead the transcendent, super-essential, infinitely spiritual nature of divine existence. The sense of God's transcendent 'super-reality' will remain a recurring theme throughout the *Periphyseon*.

The second mode of interpretation is stated in terms of an order or hierarchy of existence, and is based on the assumption that there are degrees of existence, or higher and lower forms of existence. At the uppermost level are purely spiritual or rational beings, those beings closest to God; at the lower end of the scheme of things lie the physical, non-rational, non-spiritual things which are furthest away from God.

The difference between upper and lower levels is stated in terms of truth. What is true of beings at one level will not necessarily be true of beings at another. What is true of human beings, for example, will not be true of beings above them, such as angels, or of beings below them, such as the non-rational animals. Moreover, beings at a lower level cannot comprehend or 'know' those above them. For that reason, beings of a higher order do not exist for those of a lower one. Human beings do not exist for the lower animals – that is, they do not exist *as* human beings for the lower animals, since the animals have no conception of what it is to be human. Analogously, supernatural beings, such as angels, do not exist for humans – that is, human beings do not know what it is to be an angel. We think of angels as attenuated or 'spiritualized' humans, as indeed is indicated by artistic representations of angels as attenuated humans with wings, but such attenuations do not capture the angelic essence. We might say that our attempts to comprehend angels and other supernatural beings are no better than the dog's attempt to comprehend its human handlers.

A third mode of categorizing and classifying things is expressed in terms of potentiality and actuality (or plenitude) – in terms, that is, of the completeness or 'fullness' of their being. Some things belong to 'the visible plenitude' of the world and are therefore said to *be* in the fullest sense of the term. Others exist only potentially, 'in the most secret folds of nature', and are said not to be. The latter do not yet exist and therefore do not, strictly speaking, exist at all. An acorn, for example, has the potential to become a tree but is not (yet) a tree. Eriugena's intuition is that potential existence is a kind of non-existence. Given the reality that the acorn has the potential to become, it cannot be said to belong yet to the realm of actual, fully realized things. What makes Eriugena's point intelligible is the notion that there are greater and lesser degrees of existence, depending on the extent to which the potential of a thing has been realized or not. This should not be considered an alien notion, since our everyday uses of such terms as 'realization' and 'actualization' carry similar connotations, i.e., the connotation that things may be considered more or less real, and can become more fully realized – more completely real – than they currently are.

The fourth mode is rather more remote from our everyday modern conceptions of things. It trades on the philosophical and Platonic assumption that 'only those things which are contemplated by the intellect alone truly are', while those which belong to the material, transient world of the bodily senses 'are said not to be truly' (45). This comes across as a disconcerting inversion of the first mode, the mode which assigned most reality to the sensible, tangible, physical world. In the fourth mode it is precisely those things which cannot be seen, touched, or felt that are really real. What is thinkable – what makes itself available to the contemplative intellect – possesses more reality than what is available to the physical senses. Things of the intellect or of the spirit are permanent, necessary, truly real; things of the senses are ephemeral, contingent, essentially unreal. Eriugena is not guilty of incoherence here. Each mode of interpretation is assumed to possess its own validity, and is autonomous relative to the others. Each mode, in other words, is a valid 'take' on reality and may co-exist with the others, much as a scientific worldview may co-exist with a mythological, metaphysical, theological, or 'poetic' worldview. Modern thinkers would prefer to make this point in terms of discourses or vocabularies that may not be compatible or interchangeable but that are nonetheless available to the individual thinker or interpreter (see, for example, Putnam 1981 and Rorty 1989). It is perhaps not wise to mix or conflate these different modes, discourses, or vocabularies but it is possible to move from one to the other in order to enrich one's understanding of reality. While Eriugena's first mode cannot be reconciled internally with the fourth mode, it is nonetheless possible for any knowledge-seeking individual to switch from one mode to the other without the risk of incoherence, just as it is possible to switch from a microscope to a telescope without risk of incoherence. What counts as real at the end of a microscope will not be visible to the eye squinting through the telescope and vice versa, but both are necessary to achieve a full, multidimensional understanding of reality. In Eriugena's scheme of things, different modes of interpretation provide different registers of reality, different registers of what does or does not exist. By shifting into any particular interpretive mode we bring some realities, or features of reality, into focus at the expense of others. What is in focus under the auspices of a particular mode of interpretation is what counts as real. What is not in focus does not

24

exist for the interpreter and will not begin to exist – will remain off the 'reality register', as it were – until the interpreter shifts to a different mode.

Finally, Eriugena's Nutritor identifies the religious mode of interpretation. This mode, somewhat surprisingly, offers the narrowest focus. It applies only to nature in its human form. The key concept here is sin or sinfulness. Humankind in its sinful state deservedly loses its proper status or reality 'and therefore is said not to be' (1968: 45). The state of sinful, fallen human nature is a state of relative non-existence. Sin somehow threatens to deprive us of our full human reality. All is not lost, however. Humankind has been restored by divine grace to 'the former condition of its substance' (45). Grace, therefore, is the antidote to sin, and the power of grace is a power to restore a being, an essence – namely, the human essence – to its full reality. Eriugena's assumption is that even particular theological concepts such as those of sin, fallenness, and grace, can be understood as interpretive categories which enable us to think in terms of what is real or unreal, what has or lacks real substance.

THE FOUR CONCEPTIONS OF NATURE

After the discussion of the five modes of interpretation, Alumnus raises a question which leads to a discussion of the first conception or 'division' of nature, namely, nature understood as *that which creates and is not created*. This species of nature is, of course, God in his capacity as creator, as 'the principal Cause of all things which are made from Him and through Him' (59). (Later, God will be considered in an entirely different way – indeed, will be defined, according to the fourth division of nature, as 'that which neither creates nor is created'. It sounds paradoxical, if not contradictory, to treat God as both creator and non-creator but it will make sense within Eriugena's scheme of distinctions.) From very early in these reflections on the divine nature it becomes obvious that Nutritor will emphasize the 'otherness' of the creator by showing how human categories, even at their most sublime, must fail to capture the divine essence. The most interesting feature of these reflections is the distinction between an affirmative and a negative theology. An affirmative theology is a way of thinking about

25

God that attempts to characterize God in appropriate superlatives 'by transference from the creature to the creator' (77). Attributes of goodness, mercy, wisdom, truth, justice, though normally attributed to human beings, can be attributed in a symbolic or metaphoric way to God. A negative theology, however, acknowledges that the nature of God is ineffable and is therefore irreducible to human terms, even when those terms are being used in a superlative sense. As Alumnus reminds his teacher, 'that is not ineffable which can be spoken of in any way' (81). The negative theologian therefore believes that we gain more of a sense of the transcendent otherness or ineffability of God if we deny of God even the most superlative or sublime attributes. God is not wise, good, or just in any human sense of those terms, not because God falls short of the criteria implicit in such concepts but because God's true nature − if he can be said to have a nature − is infinitely beyond the reach of such limited and limiting concepts. Ascribing such terms is not entirely pointless, however. The more we deny such terms of God, the more we grow in awe of God's surpassing difference from all creaturely things.

Although Eriugena, through his mouthpiece Nutritor, seems to favour the negative approach, he prefers to regard both theologies as complementing rather than contradicting each other, with the affirmative preceding the negative in the order of thought. We may begin by affirming, for example, that 'God is truth'; but no sooner do we make this affirmation than we should realize that the divine nature is in fact incomprehensible to us and we should forthwith negate what we have just said by thinking 'God is not truth.' Rather than leave one's thought in this negative state, however, we should conclude by saying that God is more-than-truth, and so on though the range of appropriate attributes. This is sometimes characterized as a 'third way' of thinking about God, namely, the *via eminentiae*, in which God is thought to be more-than-wisdom, more-than-justice, more-than-goodness, more-than-essence. By thinking and speaking along such lines we both affirm and deny; or affirm in a manner that includes but goes beyond the negative intuition. We approach God in thought but then withdraw in the realization that God is, in the most sublime sense, unapproachable − unapproachable, that is, by the inquiring mind of the finite creature. Eriugena's greatest mentor, the Pseudo-Dionysius, is the source of this mystical intuition of the unthinkability of God, an intuition that is encapsulated in the statement that 'one can neither discuss or understand the One, the Superunknowable, the Transcendent, Goodness itself' (Pseudo-Dionysius 1987: 53).

The paradoxical synthesis of the affirmative and negative theologies serves a useful purpose in Eriugena's philosophy. It enables him to take on board and integrate into his system the ten categories of Aristotle. A substantial portion of the first book is given over to a detailed discussion of the extent to which the categories of essence, quantity, quality, relation, situation, condition, place, time, motion, and rest are applicable to the creator. We can predict how this part of the story is going to unfold. Affirmatively speaking, God is pure essence; negatively speaking, he is not essence in any human sense of the term; in Eriugena-speak, he is more-than-essence. Likewise – but more challengingly – with the category of quantity. At first glance, it looks as if this particular category cannot be easily ascribed to God at all, since in its conventional usage it implies spatial or physical dimension. Since there is no physical dimension in God, it seems inappropriate to begin by affirming quantity of God. And yet, according to Eriugena, the divine substance 'may not inappropriately be called quantity in two ways: either because "quantity" is often used in the sense of abundance of power, or because it is the origin and cause of all quantity' (1968: 89). When we speak of the 'greatness' of God we are confirming Eriugena's observation here. Greatness, understood literally, implies mere physical quantity and dimension, but applied analogically or metaphorically it connotes omnipotence, sublimity, exaltation, infinite largesse.

Metaphoric equivocation reaches a poetic pitch in the course of Eriugena's attempt to apply the other 'physical' categories of place and time to God. God is neither place nor time, and yet, metaphorically, he may be called the place and time of all things. He is 'the Place of all places by which all places are defined, and, since He is not fixed in place by anything but gives place to all things within Him, He is not place but More-than-place' (99). God is also the cause of time and times: 'The Cause of times moves the times, but itself is not moved by any time in any time: for it is More-than-time and More-than-motion' (99). The category of place, even in its primary physical sense, has a particular fascination for Eriugena, and some of his comments have a curiously 'modern' ring to them, perhaps because they seem to anticipate the emphasis which modern, post-Kantian philosophy has given to innate mental structures. He is intrigued by the thought that place is distinct from body and therefore not a body or thing in itself. This leads to the more radical thought that place is nothing but boundary – the boundary by which every particular thing is defined or spatially enclosed. Alumnus at one point finds himself concluding that 'place exists in the mind alone' (113), and later adds that the world itself is not a place. Nutritor does not contradict him. Place is in a sense incorporeal because it has to do with the ability of the mind or rational soul to define and thereby 'situate' things in space.

NATURE, THEOPHANY, AND PANTHEISM

The aim of Book II of the *Periphyseon* is to discuss the second conception or division of nature – *that which is created and creates* – though this aim is only realized in the midst of several digressions on other matters, including a lengthy reflection on the idea of the Trinity. This second conception of nature is also the most difficult for the modern mind to grasp. Our contemporary commonsense understanding of the universe, especially where it is informed by the concepts and models of modern science, would never guess what Eriugena means by the expression 'that which is created and creates'. We will be tempted to think that it refers to the human species but we will be greatly mistaken. To begin to understand Eriugena we must appreciate that his philosophical influences are those of Neoplatonism. To understand Neoplatonism it will help to remind ourselves of the original intuitions of Platonism itself. One of the central claims of Platonic thought is that over and above the ephemeral, unstable, changeable world of everyday experience there exists a kind of super-world consisting of ideal forms or essences which are more real than anything in our world of experience and also give our empirical physical world whatever intelligible qualities it has. Wherever we find structure or design in our lived-in world we can take it that this is made possible by things 'participating' in the ideal forms or essences. In the Platonic metaphysics, then, an everyday ephemeral flower is beautiful only to the extent that it participates in, or 'mimics', the ideal form of

Beauty. The form of Beauty serves as a kind of permanent mould or template which hovers out of reach of our physical senses but which nevertheless actively confers beauty, albeit of a transient nature, on mere physical objects, such as flowers. The immateriality of the essential form of Beauty renders it impervious to the passage of time, while the materiality of the summer flower renders it susceptible to change and decay. It is not beauty itself which passes away but the individual material thing which is unable, because of its material nature, to maintain its participation in the essence of Beauty. As the summer passes, the flower loses its membership, as it were, of the form of Beauty, and returns to the state of formless matter. Decay is merely the loss of form and the return to an unformed material state. Yet even the most material things can become briefly beautiful and acquire other qualities in the measure that they can participate for the time being in the immaterial and transcendent forms.

Much of later Neoplatonic thought is concerned with understanding the relationship between the super-world of forms and the lived-in world of material objects and creatures. Plotinus, for example, will ask: 'What likeness is there between beautiful things here and The Beauty There?' (1908: 13). He will want to know, in other words, what likeness obtains between the ephemeral things of the material world and the shaping forms or 'ideas' of the transcendent world. The Christian thinkers are further concerned to understand the relationship between the super-world of ideal forms, as conceived by the Neoplatonic philosophers, and the created world as understood by Christian believers. How can the philosophical divisions of nature be reconciled with the Christian divisions? The Christian thinkers do not think of the lived-in physical world as simply a regrettable arrangement of transient physical objects – they think of it as *creation*, as the product of an act of God. The Neoplatonist is at liberty to disown the physical world and see it as something almost illusory, but the Christian thinker must take a more positive view of physical creation, just because it is creation. Hence Eriugena's repeated recourse to the terminology of creation. His whole philosophy is couched in terms of 'what creates' and 'what is created'. It is while trying to characterize the second division of nature that he reveals his Neoplatonic sympathies. He does so by slipping a Neoplatonic element into the relationship between creator and creation. The creator does not create in a direct, hands-on manner, like a potter shaping a vessel. Rather, he creates indirectly by thinking into existence the essences or forms of things; and these divinely thought essences or forms somehow bring about the existence of the particular things in which they are at the same time realized or manifested. These essences Eriugena prefers to call primordial causes or original exemplars (*primordialia exempla*), or, alternatively, predestinations, predefinitions, divine volitions, or 'the immutable reasons of things that are to be made' (1972: 15). He proceeds to give an ingenious, if difficult, Neoplatonic gloss on the biblical references to the word of God. The word is interpreted to mean that which is first formed by God and which effectively gives form to what would otherwise remain formless. (In Book III, Eriugena points out that the Greek term Logos means not only word but also reason or cause, so that the relevant Greek gospel text, normally translated as 'In the beginning was the Word' may just as well be translated 'In the beginning was the Reason' or 'In the beginning was the Cause' (1981: 79)). The primordial causes are so called 'precisely because they are first created by the one creative Cause of all things, and (themselves) create the things that are below them' (1972: 53). In sum, the reality and nature of individual things begins as a divine idea, and from this idea individual things proceed. It is as if the potter could cause a vessel to be thrown by simply having the idea of it present to his mind. The potter does in fact have such an idea (otherwise he wouldn't know what he was about), but, as a created and embodied being, he must realize his idea by physically working on his materials. In the case of the creator, however, no such laborious or time-consuming mediation is necessary. In the case of the creator's ideas, the ideas themselves are creative of the very things of which they are the forms or essences. Thus the divine ideas constitute the second division of nature, viz., that which is created (as an idea in the mind of God) and which also creates (that is, brings into existence the very thing or things in which the idea is realized). Eriugena has managed to yoke together key elements from both Neoplatonic philosophy and the biblical account of creation.

Eriugena is not afraid to extend his Neoplatonic gloss to some of the most metaphoric passages in the creation story. When the Bible reports that the earth was waste and void and that 'darkness was over the face of the abyss' (1972: 35), Eriugena is happy to interpret this text as a figurative reference to the divinely conceived primordial causes. The waste or void earth was the 'mystical earth', the obscure and unformed state of the world before things were brought into formal, specific, or visible existence. The terms 'darkness' and 'abyss' are treated similarly and given an affirmative rather than a negative gloss. The primordial causes have earned the name of 'darkness' because of their unfathomable depth and obscurity and their infinite diffusion through all things, and 'because of the ineffable excellence of their purity' (1972: 59). The abyss is taken to be a figurative reference to the chasm that exists between the nature of the divinely produced primordial causes and the nature of finite human intelligence. The primordial causes are not for human grasping, but remain 'eternally concealed in the darkness of their excellence' (1972: 61). The pertinent text, which reads 'The Spirit of God was borne above the waters', is interpreted to signify the super-eminence of God over all created things, including the primordial causes themselves.

Despite the obscurity of the primordial causes, Eriugena nevertheless attempts to convey some impression of the role they play in the process of creation. Instead of naming specific forms or modes of existence, he offers abstractions which are best understood as formal principles manifested to varying degrees in all things that have been created. These include goodness, being, life, wisdom, truth, intellect, reason, power, justice, health, magnitude, omnipotence, eternity, and peace, and are arranged hierarchically and interdependently. That is, the concept or principle of goodness precedes that of being, while being precedes life. This is not quite as obscure an idea as it looks. If we consider being vis-à-vis life, we can see that there are forms of being, such as the four elements of air, earth, fire, and water, that can exist before there is life, and that – to put the point in modern terms – organic life not only comes later in cosmological time but is in fact dependent on those inorganic elements that preceded it. Justice likewise presupposes the existence of life, wisdom, and reason. The term used most frequently by Eriugena to describe the relationship between the different causal principles of nature is the Neoplatonic term *participation*. Each order or level of causality participates in the one above it, and is participated in by the one below it. Only the highest cause – namely, God – does not participate in anything above Him, since there cannot be anything above Him; by contrast, only the lowest order – namely, visible bodies – is not participated in by anything below it, since there is nothing below it. The idea of participation is intended to show that there is a very real and active interdependence at work in nature, with everything originally and ultimately dependent for its existence on God. So absolute is this dependence of everything on God that Eriugena is eventually faced with the problem of pantheism. Alumnus points out to Nutritor that he is very close to saying that God is all things and all things are God, a proposition which he fears will be considered monstrous 'even by those who are regarded as wise' (1981: 99). Nutritor, in the course of a lengthy answer, seems to be prepared to give hostages to fortune, such indeed is his insistence on the absolute dependence of all created things on their creator. The relationship, moreover, is perceived to be an internal rather than an external one. That is, there is nothing outside divine nature, not even the material universe. Everything, therefore, is contained within God; we ought not to understand creator and creation as two distinct realities, but as one and the same:

> For both the creature, by subsisting, is in God; and God, by manifesting Himself, in a marvellous and ineffable manner creates Himself in the creature. . . . So it is from Himself that God takes the occasions of His theophanies, that is, of the divine apparitions, since all things are from Him and through Him and in Him and for Him. And therefore even that matter from which it is read that He made the world is from Him and in Him, and He is in it in so far as it is understood to have being.
>
> (163)

The apparently pantheistic logic of this argument is reiterated in the subsequent assertion that 'every visible and invisible creature can be called a theophany, that is, a divine apparition' (167), and seems finally confirmed when it is concluded, in terms prompted by Dionysius, that 'God is the maker of all things and is made in all things' (171). The process of creation is understood, moreover, as a kind of progressive descent on the part of God: 'descending first from the superessentiality of His Nature, in which He is said not to be, He is created by Himself in the primordial causes and becomes the beginning of all essence, of all life, of all intelligence, and of all things' (173). Then, descending

from the primordial causes – which occupy a kind of intermediate position between God and his creature – God is 'made' in the effects of
these primordial causes, and is openly revealed in His theophanies:

> [T]hen He proceeds through the manifold form of the effects to
> the lowest order of the whole of nature, in which bodies are
> contained; and thus going forth into all things in order He
> makes all things and is made all in all things, and returns
> into Himself, calling all things back into Himself, and while
> He is made in all things He does not cease to be above all
> things and thus makes all things from nothing.
>
> (173)

In these lines we are presented with a very dynamic, Neoplatonic
picture or model of creation, a fountain-like or emanation model
that envisages creation proceeding from the source and always at the
same time returning to the source. The problem with the fountain
image is that it leads us to think, in the manner of the pantheist,
that the divine nature is of a piece with the lowliest order of nature
– that God is literally present in creatures and bodies. Despite the
pantheistic thrust of the fountain image, it is rash to infer that
Eriugena is a pantheist. Arguably, the point of the concluding words
of the passage just quoted – 'and while He is made in all things He
does not cease to be above all things' – is to affirm the infinite difference
between the divine nature and the creaturely natures. The *existence* of
things depends absolutely on the creative activity of God, but it
does not follow that their creaturely natures share literally or numeri-
cally in the divine nature. Without the divine creativity there would be
nothing. Indeed, it is in this sense that creation out of nothing is to be
understood – that is, as the absolute dependence of every existing thing
on the creator. It is for this reason that the third division of nature is
defined as *that which is created and does not create*, namely, the created
universe, including all creaturely and bodily things. While the modern
reader is determined to think that the growth of plants and the reproductive activity of animals are instances of creative activity within the
created universe, Eriugena prefers to think that creation in the strict
and proper sense of the term belongs to God alone. Nutritor quotes
with approval a delightfully lyrical passage from St Basil's homily

on Genesis: 'For neither when the earth heard, Let it bring forth the growing grass and the fruit-bearing tree, did it produce grass which it held hidden, nor did it bring out to the surface palm or oak or cypress which, before coming into sight, were hidden in its womb. But the Divine Word is the nature of the things that are made' (177–9). The fact that created nature is not itself creative emphasizes the essential difference between creature and creator, as does the fact that created things have a creaturely nature or essence. God, we must remember, does not have a nature or essence.

Having established his general points about the relationship between God and the created universe, Eriugena proceeds to give a Neoplatonic or philosophical account of the six days of creation as described in Genesis. While the detail of this account is of little interest to most modern readers, it does serve as an example of radical interpretation – an example, that is, of virtually replacing the terms of one discourse with terms from another, while yet remaining purportedly true to the logic or spirit of the original text. Indeed, Eriugena's defence of the kind of interpretation in which he is about to engage has a modern ring to it. He justifies his approach by arguing that the Holy Spirit, as the infinite founder of Holy Scripture, 'established therein infinite meanings, and therefore no commentator's interpretation displaces another's, provided only that what each says is plainly consistent with the Faith and with the Catholic Creed' (189). Eriugena is, in other words, an interpretive pluralist in the sense that he is prepared to accommodate a variety of interpretations, provided they remain consistent with the background framework of Christian belief. A typical and ingenious example of Eriugena's radical interpretation occurs in the course of his account of the first day of creation. He takes the biblical text, 'And God said, Let there be light' and glosses the divine command as: 'Let the primordial causes proceed from the incomprehensible hiding-places of their nature into forms and species comprehensible and manifest to the understanding of those who contemplate them' (195). His account of the remaining days of creation is stated in similar terms. Whenever Scripture relates 'God said, Let there be light, etc.', this is taken to mean the establishment of the primordial causes followed by the downward procession of these same causes 'into their effects through the genera and species' (205).

THE GENDERED AND THE PRISTINE BODY

Though it would make for a certain easy symmetry if Book IV had dealt with the fourth division of nature, the fourth book is for the most part a continuation of the project of the third book, namely, the close philosophical analysis of the six days of creation (or the six primordial days as Eriugena prefers to put it). It continues the discussion of the created universe begun in the concluding sections of Book III, with particular attention being given to the divine command 'Let earth bring forth the living soul'. Alumnus is troubled by the fact that man, who is believed to have been created in the image and likeness of God, was created along with the lower animals. He finds it strange, he says, 'that man was brought forth from the earth with cattle, reptiles and beasts of the field; and yet he alone is formed in the image of God' (1995: 21). He is not prepared to accept a simple answer to his enquiry and so a lengthy discussion follows. The main theme of Nutritor's reply is that man is indeed an animal. He has a body like the other animals and is, like them, capable of irrational appetites. But he also possesses a higher nature in the form of reason and mind. These spiritual attributes he shares with 'the celestial essences'. Therefore, it may be claimed of man that he is, and is not, an animal. He is, in other words, a twofold creature. Indeed, he is the universal creature, enjoying like the angels the use of mind and reason, while enjoying like the animals the use of physical sense and the capacity to move about in the physical world. His nature may be understood to include that of every other kind of creature, given that he is a complex union of matter and living organism, and possesses both a rational and a spiritual essence. This seems to suggest that man is an incoherent or contradictory being, but it is better to think of him in terms analogous to those of negative theology. Just as we may say of God that he is truth and not truth (in the sense that he is more than truth), so we may say of man that he is an animal and at the same time not an animal (in the sense that he is more than an animal). This makes man a unique creature, more universal even than the higher spiritual creatures, 'for the whole of creation is understood to inhere in man' (53). It is not just living creatures that inhere essentially in man but also the non-living forms of nature, such as the firmament, the sun, the moon, the stars, not to mention earth, water, grasses, and shrubs. The sun, for example, is represented in man's unclouded judgement – what we might call the light of his reason. The moon, on the other hand, is represented in his capacity to be deceived by distorted images, illusions, and echoes; while the stars are represented in the varieties of judgements, opinions, and images to which the mind is subject. Earth is represented in a certain 'stability of substance' that forms the hard frame or skeleton of the body, while water is represented in 'the instability of the transient accidents' that are also part and parcel of human nature (101).

Eriugena is anxious to make and maintain a distinction between human nature before and after the fall. The divisions which exist in the human being are a result of the first sin in the Garden of Eden. Even the fact that human beings are gendered is regarded as a consequence of sin. In its original state of creation, as it was conceived in the mind of God, the human being was a simple and perfect unity, neither male nor female. If man had not sinned,

> he would not be suffering the division of his simplicity into the sexes. And this distinction has absolutely no connection with the Divine image and likeness, and would never have existed had man not sinned, nor will it exist after the restoration of our nature to its pristine conditions, which will be manifested after the general resurrection of all men.
>
> (137)

The text which gives Eriugena a serious difficulty at this point is the Genesis account of the creation of human nature itself. On the one hand we are told, 'God created man, in the image of God created He him'. But then are added the words, 'Male and female created He them'. The Genesis text states explicitly that God both created the first human being in His own image and at the same time created a gendered human being. Eriugena cannot accept the idea that God is both male and female, and so he attempts to reinterpret the Genesis text to suit his Neoplatonic obsession with indivisible unities and perfections. His less than cogent solution is to suggest that the creation of male and female was a providential decision that accompanied the original act in which God created the first human. God did originally create a perfectly ungendered human being made in the likeness of God himself, but He at the same time foresaw that this originally perfect human would soon fall away from his angelic nature and from the angelic mode of propagation – 'the glorious fecundity of the angels' – and therefore, in a pre-emptively providential move, He superimposed on the human creature an alternative mode of propagation, i.e., the irrational or animal mode in which human nature reproduces itself after the manner of the beasts of the field. In more contemporary and colloquial terms, we could say that the superadding of male and female characteristics was part of the creator's plan B, albeit a plan which came into force at the same moment as plan A. The originally perfect human form has not been quite lost, however. Human beings still retain the underlying form of the original spiritual body. In all human bodies there is one and the same common form 'and that abides ever unchangeable in all' (143). What makes each human being *human* is that original genderless form, and not these irrational, corruptible, gendered bodies that they have been stuck with after the Fall. There is, as it were, no essential difference between the primordial human essence that inhabits a male body and the primordial human essence that inhabits a female one. The gendered external body is something superadded and superfluous, like a garment, 'and is not properly regarded as the seal of the internal and natural [simple, interior, spiritual] body' (143).

THE RETURN TO GOD

So far, demandingly and digressively, we have been presented with Eriugena's elaborately philosophical account of creation. It has been for the most part an attempt to reconcile apparent contraries – not only the contraries of paganism and Christianity, philosophy and scripture, faith and reason, but also those of the natural and the supernatural, the finite and the infinite, the temporal and the eternal, the physical and the spiritual, the comprehensible and the incomprehensible. The picture of creation that has emerged is a dynamic and dialectical one that so emphasizes the absolute dependence of the creature on the creator that Eriugena has some difficulty stopping short of pantheism. In Book V the Neoplatonic logic of Eriugena's philosophy reaches its furthest remove from modern scientific thought in its account of the fourth division of nature, namely, *that which is not created and does not create*. If we grasp what Eriugena means by this, then we have grasped a concept of God that is very different from modern conceptions – a concept that is in fact utterly Neoplatonic. The reader is asked to dwell on the idea of God not as creator, originator, or initiator, but as something very different – as the goal or end of all creation, as that to which all created things finally return. It is suggested that things proceed from God only in order to return, as a point on a rotating wheel sets off on its circular motion only to return to the place from which its motion began; or as a drop of water in a fountain proceeds upwards only to return to the source from which it was projected. In other words, the end or goal of each created thing is already contained in its beginning – its sets out, or proceeds from a starting point, only to return there eventually, as if it had never left. This process of outset and return serves to emphasize the dynamic and ultimate unity of creation, a unity in which all change and division are finally cancelled out. If we think in terms of this model, we will come to think of God less as creator and more as source. Hence, we can think of God not only as that which is not created but, equally profoundly, as that which does not create. He does not create, because nature is that which necessarily proceeds from Him and duly returns to Him. Nature is, on this conception, best understood as emanation rather than creation.

The central organizing concept of the fifth book is that of the return – that is, the final return of all created things to the cause or source from whom they proceeded. Examples or instances of return are already easily found in the physical world itself. The heavens are in a constant state of revolution, perpetually returning to their original positions, while the two principal luminaries, the sun and the moon, follow their own patterns of outset and return. In the living or creaturely world, death itself can be understood as a kind of return – the return of creatures to those elements out of which they are composed. These, however, are only partial and local returns, and they do not imply renewal, restoration, or resurrection. Better examples of return and renewal include the day that dies and is born again, the seed that dies in order to spring to life, the phoenix that expires and is regenerated. Human nature itself provides the most exemplary instance of dissolution and return. Man, because of his sin, fell furthest from his original form. His fall was the greater for being a descent from a well-nigh angelic nature to the lowest depths of a corruptible, irrational, bestial, bodily existence. But all is not lost, for man's return effectively begins with the dissolution of the body in death. Bodily death is not the end of man's existence but the first step in a process of return. First, there is the dissolution of the body, which is merely the return of the physical body to the four elements of the sensible world. Then comes the resurrection of the body, followed by the conversion of that body into spirit, and finally the ascent or absorption of the spirit into God. The return of human nature to God represents the grand return which is at once complete and final. It represents a general resurrection and return of all created things to a primordial unity:

> In the resurrection sexual differentiation will be done away with and human nature will be made one, and there will be only men as it would have been if man had not sinned. The inhabited globe will be transformed into paradise. Earthly bodies will be changed into heavenly bodies. Next there will be a unification of the whole sensible creature, followed by a transformation into the intelligible, so that the universal creature becomes intelligible. Finally the universal creature will be unified with its Creator and will be in him and one with him.
>
> (O'Meara 1988: 140)

So total is Eriugena's vision of the final return that he is prepared to include hell itself in the grand denouement. Regardless of one's conception of hell, it is contained among the things that must return to God. Like everything else, it goes to make up the perfection of the whole of nature and must be taken up into the perfect harmony of the whole visible and invisible world, a harmony in which no discordant note may be heard.

ERIUGENA AND THE CULT OF THE FREE SPIRIT

Apart from an immediate regional influence among some of his contemporaries, Eriugena seems to have made the greatest impression on later thinkers, especially during the twelfth and thirteenth centuries. Many manuscripts of the *Periphyseon* date from the twelfth century in particular, suggesting a significant level of popularity among scholars and students (Moran 1989: 276–7). Ominously, one piece of evidence pointing to the popularity of the *Periphyseon* in the following century is linked to the papal condemnation of it in 1225. In the course of his condemnation, Pope Honorius III notes disapprovingly that it 'is being read by monks and students in many monasteries and other places' (Cappuyns 1933: 247; Moran 1989: 276). Among the thinkers in whose work Eriugena's influence has been detected are the important thirteenth-century English theologian Robert Grosseteste (see McEvoy 1987) and the fifteenth-century German philosopher Nicholas of Cusa (see Moran 1989). His most dramatic influence, however, seems to have been on a heretical sect associated with the thirteenth-century academic Amaury of Bene. Amaury was an Aristotelian scholar and teacher of logic and theology at the University of Paris. All that is known of his teaching – none of his work is extant – is that it owed much to the Neoplatonic tradition and made the case for some form of pantheism. It seems that Eriugena's *Periphyseon* was also an influence on Amaury. The evidence for this lies in the fact that the same Synod of Sens that condemned Amaurianism in 1225 also condemned the *Periphyseon*, along with other works which were presumed to have influenced Amaury and the Amaurians, including Arabian summaries of, and commentaries on, Aristotle. This was not the first time that Amaurianism had been condemned as heretical. Shortly before his death in 1206 or 1207 Amaury had been denounced for teaching erroneous doctrines and had been forced to make a public recantation, an experience that may have precipitated his death (Cohn 1970: 153). So great was the unease around Amaury's teaching and influence that in 1215 Robert of Courçon, the cardinal and papal legate with responsibility for the University of Paris, prohibited the study of even 'the summary of the doctrine of the heretic Amaury' (Cohn 1970: 153).

Amaurianism was not an isolated heretical sect but seems to have been part of a broad, elusive heterodoxy identified as the cult of the Free Spirit. According to Norman Cohn, this movement belongs to the history of 'revolutionary eschatology' and had its origins in the unorthodox forms of mysticism that flourished in Western Christendom from the eleventh century onwards (1970: 150). Insofar as the cult can be associated with a particular doctrine, it seems to have preached a kind of quasi-mystical anarchism or antinomianism, affirming a complete freedom of conscience, a rejection of authority, and the possibility of direct personal ecstatic communion with God. Sometimes this antinomian individualism took the form of self-deification, a rather extreme spin on the pantheistic belief that God is 'all that is', which was taken to mean that every created thing, including every human being, is essentially divine. Virtue or holiness, on this alarmingly immodest view, consists in recognizing, asserting, and living one's divinity. In other words, while traditional Neoplatonism encouraged the belief that there would be a return of the soul to God after death, the Brethren of the Free Spirit went somewhat farther in asserting that the soul was already divine this side of death. Cohn quotes the following lines from what is believed to be one of the few surviving texts of the Free Spirit movement: 'The divine essence is my essence and my essence is the divine essence. . . . From eternity man was God in God. . . . From eternity the soul of man was God and is God. . . . Man was not begotten but was from eternity wholly unbegettable; and as he could not be begotten, so he is wholly immortal' (1970: 173).

The pantheistic strand in the Free Spirit philosophy clearly owes something to the Neoplatonism of thinkers like Eriugena. While a careful reading of Eriugena reveals him not to be a pantheist, a more eclectic approach, such as one might expect from some adepts of the Free Spirit, could easily find and isolate passages in the *Periphyseon* that point in a pantheistic direction. For example, Eriugena quotes with apparent approval the following declaration by Dionysius: 'Therefore God *is* everything that truly is because He makes all things and is made in all things' (1981: 59). The following important passage – already quoted above – appears later in the same book, and also strikes a pantheistic note: 'and thus going forth into all things in order He makes all things and is made in all things, and returns into Himself, calling all things back to himself, and while God is made in all things He does not cease to be above all things and thus makes all things from nothing' (173). While the passage ends by asserting the absolute transcendence of God, a determined pantheistic reader could interpret the concluding clause not as an abrupt retreat from the pantheistic drift of the preceding propositions but simply as a way of reminding us of God's infinite creativity. God's being above all things (the determined adept could argue) does not describe his absolute and transcendent separateness from the world he has created but simply affirms his all-embracing omnipotence, his original power to create the world from nothing and sustain it in existence. In any case, it seems that it was not only the adepts of the Free Spirit who were able to isolate and amplify the pantheistic voice warbling in the pages of the *Periphyseon*. Those who condemned the book at the Synod of Sens seem to have heard the same voice.

SCHOLARS OR THINKERS?

A postscript on Peter of Ireland and Richard Fitzralph

Before we leave the medieval period, it is worth considering the contribution of the thirteenth-century scholar, Peter of Ireland, to the history of medieval thought. Born (it is believed) into an Anglo-Norman family in Ireland, Peter became a teacher of logic and natural philosophy at the University of Naples, and it was here that he almost certainly exercised some influence on a young Dominican student who was to become the greatest philosopher-theologian of the medieval period, namely, St Thomas Aquinas. Not much is known with certainty about Peter, but the early biographies of Aquinas, written between 1310 and 1320, do make references to a Master Peter of Ireland (see Crowe 1956; Dunne 1992). One of these biographies informs us that at Naples St Thomas was educated 'by Master Martin in grammar and in logic and by Master Peter of Ireland in the philosophy of nature', while the other mentions that at one point in his course of studies, St Thomas 'was entrusted to Master Peter the Irishman, who instructed him in logic and the philosophy of nature' (Dunne 1992: 202). The works of Peter that survive are in fact on the philosophy of nature, and this goes some way towards confirming the claims of the biographies. The philosophy of nature is, of course, Aristotle's philosophy of nature. Peter's surviving texts are essentially academic expositions of, and commentaries on, various aspects of Aristotle's thought. It was through Peter's teaching that St Thomas had his first sustained exposure to the ideas of Aristotle, the philosopher who would have a lasting and deeply formative influence on him. Peter, unlike his ingenious pupil, did not develop Aristotle's philosophy in a new direction. His use of Aristotle is essentially scholarly and pedagogical. A summation of his views would be little more than a somewhat eclectic summation of the views of Aristotle. He is not an original thinker. According to Michael Dunne, who has produced an edition of Peter's surviving texts, 'he falls into that category of scholars of the mid-thirteenth century who are more exegetes than personal thinkers, belonging to that second phase of Aristotelianism, that of the literal commentaries, inaugurated by the commentaries of Averroes after 1230' (1992: 217). This is succinctly said, and it is as much as can be said about Peter's contribution to intellectual history.

Dunne's judgement also provides an opportunity to make a more general point about the relationship between scholarship and thought. The work of most scholars, whether medieval or modern, contributes impressively to the history of research, exegesis, commentary, and interpretation, but only infrequently to the history of thought. For the most part, the best scholars are not original thinkers, even to a minor degree, and for that reason they do not receive extensive treatment in a book such as this. Peter of Ireland has merited a brief discussion only because of his association with the original, capacious, and influential thinker who had been for a time his student. Ireland, of course, continued to produce scholars during the medieval and early modern period. One of the most noteworthy Irish scholars of the late medieval period is Richard Fitzralph (*c.* 1299–1360), an archbishop of Armagh who became so closely identified with his diocese that he was known to his peers as *Armachanus*. Born into an Anglo-Norman family, probably in Dundalk, he was educated at Oxford when William of Ockham was at the height of his influence there. An earnest and conscientious churchman, he was keenly aware of the fundamental divisions of religion and identity within Ireland as a whole, and is known to have preached numerous sermons pleading for better relations between the Irish and Anglo-Norman communities. His sermon diary makes frequent references to the Irish or *Hiberni*, and his recurring message is that 'justice and mercy must be shown to them as to all others' (Gwynn 1933: 395). One of the implications of these Irish references is to show that the process by which the Anglo-Norman settlers became 'more Irish than the Irish themselves' was not a particularly expeditious one. Famous for his criticisms of the mendicant orders, including the Franciscans, he disputed the friars' interpretation of the significance of Christ's poverty. His anti-mendicant campaign took him to Avignon in 1357 to preach against the orders before Pope Innocent VI. Fitzralph's main intellectual concern was with contemporary problems and debates in doctrinal theology, ranging from a dispute about sin and grace to a dispute about the nature of the beatific vision enjoyed by the blessed immediately after death (see Walsh 1981: 58–60, 85–107). In his approach to these questions Fitzralph tended to steer a middle course between one side and another, often appealing directly to the authority of scripture in the course of argument. As an authority on biblical theology, he engaged in lengthy reflections on the long-standing differences between Rome and the Eastern churches. These differences are the subject of his *Summa de questionibus Armenorum* in which he devoted particular attention to the doctrinal divisions between Rome and the independent Christian church of Little Armenia, especially on the vexed question of the two natures of Christ. Fitzralph's approach is surprisingly undogmatic and respectful, involving little appeal to tradition or to patristic or liturgical argument (Walsh 1981: 147). Among those who claimed an indebtedness to the theological writings of Fitzralph was John Wyclif, the fourteenth-century English philosopher, theologian, and reformer who had argued that the Bible was the sole criterion of true doctrine, that papal authority was not well-grounded in scripture, and that monastic life did not have a biblical foundation.

Fitzralph died in Avignon in 1360 while still campaigning against the friars. Such was his reputation as a churchman that a campaign for his canonization got underway after his death, which, though unsuccessful, resulted in the emergence of a cult of 'St Richard of Dundalk' in his own native area of Counties Louth and Meath. That Fitzralph's tomb became a local centre of pilgrimage is suggested by a fifteenth-century primates' register which records the fate of an erring chaplain of Athboy who was required, as part of his penance, 'to visit barefoot the relic of the True Cross in Christ Church Cathedral in Dublin and the shrine of "St Richard of Dundalk"' (Walsh 1981: 461).

3

NATURE OBSERVED

Robert Boyle, William Molyneux, and the New Learning

By the time we pause again to consider the work of a significant Irish-born thinker great and lasting changes have taken place in Irish political and cultural life. While the Middle Ages in Ireland had witnessed the Anglo-Norman invasion and the establishment of an Anglo-Norman colony, the native Irish lords, even when submitting formally to Anglo-Norman or English kings, had not been comprehensively conquered or subjugated. Rather than developing apace, the colony eventually found itself in an increasingly defensive position. By the 1450s, the Dublin administration was 'concentrating almost exclusively on the defence of the English districts nearest to the centre of government, and the "land of peace" of the fourteenth century had shrunk to the English Pale' (Ellis 1985: 28). By the sixteenth century, however, and in the context of radical changes taking place in European cultural and political life, the conquest of Ireland was prosecuted in earnest under the Protestant sovereigns of the house of Tudor. Under Elizabeth in particular, and under the aegis of the Protestant reformation, there began a phase of intensive and centrally planned colonization that would continue deep into the next century, culminating in the Cromwellian land settlement of the 1650s. Moreover, plantation and settlement in the name of reformation would profoundly and permanently reconfigure the Irish political and cultural landscape, mainly by sectarianizing politics and government allegiance. The Gaelic Irish would remain defensively Catholic, identifying Protestant

45

settlement with conquest and anglicization, while the 'Old English', the descendants of the first wave of Anglo-Norman colonizers, would also remain Catholic and eventually come to be regarded as *Éireannaigh* along with the Gaelic Irish (see Lydon 1998: 168). The restoration of Charles II to the English throne in 1660 led to the partial restoration of Catholic Irish proprietors and to the abatement of religious persecution, but the net historical result of plantation and settlement – the establishment of a Protestant landed aristocracy – was not reversed. A more assertive Catholic resurgence during the reign of James II brought only short-lived gains, and was indeed the prelude to events that would lead to the wholesale defeat of the Catholic Irish cause. James was deposed by William of Orange in the Glorious Revolution of 1688, and the following year a civil war began in Ireland between the supporters of the deposed king and the supporters of William III. By 1691 the Irish Jacobite forces were defeated, and the Protestant domination of Irish political and public life was finally assured. By the end of the century Ireland had become a highly organized satellite kingdom, English and Protestant at the top, Irish and Catholic at base, its inferior constitutional status confirmed by the presence of a viceroy in Dublin (see Canny 1989: 156).

These upheavals of the sixteenth and seventeenth centuries were not just political and economic but also profoundly social and cultural, a fact that is, from the Catholic Irish point of view, mordantly reflected in the Irish poetry of the period (see Canny 1982b; Ó Buachalla 1992; Caball 1998). It is also reflected in the historical and political writing of the period, with writers from the different communities seeking to describe the Irish reality and reclaim the Irish past in terms of their own religious and cultural allegiances. Irish historical commentary in this context tends to diverge into 'offensive' and 'defensive' lines of reflection on the Irish and their cultural pedigrees. The offensive characterization of the Gaelic Irish had begun in the twelfth century with two Latin texts – the *Topographia Hiberniae* and the *Expugnatio Hibernica* – by the cleric and historian Giraldus Cambrensis (Gerald of Wales). The *Topographia* was the more offensive of the two. In the third part of the book, which deals with the inhabitants of Ireland, Giraldus described the Irish as treacherous, violent, inhospitable, filthy, innately lazy, steeped in vice, living like beasts, and ignorant of the rudiments of the faith (1982: 100–25). This influential text initiated a tradition of anti-Irish historical scholarship, ensuring that from the middle of the twelfth century the term 'barbarity' would become a favourite cliché in the lexicon of colonial ideology (see Bethell 1971 and Gillingham 1993). The tradition of racial calumny reached its most intense and most discursive level of antipathy, condescension, and presumption in the prose and verse of the Renaissance poet and New English settler, Edmund Spenser. His *View of the Present State of Ireland* (written in the 1590s but not published until 1633) rings the changes on the theme of the barbarous Irish and puts forward a hard-line policy of 'reformation' and violent redress, suggesting that all existing evils will need to be cut away by a strong hand before the planting of good can begin (1997: 93). His verse epic *The Faerie Queene* (1590–6) can be read as a sustained, imaginative, deeply troubling attempt to aestheticize and glorify the forceful extension of religious, civil, and moral values (see Coughlan 1989; Canny 2001: Ch. 1). A more ambivalent critique of the Irish and a more benign advocacy of anglicization found expression in the work of Spenser's Dublin-born contemporary, Richard Stanihurst (1547–1618). Stanihurst, writing as an Old English Catholic, makes his criticisms from the perspective of the counter-reformation, focusing on those aspects of Irish culture that fell short of the standards of urbanity and civility to be found in the 'English province' of the Pale. The source of his critique of Gaelic Irish culture is not racial antagonism, according to recent historians, but rather the 'exigencies of reform' (Bradshaw 1979: 283–4; Lennon 1981: 123). In his 'Description of Ireland', written for Raphael Holinshed's *Chronicles of England, Scotland, and Ireland* (1577), Stanihurst describes the 'meere Irish' as religious, frank, amorous, war-like, generous, and 'passing in hospitality', before going on to express serious regret about their 'execrable superstitions' (1979: 113–15). He prays that God will open the eyes of this rude people to the errors of their ways, and that the governors of the country will become more industrious in reducing the Irish from rudeness to knowledge, from rebellion to obedience, from treachery to honesty, from savagery to civility, from wickedness to godliness (115–16). In a later work Stanihurst would make an explicit appeal to the fair-minded among his readers, inviting them to see that he had avoided the role of 'the bitter critic' on the one hand and that of 'the smooth flatterer' on the other (1981: 145).

The first substantial antidote to these more or less offensive characterizations of the unanglicized – that is to say, uncivilized – Irish is to
be found in Geoffrey Keating's *Foras Feasa ar Éirinn* (*Groundwork of
Knowledge about Ireland*, more usually rendered *The History of Ireland*).
Completed by about 1634, Keating's book is an extraordinary amalgam of lore, history, genealogy, and bardic chronicle, and has been
fittingly described as 'an origin-legend for the Catholic community
of seventeenth-century Ireland' (Bradshaw 1993: 184). Like Stanihurst,
Keating belonged to the Old English Catholic community in Ireland,
but, unlike Stanihurst, he took a defensive, constructive, and revision-
ist line on the relationship between Gaelic and Old English culture.
He represents the people of Ireland, both the native Irish and the
'old foreigners', as an independent, kingly, cultured people, capable
certainly of battling among themselves, but also capable of hospitality,
generosity, and piety. The nobility and magnanimity of the native Irish
is reflected in the first instance in their acceptance of Christianity. The
transition from a pre-Christian to a Christian culture is presented as a
natural one, involving mutual accommodations, with the process of
conversion occurring under the aegis of well-established and flourishing Irish kingdoms. The arrival of the Old English is also presented
in terms of a natural transition, with the colonists undergoing eventual
absorption into the native culture. The foreigners (or *Gaill*) are
described as having pursued a largely 'Christian-like' conquest, as indicated by the fact that they did not set out to extinguish the Irish
language (1902: I, 35) and 'did much good in Ireland' by building
abbeys and churches (1906: II, 369). Keating refuses to acknowledge
any fundamental rift between the two historical, Catholic communities, and arrives at the general conclusion that the *Éireannaigh* –
native Irish and Old English alike, Gael and Gall together – are the
equal of any nation in Europe 'in valour, in learning and in their
being steadfast in the Catholic faith' (1902: I, 78).

While Keating attempted, in the name of a strong and honourable
cultural lineage, to claim the early Irish church for Catholicism, a
quite contrary reclamation of early Irish Christianity was pursued by
Richard Stanihurst's Protestant nephew, James Ussher (1581–1656),
who had been appointed archbishop of Armagh in 1625. Ussher
turned to historical scholarship in an attempt to demonstrate that it
was the Protestant church that had what Hugh Trevor-Roper calls

'the warrant of history' (1989: 127). He cherished the idea that Protestantism, including Irish Protestantism, was essentially a return to the values of an earlier style of pure and unadorned Christianity, while at the same time contending that Popery was a serious historical deviation — a deviation that was indeed directly attributable to the reign of the Antichrist which had begun towards the end of the first Christian millennium (see Knox 1967: 109). The influence of Popery in Ireland is presented in terms of a corruption that had happened little by little, 'until the devil was let loose to procure that seduction which prevailed so generally in these last times' (Ussher 1631: 238). While the appeal to a lost golden age of Christianity was a standard element of the Protestant philosophy of history, Ussher's originality consists in applying this general framework to the Irish church in particular (see Ford 1986). In both the general and specific case papal domination is equated with aberration and corruption, while Protestantism is equated with the restoration of 'the true, original, Christian tradition' (Trevor-Roper 1989: 136). In his *Discourse of the Religion anciently professed by the Irish and British* (1631) Ussher accumulates citations and quotations from a number of early Irish authors, including Adamnán and Sedulius, to show that the religion professed by the ancient bishops, priests, and monks in Ireland was in substance 'the very same with that which now by public authority is maintained therein, against the foreign doctrine brought in thither in latter times by the bishop of Rome's followers' (239). On the nature of the eucharist, for example, Ussher quotes from Sedulius a passage that has clearly 'Protestant' resonances. Commenting on Christ's words *Do this in remembrance of me*, Sedulius writes: 'He left a memory of himself unto us: even as if one that were going a far journey, should leave some token with him whom he loved; that as oft as he beheld it, he might call to remembrance, his benefits and friendship' (284). Ussher's historical philosophy, turning on a model of origin, aberration, and restoration, enabled him to make a case for an Irish version of Christianity that owed little or nothing to Catholicism, that was in fact originally Protestant in essence. It follows that Ussher's support for continued reformation in Ireland does not imply a wholesale disparagement of all aspects of pre-Norman Irish culture. Rather, it can be understood as an argument for the restoration of precisely the kind of true Christian culture practised in Ireland in the centuries before the advent of the 'Romish corruption'. The general effect of Ussher's work was to show unity-in-difference 'and to establish a common ecclesiastical heritage as well as a common Saviour for British and Irish Christianity, despite ancient and modern tensions and divisions' (Vance 1999: 47).

ROBERT BOYLE, THE CHRISTIAN VIRTUOSO

Though he was the greatest Irish scholar and antiquarian of the seventeenth century, James Ussher was not the greatest Irish thinker of the period. That honour must go to Robert Boyle, whose advocacy of the new experimental philosophy would offer a powerful alternative to the kind of scholarly knowledge valued by Ussher. Born at Lismore Castle, Co. Waterford, in 1627, Robert Boyle was the fourteenth child of Richard Boyle, an Elizabethan adventurer who had moved from Canterbury to Ireland in 1588, eventually accumulating such lands and offices as would earn him the earldom of Cork and the position of lord high treasurer of Ireland. The young Robert was educated mainly by private tutors, though he spent three years at Eton from the age of eight. He did not have a university education but followed his own course of studies, travelling widely in Europe, often seeking the assistance of other individuals with reputations in natural philosophy. He was in Florence with his tutor when Galileo died 'and learnt Italian to be able to master Galileo's writings' (Stewart 1991: xii). While still in his early teens he inherited the family estate at Stalbridge in Dorset, and it was during his time there that he began to develop his interest in natural philosophy. He became a founding member of the 'Invisible College', a short-lived and informal fraternity of like-minded thinkers who were active promoters in England of the 'new learning' or the 'new philosophy' – an approach to knowledge that owed much to the influence of the philosopher Francis Bacon. Bacon had rejected the speculative, fanciful researches of both the humanist scholars and the hermetical occultists and had advocated instead a systematic, fact-gathering, cooperative approach to the study of the natural world. It was part of the Baconian ideology of Boyle's fraternity to reject traditional, scholastic, 'bookish' forms of learning in the name of an approach that would value only 'useful' knowledge (Webster 1975: 57–67).

In 1652 there came, according to Marie Boas Hall, a great change in Boyle's life, one which brought to an end his period of relative seclusion at Stalbridge, 'and threw him ultimately into the scientific world' (1966: 19). The change began as a rather practical one involving property and inheritance. The Cromwellian 'pacification' of Ireland was now virtually complete, and Boyle took steps to secure title to the Irish estates left to him by his father. This led to a period of residence in Ireland, during which time he studied anatomy and other matters of scientific interest with William Petty (then in Ireland as physician-general to Cromwell's army). Shortly after returning to England, Boyle decided to move to Oxford, then the centre of scientific activity in England. It was with this move to Oxford, made in the aftermath of his Irish sojourn, that Boyle's professional involvement in scientific research and experiment really began. The Oxford group of mathematicians, astronomers, and physicians (which included Christopher Wren before he turned to architecture) saw in Boyle someone who was, like themselves, 'addicted to the new learning as espoused by Bacon and Galileo' (Hall 1966: 22). By the early 1660s, mainly as a result of the political events that would culminate in the restoration of Charles II to the throne, many of the individuals who formed the Oxford group had returned to London. At the end of 1660 the newly formed London group was already meeting in the rooms of Christopher Wren to organize an association 'for the promotion of experimental philosophy', thus ushering in the productive era of restoration science. This informal group soon became the Royal Society, receiving its royal charter in 1663. The Society's revolutionary motto was 'Nullius in verba', an extrapolation from a line in Horace's *Epistles*, 'Nullius addictus jurare in verba magistri', which may be translated 'I am not bound over to swear as any master dictates' (More 1944: 110). Just as Horace had asserted his refusal to be bound by the formula of any school or philosophy, so the members of the Royal Society were signalling their independence of any dogmatic or traditional doctrine, such as Aristotelianism. Boyle was a key figure in these revolutionary and formative years in English intellectual history, and during the 1660s he would publish some of his most important works, including *New Experiments, Physico-Mechanical, Touching the Spring of the Air, and its Effects* and *The Sceptical Chymist*.

Given the depth and extent of Boyle's involvement in English cultural and intellectual life, it may seem appropriate to question his inclusion in Irish intellectual history. But his inclusion is easily justified. His material background is undeniably Irish, and it is this background that grounds his identity as an Irish thinker. Of course, insofar as Boyle's mindset was informed by familial inheritance it was informed by the culture and ethos of the New English – the ethos, that is, of those recent English settlers whose outlook had been conditioned by Puritanism, and whose ideological justification for being in Ireland was often stated in terms of bringing civilization to the barbarous Irish. In keeping with the ethos of the new settlers, Boyle would certainly not have identified with anything natively Irish. And yet, for all his predictable antipathy to the native Irish, he was as Irish-born as John Scottus Eriugena. Indeed, his birth in Ireland is more verifiable than that of Eriugena, and for that he must duly receive the reward – or pay the price – of inclusion in the intellectual history of the country that enriched his family and effectively funded his own lifelong dedication to scientific study and research. Robert Boyle, like the majority of those who came to form the Anglo-Irish elite in the next century, is not only formally Irish by birth but is also 'Irish by privilege'. That is to say, he is Irish because the material base of his wealth, power, and status was provided largely from Irish resources – resources, moreover, that were acquired in the first place by cunning and ruthlessness, by foul means as well as fair (see Canny 1982a). The Boyle family – seriously propertied, privileged, and empowered – had appropriated to itself a substantial proportion of the land of Ireland, and drew their disproportionate sustenance from it. This historical and economic fact is sufficient to ground and locate Robert Boyle in Irish history, including Irish intellectual history. The least that a seventeenth-century Boyle can be obliged to do is to lend his reputation to the intellectual history of a country whose own pre-colonial history and cultural evolution was disrupted permanently by invasion and plantation, and by adventuring and profiteering on a massive scale – a disruption from which the Boyle family benefited more than most. Not only is this not too much to ask, it is no more than a small compensatory adjustment in the scales of poetic justice.

In some few respects – and some few respects only – Boyle's concerns seem to echo those of his most notable Irish predecessor, Eriugena. Like

Eriugena he possesses a strong religious conviction and shares with him the belief that there exists a creative and providential God. He has no doubt that the natural world is a divine creation, that there is a purpose to its existence, that its laws are divinely instituted. Like Eriugena he believes that the natural world is intelligible, and that human reason is capable of arriving at some understanding of it. He acknowledges, in other words, the difference between reason and revelation and sees them as different ways to the truth. Like Eriugena he is aware of the limits of reason, even where it is supplemented by scripture, and acknowledges the extent to which God's perfections elude human understanding. Since God is a being absolutely different from all other beings, it follows that there may be aspects of his nature which are 'without all example, or perfect analogy, in inferior beings' (1772: IV, 159). He comes close to rehearsing the logic of Eriugena's negative theology when he observes that our ideas of God 'will fall extremely short of being worthy of the incomprehensible God', adding that even the brightest idea we can frame of God 'is infinitely more inferior in reference to him, than a parhelion is in reference to the sun' (V, 155). In his characterization of the divine intellect he reaches for imagery that is reminiscent of Eriugena's Neoplatonic vocabulary. The human intellect, when compared with the divine, is like the moon in comparison with the sun:

> For as the moon, at best, is a small star in comparison of the sun, and has but a dim light, and that too but borrowed; and has her wane as well as her full, and is often subject to eclipses, and always blemished with dark spots: so the light of human reason is but very small and dim, in comparison of his knowledge, that is truly called in scripture the *Fountain*, as the *Father*, of light; and this light itself, which shines in the human intellect, is derived from the irradiation it receives from God, *in whose light* it is, that *we see light*.
>
> (V, 155)

What looks like the most startling resonance with Eriugena's Neoplatonic vision occurs in his essay 'About the Excellency and Grounds of the Mechanical Hypothesis' in which he expresses disagreement with those modern philosophers who think that God merely set matter in motion and then allowed the material parts to form a system by their own unguided motions. Boyle argues that God not only set matter in motion but established certain internal laws of motion – which Boyle is prepared to call the laws of nature – while at the same time furnishing matter with 'the *seminal* principles and structures or models of living creatures' (1991: 139). The 'seminal principles' are part and parcel of the mechanically evolving universe. Things are not formed accidentally or haphazardly as a consequence of chance interactions among particles but in accordance with divinely instituted principles and models that are integral to matter itself.

This emphasis on law, design, and seminal principles reminds us of Eriugena's primordial causes. But it should do no more than remind us. Once we enter into the detail of Boyle's natural philosophy and apprise ourselves of the world-picture which informs it we soon realize that the contrast between Eriugena's Neoplatonic universe and Boyle's mechanical universe is very great indeed. Whereas Eriugena's God is somehow continuously and dynamically implicit in the universe, Boyle's God has created the world once and for all, and has set it in motion according to certain laws or principles which continue to operate mechanically. In the very passage in which Boyle seems to strike a resonance with the Neoplatonic world-picture he insists that 'the universe being once framed by God, and the laws of motion being settled and all upheld by his incessant concourse and general providence, the phenomena of the world thus constituted are physically produced by the mechanical affections of the parts of matter' (139). The laws of nature, working mechanically, are sufficient to keep the universe in motion and to explain any natural phenomenon. Whereas Eriugena had to defend himself against the charge of pantheism, so close was the relationship which he posited between God and creation, there could never be any question of mistaking Boyle for a pantheist. The stark distinction he makes between the nature of God and the nature of the physical world is carried over into the clear distinction he maintains between theology and science. While he writes extensively on theological matters and is eager to engage with theological questions on their own terms, he maintains a clear distinction between the language of theology and the language of science. He regards revelation as 'a foreign principle' in the context of philosophical (or scientific) enquiry and undertakes 'to consult only the light of reason' when discussing questions about the formation of the universe. He explicitly rejects the practice of those who use the term 'nature' to signify 'that *Author of nature* whom the schoolmen, harshly enough, call *natura naturans*' (176), and he recommends the avoidance of any expression which 'seems to make the *Creator* differ too little by far from a *created* (not to say an *imaginary*) being' (178). So anxious is Boyle to remove any suspicion of animism or magical thinking from his conception of nature that he has reservations about the expression 'laws of nature'. The notion of law suggests a normative rule imposed by a superior will and directed towards some intelligent being capable of obeying or disobeying it. Boyle rejects the fanciful idea that an inanimate body, devoid of understanding and sense, 'can moderate and determine its own motions' (181). Over against such a vulgar idea he poses the contrary idea of unintelligent mechanism. It is precisely this idea which lies at the core of his mechanical philosophy. He prefers to think of the whole physical universe as functioning like a clock or a machine, since in machines 'we see many motions very orderly performed, and with a manifest tendency to particular and predesigned ends' (182). The whole of physical nature is to be reconceived as a great automaton, an engine, a 'cosmical mechanism' (188).

The notions of automaton, engine, and mechanism enable Boyle to mark the difference between his approach and that of the scholastic Aristotelians and Renaissance alchemists who impute too many unanalysed powers to nature. His most protracted debate is not with the earlier worldview of the Neoplatonists (such as we find in Eriugena) but with the Aristotelian scholastics or 'schoolmen' who prefer to study the texts of Aristotle than to explore and observe the physical world itself. His long essay on the origin of forms and qualities is directed explicitly against the Aristotelians who describe the world in terms of certain essential forms that are supposed to be present in things but which do not readily lend themselves to experimental observation. Whereas the Aristotelians tend to complicate the process of explanation by adding new entities, such as abstract forms and essences, Boyle, drawing on the premises of his mechanical or corpuscularian philosophy, wants to simplify the process of explanation by positing a small number of explanatory principles and terms. The Aristotelians talk of abstract qualities (whiteness, heat, coldness, healthiness) as if they really inhere in things and are therefore attenuated entities themselves. They consequently devote much thought to their own tendentious distinction between accidental and essential qualities. Some qualities are supposed to be accidental in the sense that they are not definitive of what a thing essentially is, while other qualities are believed to be part and parcel of the essential nature of a thing. Rationality, for example, is supposed to be part of the essence of being human, while having a fair or dark complexion is merely an accidental property of any particular human being. Without rationality, or at least the capacity to reason, we would not be human; having a fair complexion, on the other hand, does not make us more or less human than someone who has a dark complexion. Boyle is not impressed by this kind of elaborate redescription of the world in terms of essential and accidental qualities. Such redescription not only fails to be explanatory but also begs more questions than it answers. As well as the physical objects that make up the visible world we now seem to have an additional array of abstract objects, namely, the essential or accidental qualities that inhere in physical things.

For the Aristotelians, then, there exists a whole other abstract realm of essences that serves to explain the world of particular things and events. For Boyle there is no such formal realm. Where the Aristotelians are bountiful in their positing of explanatory principles, Boyle, the mechanical philosopher, is economical and reductive. Everything is to be explained in terms of the two 'grand and most catholic principles', namely, matter and motion (20). The variety of natural bodies in the world can be accounted for in terms of the motion of the variously shaped and variously sized corpuscles that fundamentally and universally constitute matter itself. An object is no longer a distinct, free-standing portion of 'formed' matter but a functional part of the universe, acting upon and being acted upon by other bodies in many different sorts of ways. A very few mechanical features, such as the shapes and sizes of basic particles, can give rise to a great number and variety of formations, interactions, and relationships among different bodies. Just as the nature of individual things can be explained in terms of particles in motion, so also the 'powers' of things can be explained in terms of the law-governed interactions of different parcels of particles. The sun, for example, has the power to harden clay, soften wax, melt butter, thaw ice, turn water into vapour, ripen fruit, hatch the eggs of silk-worms, and produce many other effects, 'and yet these are not distinct powers or faculties in the sun, but only the productions of its heat (which itself is but the brisk and confused local motion of the minute parts of a body), diversified by the differing textures of the body that it chances to work upon, and the condition of the other bodies that are concerned in the operation' (27). Although the human mind is prone to conceive everything under the concept of 'a true entity or substance', many of the qualities we perceive things to have are simply the functional, circumstantial, or mechanical effects of bodies interacting in various ways. The Aristotelian distinction between essential and accidental qualities has no explanatory role to play in Boyle's mechanical, corpuscularian scheme of things. The most we can say in Aristotelian terms is that all qualities are in some sense accidental, but even this can be a misleading way of thinking about the world since it gives credence to the notion that there are such *things* as qualities. The whole point of the mechanical philosophy is to get people to reinterpret visible phenomena 'which, however we look upon them as distinct qualities, are consequently but the effects of the . . . catholic affections of matter, and deducible from the size, shape, motion (or rest), posture, order, and the resulting texture, of the insensible parts of bodies' (6–7).

This mechanical reinterpretation of qualities leaves Boyle with a problem. Having apparently dispensed with the notion of inherent essences and substantial forms, he must now account in his own terms for the fact that things in the natural world do seem to fall into species and genera. In other words, things do seem to exhibit certain fixed and recurring characteristics which give them whatever identity they have and which enable them to be objectively classified according to both species and genus. Different individual pieces of a yellow substance, for example, have enough in common with each other to justify calling them *gold* (species), and this species has in turn enough in common with other groups of substances to justify calling it a *metal* (genus). It is these seemingly objective features of things that lend some plausibility to the Aristotelian notion that there exist inherent substantial forms or patterns of essential properties that are somehow as real as individual things themselves and that indeed invest these individual things with their objective identity or classifiable 'nature'. There is, it seems, a certain objective combination of features that an object or a piece of matter must have if it is to qualify for, say, the designation *gold*. And it is this objective combination that we may feel compelled to identify as the essence or substantial form of gold. How can Boyle, given his emphasis on purely mechanical interactions, account for this sustained recurrence of certain patterns of objective features? Why is it that some 'affections' of matter seem to go naturally and inseparably together, as if they were indeed held together by some internal essence? Some combinations of qualities seem destined for each other in a much more specific and meaningful way than Boyle's mechanical principles would seem to allow.

Boyle simply rejects the notion that any substance or body possesses a natural state – that is, 'a certain state wherein nature endeavours to sustain it' (61). Rather than focusing initially on relatively stable bodies which may lead us to overstate the case for permanent or substantial forms, Boyle begins by reflecting on the lesson of fluid bodies – those bodies that instructively change their state according as they are acted upon by the sun 'and other considerable agents in nature' (61). Bodies of fluids, for example, subject as they are to heat and cold, rarefaction and condensation, do not have a fixed natural state. The state of a body of water at the beginning of the spring in London is not the same as it is in either more torrid or more frozen zones. Such fluid or unstable bodies exhibit more clearly than solid bodies the mechanical axiom of Boyle's philosophy, namely, that all the phenomena of nature are caused by the local motion of one part of matter hitting against, or interacting with, another. The difference between fluid bodies and their more solid neighbours is not as significant as it looks. The apparently stable or 'natural' state of solid bodies is simply their most *usual* state, and they remain in that state not because of the presence of some internal essence but because of the presence or absence of certain external or environmental factors. That is, they remain in a particular state only until such time as some external agent alters them. The presence or absence of certain external or environmental agents is more significant than the presence or absence of some obscure internal principle or essence.

This constant recourse to mechanical principles would suggest a cold, lifeless, hard-edged world-picture in which it is hard to find space for, say, a caring, supervisory deity. Boyle, however, does not see any inconsistency between his Christian beliefs and his belief in the explanatory virtues of his mechanical, experimental, corpuscularian philosophy. Using the term 'virtuoso' to describe any person with expertise in scientific experimentation, he maintains that such a person, precisely because he searches deep into the nature of things, 'has great and peculiar advantages to discover and observe the excellent fabric of the world' (1772: V, 518). In *The Christian Virtuoso* he sets out to show that experimental philosophy 'might afford a well-disposed mind considerable helps to natural religion' (V, 522). First, the virtuoso will appreciate better than most that the universe is a machine of such immensity, beauty, and complexity that it could not have been the effect of mere chance, 'but must have been produced by a cause exceedingly powerful, wise, and beneficent' (V, 519). Secondly, the mechanical philosophy will induce in the virtuoso a sense of God's continued concern for the universe, since the stupendous motions of the vast numbers of astronomical bodies are so swift, and the masses of matter involved are so great, that any irregularity could soon reduce the cosmos to chaos. The experimental philosopher has a sense, therefore, that God has not abandoned the universe, 'but does still maintain and preserve it' (V, 519). And thirdly, the virtuoso will have such a sense of divine providence that he will see this providence at work not only on the grander aspects of the universe but also in its smallest and homeliest aspects. He will see a perfection of design in such small and 'abject' creatures as flies, ants, and fleas, and will reject any suggestion that these creatures are somehow beneath God's concern and must therefore be the offspring of putrefaction. From its highest to its lowest forms of life, the visible world is evidence of God's all-pervading wisdom and exuberant beneficence (V, 520). There is every reason, then, why a good virtuoso should become and remain a strong believer in the existence of a providential God.

Another important – and surprising – theological defence of the mechanical philosophy occurs in an earlier work by Boyle, *A Free Enquiry into the Vulgarly Received Notion of Nature* (1686), in which he warns against the tendency of some natural philosophers or 'physiologers' to give an excessive veneration to nature, to see nature as itself intelligent and god-like. Such a view causes philosophers to deny God. But the mechanical philosophy, precisely because of its emphasis on mechanism, finds no evidence of intelligence in nature itself. It finds only corpuscles acting and reacting in accordance with the laws of motion. There is evidence of intelligence, certainly, but it is evidence for the existence of an external intelligence, namely, the infinite intelligence of the creator who fashioned the materials of the universe and set them in motion in the first place.

> I conceive, then, that the most wise creator of things did at first so frame the world and settle such laws of motion between the bodies that as parts compose it . . . that, by the help of his general providence, they may have their beings continued and maintained as long and as far forth as the course he thought fit to establish amongst things corporeal requires.
>
> (1996: 112)

In thus stressing the degree of mechanism in the universe, Boyle in his earlier essay tends to place God at a greater distance from his creation than he does in *The Christian Virtuoso*. In *The Christian Virtuoso* he is so anxious to establish God's providence that he brings God into a relatively close, caring, monitoring relationship with his creation, whereas in the earlier work, anxious to remove all signs of intelligence from nature itself, he tends to emphasize God's 'absence' from the day-to-day internal workings of the world. In *A Free Enquiry* God is the distant, infallible, subsequently uninvolved creator; in *The Christian Virtuoso* God is the ever-vigilant paternal engineer, permanently on standby lest something begin to go wrong with the great machinery of his creation.

TOUCHING THE SPRING OF THE AIR

A new departure

Some of Boyle's experimental observations are designed to demonstrate the extent to which any substance or body can be radically altered under heat, pressure, or the influence of some other external force – that is, the extent to which the features of a thing have no necessary internal connections but can be prised apart and effectively reshuffled to make an entirely new object. If, for instance, you expose a bullet of lead to a strong fire, it will quickly lose its figure, coldness, colour, consistency, malleability, flexibility, and a number of other qualities – and all this, Boyle adds, 'in spite of the imaginary substantial form, which, according to the Peripatetical principles, in this case must still remain in it without being able to help it' (1991: 63). Again, Boyle denies a theoretical place to the idea of substantial form, given the stark contrast that exists between the properties of a bullet's solid 'cold' state and those of its fluid 'hot' state. True, if the lead is allowed to cool, most of its previous properties will return, but this only goes to show how much the properties in question depend for their existence on the temperature of the air, 'an extrinsical thing to the lead' (63). Moreover, if the lead is exposed for long enough to a sufficiently intense fire it will be turned into a kind of glass, losing all its leaden qualities and acquiring a colour, a transparency, a brittleness, and other qualities it did not have before; 'and let the supposed substantial form do what it can . . . to reduce or restore the body to its natural state and accidents, yet the former qualities will remain lost as long as these preternatural ones introduced by the fire continue in the matter' (63). If this new substance is to be restored to its previous state it will take 'a sufficiently powerful extrinsic agent' to effect the change. These powerful extrinsic agents effectively usurp the role once played in theory by substantial forms.

Here again Boyle has recourse to the clockwork analogy in order to show that the manner in which the parts of a natural object are put together is not significantly different from the manner in which the parts of a mechanical device are put together. The parts and properties of natural bodies are as much mechanically connected as those of a watch: 'a natural body, being dissipated and, as it were, taken in pieces like a watch, may have its parts so associated as to constitute new bodies, of natures very differing from its own and from each other' (72). Boyle includes gunpowder among his examples of such dissipation and reassembly. The blending of nitre, charcoal, and brimstone produces a new body whose operations are 'more powerful and prodigious' than almost any of nature's own compounding. In such a case, moreover, the change is not brought about by great heat or other application but by a simple blending or 'comminution'. A mere rearrangement of substances is sometimes enough to bring about an explosively new entity. It is an implication of Boyle's version of corpuscularianism that all kinds of transmutations are possible if the right sorts of rearrangements are made under the right environmental conditions. Though he frequently attacks the methods of the alchemists (or 'spagyrists'), he has no difficulty in allowing in principle for the transmutation of base metals into gold. Since all things are made out of the same basic material particles which differ from each other only in shape and size, and since the basic differences between things can be accounted for in terms of motion and its effects on different parcels of particles, it follows that there are no *essential* differences between substances. By rearranging the particles and changing the rate or direction of local motion we can in theory bring about the transmutation of one substance into another. By rearranging, for example, the particles which happen to constitute a particular lump of base metal it may be possible to produce a nugget of gold. The principle at work here is the principle that lies behind all transmutation, namely, that the same agents that can undo the frame and texture of one body or substance can also, 'by shuffling them together and disposing them after a new manner, bring them to *constitute* some new sort of bodies' (46).

So opposed is Boyle to the notion of real essences that he reduces all specific or generic differences to a matter of contingent or 'accidental' properties, thus allowing in principle for the occurrence of quite dramatic transmutations, not only from metal to metal but also from mineral to vegetable and from vegetable to animal. He believes (on the basis of experimental results which he misinterprets) that water can be transformed into earth, that plants can be produced directly out of water, that stones are formed from water, that dead or putrefying matter can be directly transmuted into animals – e.g., milk into maggots or cheese into mites; and he was prepared to accept the claims of Sir James Lancaster that he had in his travels come upon a type of worm which generated a tree, the timber of which in turn developed into white stone.

The fact that Boyle's version of corpuscularianism does not rule out the claims of alchemy should not be taken to mean that his science is primitive, or that he displays no more than an inchoate sense of scientific method. His 1660 work, *New Experiments, Physico-Mechanical, Touching the Spring of the Air, and its Effects* belongs to the early history, not the pre-history, of the modern scientific paper. While his essays on theological or philosophical matters reflect the concerns and arguments of other seventeenth-century thinkers, the *Spring of the Air* is more than just an argument. It describes in detail the design and construction of an apparatus, reports a series of forty-three experiments performed with that apparatus, and arrives at observations and conclusions on the basis of the data produced by the experiments. Instead of struggling to reconcile his experimental conclusions with those of earlier authorities, Boyle has no difficulty in exposing the errors of his respected pre-decessors, from Aristotle to Descartes. His experiments show that air is not a simple universal element supposedly present in some degree in all parts of nature. Rather, air is understood in the same basic mechanical terms as everything else in the material universe. Like any other body, it is divisible into particles and has characteristic features that can be accounted for in terms of the activity of these particles. The first series of experiments shows that air has a 'spring' – a tendency, that is, to resist compression and to duly expand when pressure is removed. According to Boyle's own rather ungainly account, the springiness or elasticity of the air consists in the mechanical fact that

> our Air either consists of, or at least abounds with, parts of such a nature, that in case they be bent or compress'd by the weight of the incumbent part of the Atmosphere, or by any other Body, they do endeavour, as much as in them lies, to free them-selves from that pressure, by bearing against the contiguous Bodies that keep them bent; and, as soon as those Bodies are removed or reduced to give them way, by presently unbending and stretching out themselves . . . and thereby expanding the whole parcel of Air, these elastical Bodies compose.
>
> (1999: I, 165)

Another series of experiments demonstrates the relationship between air and combustion. By extracting the air from a flask in which a lighted match, a lighted candle, or a live coal has been placed, he shows that the flame or ember dwindles and quenches according as the air is removed. The dependence of fire on the presence of air indi-cates that fire itself is a complex process rather than a basic element. One of the most elaborate experiments – Experiment 33 – was designed to show that air, like any other physical thing, has weight. The lesson that Boyle takes from his vacuum experiments is that there is no truth in the 'vulgar axiom' that nature abhors and flees a vacuum. This axiom, which he attributes to the Aristotelians, also had a theological slant. It was thought that a vacuum was so contrary to nature that no human power could create one, since a true vacuum could cause heaven and earth to change places and generally cause all bodies to 'act contrary to their own Nature' (I, 244). The traditional, quasi-animistic notion that nature abhorred a vacuum is reinterpreted by Boyle in terms of mechanical forces, though it must be noted that the words he chooses to characterize these mechanical forces have their own animistic connotations. What looks like a 'determination' by nature to fill a vacuum is a perfectly mechanical effect caused by the sheer physical weight or pressure of air 'whose restless endeavor to expand it selfe every way, makes it either rush in it selfe, or compel the interpos'd bodys into all spaces, where it finds no greater resistance than it can surmount' (I, 245).

'A PIECE OF GREEN-WOOD BURNING'

Boyle against the elements

In his best-known work, *The Sceptical Chymist*, Boyle sets out to show the superiority of the new experimental methodology over the approaches of the Aristotelians and the alchemists or 'chymists'. The Aristotelians believe that all 'mixt bodies' are composed of varying proportions of the four elements (air, earth, fire, and water); the modern alchemical school follows Paracelsus in claiming that everything is compounded of the three 'principles' of salt, sulphur, and mercury; while the more seemingly experimental sorts of chymists or 'sooty empirics' make the mistake of not giving due attention to the theoretical or philosophical implications of their work. Boyle's explicit aim in *The Sceptical Chymist* is not to completely discredit either alchemy or 'chymistry' but to exhort their practitioners to avoid 'Phantastick and Unintelligible Discourses' (1999: II, 373). This, it should be noted, is his *stated* aim, and may have more to do with the requirements of civility than with his heartfelt convictions. For the most part, *The Sceptical Chymist* reads like a sustained critique of both the doctrine of the elements and the theoretical assumptions that support alchemy and chymistry. Boyle registers a certain respect, however, for the alchemists and chymists, especially for their preparedness to carry out 'sooty' experiments. He is no doubt speaking truthfully when he describes the experiments of the hermetic philosophers as 'Substantial and noble' (II, 374), and again when he acknowledges that the alchemical experimenters have done the commonwealth of learning some service by helping to destroy 'that excessive esteem, or rather veneration, wherewith the Doctrine of the four elements was almost as generally as undeservedly entertain'd' (II, 329). It is clear, though, that he acknowledges such usefulness 'upon the score of their experiments, not upon that of Their Speculations' (II, 329). In the end, his objections to alchemical theories are as strong as his objections to the doctrine of the four elements (see Alexander 1985: 23–4).

The main concern of *The Sceptical Chymist* is the composition of material bodies. The time-honoured claim of the Aristotelians – that all material bodies are composed of proportions of the four elements – is presented by Themistius, who expresses a preference for the deliberations of reason over the testimony of the senses, and refers to experimental results only in order to satisfy 'those that are not capable of a Nobler Conviction' (Boyle 1999: II, 221). He asserts indeed that one experimental example is all he needs to illustrate his general position. It is in fact a very good example. He invites his companions to consider a piece of green-wood burning in a chimney. If they examine the burning or burnt wood, they will 'readily discern in the disbanded parts of it the four Elements' (II, 222). The most apparent element is, of course, the fire itself; the smoke ascending from the fire is air from the wood returning to where it belongs; the water boiling and hissing at the ends of the burning wood manifests itself to more than one sense; 'and the ashes by their weight, their firmness, and their dryness, put past doubt that they belong to the Element of Earth' (II, 222). Before he concludes his knock-down argument, Themistius, the Aristotelian, makes it clear that he rejects not only the theories and experiments of the modern innovators, such as are represented by Boyle's mouth-piece, Carneades, but also the sort of chemistry practised by the followers of Paracelsus. All experimenters alike are dismissed by Themistius as 'sooty empirics', just because they persist with dirty experiments instead of reflecting on the noble truths of reason.

Carneades proceeds to reply at length to the claims not only of Themistius but also of the alchemists and chymists. He weaves together a number of objections which challenge the basic assumptions that his rivals make about the role of fire in experiments, about the nature of the 'precipitates' produced by fire, and about the number of ingredients that are supposed to make up every compound substance. He rejects the claim, which he imputes to both Aristotelians and alchemists, that fire is the only means of separating a compound into its supposedly component elements, and cites experiments which demonstrate that there are some compounds which can be easily separated into their components by 'cold' chemical means – that is, by applying acids and other specially prepared solutions. Fire will not separate gold and silver if they are combined in one mass, 'whereas they may be very easily parted by the Affusion of Spirit of Nitre or *Aqua fortis*' (II, 240). Even in those cases where fire reduces a compound to a number of substances, there is no guarantee that these residual substances are the original, let alone the elementary, components of the compound. These by-products or residues may be nothing more than new compounds produced by the very action of the fire and may not be any simpler than the original compound. If subjected to further heat they may produce further new by-products which yet again constitute new compounds. In any case, even where fire does reduce a compound to its original components, it does not follow that the number of elementary components must always be four, as the Aristotelians argue, or three, as the alchemists argue. Boyle again cites examples where the number of separated elements is more than four or less than three. He has particularly interesting observations to make about the ability of gold to resist analysis. Although he stops short of discovering that gold is in fact an element (possibly because he is unduly suspicious of the concept of *element*), he writes intriguingly of attempts to reduce gold to its 'components', and is incredulous of reports that some experimenters have recovered salt from gold. His own position on the theory of elements is that some things which are assumed to be compounds (such as gold) may not be compounds at all, and that all genuine compounds are composed of varying numbers of elements, sometimes less than three, sometimes more than four.

The closest that Boyle comes to the modern theory of elements is in the following summation of his corpuscularian position: '[I]f it be granted rational to suppose . . . that the Elements consisted at first of certain small and primary Coalitions of the minute Particles of matter into Corpuscles very numerous, and very like each other, It will not be absurd to conceive, that such primary Clusters may be of far more sorts than three or five' (II, 279). In this passage he is postulating not only the existence of primary particles but also the bonding of some particles into primary clusters or elements. Though he is a long way from postulating the complex atomic structure of elements in the modern sense, nevertheless he is groping in the right direction. Despite the fact that Boyle 'failed' to discover the modern elements, he is nonetheless entitled to his place of importance in the history of modern chemistry. Under his influence alchemy and 'vulgar chymistry' were transmuted into natural philosophy, and it became the task of later scientists to transmute Boyle's mechanical philosophy into the modern science of chemistry. Though it is perhaps too much to claim that he was the father of modern chemistry, he was certainly 'a great and influential preceptor who infused chemistry with an exceedingly fruitful and rewarding attitude and method of attack' (Hall 1966: 113).

Research by modern scholars has shown that Boyle is important not only for his contribution to natural philosophy but also for his contribution to the wider intellectual universe. Rose-Mary Sargent has argued that Boyle developed a philosophy of experiment that is significantly different from the traditional forms of empiricism and inductivism, and that now merits consideration in its own right. She also suggests that a retrieval of Boyle's attitude to experimental enquiry would lead to a much-needed modesty of mind among scientists and a greater reverence for the world, and might go some way towards curbing 'a technological hubris that has resulted in the near devastation of crucial parts of the earth's delicate ecosystem' (1995: 216). Peter Anstey has made a strong case for Boyle's status as a philosopher, pointing out that he had an original conception of matter and its properties, and was the first of the mechanical philosophers to pay due attention to the objective or 'ontological' status of the perceivable qualities of things (2000: 205). In *Robert Boyle Reconsidered*, Michael Hunter has edited a collection of articles on so many aspects of Boyle's work that it is the best contemporary evidence of the range, diversity, and depth of the Irishman's contribution to intellectual history, tending to 'enhance one's respect for Boyle's sophistication as a thinker' (1994: 10). One aspect of Boyle's diversity – namely, his interest in the theological idea of 'things above reason' – is examined in precocious detail by Jan W. Wojcik. Wojcik undertakes to show that Boyle denied the competence of human reason to judge the content of revelation, and that his acceptance of the limits of reason shaped his conception of natural philosophy or 'science' (1997). And finally Lawrence Principe in his book *The Aspiring Adept* has argued the case for Boyle's indebtedness to both the theory and practice of alchemy. Principe's 'crucial note' on the 'value-laden baggage of the terms *alchemy* and *chemistry*' (1998: 8) is indeed essential reading for anyone setting out to read *The Sceptical Chymist*.

A THINKING GENTLEMAN

William Molyneux, new learner and patriot

William Molyneux (1656–1698) was born in Dublin into a wealthy and influential family that held a relatively secure place in the ascendancy network that dominated economic, political, and social life in seventeenth-century Dublin (see Simms 1982). He was educated at a city grammar school and at Trinity College, Dublin, from which he graduated in 1674, travelling to London the following year to study law at the Middle Temple. When he completed his courses there he returned to Ireland in 1678 and shortly afterwards married one of the daughters of Sir William Domville, Chief Justice of Ireland. An anxious period of Molyneux's life began when his young wife, Lucy, contracted a sudden and debilitating illness that led to rapidly failing eyesight. Visits to doctors in Dublin and later in England were to no avail. During this troubled period Molyneux, between journeys to doctors, occupied himself by translating Descartes' *Meditations*, an exercise that reflected his interest in the new methodic approach to philosophy. When it became clear that a cure for Lucy's disability was not forthcoming, she and Molyneux became resigned to their situation and turned towards occupations that were congenial and absorbing, she to music, he to science and optics. In 1689 Lucy gave birth to a child, Samuel, but her own life ended in 1691.

Molyneux became an advocate of the new scientific learning and the ideology of social improvement which surrounded it. In 1683, assisted by a like-minded contemporary, St George Ashe, and with the support of the Royal Society of London, he established the Dublin Philosophical Society. Though the new society would cease to function by 1708, its founding members were no less enthusiastic about natural philosophy and the value of scientific research than were their more numerous peers in the more successful Royal Society. As with the more established mentor society, the emphasis was on experiment rather than scholarship, and on cooperative rather than private effort. The first rule of William Petty's advertisement for the Dublin society expressly advises that its members 'apply themselves to the making of experiments, and prefer the same to the best discourses, letters and books they can make or read, even concerning experiments' (Hoppen 1970: 202). If the first rule serves to highlight the difference between the old and the new learning – between, respectively, the scholastic and the experimental approaches to knowledge – the sixth rule might well be directed against the hermetic secrecy of the traditional alchemist: 'That [the members] provide themselves with correspondents in several places, and make such observations as do depend upon the comparison of many experiments, and not upon single and solitary remarks' (Hoppen 1970: 203). The 'improving' or public-service ethos of the society is expressed in the second rule: 'That [the members] do not contemn and neglect common, trivial, and cheap experiments and observations; not contenting themselves without such, as may surprise and astonish the vulgar' (Hoppen 1970: 203). This rule seems in fact to encourage not only the edification of the vulgar but also their entertainment, suggesting that good public relations, even to the extent of playing to the gallery, was to be an important part of the society's enlightening mission.

The members of the Dublin society, like the members of the sister organizations in London and Oxford, had a penchant for researching abnormal phenomena, whether in the form of 'monsters' – that is, animals with deformities – or uncommon events and formations in the natural world. William Molyneux was as responsive to nature's curiosities as were his fellow members, and he duly performed dissections, examined 'monsters', and inquired into uncommon features of nature, such as the petrifying properties of the waters of Lough Neagh. He did so, however, without sensationalism and with due scientific caution. His two papers on Lough Neagh indicate the extent to which he was himself a 'new learner', capable of error but also capable of self-correction. In his first paper on Lough Neagh he was prepared at first to accept popular local belief that pieces of wood immersed for a number of years in the lake would turn to stone, but in a follow-up paper presented several months later he raised a series of questions over such local reports, specifically over the Lough Neagh 'holly stone', a particular example of which had aroused the interest of the Oxford Philosophical Society. Molyneux does not attempt to answer his own questions, but in the course of raising them he places emphasis on the need for further enquiry and careful observation. His commitment to enquiry and careful observation is also effectively and simply illustrated in his 'Account of the Connaught Worm' in which he discounted popular beliefs about this particular monster, successfully identifying it as a specimen of the elephant caterpillar (see Simms 1982: 40–4).

Like many other Protestants, especially those associated with the ruling intelligentsia, Molyneux left Ireland during the Williamite War of 1689–91, moving to Chester with his family and his brother, Thomas. While in Chester he concentrated on compiling and preparing for publication his extensive work on optics, though he seems to have regarded his interest in this area as more diversionary or 'idle' than his other pursuits. In a letter in 1690 to the English astronomer, John Flamsteed, he explained that 'whenever the troublesome thoughts of the misery of my poor country would permit me (which indeed was but seldom), I have diverted my mind by the consideration of dioptrics, and have put the last hand to an idle work of this kind, which I now design for the press' (Simms 1982: 65). The result of the concentrated work at Chester was his substantial treatise, *Dioptrica nova*, published in 1692. Although the treatise does not lend itself to summation in general terms, since it consists of detailed diagrams and theorems on the 'geometry' of lines of light passing through lenses of different shapes, one of the theorems, Prop. XXXI, is of particular significance in Irish intellectual history. This theorem would form the basis of the radical theory of vision and perception developed by a later

Irish philosopher, George Berkeley. The topic of the theorem is 'the Apparent Place of Objects seen through Convex-glasses'. The most surprising and provocative claim made in the course of the theorem is that distance is a matter of judgement or inference rather than of direct perception. Distance as such is not perceived, according to the theorem, but is 'a line presented to our Eye with its End towards us, which must therefore be only a *Point*, and that is *Invisible*' (Molyneux 1692: 113). Distance, then, is perceived more or less indirectly, by means of inference from 'interjacent bodies', such as familiar features of the landscape, including mountains, hills, fields, trees, and houses; and also by estimating the comparative magnitudes and colours of things arranged before us. This will be discussed again in Chapter 5, a section of which deals with Berkeley's theory of vision.

The fact that Molyneux spent most of his life in Ireland and that he was an enthusiastic founder-member of the country's first scientific association already implicates him more deeply than Robert Boyle in Ireland's cultural and intellectual life. But it was the publication of his influential political tract making a case for Ireland's legislative independence that earned him his reputation as an Irish patriot. When Henry Grattan, the political reformer of a later generation, famously exclaimed 'Spirit of Swift! spirit of Molyneux! your genius has prevailed! Ireland is now a nation!' (1874: 70) – this in the aftermath of constitutional reforms achieved in 1782 – he secured for Molyneux an identity and place in Irish history that later and more critical readings of Molyneux's book would not remove. Molyneux's intervention in the history of Ireland's troubled campaign for legislative independence occurred in the latter years of his life, the years following his return to Ireland after the battle of the Boyne. His active involvement in public affairs began when he was elected to the Irish parliament in 1695 as a representative for Trinity College. Three years later he published *The Case of Ireland's being Bound by Acts of Parliament in England, Stated*, drawing heavily upon the social contract principles that informed Locke's political philosophy, and applying these in a potentially radical way to Ireland's relationship to the English crown and parliament. He begins by declaring that the historical relationship between England and Ireland is founded on contract, not conquest. It is not possible, he argues, to find a better example of a 'fair Original Compact' than that which took place between Henry II and the people of Ireland in the second half of the twelfth century. The time-honoured account of the transactions between Henry and the Irish kings is an account of allegiance and contract, not of coercion, subjugation, or conquest. The essence of that original contract was that the people of the Irish kingdom should 'Enjoy the like Liberties and Immunities, and be Govern'd by the same Mild Laws, both Civil and Ecclesiastical, as the People of England' (1698: 46). From this royal guarantee it follows for Molyneux that no laws can be rightfully imposed by an English parliament 'but by the *Consent* and *Allowance* of the People of *Ireland*' (46). He is most anxious to show that, historically, Ireland has enjoyed the status of a separate kingdom, and should not be looked upon as a colony. Of course, he accepts without question that Ireland owes allegiance to the English crown, but the allegiance in question is the voluntary allegiance of an independent kingdom, freely given under the terms of an original contract, and not at all the coerced allegiance of a conquered and subjugated people. It has ever been acknowledged, he writes, 'that the Kingdom of *Ireland* is inseparably annex'd to the Imperial Crown of *England*' (102), but there exist statutes and acts which show conclusively that Ireland, though annexed to the crown of England, 'has always been look'd upon to be a *Kingdom Compleat within it self* . . . and Subordinate to no Legislative Authority on Earth' (103). His thinking here is grounded philosophically in Locke's *Second Treatise of Government* and is duly articulated in the language of natural rights and social contract. Having established that Ireland's being bound by acts of parliament made in England is contrary to the historical record, he proceeds to show that it is also contrary to reason and to 'the Common Rights of all Mankind' (116). He takes it as self-evident that all men are by nature in a state of equality, that they are 'promiscuously born to all the same Advantages of Nature, and the use of all the same Faculties' (116), and that it is therefore inconceivable that anyone should be naturally subordinate or subject to another. On this equality of nature is founded 'that Right which all Men claim, of being free from all Subjection to Positive Laws, till by their own *Consent* they give up their Freedom, by entring into Civil Societies for the common Benefit of all the Members thereof' (117). On this popular consent – which is the consent of the social contract – depends the validity and enforcibility of all subsequent 'humane' or civil laws. The radical implication which Molyneux is able to take from such thinking is that it must be contrary to justice and reason that a kingdom with its own laws and parliament, such as Ireland has had historically, should now be bound without its consent 'by the Parliament of another Kingdom' (120). A further radical implication of Molyneux's political thought is that, as Joep Leerssen emphasizes, he does not see government as the self-evident and inevitable concomitant of a social community of individuals, 'but considers it in constant need of being justified through its serviceableness to that social community, to the common good' (1996: 298). It is this appeal to consensus, and his insistence on the relationship between government and the public good, that makes Molyneux such a crucial figure in the history of Irish political thought.

That Molyneux was concerned primarily and exclusively with the rights and liberties of his fellow Protestants is perfectly clear from his derogatory references to 'papists' in the text of *The Case of Ireland*. But two points need to be made here, and made together. First, as Caroline Robbins reminds us, the Irish Protestants in this period were not republican, nor were they for the most part Commonwealthmen, 'but their own situation forced from them expression of ideas potentially revolutionary and useful to rebellious colonists . . . and to supporters of full civil and religious liberties for all mankind' (1968: 135). In their determination to be granted the same rights and liberties as other subjects of the English crown, they were obliged to plead equality before the law; and in order to make the strongest possible case for their rights as Irish subjects, they were obliged, first, to recognize the unfair treatment of Ireland by recent English parliaments, and, second, to speak the language of rights, equity, and moral entitlement. This recourse to the language of rights had the effect, whether consciously intended or not, of developing a sense of grievance on behalf of all Irish subjects of the English crown. The fact that the sense of grievance was articulated by a relatively privileged minority does not compromise the historical importance of the kind of Irish Protestant patriotism articulated by Molyneux. What is significant is that, under the moral aegis of Molyneux, a protracted history of grievance began in Ireland in response to acts and laws imposed unilaterally by English parliaments. This history, though originating with a Protestant minority, would be volleyed forward subsequently by even more aggrieved groups, including the insolent and barbarous Irish papists of whom Molyneux speaks in passing. What is especially noteworthy here is that the language used originally by the Protestant patriots – the language of natural rights and liberties – cannot be confined to a minority or used to justify the privileges of a minority. The universal import of the language of rights adopted by the Protestant patriots, beginning with Molyneux, was carried far beyond the confines of their own regional and timely concerns and became audible to others, including those whom they did not at first recognize as full citizens of the commonwealth of entitlement. This combination of special regional circumstances with the universal language of rights proved in any case to be a potent mix. Molyneux's *Case of Ireland* became such an influential document that it came to be described as 'the Manual of Irish Liberty', and would be cited and quoted by other advocates of right and liberty, both conservative and revolutionary, from Swift to Wolfe Tone (see Kelly 2000: 106).

MR MOLYNEUX TO MR LOCKE

An Anglo-Irish correspondence

The dedicatory epistle which prefaces Molyneux's *Dioptrica nova* is of particular interest since it provides another important link between Molyneux and one of his most influential mentors, a mentor with whom his name is still linked. In his dedicatory epistle Molyneux, after dismissing scholastic philosophy as 'an heap of froathy Disputes' and the greatest cheat ever imposed on the mind of man, had expressed his indebtedness to John Locke in terms that were highly complimentary, even by seventeenth-century standards of exaggerated civility. He refers to 'the incomparable Mr. Locke', who, in his *Essay concerning Human Understanding*, 'hath rectified more received Mistakes, and delivered more profound Truths, established on Experience and Observation, for the Direction of Man's mind in the Prosecution of Knowledge . . . than are to be met with in all the Volumes of the Ancients' (1692: [v]). Molyneux clearly intended Locke to see this laudatory dedication since he had a copy of *Dioptrica nova* delivered to him. Locke was duly impressed. In his first letter to Molyneux, dated 16 July 1692, he thanks Molyneux for his 'extraordinary compliment' and asks him to provide some assistance to the bearer of the letter, a Dr Sibelius, who intended to settle in Dublin. In his second letter he earnestly requests Molyneux's 'advice and assistance' about a proposed second edition of the *Essay*. As the correspondence between the two men develops, Locke becomes increasingly specific, even insistent, about the kind of advice he has in mind. He suspects that Molyneux's reluctance to find major faults in the first edition has less to do with the excellence of the *Essay* than with the civility of his correspondent. Even when Molyneux identifies several passages in the *Essay* which could benefit from further clarification, Locke is still not satisfied and continues to press him for further comments. It is clear that Locke is anxious to pre-empt future criticism by having as many flaws as possible uncovered and dealt with before the second edition goes to press – and that he trusts Molyneux to detect them. He is not merely being civil when he praises Molyneux for his 'penetration and quickness'. A number of important revisions made in the second edition were in fact prompted by Molyneux's criticisms and requests for explication. The most extensive of these revisions occurs in Book II, ch. xxi, in which Locke deals with the question of liberty and the determinants of human action.

The addition to the *Essay* with which Molyneux is most famously credited arose out of a 'jocose problem' that he put to Locke in his letter of 2 March 1693. This problem is best understood in the context of Locke's account of the nature of simple ideas. In Book II of the *Essay* Locke identifies four categories of simple ideas – those, such as colour or sound, that are registered by one sense only; those, such as shape or figure, that are registered by more than one sense; those that are acquired through 'inner sense' or reflection – that is, by inward observation of our own internal psychological states or processes; and finally those ideas, such as pain and pleasure, that are registered by all the senses, including the internal sense. In the context of Molyneux's 'jocose problem', we are concerned only with the second category of simple ideas, though it helps to appreciate a difficulty with the second category if we have a clear understanding of the first, that is, the category of ideas that register through one sense only. Colours come through one sense only, namely, the sense of sight; sounds through hearing only; solidity through the sense of touch only.

In other words, a colour is precisely that 'idea' or quality that cannot be heard or touched, only seen; a sound is that quality that can be heard but not seen or touched; solidity that quality that comes through the sense of touch but not through sight or hearing. If we lack any one of these senses, then we will lack the simple ideas that might have entered the mind through that sense. If we lack sight, for example, we will not acquire the simple idea of 'red', 'blue', or of any other colour. In the case of the second category of simple ideas, however, more than one sense is involved in the formation of the appropriate simple ideas. The simple idea of shape or figure, for example, can register through both the sense of sight and the sense of touch. We can see a shape and we can also feel or touch it. Shape, in other words, is a visible feature of things but it is also a tangible feature – we can *see* the roundness of an apple but we can also *feel* this roundness. However – and this is the crux of what has come to be known as 'Molyneux's problem' – the idea of a shape as it registers through sight is not directly inferable from the idea of the same shape as it registers through touch. You can feel the shape of something as well as see it, but you cannot infer the visible shape from the felt shape, or vice versa. The visual representation or 'look' of a thing's shape is different from the tactile representation or 'feel' of it, even though both experiences are effected by the same primary quality in an object, namely, its objective shape. The look of a thing cannot be inferred from the feel of it, as far as shape is concerned. This at least appears to have been Molyneux's understanding of Locke's position when he wonders whether a blind man, on recovering his sight and being presented with a sphere and a cube, would be able to identify them on the basis of having previously experienced them through touch alone. Molyneux presents the problem as follows:

> Suppose a man born blind, and now adult, and taught by his touch to distinguish between a cube, and a sphere (suppose) of ivory, nighly of the same bigness, so as to tell when he felt one and t'other, which is the cube, which the sphere. Suppose then the cube and sphere placed on a table, and the blind man to be made to see; query, Whether by his sight, before he touched them he could now distinguish and tell, which is the globe, which the cube? I answer, not; for though

he has obtained the experience of how a globe, and how a cube affects his touch; yet he has not yet attained the experience, that what affects his touch so or so, must affect his sight so or so; or that a protuberant angle in the cube, that pressed his hand unequally, shall appear to his eye as it does in the cube.

(Locke 1794: 311)

It is Molyneux's view, then, that as far as simple ideas or sensations are concerned, we cannot make immediate inferences from the ideas of one sense to the ideas of another, even when the same objective feature is in question. The distinctively tactile idea of roundness, angularity, or cubeness that we receive through the sense of touch cannot be translated directly into the visual idea of roundness or squareness derived from sight. In order to recognize by sight the same shapes that are familiar to us through touch we first have to acquire the appropriate visual ideas, and subsequently build up associations between the visual and tangible impressions. The basic conditions of visual recognition are not yet available to the man who is seeing for the first time.

In his letter in reply to Molyneux, Locke makes only a brief reference to the problem of the sphere and the cube, but it is a significant one. Your ingenious problem, he tells Molyneux, 'will deserve to be published to the world' (1794: 314). And, true to his implicit promise, Locke does indeed publish Molyneux's problem to the world. In Book II of the second edition of his *Essay concerning Human Understanding* he indicates to the reader that he is about to interpolate a problem 'of that very ingenious and studious promoter of real knowledge, the learned and worthy Mr. Molineux, which he was pleased to send me in a letter some months since', and then goes on to present a slightly modified version of the relevant passage from Molyneux's letter (1975: II, ix, § 8). Having stated Molyneux's question Locke immediately expresses agreement with Molyneux's solution:

I agree with this thinking Gent. whom I am proud to call my Friend, in his answer to this his Problem; and am of opinion, that the Blind Man, at first sight, would not be able with certainty to say, which was the Globe, which the Cube, whilst he only saw them: though he could unerringly name them by his touch, and certainly distinguish them by the difference of their Figures felt.

(II, ix, § 8)

Molyneux's query became, and has remained, a touchstone of funda-mental differences between philosophers, especially those who are concerned with the respective roles of mind and sense, or reason and experience, in the formation of ideas. Those sympathetic to an empiri-cist epistemology have tended to side with Molyneux and Locke, while those (such as rationalists and idealists) who wish to make ideas relatively independent of the senses have tended to give an affirmative answer to the query – that is, have tended to say that the man who has recovered his sight would in fact be able to visually distinguish globe and cube on the basis of prior tactile experience. The exemplary ration-alist or idealist response to the query was stated by Locke's contem-porary, the German philosopher G.W. Leibniz, who argued that the blind man whose sight is restored could discern the cube and the sphere by applying rational or geometrical principles to the sensory knowledge he has already acquired by touch (1996: 136–8).

AGAINST THE SELF-IMAGE OF THE AGE

Michael Moore, a Paris Aristotelian from Ireland

The new scientific learning promoted by Boyle, Molyneux, and the members of the Royal Society and the Dublin Philosophical Society had its origins in the thought of the English philosopher Francis Bacon and the French philosopher René Descartes, both of whom deliberately turned away from traditional scholarly modes of enquiry. Though there were important differences of emphasis among the new learners – some, the 'deductivists', following Descartes in their advocacy of reason, others, the 'inductivists', following Bacon in their advocacy of observation – they were united in their opposition to 'the verbose philosophy' of scholasticism and Aristotelianism. Their typical criticism of the Aristotelians was that they were 'more committed to Aristotle than to the pursuit of truth' (Mercer 1993: 35). Bacon dismissed the scholastic texts as 'laborious webs of learning' based on the study of a few authors, chiefly Aristotle, their 'dictator' (1857: 285); and Descartes proudly recorded his intention to leave the scholarly study of letters and turn instead to 'a practical philosophy in the place of the speculative philosophy taught by the Schoolmen' (1970: 46). Recent research has cast an interesting side-light on the historic rise of the new learning, and has shown that, while the new learning had able defenders in Ireland, some of its ablest critics also hailed from Ireland. These critics, however, did not for the most part reside in Ireland. They were those Catholic scholars and clerics who did not have access in a Protestant-controlled country to the kinds of institution that could train them in theology and philosophy and who therefore tended to go to Continental universities for their education and training. In the aftermath of the Council of Trent (1545–1563), and throughout the seventeenth century, these scholars and students came to constitute a kind of university in exile, attending seminaries or colleges in Salamanca, Louvain, Rome, Bordeaux, Toulouse, Prague, and Paris. Liam Chambers has shown that one of these exiled Irish scholars, Michael Moore (1640–1726), was not only a capable defender of the 'old learning' (or Aristotelianism) but was also actively engaged in attacking the Continental version of the new learning, namely, Cartesianism. In a trilogy of Latin texts, the most important of which was his *De existentia Dei* (1692), Moore launched an impressive critique of Descartes' theory of knowledge, arguing that the Aristotelian conception of ideas and their relationship to the world was a more promising foundation for a truly scientific knowledge of the world.

Moore's reason for attacking Descartes in particular had to do with the centrality of France in his own curriculum vitae. Born in Dublin in 1640, he was educated in France, graduating from the University of Paris with a Master's degree in 1662. For the next twenty years he pursued a teaching career at the University of Paris, becoming a vice-principal of one of its colleges by the 1680s. He returned to Ireland during the reign of James II and was appointed vicar general of the archdiocese of Dublin. He was also appointed provost of Trinity College, Dublin, the first Catholic to occupy the position. His unlikely and short-lived appointment was brought about by the influence of the powerful Richard Talbot, earl of Tyrconnell, who was commander-in-chief of the Jacobite army in Ireland, later lord deputy. Talbot, a member of an Old English Catholic family, had wanted Catholics in positions of military and civil power, and his appointment of Moore to the provostship of Trinity College was part of a general plan of 'Catholicization' (see Connellan 1992: 263). Moore's untimely departure from the position of provost was precipitated not by the collapse of the Jacobite cause but, reportedly, by his own indiscretion. In the course of a sermon at Christ Church he seems to have made a slighting reference to a Jesuit friend of King James, and the offended king subsequently gave orders that Moore should quit the kingdom. This Moore promptly did, but not without remarking, 'Go, I will, without doubt, but remember, the King himself will soon be after me' (Connellan 1992: 266). By 1691 Moore was back on the Continent, spending some years in Rome before eventually returning to the University of Paris where he was twice made rector.

Moore's philosophical position – what L.W.B. Brockliss (1981) calls 'Paris Aristotelianism' – has been described as a dynamic and sophisticated one, not a mere reiteration or recycling of Aristotelian postulates and definitions (see Chambers 2000). Certainly, his criticisms of Cartesianism are lively and deserved to be answered by the followers of Descartes. He is particularly strong in his critique of the Cartesian theory of knowledge (1692: 56–67), and offers in place of Cartesian rationalism a conception of ideas that gives due importance to sensation and experience. This emphasis on the role of sensation suggests, at first glance, a bias against rationalism and towards empiricism. But only at first glance. It is clear that Moore's conception of knowledge is not only very different from that of Descartes but also very different from the new experimental approach pursued by the Baconian observers. Moore's own theory of 'scientia' – of knowledge as it is understood in the Aristotelian tradition – is revealingly different from the kind of scientific treatise that one might associate with such new learners as Boyle and Molyneux. Whereas the latter engaged in detailed experiments, measurements, and observations, Moore has recourse to schematic definitions and demonstrations, all interspersed with respectful references to Aristotle. His promisingly titled *Vera sciendi methodus* (1716) is not an account of scientific methodology in the modern sense, certainly not in any sense that would be acceptable to Boyle, Molyneux, or the new natural philosophers. Indeed, in his preface to this work Moore cannot contain his contempt for the new atomistic, mechanical philosophy, observing that in the French schools of physics 'you will hear of nothing but subtle, spherical and fluted matter, fanciful illusions which have no connection with the nature of things; nor in most cases is our physics anything more than a commentary on Descartes' fanatical fable of the origin of the world' (Brockliss 1981: 53–4). In other words, his own theory of knowledge is not based on the kinds of observations that might be made in a laboratory or discovered as the result of experiment – it is instead an elaboration of Aristotelian and scholastic conceptions, definitions, and propositions. It serves in the end to highlight the contrast between the old and the new learning, and to confirm indeed some of the suspicions of the new learners. This is not to say that the tradition to which Moore belonged was universally vanquished by the new learning. While Aristotelianism has long ago ceased to offer a competitive alternative to the modern modes of scientific enquiry, it has found a niche in classical studies and in certain departments of philosophy, and has continued to attract scholars or 'old learners' who possess a knowledge of classical Greek and Latin.

4

JOHN TOLAND AND THE ASCENDANCY OF REASON

In a letter to John Locke on 16 March 1697, William Molyneux refers in passing to an essay entitled *Christianity not Mysterious* and identifies the author simply as 'Toland'. It is obvious that Molyneux at this point has only hearsay knowledge of this newly controversial author. He describes him as 'a stranger in these parts', adding that 'if he belongs to this kingdom, he must have been a good while out of it, for I have not heard of any such remarkable man amongst us' (Locke 1794: 404). It is an indication of the urgency of John Toland's self-propelled rise to fame and notoriety that Molyneux, in a follow-up letter to Locke a few weeks later, is able to report that he has just had a visit from Toland. The impression Molyneux has of his visitor at this point is largely positive, though he appears to be alarmed at his penchant for controversy. He is impressed by the fact that Toland has travelled to Europe and studied under 'the great Le Clerc' (about whom Molyneux and Locke have much to say in their correspondence), and even more so by the fact that his well-travelled visitor has expressed admiration for Locke. He is pleased too with Toland's conversation, finding him to be 'a candid free-thinker, and a good scholar' (405). He adds, however, that 'there is a violent sort of spirit that reigns here, which begins already to show itself against him' (405). Subsequent letters confirm that Toland has indeed drawn upon himself 'the clamours of all parties', not just because of the dis-agreeableness of his point of view but because of 'his unreasonable way of discoursing, propagating, and maintaining it' (421). By September Molyneux is reporting to Locke that Toland has been at last driven out of the country, having raised such an outcry 'that it was dangerous for a man to have been known to converse with him' (434). Who is this petulant figure who makes a series of fleeting and unsettling appearances in the correspondence between Molyneux and Locke, eliciting their praise but also their disapproval and apprehension? Who is this 'candid free-thinker' who does not seem to belong to the Irish intelligentsia of Molyneux's acquaintance, yet has the audacity to make himself known to the leading political and cultural figures of the day? And how did such a controversial and enigmatic figure come to be described as 'the father of modern Irish philosophy' (Berman 1985: 120)?

Sometime during the year 1670 John Toland was born in the Inishowen peninsula in Donegal, probably in the townland of Ardagh, and almost certainly into a Gaelic-speaking Roman Catholic family. Apart from his year and place of birth, little else is known about his early life in Donegal. His own account of his early life is not always reliable, tending as it does to project the mind of the mature and controversial man back into the formative years – the mind, moreover, of a man determined to forge a particular sort of identity for himself. The difficulty of establishing the early details of Toland's life begins with his very name. He claimed that he was christened Janus Junius but subsequently called himself John in order to avoid the derision of other children. Some recent scholars (Sullivan 1982 and Harrison 1994) have rejected the name Janus Junius as fanciful, since neither of the names would have been derived from local Irish ones and would therefore have been contrary to the baptismal canons of the local, Gaelic-speaking church. It is more likely that the new-born Toland was given the name Seán or Seán Eoghain (Sean Owen), which could have been latinized as Johannes Eugenius and further modified by Toland into the more suggestive Janus Junius. Janus invokes the two-faced Roman god who looked forward and backward at the same time (hinting perhaps at Toland's own ambivalent identity), while Junius alludes to Marcus Junius Brutus, the great Roman orator and philosopher whose republican credentials would have appealed to Toland. The surname itself is one of the common anglicizations of the Irish family name, Uí Thuathalláin. Though we can only speculate on Toland's reasons for perpetrating a fanciful gloss on the latinized version of his Gaelic name, it is all too easy to suspect that he wished to 'gloss over' his native Irish identity, the better to translate himself into his adopted identity as a freethinking member of the Protestant and dissenting intelligentsia. It is as if Toland was well aware of the political and cultural forces that were then in the ascendant in his country, and knew therefore that any future thinker who bore a name like Seán Eoghain Ó Tuathalláin was unlikely, at least for the time being, to make a contribution to the cultural or intellectual life of Ireland.

Toland also gives a somewhat romanticized account of his early conversion to Protestantism. He claims in the preface to his most important and most controversial work, *Christianity not Mysterious* (1696), that he was educated from the cradle 'in the grossest Superstition and Idolatry', adding immediately: 'God was pleas'd to make my own Reason, and such as made use of theirs, the happy Instruments of my Conversion' (1696: viii–ix). This account of his conversion to Protestantism can be interpreted as an example of enlightenment *mauvaise foi*, overstating as it does the influence of rational factors and ignoring the local historical realities of late seventeenth-century Ireland. While his reference to superstition and idolatry is readily decoded as a reference to Catholicism, his reference to the instruments of his conversion, specifically to those who 'made use of their reason', may be understood as an allusion to members of the Protestant community with whom he appears to have become acquainted quite early in his life. It is very likely that while still a child he attracted the attention of a local minister or teacher who effectively became his patron, subsequently enabling him to enrol as a scholarship student at the Protestant school at Redcastle in Donegal. Alan Harrison points out that Protestant schools at this point in the seventeenth century offered a good education to promising young Catholics on condition that they changed their religious allegiance (1994: 8–9). While it is very possible that Toland was a willing convert, it is equally possible that the generous act of patronage which took him from Inishowen to Redcastle, from a Catholic to a Protestant ethos, had something to do with the urgency of his conversion. His conversion was in any case whole-hearted, and he was absorbed ever more deeply into the culture of Protestantism, quickly gravitating towards the radical and dissenting end of his adopted religion.

The journey to Redcastle was only the first stage in a kind of eventful intellectual and cultural pilgrimage that would take Toland into the centres of radical theological and philosophical thought in Britain and Europe. In 1686, probably with the support of his original Protestant patron, he went to study at the University of Glasgow where it is on record that 'he behaved himself as one trew Protestant, and Loyal subject' (Harrison 1994: 11). Three years later, for reasons that are not clear, he moved to Edinburgh, where in 1690 he was awarded an MA degree. Though his original patron no doubt expected him to return to his native community to proselytize on behalf of his adopted persuasion, Toland had other plans. Shortly after his graduation from Edinburgh he moved to London, where he became acquainted with a congenial group of dissenters. From there, and with the material support of these dissenters, he went to Holland in late 1692 or early 1693, attending the universities of Leyden and Utrecht, where he came under the influence of some of the most influential and controversial figures of the day. Holland, with its ethos of tolerance, quickly became a model of civic and intellectual culture for Toland. The Dutch Republic had, of course, already played a pivotal role in the history of the Protestant cause in England and Ireland, since it was from there that William of Orange had come to depose the Catholic king, James II, bringing about the Glorious Revolution of 1688. Two years later the same William, now King William III, had brought Irish history to one of its crucial turning points when he defeated the combined Irish and French forces of James II at the battle of the Boyne. It is a measure of Toland's immersion in the Protestant cause and ethos that he should find such a congenial niche in Holland during these years of Williamite triumph. By the time Toland left Holland he had become, according to Margaret Jacob, a changed man. If we presume that he left England as a committed Christian and Presbyterian, 'his experiences in Holland produced in him an intellectual revolution' (Jacob 1976: 212). He was now a freethinker, and the first substantial expression of his freethinking would be his highly controversial *Christianity not Mysterious*, published in London in 1696.

REASON, REVELATION, AND MEANING

To fully appreciate the intellectual origins of Toland's theological radicalism it is worth taking a brief look at the main arguments of the chapters on religion in Locke's *Essay concerning Human Understanding*. In Book IV of the *Essay* Locke sets himself the difficult task of marking the boundaries between the 'distinct provinces' of faith and reason. Reason he takes to be the ability of the mind to deduce propositions or truths from all those ideas it has formed through sensation or reflection. Faith, on the other hand, is the assent to propositions that are not based on sensation, reflection, or the deductions of reason, 'but upon the Credit of the Proposer, as coming from GOD, in some extraordinary way of Communication. This way of discovering Truths to Men we call *Revelation*' (1975: IV, xviii, § 2). There is nothing unduly controversial in this distinction, so stated. Locke has simply cleared an important space in his theory of understanding for the concepts of faith and revelation. In subsequent sections, however, we find him arguing that we can never accept as a truth anything that is directly contrary to the plain and clear dictates of reason. For example, our idea of an individual thing or body is so clearly bound up with the idea of its singularly occupying one place at a time that we can never assent to a proposition affirming a thing's appearance in two different places at the same time, even if such a proposition should be offered as a divine revelation. Given the evidence of our own intuitive knowledge about bodies and locations, it is more likely that we have deceived ourselves than that we have actually discovered the same object in two different locations at the same time. Therefore, Locke concludes,

> *no Proposition can be received for Divine Revelation,* or obtain the Assent due to all such, *if it be contradictory of our clear intuitive Knowledge.* Because this would be to subvert the Principles, and Foundations of all Knowledge, Evidence, and Assent whatsoever: And there would be left no difference between Truth and Falshood, no measures of Credible and Incredible in the World, if doubtful Propositions shall take place before self-evident; and what we certainly know, give way to what we may possibly be mistaken in.
>
> (IV, xviii, § 5)

In sum, then, we cannot rightly or rationally accept that a proposition is a divine revelation if the acceptance of it would effectively overturn all the principles and foundations of knowledge that God has already given us, thereby undermining 'the most excellent Part of his Workmanship, our Understandings' (IV, xviii, § 5). Rather than confound our rational natures in this way, we should prefer to question the authenticity of any such supposed revelation.

While Locke accepts that there are things which are above or beyond the scope of reason and are therefore 'the proper Matter of Faith', he nonetheless insists that reason reserves the right to decide whether any putative revelation is a genuine one or not. The following passage encapsulates the 'rationalism' of Locke's position:

> Whatever GOD hath revealed, is certainly true; no Doubt can be made of it. This is the proper Object of *Faith*: But whether it be a divine Revelation, or no, *Reason* must judge; which can never permit the Mind to reject a greater Evidence to embrace what is less evident, nor allow it to entertain Probability in opposition to Knowledge and Certainty.
>
> (IV, xviii, § 10)

Even in those areas, then, where reason and experience have nothing substantive to offer, and where revelation alone may be the source of new truths, reason must remain wary of anything that is contrary to its own principles of evidence and consistency. Reason is not in opposition to faith or revelation – indeed, it is reasonable to acknowledge that revelation may yield up truths which reason cannot itself deliver – but anything purporting to be a truth of revelation must not be repugnant to reason. We may believe what is improbable, but we should not be prepared to believe what is contrary to, or subversive of, reason. While Locke professes to emphasize the complementary roles of reason and revelation, it is easy to read him as tipping the balance very much in favour of reason and effectively preparing the way for arguments that could be used to make a case for forms of religious belief, such as deism, that purport to be altogether rational in origin and character. Locke in *The Reasonableness of Christianity* expressly rejected deism, claiming it to be a subversion of Christianity, but in

Book IV of the *Essay* he has provided thinkers more radical than himself with the makings of the deistic argument.

Toland is one such radical interpreter of Locke. In *Christianity not Mysterious* he sets out single-mindedly to show that there is nothing in the Christian gospel that is either contrary to or above reason, or that is mysterious or unintelligible. Like Locke, he is sure from the outset that the doctrines of the gospel, insofar as they really are the word of God, cannot be repugnant to our clear and distinct ideas, 'nor to our common Notions' (1696: 25). His objective is to remonstrate with those who would claim that we are bound to 'adore what we cannot comprehend' (26). He dismisses this claim as irrational, as the source of all the 'absurdities' that beset Christianity. By absurdity he means not merely something that is highly improbable or factually incredible but, more fundamentally, a use of words to which no meaning can be attached – that is, an expression or sentence that will prove unintelligible once we dwell on the meanings of the terms which compose it. By way of example he targets the idea of limbo, placing the sentence 'Children dying before Baptism are damn'd without Pain' on the same level of intelligibility as the self-contradictory assertion that '*a Ball is white and black at once*' (29). Both sentences are 'well put together' and therefore appear meaningful, but in fact they signify nothing at all. The latter loses its meaning as soon as we realize that the named colours are incompatibly ascribed to the same object. And the former fares no better once we attend to what is implied by damnation and pain. If the souls of the unbaptized children are 'intelligent creatures' in the other world, then their being excluded from God's presence and from the company of the blessed must be ineffably painful to them. On the other hand, if they lack understanding, or the capacity to experience pain, then it makes no sense to speak of their being damned. In short, the notion of damnation without pain is unthinkable, and any reference to such a notion is unintelligible. Such notions and such expressions cannot be 'the Ground of a *reasonable Service*, or Worship' (30).

To say that revealed truths must be presented in intelligible terms and in accordance with rational principles seems to place serious constraints on the omnipotence of God. Is it not a kind of blasphemy to limit the omnipotent creator to the terms of human reason? Is an omnipotent God not capable of doing and revealing things which go beyond what is expressible in human terms? To this sort of objection Toland replies that the real blasphemy is to presume that God would require us to believe what is manifestly unintelligible or impossible. If we call that person a fool who asks us to believe something impossible, such as that he saw a cane or staff without two ends, 'how dare we blasphemously attribute to *the most perfect Being*, what is an acknowledg'd Defect in one of our selves?' (42). Toland reiterates his principle that whoever wishes to reveal anything to us must utter words that are intelligible and speak of matters that are possible. This rule holds good regardless of whether the revealer is God or a fellow-human. We cannot begin to believe unintelligible revelations, even when they purport to come from God, 'for the conceiv'd Ideas of things are the only Subjects of Believing, Denying, Approving, and every other Act of the Understanding: Therefore *all Matters reveal'd by God or Man, must be equally intelligible and possible*' (42).

Toland finds evidence in scripture itself to support his claim that Christianity was intended to be a 'rational and intelligible religion' and not at all a religion of mystery and paradox. He even identifies examples of key figures ostensibly exercising their rational faculties. The Virgin Mary did not believe that she would bear a child who would be called the son of God 'till the *Angel* gave her a satisfactory Answer to the strongest Objection that could be made' (44). Even the story of Abraham's preparedness to sacrifice his own son on a command from God is not to be read as an example of irrational or unquestioning belief. Abraham must have been aware of God's promise that his descendants would be as 'numerous as the Stars of Heaven, or the Sand upon the Sea-shore' (131), and, duly deducing that all these future descendants must come from his only son, Isaac, he would have concluded that God must intend to revive Isaac miraculously after his sacrificial death. In this way Abraham, as a rational human being, would have inwardly resolved the apparent contradiction between God's present command and his former promise. What is there in all this, asks Toland rhetorically, 'but very strict Reasoning from Experience, from the Possibility of the thing, and from the Power, Justice, and Immutability of him that promis'd it?' (132).

In his opening critique of what he calls 'the irrational hypothesis' Toland concentrates on pressing home his claim that unintelligible expressions cannot constitute the matter of revelation or belief.

In Section Three he turns his attention to a more moderate version of the irrational hypothesis, namely, that though revealed doctrines cannot be contrary to reason, nevertheless they may sometimes be above reason in the sense that they be 'mysterious' or not fully understood. Toland accepts that there is a legitimate use of the term 'mystery', but denies that it refers to anything that lies beyond or above reason. He identifies many passages in scripture in which there are references to such things as the 'mystery' of the Gospel (Eph. 6: 9), the 'mystery' of Christ (Col. 4: 3, 4), or the 'mystery' of the Kingdom of God (Mark 4: 11), but suggests that mystery in these contexts refers to the fact that something of great significance was hidden or unknown until it was subsequently revealed. In its most general application, the term refers to the fact that 'the future Dispensation' described in scripture 'was totally hid from the *Gentiles*, and but very imperfectly known to the *Jews*' (Toland 1696: 95). In other words, a phrase such as 'the mystery of the gospel' simply reminds us of that condition of human knowledge that preceded revelation and which is put into perspective by revelation, but it does not refer to some incomprehensible condition or feature of revelation itself. Toland reinterprets the term mystery to mean something like 'awesome recognition' rather than a state of puzzlement.

Toland does not argue that the biblical testaments are so simple that they do not need study and close reading; nor does he advocate a hubristic conception of human reason, as if to say that all things are wholly transparent to the human intellect. He accepts that in fact nothing is ever fully understood, though this consideration applies to all the objects of our experience and knowledge, regardless of whether they are natural or supernatural. He makes a clever use of Locke's distinction between nominal and real essences. A thing's nominal essence is the set of its known properties to which we attach a particular name. The nominal essence of the sun, for example, will include its brightness, heat, roundness, and motion. To have an idea of the sun is to be able to bring to mind such properties whenever references are made to it. Likewise the nominal essence of honey consists in its colour, taste, redolence, and other known properties. We cannot assume, however, that such observable properties constitute the *real* essence of a thing. For one thing, we know only those properties of things which it is necessary and useful for us to know. We cannot therefore claim to know all the essential properties of a thing. Moreover, it stands to reason that all observable properties inhere in an underlying substance – matter in the case of physical properties, spirit in the case of psychological or intellectual properties – and that this underlying substance or foundation of properties is not accessible to us since it is not itself a property, e.g., a colour, sound, taste, shape, or smell. It is precisely this internal substance which constitutes the real essence of anything. Following Locke, Toland defines real essence as *'that intrinsick Constitution of a thing which is the Ground or Support of all its Properties, and from which they naturally flow or result'* (82). He concludes that nothing can be said to be mysterious or above our reason merely because we do not know all its properties or its real essence. If we were to conclude otherwise, then everything would be as mysterious as everything else, and a blade of grass or a drop of water should be considered as mysterious as God or eternity. Rather than mystify everything we should take the opposite view and demystify everything. We should acknowledge that we have a working knowledge of many things, including such attributes of God as are necessary and useful for us to know. Thus what is revealed in scripture may be as easily comprehended, 'and found as consistent with our common Notions, as what we know of Wood or Stone, of Air, of Water, or the like' (79).

When Toland reflects on the reasons for the introduction of mystery into Christianity he very quickly decides that the main guilty parties, historically, were, first, the early Christian proselytizers who made too many concessions to the Gentiles' love of ritual, and, secondly, the early Christian philosophers who sought to graft their sectarian and disputatious theories on to the new religion. Some of the early Christian proselytizers were faced with potential converts who had been accustomed all their lives to the pomp and ceremony of the pagan forms of ritual and priestcraft. In their anxiety to make the new religion as acceptable as possible these proselytizers unwisely introduced ceremonial and other mysterious elements into their religious practice. They proceeded not only to add unnecessary mystical rites to the originally simple ceremonies of baptism and supper, but also began to administer these rites with the utmost pomp and strictest secrecy. They soon introduced a lengthy process of priestly initiation, giving the impression that there were 'tremendous and unutterable mysteries' to be mastered. Thus, 'lest *Simplicity*, the noblest Ornament of the Truth, should expose it to the Contempt of Unbelievers, *Christianity* was put upon an equal level with the *Mysteries* of *Ceres*, or the *Orgies* of *Bacchus*' (153). In Toland's view, then, the highly ceremonial forms of Christianity are really a kind of paganized Christianity.

If the early 'Christianized' pagans were responsible for introducing mystifying rituals into Christian practices, the early converts from among the philosophers were responsible for obscuring the text of the gospel and giving rise to the traditions of learning, dispute, and interpretation. Although the philosophers purported to defend Christianity, they effectively conflated philosophical and religious vocabularies, and soon produced a theology so abstruse that it became intelligible only to the learned, 'so making themselves sole Masters of the Interpretation' (154). The craft and ambition of priests and philo-sophers alike has had the effect of causing Christianity to degenerate into mere paganism. The chief effect of this paganization has been to place mediators between the gospel and the people, and to place undue emphasis on ceremony. Priestcraft thrives on mediation; and in the case of Christianity it consists in a clergy that reserves to itself the sole right or power of interpretation. It also thrives on ceremony, which is in Toland's view an even greater corruption of the gospel than the priestly office of interpretation, since 'there is nothing so naturally opposite as *CEREMONY* and *CHRISTIANITY*' (167).

In his later work, despite many changes of mind and tack, Toland remained consistent in his rejection of mystery and ceremony in religious practice. His essay *Vindicius liberius* (1702) is instructive for its ambivalent combination of apology and reiteration. The uncharac-teristic apology is motivated by the fact that the hostile reception of *Christianity not Mysterious* had been more robust and sustained than even a controversialist like Toland would have relished. In 1697, the year after its publication, it had been publicly burned by the hangman outside government buildings in Dublin, on the orders of the Irish parliament, and had provoked a series of angry and accusatory responses from influential churchmen. Toland himself had been obliged to flee the country. In *Vindicius liberius* he ostensibly disowns *Christianity not Mysterious*, describing it as a work of which he no longer wholly approves, and goes on to seek pardon for any public or private scandal it may have caused. And yet he only offers this apology after he has already devoted numerous pages to reiterating and clarifying his criticisms of ritual and mystery, making it particularly clear that his words were not directed at the reformed churches but were 'only applicable to *Papists, Mahometans, Heathens,* and such others' (1997: 178). His apology is as selective as his retraction is partial. Indeed, no sooner has he offered his apology than he quotes a long passage from his *Anglia libera* (1701) in which he expresses antipathy towards 'the Idolatry and Tyranny of the Romish Clergy' and describes Popery in general as 'an Extract of whatever is ridiculous, knavish, or impious in all Religions' (1997: 184). In some of his later works, including his revisionary historical tract *Nazarenus* (1718) and a follow-up essay entitled 'Mangoneutes' in *Tetradymus* (1720), he is still making the case against mystifying rituals in favour of simple ideas and simple modes of worship. He tries to show that his position is not outrageously novel, that it has exemplary precedents in the earlier forms of a simple and unpriestly Christianity, especially in those forms practised by the first Jewish converts, the Nazarenes and, in later times, by the first Irish Christians who had developed a monastic church 'before the Papal Corruptions and Usurpations' (1720: 173).

TYRANNY, SUPERSTITION, AND THE POLITICS OF PANTHEISM

While Toland maintained a certain consistency in the more negative or critical aspects of his philosophy – specifically in his critique of the tyranny of mystery and ceremony – he is less consistent in his attempt to formulate a positively alternative position. His claim in *Vindicius liberius* that he willingly and heartily conformed to the doctrine and worship of the Church of England is not borne out by the heated controversy that his views continued to arouse throughout his life. Certainly, his contemporary critics from within the Anglican community did not accept his professions of orthodoxy. At the same time, Toland himself rejected claims that he was either a deist or an atheist, and his eventual endorsement of pantheism may be understood as the expression of a genuine religious impulse. His version of pantheism, ironically for an advocate of conceptual clarity, is not without ambiguity. In his *Letters to Serena* he seemed close to rejecting pantheism in the course of his critique of the Dutch philosopher, Spinoza, who had argued that there exists only one substance which presents two different aspects, thought and extension. But in fact his critique of Spinoza is a very particular one and does not imply a rejection of the pantheistic idea. He criticizes Spinoza for his failure to find a place for motion in his one-substance universe. For Toland, matter is not 'an inactive dead Lump in absolute Repose' but is essentially active or dynamic (1704: 159). All the parts of the universe are in a constant motion, one thing living by the destruction or decay of another. There is an endless round of 'destroying and begetting, of begetting and destroying' (188). The crucial question then arises: If motion is an intrinsic feature of matter, does motion then take the place of God? If so much activity can be attributed to matter-in-motion, what need is there for a creator? Having insisted on the essential dynamism of matter 'there seems to be no need of a presiding Intelligence' (234). Toland does not think that a dynamic conception of matter accounts for all aspects of the world, and does not therefore accept that atheism is an implication of such a view. He suggests that motion alone could not account for the present degree of order and variety in the world, 'nor cause the Organization of a Flower or a Fly' (235).

In his *Pantheisticon* (1751) Toland has more to say about pantheism as a doctrine but he does not further clarify his conception of the close relationship between God and nature. The language he uses to describe the relationship between God and the universe is pantheistic in tenor, but does not always univocally assert the identity of the two realities. The force and energy of the universe, the creator and ruler of all, is God, 'whom we call the *Mind*, if you please, and *Soul* of the Universe' (1751: 17). Terms like force and energy suggest a materialistic pantheism, while creator and ruler suggest the opposite, namely, God's separate existence; but by the end of the sentence we are told that the force or energy in question is 'not separated from the *Universe* itself, but by a Distinction of Reason alone' (18). This qualification now suggests that the distinction between God and the universe is a formal one, that there is only one reality when all is said and done. In a later section, and without warning or preamble, he introduces the notion of the 'ethereal fire' that surrounds, permeates, and rules all things, that makes thought possible, that contains soul, mind, motion, and that 'never suffers celestial and terrestrial Beings to be at Rest' (24). This talk of ethereal fire, obscurely evocative as it is, reinforces the original impression of pantheistic materialism, though it is a very dynamic and animated sort of materialism. In one of the most provocative and visionary parts of the book he brings the earth to life (as in the modern Gaia hypothesis), insisting that everything on and in the earth is organic — so organic, indeed, that minerals, metals, and stones are considered to be part of the anatomy of the living earth. He reports that, when asked by an inn-keeper what country he came from, he had replied: 'The Sun is my Father, the Earth my Mother, the World's my Country, and all Men are my Relations' (33), thus yoking together both a very old and a very new idea, both a kind of pagan or alchemical earth-mysticism and a kind of universal humanism.

Though Leslie Stephen dismissed *Pantheisticon* as 'scarcely serious' (1962: 87), it is in fact one of the most remarkable works of the eighteenth century, albeit for qualities that are perhaps more apparent to the modern reader than they were to earlier readers. The style and composition of the text mimic the substantive content of its argument. What looks like an uneasy, almost bewildering, conflation of ideas from disparate sources, from the most ancient to the most modern, from the pre-scientific to the scientific, can be read as a kind of stylistic reflection or rehearsal of the esoteric version of pantheism that is argued for in the course of the text. Divisions and hierarchies are abolished; genres are collapsed in upon themselves; authorities are cited in a mixum-gatherum way and without deference; and the conventional distinctions between the reverent and irreverent are elided or blurred in every direction. It is easy to see the pseudo-liturgical format of the closing sections of *Pantheisticon* as the irreverent sending up of an orthodox and time-honoured convention, but it is also possible to see the use of that format as playfully celebratory rather than irreverent, as part and parcel of the upbeat pantheistic 'fusion' that is taking place in the form as well as in the argument of the text. Read in this light, with due attention to the levelling, conflating, anarchic impulse that pervades it at every turn, this esoteric and uncontainable text may be regarded as one of the most astonishing, even thrilling, documents to emerge from an eighteenth-century Irish thinker.

The importance of *Pantheisticon* is further confirmed by the role it has come to play in recent scholarship on the ideologies, philosophies, and mindsets of the eighteenth century. Some scholars, most notably Margaret C. Jacob, have emphasized the materialistic, naturalistic, secularist, 'levelling' tendency implicit in the work of enlightenment radicals like Toland, suggesting that the Irishman was part of an underground enlightenment that drew on a range of subversively secular philosophies, including republicanism, pantheism, and Free-masonry. Classical republicans like Toland 'knew that in religious consensus, in a civil and universal religion, lay the key to the reform of the old order. For them, republicanism and pantheism were of a piece, and Freemasonry provided one possible model for its ethical and social expression' (Jacob 1981: 155). *Pantheisticon* becomes on this view a revealing document to the extent that it contains both theological and political elements, all cheerfully thrown together. It contains the makings of a materialistic, naturalistic pantheism in keep-ing with the claims of the new science, but it also lays out a programme for the establishment of a secret 'Socratic' society – a kind of phil-osopher's Masonic lodge. More implicitly, in the references in its 'litur-gical' sections to Roman republicans like Cato and Cicero, as well as in its prayer-like declaration that 'We are therefore Votaries of Truth and Liberty, that we might rescue ourselves from Tyranny and Superstition' (Toland 1751: 65), it gives expression to the republican philosophy. In other words, *Pantheisticon*, instead of being an isolated, esoteric, or marginal text, affords an insight into a forgotten but important aspect of the radical enlightenment, namely, that thrilling under-current of thinking that blended together a religious naturalism, a civil theology, and a celebratory stoicism.

More recently, Justin Champion (1992) has emphasized the central-ity of religion in the eighteenth century, even among those enlighten-ment radicals who were pursuing anticlericalist and ostensibly secularist programmes. He takes issue with David Berman for sug-gesting that Toland, like other freethinking radicals of the period, practised 'the art of theological lying' and is really an atheist in disguise. Berman's intriguing thesis is that the freethinkers lived in such dangerous times that it was necessary for the atheists among them to protect themselves by loudly disclaiming their atheism in the very same texts in which they were setting out to subvert not only orthodox belief but all religious belief. Toland's pantheism in particular is really a kind of disguised atheism, since the material God of pantheism 'is really no God at all' (Berman 1992: 272). There is much circumstantial evidence to support Berman's view, but Champion does not find it wholly persuasive. It is possible, he thinks, to overstate the secularist tendency in Toland and other radicals. The reason for this overstatement lies in the tendency of some modern scholars to assume too readily that anticlericalism implies secularism. In Champion's view, the rejection of priestcraft does not – and in the seventeenth century did not – imply the rejection of religion. Certainly in Toland's case the rejection of the one should not be taken to mean the rejection of the other. While some scholars have been sceptical of Toland's protestations that he is not an atheist or an enemy of religion, Champion accepts these protestations at face value, and finds significance in them. Their significance lies in the fact that for classical republicans like Toland the enemy is not religion as such but priestcraft. And priestcraft is anathema not because it is religious but because it corrupts true religion and draws it into structures of power and tyranny. Toland, like other seventeenth-century radicals, accepts with Hobbes that the worship of a deity is natural to humankind and necessary for good government. This conviction should explain Toland's very real defensiveness about early forms of Christianity. A true secularist would have been no more defensive of simple worship than of the overwrought, ritual-ridden worship of the corrupted church; but Toland is emphatic in his defence of the simple modes precisely because his target *is* priestcraft and not religion itself. The importance of *Pantheisticon* to Champion's perspective is that it confirms the importance for Toland of the Ciceronian distinction between *religio* and *superstitio*, and of the necessity for popular religion. In the *Pantheisticon* Toland does indeed distinguish between, on the one hand, the mythical and fabulous religion that appeals to the generality of people and, on the other hand, the more rational sort of religion that appeals to – and that should be practised secretly by – those who have educated themselves in philosophy. This may look like a rather elitist, self-privileging position, but in any case it serves to indicate that there is in Toland an earnestness about religion – that is, an earnestness about religion understood in its simple, unpriestly, unauthoritarian, 'republican' sense. In the light of these sorts of consideration, the seemingly irreverent liturgical sections of *Pantheisticon* can now be read as a serious attempt to find a formal vehicle for the private religious impulse of that freemasonry of intellectuals who 'talk with the people, and think with the philosophers' (Toland 1751: 57; Champion 1992: 193–4; see also Eagleton 1998: 57–8).

'AS IN A GLASS DARKLY'

Peter Browne and the argument from analogy

One of Toland's critics (whom Toland would have included in his derogatory reference to the 'Partizans of Mystery') was his fellow countryman, Peter Browne (1665–1735). Provost of Trinity College, Dublin, from 1699 to 1710, and bishop of Cork and Ross from 1710 to 1735, Browne was first introduced to Toland's work in 1697 when the archbishop of Dublin, Narcissus Marsh, sent him a copy of *Christianity not Mysterious* and invited him to make a reply to it. Browne's reply, *A Letter in Answer to a Book entitled Christianity not Mysterious* (1697) is in fact a substantial essay in which the orthodox argument on behalf of 'revelation and mysteries' is articulated at some length, sometimes in vehement terms. Browne is prepared to accept little of what Toland says, even to the extent of questioning the Lockean premises on which Toland bases his reasoning. He identifies as the fundamental error of all promoters of reason and evidence that, while they purport to accept authority or revelation as a source of information, yet they still insist that reason and evidence are the ultimate grounds of persuasion or assent. But by thus making evidence one of the grounds of persuasion they effectively eliminate revelation as a source of information, since it is the authority or status of the revealer that provides the only ground of assent to a revealed proposition. Revealed propositions by their very nature are ones for which we do not have sensory evidence since they refer to unearthly, unobservable realities. Our grounds for believing revealed truths cannot therefore have much to do with earthbound experience or evidence:

> It will follow that no Person, either God or Man, can be believ'd on their word. For what they relate is evident to the Mind, or it is not; If it be, then they give their assent to

that *Evidence*, and not to the person who relates it. If it be not evident . . . he must utterly reject it. And thus in a few words he destroys all Faith, both Human and Divine.

(Browne 1697: 31)

Browne's intuition is that Toland's rationalistic, evidence-seeking approach leaves no room for the acceptance of the kinds of proposition that lie at the heart of any religion. This does not mean that in order to defend religious belief it is necessary to deny the importance of clear and distinct ideas, or of reason and evidence. Browne acknowledges that clear and distinct ideas are indeed the foundation of all our knowledge, but he refuses to accept that we can 'believe nothing but what we have a clear and distinct idea of' (33). Knowledge and faith are different but related modes of cognition. It is true that we cannot have immediate and proper ideas of 'those things of another World which are revealed to us' (37) – we can have immediate and proper ideas only of the ordinary phenomena of nature. But we can form mediate and 'improper' ideas of the things of another world 'by Analogy or Similitude' (38). In other words, we can frame to ourselves conceptions of another world 'from those things in this World whereof we have clear and distinct Ideas' (39). God has adapted the terms of his revelations to those faculties and ideas that we already have, and makes use of words and ideas with which we are already familiar in our dealings with each other and with the natural world. While we cannot form an immediate and proper idea of the real nature of God or of the nature of supernatural realities, we can nevertheless comprehend something of both. We can 'see as in a glass darkly' – that is, we can dimly comprehend the realities of another world by finding analogies for them among the things of this world.

In Browne's view a revelation about the supernatural world is never either wholly intelligible or wholly obscure. Every revelation gives us something that we can understand while at the same time pointing to something of which we can have no notion at all. If a revelation did not give us something to grasp, then it would not merit the name of revelation. At the same time, it is not possible for a revelation to make the supernatural world as intelligible to us as the natural one. The reality of God himself is so other-worldly, for example, that we cannot expect to comprehend it with our finite intellects. But since it is necessary for us to believe in God we must have some idea, no matter how inadequate, of his existence and attributes. While we cannot form an adequate idea of the true essence of God, we can nevertheless form a usefully negative idea of him 'by removing from him all the Imperfections of the Creatures' (41). To know that God is not finite, not material, not limited in wisdom, not vengeful, not unjust, and so on, is to know something about God. We can also approach him more affirmatively by enlarging to perfection the excellencies we find in his creatures, and then attributing these enlargements to him. Thus we can attribute to God infinite degrees of wisdom, power, justice, holiness, mercy, and so on, through the range of the attributes of excellence, though it must always be borne in mind that even after we have framed 'the biggest Idea of God our Minds are capable of, by the greatest enlargement of these perfections . . . 'tis as gross a representation of him as Darkness is of Light' (47).

Later in the *Letter* Browne makes the helpful suggestion that the object of any revelation may be thought to have four aspects: existence, essence, real properties, and the relationship in which it stands to us. Only two of these, existence and relationship, can be revealed to the finite human understanding. The internal essence and real properties of any divinely revealed object or event remain as obscure to us after revelation as before, but the bare existence of such divine things, and the extent to which they have a bearing on our moral lives, can at least be made known to us. That Christ is the Son of God is a revelation in the strictest sense of the term, as is the belief that he was sent to redeem humankind, but Christ's supernatural essence remains beyond our understanding and cannot be a matter of revelation. We learn something of importance through the act of revelation, but we do not learn everything and we do not learn anything at all of the divine essence itself. We may accept that the veil is taken away *in* Christ, in the sense that Christ's existence and his redemptive relationship to humanity is a matter of revelation, but it does not follow, as Toland would wish to claim, that the veil is taken away *from* Christ. To insist that the veil is taken away from Christ would be tantamount to denying the redeemer's supernatural reality and divinity.

In *Christianity not Mysterious* Toland had suggested that a God who chose to speak in obscure or unintelligible terms – in terms that did not agree with our common notions – would be a God who spoke a kind of nonsense, a God who would be capable of asking us to believe, for example, in the existence of something called Blictri without revealing anything about the nature of Blictri. In Toland's view it is not possible to assent to, or believe in, the existence of Blictri or of anything of which one has no conception, and he concludes that God, since he is not a confounder of human sense and reason, would not choose to speak in riddles or mysteries. He chooses rather to speak in terms that are intelligible to us – terms that reveal rather than obscure and mystify. Browne responds to this point by comparing two terms, 'Blictri' and 'glory'. He accepts that 'Blictri' is indeed a nonsense word – it is not even meaningful enough to be properly obscure or mysterious. 'Glory', on the other hand, is a significant term, despite the fact that we know as little of the reality it signifies as we do of the reality signified by 'Blictri'. It is obscurely significant, or significant in an analogical sense, because the reality it signifies – the glory of God and of the saints in heaven – is represented by the brightness of the sun and the glory of an earthly kingdom, which are the greatest images we are able to frame of it (162). As well as this analogical meaning there is the relational or moral significance of the term. The word 'glory' invokes a future happy state, the reward of a virtuous life. The word itself, despite its obscurity, is semantically promising – that is, it induces or evokes a kind of expectancy or hope, namely, 'That it expects me in the Heavens, that I shall enjoy it, and be made partaker of it; and that it will render me happy beyond all imagination' (162–3).

The problem of how to precisely characterize the ability of human beings to understand something of the supernatural world, while at the same time preserving the mystery of the divine essence, continued to preoccupy Browne long after the initial controversy triggered by Toland's book. In his *Procedure, Extent and Limits of Human Understanding* (1728) he set out to develop a more detailed and comprehensive account of analogical understanding. His basic intuition, however, has not changed. He is anxious to clarify what he understands by analogy, for 'without a judicious and cautious application of *Analogy*, men will be apt to mistake it for pure *Metaphor*, and by that means resolve all Religion into nothing more than mere Figure and Allusion' (9). His concern is not just with the heretical demystifiers – the Arians, Socinians, deists, and Freethinkers – but also with those who wish, like himself, to preserve the mystery of Christianity. In 1709 the arch-bishop of Dublin, William King, had cogently argued in his *Sermon on Predestination* that human beings cannot have a direct or proper conception of God, nor of any aspect of the supernatural world. King had gone on to claim, equally cogently, that the divine or supernatural realities cannot be approached by finite human minds except through the language of analogy. But in Browne's view the learned prelate fails to distinguish carefully between metaphor and analogy, and has there-fore left himself open to the charge that he has reduced the language of revelation to a fragile tissue of figures, conceits, and fictions. A full-blown atheism is only a short step away, since the atheist can avail of King's confusion in order to argue that the language of revelation is after all just a human construct, 'a Creature only of the *Imagination*' (41). To help prevent any further, albeit inadvertent, concessions to heretics or atheists Browne undertakes to state the true nature of analogical understanding.

His main objective is to show that analogical conceptions of things, especially of things supernatural, occupy an important half-way house between literal and metaphoric conceptions. What seems to make his task a difficult one is the fact that the terms and ideas we use to under-stand the supernatural world have originated in our experience of the natural world. Though dismissive of many aspects of Locke's theory of knowledge, Browne accepts that all our basic ideas originate in our experience of the natural world, and that the only experience we can have is of that world. We cannot experience the supernatural world, nor can that world directly form ideas in us. Unlike Locke, Browne denies that we have any simple or direct idea of even the spiritual or purely mental side of our own individual human natures. While Locke had accepted that we form, through reflection or intro-spection, certain ideas of our own minds or souls, Browne insists that the bodily senses can lay down only ideas of bodily things, and that we do not have the least direct idea or perception of the purely spiritual part of us, 'nor do we discern any more of its *Real Substance* than we do that of an Angel' (97). How then, if our ideas are so rooted in physical sensation, can such worldly ideas be used to express revelations about an otherworldly order of reality? How is it possible to think, or make any intelligible statements, about a transcendent God or a supernatural world? How can ideas produced in the course of sensational encounters with the natural world at the same time serve to report a reality that is beyond the reach of sensation? If the supernatural world is beyond the reach of our natural experience, is it not also beyond the reach of ideas formed on the basis of that experience?

In order to make a case for revelation and faith, Browne, because he accepts the Lockean premise, must try to show that ideas derived from natural experience can be used to provide some degree of information about another order of reality. He does so by reiterating his argument that ideas can be used analogically – that is, they can be used to provide information about things other than those that produced them in the first place. Maintaining a distinction between metaphor and analogy becomes important at this point. Metaphor has its uses. It is frequently deployed in scripture to give expression to certain edifying images of God. The image of God's ubiquitous or all-seeing eye is used to convey an impression of his omniscience, while the image of his strong hand conveys an impression of his power. But such figurative words and ideas are used 'without any *Real Similitude* or *Proportion*, or *Correspondent Resemblance* in the things compared' (106). Since God is a purely spiritual being, he cannot be really thought to have such physical attributes as an eye or a hand. Such metaphors serve only to clarify or reinforce already existing knowledge but do not themselves add to our knowledge. They are therefore not absolutely necessary to our way of conceiving or expressing the nature of purely spiritual things. They affect the imagination but do not inform the understanding. Analogical comparisons, however, are more crucially informative and are essential to our understanding of revelation. There must exist a real correspondence between the properties of a heavenly or spiritual reality and the properties of those natural things 'which are justly substituted to represent them' (137).

This does not mean, however, that our analogical conceptions enable us to really understand the divine essence or the spiritual world. The difficulty of Browne's position is highlighted by his claim that our analogical conceptions represent 'a real and *Correspondent*, but *Inconceivable* Nature or Perfection, of which we cannot in our present State form any *Abstract Idea* or Notion' (199). Here he is close to making an incoherent statement, namely, that we have, and yet do not really have, a conception of divine or spiritual realities. He barely succeeds in avoiding incoherence when he introduces a distinction between the simple or compound ideas formed in sensation and the more complex conceptions or notions that arise from the operations of the mind upon those more basic ideas (99–103). The concept of charity is just such a complex notion – it brings together the basic ideas of man, misery, relief, and money, but also involves such subjective states as consciousness of pain, a sense of duty towards God, and a capacity to feel compassion for fellow creatures. It is such appropriately complex notions, which have as much to do with the operations of the intellect as they do with the ideas derived immediately from experience, that are most useful in providing analogical conceptions of spiritual realities. This helps us to understand the distinction between metaphor and analogy. When God is said to have a mighty arm we cannot take the expression literally – we can only take it as metaphor. But the expression is more than mere metaphor since it refers implicitly to the power of God. It is this implied complex notion of power, rather than the explicitly literal idea of a muscular arm, that is properly analogical here – and therefore revelatory. Likewise with other notions, such as wisdom and goodness. When God is said to be powerful, wise, and good, 'we don't only mean something true, and solid, and real; but also inconceivable Perfections in his real Nature *Correspondent* and answerable to Power, and Wisdom, and Goodness in us' (1728: 145). Precisely because of their complex origin in intellect as well as in sensation, these notions are sufficiently 'spiritualized' already to warrant their role in the vocabulary of belief and revelation. The power, wisdom, and goodness of God are beyond our understanding, but at least we know that these are the kinds of attributes possessed by God.

Browne's chief difficulty is not fully resolved in the *Procedure*, mainly because the concept of analogy remains more problematic than he might have wished. On the one hand, he needs to emphasize the mystery of divinity and the inability of the human mind to grasp the essential nature of spiritual or divine existence; on the other hand, he also wishes to make a case for revelation – that is, for the idea that God is not wholly incommunicado, that he speaks to his creatures, that some information about the divine will and the supernatural world is available to human beings. The dilemma can be put like this – too little mystery leads to deism or natural religion, but too much denies the possibility of revelation. Revelation, in so far as it implies the conveyance of information from God to humankind, implies some reduction of the mystery. The nature of God, in the aftermath of any instance of revelation, is a little less mysterious than it was before. Browne's problem is that he does not want the process of demystification to go too far. By introducing the concept of analogy to account for the nature of revelation, he is in danger of making God too intelligible – not directly intelligible, as he is for the deists, but too intelligible nonetheless. Instead of abandoning analogy, however, he continues to refine his conception of it. In his next major work, *Things Divine and Supernatural conceived by Analogy with Things Natural and Human* (1733), he once again restates his conviction that human beings do not have any direct or immediate knowledge of things divine, but that nonetheless these things can be known indirectly or analogically – by means, that is, of 'lively semblances' conveyed in humane and worldly terms. But the addition of further detail and example does not alter the difficulty that has by now attached itself to Browne's conception of divine analogy. Once it is accepted that knowledge of God is possible in any form or to any degree, it does not matter whether such knowledge – if it is knowledge – is arrived at directly or analogically. To understand something analogically is nonetheless to understand it, and whatever is understood analogically can no longer be described as beyond understanding. The same logic applies to the notion of representation, including analogical representation. If an image or idea truly represents its object to any degree, then it does not matter how indirectly that image or idea has been arrived at, or whether it is seen in a glass darkly or in a glass clearly. Either the idea represents its object or it does not. If it represents its object, whether wholly or partially, clearly or obscurely, then it gives information about the object in question, and that object can no longer be described as lying beyond the reach of human understanding. Unfortunately, Browne uses the concepts of analogy and representation equivocally and shape-shiftingly, sometimes in order to argue that analogical ideas afford some understanding of God and the supernatural realities, sometimes in order to argue the converse, namely, that the supernatural realities nonetheless remain fully beyond the reach of our finite understandings.

OTHER PARTISANS OF MYSTERY

Edward Synge and Philip Skelton

Predictably, the arguments of freethinkers, deists, and 'rationalists' drew more critics than supporters from among the ranks of the orthodox Anglican intelligentsia in Ireland. Edward Synge (1659–1741), archbishop of Tuam, attempted to establish a continuity between the intuitions of reason or natural religion on the one hand and the claims of revealed religion on the other. In his *Free Thinking in Matters of Religion* (1737a), he maintains that a rational person will be disposed to embrace the intuitions of natural religion, since the rational person's God-given reason will lead him to realize that there must be an external cause of the universe, that this cause must be supernaturally wise and intelligent, and that basic principles of behaviour can be inferred from the fact of the supernatural being's wisdom and goodness (1737a: 22–6). But over and above the doctrines and duties that derive from natural religion there are the additional and extremely important doctrines and duties communicated through revelation. Revelation is to be understood here as a kind of augmentation, a 'topping up' or crowning, of the claims and precepts of natural religion. Since revelation comes from God, however, and not from within human reason, it follows that some revealed truths will not be as 'reasonable' or as intelligible as the truths discovered by reason on its own terms and on its own earthly ground. Synge accepts that no one can be expected to give his assent to propositions that are contradictory, but 'it is no way absurd or unreasonable for any Man, upon the Testimony of those who are wiser and better informed than himself, to give Credit to such Things as are beyond the Compass of his own Understanding' (27). The implication here is that revelations may not be universally obscure – that is, they may be obscure to many but intelligible to those who are wiser and more informed. There is, as it were, a degree of understanding in the community of believers, though such understanding may not be distributed equally among all the members. Some believers may have to take it on trust that what is entirely mysterious to themselves is not quite so mysterious to some others.

Synge's main objective, however, is to show that even where there is some understanding of revelation – or of the attributes and actions of God – it cannot be clear or literal understanding. It is only necessary that a believer have *some* understanding of the propositions he believes, and this limited understanding may consist in an obscurely analogical grasp of the terms of revelation. Our general conceptions of God can only be derived 'from some faint and dark Resemblance' (1737b: 39) which we perceive to exist between the attributes of God and those of his creatures. These faint and dark resemblances do not tell us everything there is to know but they are enough to invest the propositions of revelation with such meaning as is necessary to assent to them. The position of the believer confronted with the mysteries of revelation is comparable with that of the blind person trying to come to terms with other people's references to light and colour. The blind person cannot have a literal conception of what is meant by these references, but can 'by way of *Analogy, Similitude,* or *Comparison*' come to have some comprehension of them – enough comprehension to ensure that what is being said about light and colour 'is not a multitude of Words without any Signification at all' (53–4).

Synge explores the blind person analogy most extensively in the course of his attempt to rebut the claims of John Toland. While the blind person cannot form a concept of illuminated and coloured shapes he still understands significantly more than the person who is asked to believe in the existence of Blictri. He is able to frame 'some sort of representative Conception of them, which is more than a Man can do of *Blictri*, of which he hears only the Sound, but knows not the Signification' (1752: 290). The believer's obscure but nonetheless real 'understanding' of such things as the Trinity and the Incarnation is analogous to the blind man's obscure but nonetheless real 'understanding' of the language of light and colour. The blind man knows what it is to have faculties of perception, and knows from his own sense of touch that things have shape and form. From this he can develop some idea of an additional faculty that some people possess and which affords them an additional experience of shape and form. Analogously, the believer who cannot fully understand the Trinity or Incarnation nonetheless knows what a person is, what unity and diversity are, and what it is for one being to be generated by or from another. The 'mysteries' of revelation are therefore not complete mysteries in the sense of being completely unintelligible; rather, they possess the qualified mystery of things seen in a glass darkly. The things in question are seen only darkly and partially, it is true, but they are none-theless seen to some degree.

Philip Skelton (1707–1787), amateur boxer, lover of flowers, and philanthropic curate to several Ulster parishes, produced a voluminous critique of deism in his *Ophiomaches: or Deism Revealed* (1749) in which he expresses scepticism about the claims that deists make on behalf of the power of reason. He endorses a Lockean conception of reason as that faculty by which we form propositions out of ideas already conceived, and maintains that the ideas on which reason operates are supplied from outside itself, initially by the senses (I, 82–3). The senses, how-ever, can only supply ideas of material things. They are not capable of supplying ideas of spiritual beings, least of all God. Since God is not an object of sense, reason will not be able to derive a proper idea of him from the materials of experience, nor can it generate a proper idea of him from within itself. At this point Skelton proffers a useful observation on the character of reason, describing it as 'the faculty by which we are rendered teachable', a passive faculty which 'stands extremely in need of instruction and exercise' (I, 86). In other words, reason does not come fully developed into the world but must be instructed and furnished with its contents and principles. Not only are there no such things as innate ideas but neither are there such things as ready-made, ready-to-go principles. The function of the senses is to instruct reason in the most necessary and fundamental way, but instruction may also come from culture and education – and, most importantly, from divine revelation. Left to its own devices, the uninstructed reason of any individual or community of individuals would take an immense length of time to arrive at the right idea of God. Rather than abandon his creatures to their own inadequate devices, God has chosen instead to reveal to them certain truths about himself and about his plan for human salvation. A proper con-ception of God can only come from God himself, by way of special revelation. Revelation, however, does not have to meet the rationalist's standards of literalness and clarity to be counted a revelation. When we speak of God, we are obliged to use 'such ideas as the human mind, and such words as human language, afford us', which means that God's essentially incomprehensible nature can only be understood incom-pletely and by analogy with our own nature (II, 114). God has been frugal in his revelations, taking account of our limited capacities, and has given us only so much of the truth 'as is necessary to our occasions' (II, 126).

In the sixth dialogue of *Ophiomaches*, Shepherd, the character who is Skelton's mouthpiece, accuses the deists and rationalists of arrogance. Shepherd points out to the deist, a character called Dechaine, that the whole difficulty that he, Dechaine, has with such mysteries as the doctrines of the Trinity and Incarnation arises from his determination to measure God by himself. But this the deist cannot validly do, given the finite littleness of human capacities vis-à-vis the infinite greatness of the creator. 'What is reason to God?' Shepherd asks. 'It is an inch of line to an unfathomable ocean: it is a foot-rule to infinite space' (II, 146). The very first principle of any religion worthy of the name must be the recognition that it has an infinitely mysterious being, 'the most incomprehensible and mysterious of all beings', for its object (II, 146), and cannot hope to wholly comprehend it. Disappointingly, Skelton's treatment of John Toland produces more invective than analysis. Instead of engaging respectfully and argumentatively with Toland, he dismisses him as 'a pretender to scholarship', a man 'of mean and despicable genius', a propagator of infidelity in Ireland, someone who is foremost in conceit and 'self-sufficiency', and a writer of bad Latin to boot (II, 339–41). He even has recourse to a kind of libel. In the eighth and last dialogue, he has Shepherd recount an old rumour that Toland stole a spoon while dining with some wealthy deist. Shepherd confesses himself prepared to believe such an act of anyone who, under pretence of being a Christian, gets admittance to the minds of others 'in order to steal away their principles of religion and honesty' (II, 340). When another character, as if wishing to defend Toland's reputation, wonders if a servant might not have pocketed the spoon, Shepherd retorts: 'The honourable company were best able to judge whether a Christian servant, or a Deistical gentleman, was the most likely to be a thief' (II, 341).

GOD, GOOD, AND PRIVATION

The theodicy of William King

Not all the orthodox thinkers of this period were as preoccupied with refuting deism as were Browne and some of his like-minded

contemporaries. One of the Irish thinkers who tackled other theological and philosophical issues was William King (1650–1729), an
influential Church of Ireland clergyman, described as 'a far-sighted
and strong-minded ecclesiastic to whom the Church of Ireland to
this day is immeasurably indebted' (Luce 1949: 43). He became archbishop of Dublin in 1703 and was acquainted with other noteworthy
figures of the period, including William Molyneux, George Berkeley,
Jonathan Swift, and Peter Browne. Though he addressed the problem
of divine knowledge and the nature of analogical reasoning in his
Sermon on Predestination, his most important and most substantial contribution to eighteenth-century thought is his book on the problem of
evil. His *De origine mali* (1702) was in fact important enough to attract
the critical attention of a number of his European contemporaries,
including Pierre Bayle and G.W. Leibniz. His views had perhaps
their most positive and creative influence on Alexander Pope, whose
philosophical poem *Essay on Man* (1734) contains what may be read
as a versification of the substance or theme of King's treatise. More
recently, King's views have been discussed by Arthur O. Lovejoy in
The Great Chain of Being (1960: 212–23).

The problem of evil, considered as a theological problem – as the
problem to which all theodicies are a response – may still be stated
in much the same terms in which King presented it. How can a
good and powerful God have created a world in which evil exists?
The question is prompted by the fact that God, the uncaused First
Cause, is supposed to be both infinitely good and infinitely powerful.
But if God is so good and so powerful, how is it possible that both
natural and moral evils should exist in the world that he has created?
How can evils of any kind 'come into the Works of a God of the highest
Goodness and Power'? (King 1732: I, 103). King rejects the kinds of
solutions offered by atheists, by the Manicheans, and by Catholic
theologians. According to the atheistic argument, the existence of
evil is incompatible with the existence of a perfectly good God, therefore such a being does not exist. According to the Manicheans, the
presence of evil indicates that there must exist an autonomous principle
of evil as well as an autonomous principle of good, and that the
benevolent power of God is countervailed by the malevolent power
of an Evil One. And according to the Catholics, the presence of evil
is undeniable but is a mystery that we cannot begin to understand.

Each of these positions is based on the assumption that evil exists as an objective reality, as if it were some kind of created entity or subsistent force or principle. But this, in King's view, is an erroneous assumption. His own solution is to develop an idea that is to be found in Neoplatonic philosophy, in the thought of St Augustine, and in scholastic philosophy, namely, the idea that evil, especially natural evil, is a privation or deficiency rather than an actuality. Evil is not a reality or force in its own right but a falling short of the absolute perfection possessed by God alone: 'All creatures are necessarily imperfect and at infinite distance from the Perfection of the Deity' (I, xix). Insofar as anything is a created being it cannot share in the perfection of the creator, and is therefore necessarily imperfect to some degree. The concept of an absolutely perfect creature implies a contradiction, since only the creator can be so described (I, 115). Everything that has been created is relatively imperfect along a continuum of imperfection that ranges from that which is just short of absolute perfection to that which is just short of absolute imperfection: 'There are infinite Degrees of Perfection between a Being Absolutely perfect and Nothing' (I, 119). Nothing that exists, however, is absolutely imperfect. Even matter, which is at the farthest remove from the perfection of the divine essence, is still better than nothing. It is indeed a feature of all creation that it is in varying degrees, and in all its diverse forms, better than nothing. Even the processes of generation and corruption, though they may look like serious defects in the divine work, are better than nothing. While pure nothingness cannot exist, every created thing that exists has been created out of nothing; and imperfection is the price that must be paid for this genesis out of nothing. In an extraordinary and startling image, King suggests that God enters into a kind of reproductive relationship with nothing: 'A Creature is descended from *God*, a most *perfect Father*; but from nothing as its *Mother,* which is Imperfection itself. All finite creatures partake of nothing, and are nothing beyond their bounds' (I, 217).

Every created thing then carries within it an element of nothing – it is, we might say, a mixture of existence and non-existence, a mixture of features possessed and features lacked. Instead of seeing evil as the effect of a principle of evil, or as something which actually exists in its own right, we should regard it as an inevitable feature of created or creaturely existence: 'This Mixture therefore of Non-existence supplies the place of an ill Principle in the Origin of Evil' (I, xxi). A possibility of evil 'is a necessary attendant on all Creatures, and cannot be separated from them by any Power, Wisdom or Goodness whatsoever' (I, xxii). Even God cannot eliminate imperfection from the created world. He could only do so if he were to create beings as perfect as himself, namely, other Gods, but this is impossible since such created deities would not be uncaused First Causes. The idea of a created First Cause, or a created deity, is incoherent. It follows that only beings less perfect than the First Cause can be created, from which it follows at the same time that all created beings, even pure spirits such as angels, must be more or less imperfect. And where there is imperfection there always resides the possibility of evil.

In King's theodicy, imperfection is already a kind of evil. By the evil of imperfection he understands the evil of defects, shortcomings, or deficiencies. An imperfection in this sense may be understood as a privation – as simply the lack or absence of a perfection. Such defects would include the absence of wisdom in human beings, the absence of reason in animals, or the absence of sentience in inanimate objects. These defects are not, however, created by God. They are part of the inevitable condition of created or creaturely existence. The only way that God could have avoided such defects would have been by refraining from the act of creation itself. Why, then, did God not so refrain? Would it not have been better if he had continued to exist absolutely by himself, thus ensuring that nothing imperfect could come into existence? Or, if he had to create imperfect creatures, why did he not confine himself to creating spiritual or angelic creatures whose natures would be closest to his own? To such questions King replies that God in his goodness is determined to fill the void with as many forms or species of existence as possible, since even the most imperfect species is still better than nothing. Even the most lowly form of matter, stupid and devoid of sense, is better than nothing. Moreover, it fills a space in the void in a way that it cannot be filled by any other mode of existence. If God had filled the universe with spirits and pure immaterial beings, 'yet there would be no less Room for Matter' (I, 132). Matter, despite its imperfections, fills a void in a way that spirits could not; and each species of material thing that exists likewise fills the void in a way peculiar to itself. The varieties of existence, imperfect as they are, should be seen as an expression of divine good-ness, of the divine determination to fill the void with the complete range of species of existence, from the immaterial to the material, from the least imperfect to the most imperfect: 'The Evils of Imper-fection then must be permitted in the Nature of things; and the inequality of Perfections must be permitted also, since it is impossible that all the Works of God should be endowed with equal Perfections' (I, 136).

The logic that King applies to the deficiencies or 'lacks' of creation is extended to natural evils. Natural evils are the actual or occurrent evils that befall each living species, and they have their specific origin in the basic nature of matter and motion. Wherever there is matter in motion there also will be division, disparity of parts, clashing and repulsion of parts, and eventual separation and dissolution. Living creatures in whom a soul has been joined to a body will inevitably experience all the natural evils that matter is heir to, including generation and decay, instability and death. In sentient beings a range of disagreeable passions, such as pain and disappointment, will be felt according as the range of natural evils is encountered and endured. The occurrence of such evils, however, is outweighed by the good of existence itself. Indeed, it would be a greater evil for something not to exist at all than that its existence should be attended with inevitable evils:

> All the Species of Creatures then must either have been omitted, or their concomitant Evils tolerated: the Divine Goodness therefore put the Evils in one Scale and the Good in the other; and since the Good preponderated, an infinitely good God would not omit that because of the concomitant Evils, for that very Omission would have been attended with more and greater Evils, and so would have been less agreeable to infinite Goodness.
>
> (I, 177)

In other words, the existence of a species together with the evils which necessarily attend its imperfect nature – what we might call 'existence, warts and all' – is preferable to the non-existence of that species. God, in his infinite capacity as creator, 'would rather have Creatures liable to Natural Evils, than no Creatures at all' (I, 182).

It might appear that some natural evils, such as earthquakes, storms, thunder, and floods, are unnecessary imperfections, but we must bear in mind that these are not created for their own sakes. They are the smaller features of a greater whole and are no doubt related to funda-mental natural causes 'which are necessary, and could not be removed without greater Damage to the whole' (I, 189). The earth must either not be created at all, or we accept it as it is, earthquakes and storms notwithstanding. We may take it that God has arrived at the best conceivable arrangement of matter and motion, that this arrangement could not possibly be better, all things considered, 'and that no Evil in it could be avoided, which would not occasion a greater by its absence' (I, 219). The expression 'it takes all kinds to make a world' is perhaps the best idiomatic summary of King's argument that the created world is a plenitude of different natures, each nature, for all its imperfection, forming a necessary link in the great chain of being.

The second volume of King's treatise deals with the particular problem of moral evil. This is the crux of the problem of evil, because King must deal at last with evil in its most unholy sense – the sense, indeed, in which it is normally understood. His account of both imperfection and natural evil can pass muster readily enough because we do not normally think of nature's shortcomings, or natural calamities, as evil in any moral sense. It is easy to accept that such things as earthquakes and storms may be part of the overall economy of creation. It is not so easy, however, to argue that moral evil can be accommodated in terms of some grander divine plan. The particular problem with moral evil is that it is gratuitous. That is, it is caused by free agents who have a choice between doing either good or evil, and who then choose or 'elect' to do evil. Why should an infinitely good God choose to create a being that is by its very nature capable of wilfully introducing evil into the order of creation? Would it not have been better to have left such a being uncreated, or to have created a being that would not have been capable of doing wilful evil? Drawing impressively on a vocabulary that includes *free will*, *free election*, *agency*, and *liberty*, King insists that freedom of choice or action is the mark of a relatively superior being. Physical objects, machines, and brutes are inferior precisely because they are not capable of self-willed or self-determining action, but are instead passively dependent on external or internal impulses. Such inferior beings are acted upon rather than self-active. God himself is the most perfect possible agent or self-active being, a being who 'delights in things merely because they are chosen' (II, 323). The very goodness of things depends on their having been chosen to exist: 'The Divine Election therefore is not determined by the Goodness of things, but the Goodness and Fitness of them arises from that Election' (II, 323). What is true of God is true to some extent of the most superior of his earthly creatures, namely, human-kind. We indeed continually experience in ourselves the principle of free choice or 'free election'. We are conscious that we are the true cause of our own actions, that we have an ability to act 'and please our-selves in contradicting our natural Appetites, our Senses and Reason' (II, 327). Such, however, is the power of free will and such is the pleasure of acting freely that we are capable of making decisions and choices that cause pain to ourselves and to others. Even some things that are naturally unpleasant to the senses can be made tolerable 'by the force of Election' (II, 333). Conversely, things that are naturally pleasant or beautiful can be rejected by the will and eventually rendered disagreeable. The power of the will to run counter to the natural inclina-tion of the appetites and senses extends also to reason and the under-standing. Human beings are capable of throwing away their fortune, life, and soul 'lest they should be disappointed in a foolish choice' (II, 340). In other words, rather than relinquish the special pleasure that attaches to a free choice, even a perverse, irrational, or foolish one, human agents are prepared to risk loss of property or life. This preparedness to persist in a foolish choice confirms that the peculiar pleasure to be had from the sheer exercise of the will may be greater than the pleasures of either the senses or the understanding.

This is not to say that the individual human will is essentially per-verse, or that it takes particular pleasure in being perverse. If that were so, then God would indeed have created something wicked in itself. It is of course God's intention that the chief happiness of human agents should consist in the proper use of the will. The happiest choices will be those made within the bounds prescribed by God and nature. As a rule, human agents will in fact choose the courses of action that are the most likely to bring them happiness. But it is here that certain natural imperfections or natural evils make their presence felt. Because of the natural evils of ignorance and inadvertence, people will be led to make 'undue Elections'. Decisions and choices are sometimes made in the absence of sufficient knowledge or understanding; or, where there is sufficient knowledge, there is sometimes a failure of attention or due care on the part of the hasty agent. A third source of unhappy choices is what King calls 'levity' – a casual and excessive indulgence in the making of new choices, merely for the pleasure that is to be had from the exercise of the will. Once such choices are made, they may be repeated without due thought and may become unproductive habits, 'whereupon we grow supine and negligent, and disregard the Alterations of things' (II, 376). Such habitual repetition, based on the erroneous assumption that the same pleasure will always follow the same act, may result in 'unseasonable Perseverance'. The vice of obstinacy has its origin in the fact that many people 'had rather persist in absurd Elections than undergo the trouble of altering them' (II, 378). Finally, there are the problems caused by the ever-present appetites of the body. These appetites occur naturally in a being that is composed of mind and body, but they can elicit an unbalanced response from a free agent. If agents are not on their guard, they may find themselves either unduly influenced and swayed by the bodily appetites, or, conversely, unduly negligent of them. These five sources of unhappy choices show that such choices are not the result of an innately per-verse will, but are due rather to the various contingencies, including natural evils or deficiencies, that influence the making of choices and decisions.

This still leaves the really hard question: how are evil choices and actions consistent with the power and goodness of God? It may be the case that the will is not itself perverse, but there is no denying that evil choices are made, that evil deeds are done. Could God not have done otherwise than to create a free agent capable of making such evil choices? King's reply is that he could not. In the first place, God created free agents because such beings are more worthy of creation than passively brute or mechanical beings. Without free agents the whole world would be a mere machine, 'totally brute and stupid, as much as a Wheel or a Stone' (II, 385), and therefore unworthy of the infinitely self-active being that is God. Since God will wish to create beings as near as possible to himself in self-activity, he will wish to create a being that moves and pleases itself. It is only with such self-active creatures that God can have a relationship, and it is therefore as agreeable to God that he should have made such beings as it is to the beings themselves that they should be made. The price of creating such beings is that they will be free to abuse their freedom, but it is better that this freedom should sometimes be abused by some agents than that such free agents should not have been created at all. It is no wonder then that God permits evil choices 'since for the most part they could not be prevented without greater Evils' (II, 418). In other words, a world that contains free agents capable of sin is superior to a world without such agents in it, and God in his goodness could not have failed to create such free – albeit potentially sinful – agents. He does not, of course, create the sin, only the being that, because it is free, is capable of sinning.

In the most controversial part of his argument, King rejects the suggestion that God could have created a being that was free to choose among morally good alternatives only. The will cannot be determined by good objects, because 'Moral Good and Evil are very frequently not absolute things, but merely relative' (II, 393). They are relative, moreover, to the will itself. We generally do not choose objects or actions because they are objectively good; rather, these objects or actions become good because we choose them: 'The Goodness of them therefore is for the most part determin'd by the Elections, and not that by the Goodness' (II, 394). If the will was such that it could be influenced or determined by objects or actions whose goodness was always apparent to the will, then the will would not be wholly free. Similarly, if the will could be constrained by the understanding, such that it could only make rational choices or choices based on full knowledge, it would again be less than free. The will delights in its own free exercise, but a will governed by knowledge or understanding could not take unqualified pleasure in its determinations. If the will was confined to the choice of those things that the understanding declared to be good, 'we must of necessity hesitate in many things, and be anxious and solicitous in all' (II, 398). We would subsequently fail to experience the pleasure that arises from the exercise of liberty. In one of several passages that foreshadow an existentialist conception of will and liberty, King concludes:

> It is therefore convenient for us to derive our peculiar and chief
> Happiness from the Will itself; for if it depended on the
> Understanding it would come with Difficulty, Pains and

Anxiety, and we could seldom enjoy it pure and unmix'd. 'Tis better therefore for us to be able to please ourselves without a long Speculation of Antecedents and Consequences, tho' with a danger of Sinning, than to cease from Election, and be restrain'd from the Exercise of our Faculties, till a whole train of these were perfectly apparent.

(II, 400)

His principal aim in so emphasizing the primacy of the will is, of course, to lay the blame there for the existence of evil. God in his goodness and generosity has created a free agent who resembles the creator himself in his freedom and self-activity. Unlike God, however, created free agents are prey to imperfections and natural evils, and are consequently capable of wilfully bringing about evil states of affairs, either for themselves or for others. It is not correct to say that these free agents can choose between good and evil, since that suggests that evil somehow pre-exists the choice. Rather, undue elections – that is, elections made by imperfect beings in imperfect circumstances – are directly the source of evils. That is all that a moral evil is. It is a natural evil – pain, privation, injustice, calamity, death – that has been advanced, exacerbated, or brought about by the choice or action of an imperfect free agent. Elections are wrong or undue 'on account of the natural Evils which sometimes attend them' (II, 388). If the world did not contain natural evils, then moral evils would not exist. This would seem to put the ball of blameworthiness back in God's court, but King has already argued that the created world, just because it is created, must needs be imperfect and have some natural evils in it.

The position defended by King has been described as the most influential of the eighteenth-century theodicies (Lovejoy 1960: 212), and may indeed have influenced the best-known and most accessible theodicy in English literature, namely, that presented by Alexander Pope in the first epistle of his *Essay on Man*. The aim of the first epistle is to show that evil is more apparent than real, that what looks like evil to the finite human mind may serve some good purpose in the divine scheme of things. He comes closest to King in the eighth section of the epistle where he refers to the 'vast chain of being' that extends from the Infinite to man, and from man 'to Nothing'; and in the concluding section of the same epistle in which he declares that all chance is order – or 'direction' – that one cannot see: 'All Discord, Harmony, not understood; / All partial Evil, universal Good: / And, spite of Pride, in erring Reason's spite, / One truth is clear, "Whatever IS, is RIGHT"' (Pope 1963: 515).

The strongest criticism of the 'see no evil' optimism of King and Pope is that its cogency depends on what Arthur Lovejoy calls the 'enforced revision of the notion of good' (1960: 222). In order to deny the reality of evil and re-present it as mere lack, deficiency, or privation, it is first necessary to naturalize goodness, so that goodness becomes identical with what exists, with what has been created. But such a revision of the meaning and province of goodness has two consequences – first, the reality of evil is effectively denied, and second, the concept of goodness is emptied of its usual discriminatory force. By being treated as mere privation, evil is left with no footing in reality, no space to occupy. This appears like a good day's revisionary conceptual work. But the consequence of such deep conceptual revision is that the concept of good begins to lose its meaning, since it is made to reach into or stretch over areas that are normally designated evil. If evil is glossed as privation, then good must be glossed as existence or plenitude – in other words, as that which is good just because it exists and contributes to the fullness or completeness of being. The evil is taken out of 'evil', it is true – but, by the same token, the good is taken out of 'good', and this is a high conceptual price to pay for a radical alternative to the atheistic, Manichean, or Catholic conceptions of evil, as understood by King. In other words, King's radical trans-valuation of values has the consequence that, as Lovejoy puts it, 'the desirability of a thing's existence bears no relation to its excellence' (1960: 222). The main theological implication of this revision is that the idea of divine goodness also loses its meaning, and God becomes an indiscriminate creator, preoccupied with the wholesale filling of the void.

SPIRIT AND MOTION

The philosophical animism of Robert Clayton

If John Toland's *Pantheisticon* is arguably the most startling and dis-concerting work produced in the early stages of the Irish period of

theological controversy, then Robert Clayton's *Essay on Spirit* is argu-
ably the most startling and disconcerting work to be produced towards
the end of that period. Clayton was born in Dublin in 1695, was
educated at Trinity College, and entered into a religious career, becoming bishop of Clogher in 1745. His most famous association was with
George Berkeley, whom he assisted during Berkeley's ill-fated
Bermuda project. His most important theological work is his heretical
Essay on Spirit, which turns on Clayton's keen sense of the duality of
existence, beginning with his own sense of himself as a radically
divided being. Following Descartes, but placing more emphasis on
the lived experience of duality, he finds himself to be composed of
two very different modes of existence, 'that is, of a thinking, active,
powerful, Existence, and a dull, heavy, inactive, Existence', the
former called spirit, the latter called matter or body (1752a: 6).
What impresses him most is the essential, definitive inactivity of
matter contrasted with the essentially active nature of the soul,
mind, or spirit. His thought now takes a sudden and surprising
turn. He proceeds to argue that matter, because it is essentially
inactive, cannot have the principle of motion contained within its
nature. Motion is a form or mode of activity, and since spirit is the
sole source of activity, it follows for Clayton that spirit is also the
source of motion, even when it is ostensibly material things that are
in motion. The original and recurring cause of motion – or of resistance
to motion – must be 'some Spirit or other' (9). All nature, therefore,
seems to him to be pervasively and permanently animated, the whole
world 'replete with Spirits formed with different Kinds and Degrees
of Abilities, according to the various Ends and Uses, for which they
were designed by their Creator' (12). It is not simply the case that
all things were set in motion in an initially creative act of the creator.
Rather, wherever there is motion there continues to be the activity of
spirit.

All created spirits are associated with particular forms of matter, and
are, as it were, clothed in a particular set of material 'organs' through
which they operate on the world, exercising their intelligence in the
performance of attraction and repulsion. However, when certain jarring
elements meet and break forth 'in Thunder and Lightning, and Earthquakes, or any other mechanical Operations' some spirits may become
united to a different set of material organs, including organs of a more

exquisite and delicate kind through which they may become capable of exerting voluntary motion and even of thinking and reasoning (25). Some spirits may be equipped from the beginning of their existence with bodies of so delicate a texture that they are in effect clothed in light, and 'may make the Clouds their Chariots, and walk upon the Wings of the Wind' (27). These subtly embodied beings are angels, and their existence is the key to Clayton's heretical contribution to the religious controversies of the day, especially the controversy over consubstantiality. This controversy concerned the divinity of Christ. According to the consubstantialists, Christ, as the Son of God, was divine – that is, of one and the same substance with God the Father. For those who rejected this view, Christ, as a being of spirit and flesh, is a being distinct from God, and cannot therefore be divine. This was the view of the early Christian sect, the Arians, whose heresies were condemned by the general council of the church which met at Nicea in 325. Clayton's position echoes that of the Arians (see Young 1998: 39–40), and his extraordinary vision of a universally animated nature is indeed intended to provide the metaphysical basis for his rejection of the doctrine of consubstantiality. Just as angels and other spirits are separate from God, so was Christ; just as they are sent by God, so was Christ. But for Clayton it is manifest that God does not and cannot send himself (1752a: 72), since the idea of God sending himself is an incoherent notion. Clayton's universal animism is intended to show that there are spirits active everywhere in nature but that these busy spirits are not on that account divine, nor worthy of worship or adoration. Christ, albeit a uniquely embodied spirit, should be considered part of animated nature rather than part of the divine nature, and so is not deserving of worship or adoration. The one and only invisible God cannot therefore be of one substance with that God who was supposedly manifested in the flesh (81–2). Christ is no less than the image of the invisible God, but neither is he more than that. In short, he is not God and therefore not divine. Clayton then proceeds to isolate scriptural texts that seem to him to confirm the separate identities of God and Christ.

One of Clayton's most tenacious critics was another Irishman, Thomas McDonnell, whose lengthy riposte is contained in his *Essay towards an Answer to a Book, Entitled An Essay on Spirit* (1753). McDonnell begins by dismissing Clayton's belief that matter depends for its motion on the direct activity of spirit or spirits. While he accepts that all matter and motion originated in God's creative will, he rejects the claim that motion requires constant intervention by spirits. He suggests a more naturalistic explanation in terms of mechanical laws of rest and motion, according to which all bodies remain in their original state of rest 'unless their State or Situation be altered by some external Force' (18). In the course of defending the doctrine of consubstantiality he argues that there is no contradiction between God conceived as one and invisible and God as manifested in the flesh of Christ. However, while accepting that this doctrine is not a contradiction, he does accept – indeed insist – that it is a mystery. It is also a mystery how God can send himself in the form of the Holy Spirit, yet we must believe both that he does send himself and that the Holy Spirit is a distinct 'person' in his own right. This only looks like contradiction if we take too literally the language used to describe God's relationship to his creation. But our sense of contradiction should vanish when we realize that the language used to describe the power and operations of God is a language 'suited to our Apprehension', and therefore a language that is not wholly adequate to the task of describing the supernatural realities in question. It is enough if we understand that the effects of God's goodness are communicated to us; it is not necessary for us to understand how this communication is achieved. In the case of the doctrine of consubstantiality, it is enough if we understand that God remains one, supreme, self-existent being. If we are mystified by the manner of existence of the three divine persons, then so be it. Our reverential sense of mystery is appropriate to the supernatural nature of the realities in which Christians believe.

There is no forgetting the startling and fabulous possibilities that were framed, albeit momentarily, in Clayton's curious piece of metaphysical and theological reasoning, but in reading McDonnell's rebuttal one has the sense that the doors of perception flung open by Clayton are being sensibly and firmly closed. Clayton's career as a clergyman – and possibly his life itself – was jeopardized by his persistent airing of his heretical views. Though he had held a series of bishoprics in the Church of Ireland, he was denied the archbishopric of Tuam on account of the *Essay on Spirit*. His relationship with the church worsened when in 1756 he proposed to the Irish House of

Commons that the Athanasian and Nicene creeds should be removed from the liturgy of the Church of Ireland. Within two years he was summoned to a meeting of prelates of the church, presumably to face severe censure, but before he could keep his appointment he fell seriously ill, and he died on the eve of his trial, on 26 February 1758.

5

WONDERFULLY MENDING THE WORLD

George Berkeley and Jonathan Swift

The astonishing philosophy of George Berkeley (1685–1753) is best understood as an attempt to provide a truly radical alternative to the materialistic and sceptical trends that seemed to be emerging in eighteenth-century English thought. Born into an Anglo-Irish family in Kilkenny, Berkeley was educated at Kilkenny College and at Trinity College, Dublin, from which he graduated in 1704 with a BA degree. He was ordained an Anglican minister in 1710, the same year in which he published his philosophical masterpiece, *A Treatise on the Principles of Human Knowledge*. Three years later, in 1713, he popularized his arguments in *Three Dialogues between Hylas and Philonous*. It was also in that year that he set out on a series of travels that would take him to London, to a number of European cities, and to America. Perhaps the most singularly ambitious project of his life had been to set up a college in Bermuda, for the purpose of educating both 'the English youth of our plantations' and the young native Americans, whom he refers to as the 'young American savages' (1956: 127). The extent of his naivety and presumption is best captured by his hope that these young savages might be educated 'till they have taken their degree of Master of Arts' (127). In 1726 he was granted a royal charter for the proposed college – to be called St Paul's College, with Berkeley as its president – and was promised a treasury grant by the House of Commons. The money, however, was not immediately forthcoming and for two years Berkeley waited patiently in London. In 1728, though there was still no sign of the treasury money, he made a decision to set out for America, mainly because he had received a substantial sum from private sources, and the story had begun to get about that, as his biographer diplomatically puts it, 'he was not in earnest with the scheme' (Luce 1949: 109). Still hopeful, and with a sense of obligation to his private subscribers, he set out for Newport, Rhode Island, accompanied by his wife, Anne. Rhode Island was to be a station en route to Bermuda, and was also intended to provide a mainland estate from which the remote college could be supplied with provisions. In Rhode Island he continued waiting, 'waiting in hope deferred, waiting sick at heart, and lastly waiting for recall' (Luce 1949: 125). After almost three years, he was informed that the money was not forthcoming after all. The revenues from which the grant was to be drawn had not materialized, and there was in any case some opposition in England to the funding of what looked increasingly like an unworkable project. The ambitious and perhaps quixotic plan had to be abandoned, and the Berkeleys had no choice but to return home. Domestic sorrow, as A.A. Luce notes, 'darkened their departure for England' (1949: 149), because their infant daughter Lucia, who had been born shortly before they prepared to leave for London, died on their last Sunday on Rhode Island, and was buried in Newport churchyard. The Berkeleys returned to London, where they remained until 1734 when Berkeley was made bishop of Cloyne in Cork. Much of the remainder of Berkeley's life, until his death in 1753, would be spent in Ireland and in Cloyne, where for over eighteen years or so he lived 'a busy and (on the whole) a happy life' (Luce 1949: 172).

Berkeley belonged to the Anglo-Irish elite, the politically and culturally dominant class that had come into its own in Ireland in the eighteenth century, having had its origins in the century of sustained colonization and settlement that preceded it. The ethos of this elite was predominantly and defensively Anglican, expressing itself in a tendency to interpret native Irish practices and attitudes as the embodiment of culturally regressive pre-Reformation values. And yet – as we have already seen in the political thought of William Molyneux – while the Anglo-Irish were decidedly 'unIrish' in most of their sympathies and ideological commitments, they came increasingly to identify with the kingdom of Ireland, even if in a highly tempered and ambivalent sort of way. Roy Foster observes that members of the Anglo-Irish ascendancy who would have referred to themselves in the 1690s as 'the Protestants of Ireland' or 'the English of this king-dom' were, by the 1720s, prepared to see themselves as 'Irish gentle-men' (1988: 178).

This adjustment in self-identification is reflected to some extent in Berkeley's writings. While a student at Trinity College he referred to the Irish as 'natives', which indicates that he did not identify with them and did not see himself as Irish in any sense that might confuse him with his unreconstructed neighbours. But a few years later in his philosophical notebooks he was using phrases like 'we Irish' and 'we Irish men'. He uses these phrases as a way of emphatically dissociating himself from the 'English' philosophy of Locke: 'There are men who say . . . the wall is not white, the fire is not hot etc. We Irish men cannot attain to these truths' (1948: 47). He then goes on to use the phrase again in disagreeing with those mathematicians who claim that there exist invisible lines and that a mathematical point is neither a nothing nor a something. Of invisible lines he remarks, 'We Irish men can conceive no such lines'; and of mathematical points he remarks, 'we Irish men are apt to think something & nothing are next neighbours'. He concludes the sequence by wondering whether other people have the same ideas 'as we Irishmen' (47). But even if Berkeley had not used such phrases he would still be an Irishman whether he liked it or not. Although materially less privileged than Robert Boyle, he is still Irish by privilege, and no amount of text-combing for evidence of Berkeley's attitude to the native Irish or to his own class alters this fact. Harry Bracken has suggested that 'when Berkeley is called an "Irish" philosopher no more is intended than that he was born and educated, lived and worked, in Ireland' (1965: 108). It needs to be added, however, that Berkeley is as deeply implicated in the formation of the complex historical identity of Ireland in its colonial phase as was William Molyneux. Though not as 'patriotic' as Molyneux, it is clear that some of the questions he puts in *The Querist* betray his sense of separateness and grievance – his sense that Ireland, for physical, historical, and cultural reasons, maintains a separate identity and has not in fact become an English province. Of course, Berkeley sees this separateness as regrettable, as some kind of failure rather than some kind of achievement, but his acknowledgement of the reality of separateness is significant nonethe-less. His aggrieved sense of difference and alienation is present in

Queries 271 and 273 when he asks: 'Whether we are not as far before other nations with respect to natural advantages, as we are behind them with respect to arts and industry?' and 'Whether we do not live in a most fertile soil and temperate climate, and yet whether our people in general do not feel great want and misery?' (1953: 128). Perhaps the most revealing sequence of questions in *The Querist* is one that begins with the question, 'Whether our old native Irish are not the most indolent and supine people in Christendom?' and yet ends with, 'Whether we should not cast about, by all manner of means, to excite industry, and to remove whatever hinders it? And whether every one should not lend a helping hand?' (134). These questions suggest that Berkeley is working with an environmental or social theory of the causes of indolence, and is not just making hand-wringing quasi-racist observations about the native Irish. This sequence is soon followed by the question 'Whether there can be a greater reproach on the leading men and the patriots of a country, than that the people should want employment?' (135). And later he asks 'Whether the remotest parts from the metropolis, and the lowest of the people, are not to be regarded as the extremities and capillaries of the political body?' and concludes with the most plaintive and pointed query in the text, 'Whose fault is it if poor Ireland still continues poor?' (154). He implicitly sees the solution to poverty and indolence as lying with the government, and accordingly he makes a case for direct intervention by the government, specifically recommending the establishment of a state-owned national bank that would introduce an adequate currency for the country.

Denis Donoghue has suggested that by the phrase 'We Irish' Berkeley meant only those upper-class Protestants who depended on social prestige and talent rather than on land and power, adding that these men – such as Molyneux, Swift, and Berkeley himself – were often provoked into sentiments that could be mistaken for those of modern nationalism (1986: 17). Though such men resented the mercantilist restrictions imposed by English parliaments, ranging from Poynings's Act of 1495 to the Wool Acts of 1660 and 1690, they resented them on behalf of themselves and their fellow upper-class Protestants and not at all on behalf of the Catholic peasants 'who were so low on the scale of civic life that they could be ignored, as slaves were ignored by Greek philosophers' (Donoghue 1986: 17).

However, it may be instructive in this context to reflect on why the sentiments expressed by Berkeley and others should have been so easily mistaken for modern nationalism. The 'mistake' may have to do with the fact that the sentiments in question are *moral* sentiments, and are duly expressed in the language of entitlement, rights, and justice. This language, precisely because it is a moral language, has universalist implications. Moral categories and judgements, independently of the will of the person who applies them, point indefinitely beyond the interests of individuals or groups to embrace all who have a claim to the conditions of well-being. The 'mistake' that Donoghue identifies may not really be a mistake at all, but an example of what happens when the universalist language of rights and justice is used to articulate a sense of grievance. Anyone in aggrieved circumstances can in principle make that language apply to themselves and use it to seek redress. Berkeley, in making a case for his own class, is implicitly making a case for all – including the Catholic peasantry – who suffer under unjust legislation or government neglect.

SEEING THINGS

Berkeley's theory of vision

Although Berkeley addressed important social, economic, and 'Irish' issues in *The Querist*, his reputation as a thinker rests on the original and provocative battery of arguments that he deploys against materialism, in defence of a God-centred vision of the world. His first major work, *An Essay Towards a New Theory of Vision* (1709), reveals his characteristic concern with the intimate relationship between mind and world. At first glance, this early work seems to be concerned with rather technical and questionable reflections on points made by earlier writers on optics, including William Molyneux, but in fact his study of the contemporary texts on optics elicited from him a number of observations so subtle and original that they revolutionized and had a lasting effect on the subsequent development of modern scientific theories of vision (see Atherton 1990 and Schwartz 1994). One expression of this revolutionary influence is the belief that certain supposedly objective or calculable features of the world, such as distance and magnitude, depend for their visual detection on learnt associations rather than on immediate or direct perception.

The *New Theory* begins with Berkeley's statement of his two objectives in writing the book, namely, 'to shew the manner wherein we perceive by sight the distance, magnitude, and situation of objects', and also to consider the difference between the ideas derived from sight and those derived from touch (1948: 171). He outlines his areas of agreement with other writers on optics, particularly Molyneux, whose terminology and phrasing he sometimes closely follows (see Molyneux 1692: 103). His main concern is with spatial distance and how it is perceived. It is agreed by all, he writes, 'that distance, of itself and immediately, cannot be seen' (Berkeley 1948: 171), and that the estimation of the distances of remote objects 'is rather an act of judgment grounded on experience than of sense' (171). The claim that distance is not directly or immediately seen is based on Molyneux's premise that distance is a line that is always directed end-wise to the eye. That is, distance is always extended straight-forwardly away from us, and we can never see it in perspective since it always presents its base point – and only its base point – on the retina of the eye. We cannot see along the length of the line of distance to determine how short or long it is, and consequently we cannot immediately see distance itself. If we try to 'see around' the end-point of a line of distance we simply move over to another line of distance and put ourselves in the way of yet another end-point. How then do we come to perceive, conceive of, or judge distance? Berkeley's answer is at first close to Molyneux's. Molyneux had suggested that our sense of distance is acquired by the exercise of 'a Faculty of *comparing*' (1692: 113), especially in the case of remote objects. We perceive 'Interjacent Bodies', such as mountains, hills, fields, trees, and houses, and are able to estimate their distances from each other on the basis of their relative heights, sizes, and shapes. We learn from experience, for example, that a mountain is much larger than a house, so that when a mountain appears visually smaller than a house we may safely infer that the mountain must be far off and the house relatively near. We will also have learned that mountains when observed at close quarters have particular and variegated hues but that these coalesce into a hazy blue according as we travel away from them, and this knowledge will also serve to confirm our future estimation of the distance of such a body. Generally, the relative magnitudes, intensities of colour, and other visible features of bodies play a role in aiding the estimation or judgement of distance. It is a somewhat different story with near objects. Their distance, according to Molyneux, is perceived 'by the turn of the Eyes, or by the Angle of the Optick Axes' (1692: 113). By 'the turn of the Eyes' he means the movement that the eyes make in order to focus on a nearby object. The extent to which the eyes turn inward or return to a parallel position is indicative of the relative proximity of the object in question. By 'the Angle of the Optick Axes' he means the angle formed by the straight lines that are supposed to link the eyes with a point in the perceived object, such that the angle between these two lines increases according as the object moves nearer to the eyes and decreases according as it moves away.

Berkeley, like Molyneux, accepts that our ideas of distance depend on experience and on learnt associations, including those associations between visual and tangible properties that are formed in the course of moving about in the world. Berkeley differs from Molyneux and others, however, by placing much more emphasis on the contingent nature of the learnt associations that form the basis of distance perception. There is no innate geometry at work, nor is there any necessary or natural connection between distance and, say, faintness of colour, or between distance and smallness of magnitude. The connection in every case is a learnt one, the result of repeated experiences and of associations built up over a period of time. A man born blind and made to see would not be able to perceive any connection between, say, distance and faintness of colour: 'the sun and stars, the remotest objects as well as the nearer, would all seem to be in his eye, or rather in his mind' (Berkeley 1948: 186). Berkeley accepts that the turning of eyes is indeed involved in the visual detection of distance, but emphatically denies that this movement of the eyes is accompanied by some kind of geometrical calculation of angles and distances. The eye, for Berkeley, is not 'a solver of mathematical problems' (Atherton 1990: 84). Berkeley emphasizes instead the importance of the ocular, muscular *sensations* that accompany the moving, focusing, and straining of the eyes according as objects come close or move away. He also notes that a certain confusion – a blurring of focus – is caused by the approach of an object close to the eyes, even as the eyes strain to keep the object in focus. These experiences of eye-turning, blur, and strain will help in the estimation of distance, since a telling association will come to be established between the experience of blur and strain on the one hand and the idea of (near) distance on the other. We simply learn to associate different ocular sensations or effects with different distances, always bearing in mind that there is no innate geometry involved at any point. Other associations will be established in the aftermath of experiencing repeated connections between certain degrees of distance and certain impressions of light, colour, and shade. We learn through repeated experience, for example, that faintness or haziness of colour signifies the distance of a mountain, and in this way an important association is again established between the visual cue or sign (faintness of colour) and a certain idea of distance.

By so emphasizing sensation and association, and the contingent nature of the learnt relationship between the visual and the tangible properties of things, Berkeley is effectively preparing the way for the radical empiricism that will emerge in his later work. This radical empiricism is perhaps most evidently foreshadowed in his rejection of the theory of innate geometry. Earlier optical theorists, including Descartes and Molyneux, had claimed that perceiving the distance of near objects involves a natural ability to calculate distances according to projected lines and angles. For Berkeley, however, such lines and angles have no real or perceivable existence in nature – they are no more than hypothetical abstractions introduced into optics by mathematicians, and are not therefore objects of perception at all. We do not experience these lines and angles in the course of our acts of perception, 'nor are they in truth ever thought of by those unskilful in optics' (1948: 173). It is for Berkeley axiomatic that nothing that is not itself perceived can be the means of perceiving anything else. If lines and angles are abstractions that are not themselves perceived, then they cannot be the basis on which distance is visually estimated or judged. Our estimation of distance must be dependent on our direct perception of something else, in the same way that the nature of another person's inner feelings or passions is perceived by means of the changing colours of his countenance. Distance, like another person's passion, is a matter of judgement, but it is nonetheless a perceptual judgement – that is, a judgement on the basis of what is immediately perceived, and not at all a judgement on the basis of some kind of deductive calculation or inference. Distance is not seen, but it is nonetheless 'perceived by sight' in the sense that our judgement of it typically involves learnt visual cues and signs.

Later in the *New Theory* Berkeley develops a position on the relationship between sight and touch that owes much to both Locke and Molyneux, a position that also foreshadows the more radical ideas to come. Locke and Molyneux had agreed that a man born blind and later made to see would not be able to distinguish a cube from a sphere on the basis of sight alone, though he had previously been able to distinguish them by touch. The reason suggested by Molyneux was that the formerly blind man has not yet obtained the experience that will enable him to establish 'that what affects his touch so or so, must affect his sight so or so' (Locke 1975: II, ix, § 8). Berkeley develops the suggestion that sight and touch have separate tasks into the claim that they also have separate 'objects', even when they are registering information about the same apparent feature. It must be acknowledged, he argues, that we never see and feel one and the same object: 'That which is seen is one thing, and that which is felt is another' (1948: 189). This means that shape as sensed by sight is different from shape as sensed by touch. Shape in the visual sense is conveyed through light and colour, neither of which is detectable by the sense of touch. Shape in the tactile sense is conveyed through the texture, firmness, resistance, and other tangible qualities of things, none of which is available to the sense of sight. The 'feel' of a cube is in all respects different from the 'look' of a cube, and no amount of tactile acquaintance with the cube will prepare one for the first *visual* experience of it. We do, of course, by dint of repeated experience, come to associate the visual and the tangible shapes of things. Indeed, this associative ability, based on connections established over a period of time, enables us to use the visual appearances of things as a way of usefully anticipating, or 'looking forward' to, their tangible features. Such, in Berkeley's view, is the 'habitual connexion' between visual and tangible ideas that the objects of vision serve as a kind of life-enhancing and providential language – as indeed 'an universal language of the Author of nature' (231). Like the signs and marks of a human language, the objects of vision serve to signify and mark objects that are at a distance from us, enabling us to regulate our actions and to avoid whatever may be harmful and destructive in our immediate environment. For example, if I do not see the distinctive colour and shape – 'the visible ideas' – of a car hurtling along the road in my direction, then I am in danger of being struck by it when I step off the path. By the time I make tactile contact with this particular object in motion it will be too late for me to take evasive action. Only by paying attention to visual cues and signs will I be able to negotiate my way safely through the world of cars and other objects. The existence of the whole system of life-enhancing, life-preserving connections that we have established between visible signs and the tangible world suggests to Berkeley that this system of connections is indeed a language, the language of a providential God. This extraordinary idea will lie at the centre of his expressly theological writings, which will be discussed in a later section.

SEEING (AND NOT SEEING) THINGS

Berkeley's philosophy of perception

The mind-dependence of all perceived objects, including tangible objects, is the startling message of Berkeley's *Principles of Human Knowledge*. Before examining in some detail the manner in which Berkeley advances his case for mind-dependence, it is worth bearing in mind that his main motive is to make the strongest possible case against scepticism, atheism, materialism, even idolatry. Some remarks he makes in his notebooks, eventually published as the *Philosophical Commentaries*, signal his intellectual concerns – concerns that cannot, however, be separated from his moral and theological obsessions. He writes of himself, for example, that he is the 'farthest from Scepticism' of any man, and that his own doctrines, rightly understood, undermine the philosophies of Epicurus, Hobbes, and Spinoza, all three of whom he takes to be materialists. His relationship to Locke is more complex, but it is significant that he rejects any argument in Locke's work that seems to lean towards scepticism or materialism. He is especially dismissive of Locke's claim that ideas are merely representations of objects, since this suggests that all we can know are the mental images of objects rather than the objects themselves: 'The supposition that things are distinct from Ideas takes away all real Truth, & consequently brings in a Universal Scepticism, since all our knowledge & contemplation is confin'd to our own Ideas' (1948: 75). He expresses alarm at Locke's opinion that physical matter might be capable of thought, since this implies the possibility of thought without mind or spirit. Later he makes a remark that is symptomatic of his antagonism not only to materialism but to the very idea of matter itself. He writes: 'If matter is once allow'd to exist Clippings of beards & parings of nails may Think for ought that Locke can tell Tho he seems positive of the Contrary' (87). It seems to Berkeley that in the work of Locke matter has begun to rival God as the principle of existence. If thought itself can be produced by and subsist in matter, then there is less reason to appeal to a principle of mind or spirit in order to explain any important features of reality. As if to avenge himself on the materialists, Berkeley will reassert not only the autonomy of mind, spirit, and God but also the purely spiritual and divine basis of all reality, including the reality of the perceivable world itself. In brief, God will displace matter in Berkeley's scheme of things, thereby depriving atheists and materialists of their main philosophical support.

The substance of Berkeley's theory of a mind-dependent world is set out in the opening paragraphs of the *Principles*. The key term here is 'idea'. The extent to which we can sympathize with Berkeley's philosophy of mind-dependence will depend on how much we can sympathize with his expansive and extended use of this term. To begin with, an idea will be defined simply as a mental entity, something that can exist only in a mind, but before long the term will be made to do more work than it does in normal usage. For Berkeley, ideas fall into three groups: (a) those imprinted on the senses, (b) those formed by attending inwardly to the operations of one's own mind, and (c) those formed with the aid of imagination or memory. Ideas, moreover, because of their original dependence on the senses, including 'internal' sense, may be thought of as sensations or perceptions. This is the principal way in which Berkeley stretches the idea of 'idea' – that is, he makes it stand for sensation or perception. Each of the five external senses generates ideas peculiar to itself – sight provides ideas of light and colour, touch provides ideas of texture, temperature, motion and resistance, hearing gives us sounds, and so on. We do not possess any idea that was not originally conveyed through one of the senses.

But Berkeley is not done yet. Having first stretched the meaning of *idea* to include sensations or perceptions, he next stretches it all the way to the object of sensation or perception. He invites us to think of an object or thing as nothing more or less than a collection of all the ideas or perceptions that come in by the various senses. Thus, for example, 'a certain colour, taste, smell, figure and consistence having been observed to go together, are accounted one distinct thing, signified by the name *apple*' (1949: 41). In *Three Dialogues between Hylas and Philonous* – which is Berkeley's attempt at a more accessible account of the arguments of the *Principles* - the same point is put more cogently, using a different fruit for illustration:

> I see this *cherry*, I feel it, I taste it: and I am sure *nothing* cannot be seen, or felt, or tasted: it is therefore *real*. Take away the sensations of softness, moisture, redness, tartness, and you take away the cherry. Since it is not a being distinct from sensations; a *cherry*, I say, is nothing but a congeries of sensible impressions or ideas perceived by various senses: which ideas are united into one thing (or have one name given them) by the mind.
>
> (1949: 249)

These radically revisionary conceptions of such familiar things as an apple and a cherry encapsulate the simple but mind-boggling argument that lies at the heart of Berkeley's philosophy. Berkeley has effectively defined an object in terms of the ideas or sensations that it *is*, rather than in terms of the ideas or sensations that it causes or produces. The real object is not, as it is in Locke's philosophy, an external material substance that makes its presence felt (or seen) by causing representations in the mind of a perceiver. For Berkeley, the object is the totality of the perceptions or ideas we have of it. The apple, cherry, or any other object just is a collection of ideas or sensations designated by a particular term. It is whatever has a distinctive identifiable existence, complex but unified, at the tips of our senses. Indeed, Berkeley finally stretches *idea* so deep into the world of perceived objects that he makes it cover existence itself. That is, existence itself comes to be defined in terms of ideas, sensations, impressions, or perceptions:

I think an intuitive knowledge may be obtained of this, by anyone that shall attend to what is meant by the term *exist* when applied to sensible things. The table I write on I say exists, that is, I see and feel it; and if I were out of my study I should say it existed, meaning thereby that if I was in my study I might perceive it, or that some other spirit actually does perceive it.

(42)

What this means is not merely that we perceive things because they exist but also that things exist in the measure that we perceive them (or in the measure that some other mindful being perceives them). Objects of sense are defined entirely in terms of their perceivability. The notion of an unperceived or unperceivable object of sense is unintelligible. It is for this reason that Berkeley declares of all objects of sense that their *'esse* is *percipi'* (42) – that is, their existence absolutely depends on their being sensed or perceived by a mind. For Berkeley, one can no more divide the existence of a thing from the perception of it than one can divide a thing from itself. He concludes that 'all the choir of heaven and furniture of the earth, in a word all those bodies which compose the mighty frame of the world, have not any subsistence without a mind, that their *being* is to be perceived or known' (43). Sensible or perceivable objects are therefore necessarily mind-dependent objects, since perception is a function of the mind. If anybody wants to talk about objects existing absolutely independently of the mind, then, in Berkeley's view, such a person wants to talk about something that is by definition not sensible or perceivable, something not present to the mind, something of which we can literally have no idea – and therefore something that cannot be said to exist.

What else exists in Berkeley's scheme of things, besides collections of ideas or perceptions? Only perceivers. Besides the endless variety of ideas or collections of ideas, there exists the perceiving, active being that perceives them, namely, the mind, spirit, or soul: 'there is not any other substance than *spirit*, or that which perceives' (43). Matter drops out of the framework as something that is neither perceivable nor deducible from reason. Materialists themselves acknowledge that there is no necessary connection between the having of an idea and the existence of material substance. If there were a necessary connection between ideas and the existence of material substance, then the having of any idea, including a dream-like or hallucinatory one, would imply the existence of a corresponding material substance. But this is so obviously absurd it is not argued by anyone. Given the conceivability of ideas without matter, it follows for Berkeley that it is not necessary to suppose the existence of external bodies in order to account for the occurrence of any of our ideas (48).

Berkeley has cleverly used the materialists' own scepticism or agnosticism about material substance as a way of making a case against the concept of matter itself. If material substance is by definition not perceivable and if it is unnecessary to suppose its existence in order to account for the existence of any idea, then it plays no necessary role in our account of things. But if it does not play a necessary role, surely, we might want to argue, it plays a rather useful role. How are all the properties of things held objectively and continuously together if they do not subsist in matter? What accounts for the difference between a real idea and an imaginary one if not the fact that one has a relationship with the material world, the other not? How are we going to account for the fact that things are not creations of our own minds but change and develop independently of our individual wills if we cannot make matter the principle of independent existence? If matter is not the principle of objectivity, substantiality, and external reality, what is? Berkeley's reply to such questions is that the guarantor of objectivity and reality is not an underlying material substance but an overseeing divine mind, a governing spirit, an infinite omnipresent spirit – in a word, God. Berkeley finds it evident 'that the being of a *spirit infinitely wise, good, and powerful* is abundantly sufficient to explain all the appearances of Nature' (72). The objective permanence and reality of things resides in the fact that ideas are not generated from within by the mind itself, 'but imprinted by a spirit distinct from that which perceives them' (80). Berkeley's vision of the relationship between the perceived world and God, or the Author of Nature, receives its most emphatic expression in § 146:

[I]f we attentively consider the constant regularity, order, and concatenation of natural things, the surprising magnificence, beauty, and perfection of the larger, and the exquisite contrivance of the smaller parts of the creation, together with the exact harmony and correspondence of the whole, but above all, the never enough admired laws of pain and pleasure, and the instincts or natural inclinations, appetites, and passions of animal; . . . we shall clearly perceive that they belong to the aforesaid spirit, *who works all in all*, and *by whom all things consist*.

(108)

Though not a pantheist, Berkeley strikes a pantheistic chord in these lines which suggest that God is all-supportive and omnipresent, immediately and fundamentally operative in the world around us, 'and intimately present to our consciousness' (Luce 1949: 44). This sense of an omnipresent God so animates Berkeley's philosophical and theological writings that he can be characterized as possibly the most God-centred and 'theophanic' of modern thinkers.

THE VISIBLE LANGUAGE OF GOD

Although Berkeley's essay on optics and his treatise on human knowledge are directed explicitly against the claims of sceptics, atheists, and materialists, they are not ostensibly theological essays. His most explicitly and most importantly theological work is to be found in *Alciphron; or the Minute Philosopher* (1732), where he is specifically concerned to rebut the freethinking theology of the deists. He offers two arguments of interest, one in favour of theism, the other in favour of fideism – in favour, that is, of the claim that understanding is not a prerequisite for faith. Berkeley's argument for theism is based on claims made in the *New Theory of Vision* and is a kind of argument from analogy, turning specifically on a comparison between human language and nature's visual phenomena. Berkeley claims that light, shades, and colours, variously combined, 'answer to the several articulations of sound in language' in the sense that they serve as the marks or signs of things other than themselves. Just as a language consists of the use of outward, sensible signs that arbitrarily signify various objects or ideas, so a whole range of visual phenomena come to be associated with aspects of the natural world that are not themselves visual, principally distance, shape, magnitude, and position. Moreover, these connections of visual phenomena with non-visual aspects of the world are not at all natural or necessary; the connections or associations are purely contingent and are established as a result of repeated experiences over time. That is why we can say that the faintness of a thing's appearance is a *sign* of its distance from us. It is a sign precisely because there is no necessary connection between faintness and distance and because the association in question is contingent and arbitrary, something learnt through repeated experience. Other non-visual aspects of the world – in particular its tangible aspects – are also suggested or signified by the associations we come to establish between these aspects and certain visual cues or signs. The range and variety of such contingent or arbitrary associations point not only to the existence of a network of signs, a veritable language of vision, but also to 'the immediate operation of a spirit or thinking being' (1950: 160). Just as human speech informs us of the presence of another person, so the optic language of nature should convince us of the presence of a being who 'speaks' through that language. Light and colour 'do form a language wonderfully adapted to suggest and exhibit to us the distances, figures, situations, dimensions, and various qualities of tangible objects: not by similitude, nor yet by inference of necessary connexion, but by the arbitrary impositions of Providence, just as words suggest the things signified by them' (154). You have as much reason, says Euphranor to Alciphron, 'to think the Universal Agent or God speaks to your eyes, as you can have for thinking any particular person speaks to your ears' (157).

Does this not bring God too close to the creaturely minds of human beings? It does not. Or at least it does not do so in a way that detracts from God's absolute difference. In the first place, it is not human beings who presumptuously take the initiative of bringing God closer to themselves. Rather, the initiative to communicate across the distance between God and human beings is taken by God himself in order to show that he is not a creator merely but 'a provident Governor, actually and intimately present, and attentive to all our interests and motions' (160). We might say that the act of communication through the language of vision is 'an act of God', or an act from above downwards, and not at all 'an act of man', or an act from below upwards (see Przywara 1935: 22). In the second place, God's 'intimate presence' is not in any sense a pantheistic or an immanent presence but rather a signified presence, a caring presence expressed and communicated through the visual language of nature. Of course, no particular visual sign or set of signs can in itself signify the being or nature of God. Rather, it is the existence of so much significant arbitrariness in the language of vision – 'the sensible intervention of arbitrary signs, which have no similitude or connexion with the things signified' (1950: 157) – that points to the existence of an infinitely intelligent, never-absent, and providential Author of Nature.

In the seventh dialogue Berkeley makes the case for fideism in the form of an argument that is intended as a rebuttal of the Lockean semiology promoted by Toland. A position superficially similar to Toland's is presented by Alciphron, the freethinker: 'Words are signs: they do or should stand for ideas, which so far as they suggest they are significant. But words that suggest no ideas are insignificant. He who annexeth a clear idea to every word he makes use of, speaks sense; but where such ideas are wanting, the speaker utters nonsense' (1950: 287).

Alciphron chooses *grace* as an example of an idea which is central to Christian belief but which does not bear up very well when one subjects it to the criteria of clarity and distinctness. He professes himself altogether unable to associate any distinct idea with the word 'grace', and concludes that he cannot therefore assent to any proposition concerning it, 'nor, consequently have any faith about it' (290). The main tactic of Berkeley's mouthpiece, Euphranor, is to question the assumption that verbal meaning must be linked to clear and distinct ideas. In a graphically cogent image he suggests that signs or words are analogous to counters in a card-game. The counters are not used for their own sake, as valuable in themselves; rather, they are 'signs substituted for money, as words are for ideas' (291). In order to use the counters in the game, it is not necessary to keep bringing to mind the distinct sums or values that each counter represents: 'it will suffice if in the conclusion those figures direct our actions with respect to things' (291). It is likewise with words, Euphranor quickly adds, opportunistically exploiting his antagonist's concurrence. Words can be, and often are, used meaningfully, although they do not, every time they are used, bring to the mind the ideas which they do in fact signify. It is sufficient that we have the ability 'to substitute things or ideas for their signs when there is occasion' (292).

No sooner has Euphranor thus loosened the connections between sign and idea than he takes another step – and, again, takes it rather hastily. From the fact that words can sometimes be used independently of the ideas they signify, it seems also to follow 'that there may be another use of words besides that of marking and suggesting distinct ideas, to wit, the influencing our conduct and actions' (292). As well as, or instead of, exciting ideas in our mind, words can also excite certain passions, dispositions, and emotions in us. A discourse concerned with influencing our dispositions or guiding our actions may contain terms that do not bring distinct ideas to mind. Even in technical or scientific discourse there may be no agreed definition or conception of what a particular term means. For example, no one can form a clear and distinct idea of force if they are required to abstract it from all considerations of body, space, motion, and its other visible and tangible effects. We all know what force is when we see an instantiation of it, but if we are asked what force is apart from its manifestations – what force is in the abstract – we are at a loss. We cannot contemplate force itself 'in its own precise idea', and yet there is no denying that we have constant and useful recourse to the word 'force' in both scientific speculation and practical or applied mechanics.

It is at this point that Euphranor expressly defends the view that there can be a valid credulous response to signs or terms, albeit in the absence of clear and distinct ideas. He uses a 'parity of reason' argument here, an argument based on a comparison between the use of the word 'force' and the use of the word 'grace'. It is true that we do not have a clear idea of what grace is, but neither do we have a clear idea of what force is:

> If there are queries, disputes, perplexities, diversity of notions and opinions about one, so there are about the other also: if we can form no precise distinct idea of the one, so neither can we of the other. Ought we not therefore, by a parity of reason, to conclude there may be divers true and useful propositions concerning the one as well as the other?
>
> (296)

In other words, there can be faith or assent without full understanding – that is, without clear and distinct ideas of the supernatural realities in question – just as there can be science and practical knowledge without clear and distinct ideas of the natural processes in question. Although we do not have a clear and distinct idea of grace, grace can still be a valid object of faith, and our belief in it can influence our life and actions. The same reasoning can be extended to more specific and more 'difficult' terms, such as original sin or the Holy Trinity. These terms do not bring to mind, nor can they be associated with, clear and distinct ideas, but they nonetheless belong usefully in discourses that serve to regulate our wills, passions, and conduct. A person's belief in original sin, for example, even if he doesn't have a precise idea of it, may produce in him a salutary sense of his own unworthiness and an equally salutary sense of the infinite goodness of the redeemer. From these effects may follow good habits and good actions. Faith, says Euphranor, 'is not an indolent perception, but an operative persuasion of mind, which ever worketh some suitable action, disposition, or emotion in those who have it' (301). What gives words their meaning is their usefulness and effectiveness in a discourse or practice, whether it is a scientific or a religious discourse. Across different discourses there may be many such exemplary parities of use and effect. Euphranor concludes: 'The true end of speech, reason, science, faith, assent, in all its different degrees, is not merely, or principally, or always, the imparting or acquiring of ideas, but rather something of an active operative nature, tending to a conceived good' (1950: 307). In Berkeley's theological scheme of things, human beings are put in the position that they can be moved by the language of revelation without fully understanding it, or indeed understanding it at all. In this way human understanding is duly humbled but without risk to the sources of faith and good conduct. It is as if an infinitely providential God can communicate directly with the heart and the will without going through the understanding.

Berkeley's views on religious language are, of course, unacceptable to deists like John Toland for whom all effective language, to be effective as *language*, must be meaningful. To be meaningful, language must be mediated through the understanding – that is, must give rise to ideas of some kind. To say that words can be a stimulus to emotion or action without first producing an idea in the mind of the hearer is tantamount to saying that a word can be heard and be meaningful without being understood. For Toland, such a claim cannot be coherently made.

Faith, in Toland's view, comes from hearing, 'but without Understanding 'tis plain this Hearing would signify nothing, Words and their Ideas being reciprocal in all Languages' (1696: 129). If someone were to speak to us in a language we did not understand to any degree, we could not be moved by his or her use of language, because we would, literally, have no idea what was being said to us. This is not to say that we could not be moved at all. But if we *were* moved in the presence of incomprehensible words it would be on some other account – ritual or music, perhaps – and not on account of the words considered as semantic units. Toland would not have been able to accept Berkeley's supposition that the 'popish peasant' gives his assent to the uncomprehended propositions he hears at the Latin mass (Berkeley 1948: 88). If the peasant does not understand the terms of the propositions (because they are in Latin), then he cannot be said to *hear* the propositions in the first place. What he hears are not even meaningful sentences, let alone propositions capable of eliciting his assent. Words do not move us in virtue of the brute syntax of their physical shape or sound but in virtue of their meaning – that is, in virtue of their capacity, when heard, to bring ideas to mind. This is the point of the Blictri example. If someone invites us to believe in Blictri, to adore Blictri, or to otherwise let Blictri into our lives, we cannot begin to make our commitment sensibly or rationally until we have some sense – some *idea* – of what a Blictri is.

SWIFT AND THE DRAPIER

The making of a Hibernian patriot

If Berkeley wonderfully mended the world by theoretically ridding it of matter, his friend Jonathan Swift set about mending it rather differently, by indignantly and savagely exposing its moral vices and intellectual pretensions. (The reference to 'wonderfully mending the world' occurs in a letter of 1725 in which Swift wrote to his friend Charles Ford: 'I have finished my Travells, and I am now transcribing them; they are admirable Things, and will wonderfully mend the World' (1963: 87).) Swift was born in Dublin in 1667, educated at Kilkenny College and Trinity College, Dublin, taking his BA degree in 1686.

He was still in residence at Trinity, preparing to receive his Master's degree, when the fall-out from England's 'bloodless revolution' of 1688 began to be felt in Dublin, threatening English rule and bringing normal life to a stop (Quintana 1955). As a result of the changing circumstances Swift, like many others, left Ireland in the couple of years between the 1688 revolution and Ireland's far from bloodless battle of the Boyne in 1690. He would spend most of the next ten years in England, as secretary to the retired statesman and writer, Sir William Temple, at Moor Park in Surrey. Sir William's father, John Temple, had been master of the rolls in Ireland both before and after the restoration, and had come to know members of Swift's family. It was through this family connection that Swift came to the attention of Sir William, who was at this time working on a collection of essays and saw an opportunity that would benefit both himself and the young Swift. The arrangement between Temple and Swift did indeed prove to be beneficial on both sides. Temple found himself an able secretary, and Swift found himself an inspiring mentor. Writing of the formative impact of Temple on Swift during this period, Irwin Ehrenpreis notes that Swift admired Temple's character and his mind: 'Temple's literary style, political philosophy, moral outlook, and aesthetic judgment became either models or points of departure for Swift's own' (1962: 92). Swift's career as a writer and satirist had its origins in the period at Moor Park. Although his famous satires *A Tale of a Tub* and *The Battle of the Books* were not published until 1704, they were among the works composed at Moor Park.

Temple died in 1699, leaving a disappointed Swift without place or post. Swift returned to Ireland and became resident at Dublin Castle as chaplain to the earl of Berkeley, one of the three lords justice to Ireland. In the following year he was given the vicarage of Larcor near Trim in Co. Meath, but by 1701 he had begun an active period which saw him moving between Dublin and London, engaging in church business, and at the same time becoming seriously involved in literary and political matters. When the Tories came to power in 1710 they solicited Swift's support, since he had by then earned a considerable reputation as wit, satirist, and man of letters, and was seen as a potentially powerful propagandist for any cause or party that he might choose to support. Although Swift did agree to support the Tories, successfully attacking particular Whig policies, he did not receive from them the rewards he had expected. Instead of an English bishopric he was offered an Irish deanery, the deanery of St Patrick's, which he accepted less than whole-heartedly. Back in Dublin by 1714, he lived for a while, as Ehrenpreis puts it, 'as though under house arrest, like an exile in his own country' (1983: 4). But eventually he rallied, and 'let his natural roots in Ireland feed his conscience and support his art' (Ehrenpreis 1983: 5). Gradually, as Dean of St Patrick's, he came to devote himself to the good of a nation, his dedication growing deeper until the object of his conscience and new-found allegiance became 'humble, produc-tive humanity' (Ehrenpreis 1983: 4). It was during his time as dean that Swift engaged the issues that would earn him the designation 'Hibernian patriot' and a place alongside William Molyneux in one of the most famous exclamations in Irish history (which we have already heard in Chapter 3), namely, Henry Grattan's exclamation from the floor of the Irish House of Commons on the granting of legislative independence in 1782: 'Spirit of Swift! spirit of Molyneux! your genius has prevailed! Ireland is now a nation!' (1874: 70).

Swift's patriotic reputation originated with his *Drapier's Letters*, a series of seven pamphlets written during 1724 and 1725, and directed primarily against a proposal to mint a new copper coinage for Ireland. Since Ireland did not have a national mint, it was customary to grant the minting patent to private individuals. In 1722 it transpired that an English iron merchant, William Wood, had been awarded the patent to mint £108,000 worth of copper coin, an amount greatly in excess of what the economy needed, given the total value of the Irish currency at the time. After the Irish parliament objected to Wood's patent, Swift began his campaign against 'the deluge of brass', publishing his first and subsequent 'letters' under the guise of an honest-to-goodness Protestant shopkeeper, 'M. B., Drapier'. While the first three letters deal with what we might call the 'economics' of the patent, the fourth letter takes a dramatic political turn. This letter is addressed to 'the whole people of Ireland', and its most pointed passages contain loaded references to liberty and the consent of the governed. The Drapier insists on the relative autonomy of Ireland as a kingdom, claiming that he can find no statute that makes Ireland depend upon England, 'any more than *England* does upon *Ireland*' (Swift 1935: 78). In the course of questioning the right of English parliaments to make laws binding on the kingdom of Ireland, he cites 'the famous

Mr. Molyneux' and proceeds to make one of the most radical points that Swift ever made through one of his writerly masks, namely, that 'all *Government* without the consent of the *Governed* is the *very Definition of Slavery*' (1935: 79).

In a note on the fourth letter, Joseph McMinn points out that the rhetorical ambition of the pamphlet's title – 'To the whole People of Ireland' – is deceptive, 'since Swift is largely addressing the Protestant and propertied interest' (1991: 70). And J.C. Beckett is adamant that Swift hardly thought of himself as an Irishman at all, 'but rather as an Englishman who had, by a kind of unhappy accident, been born in Ireland' (1971: 155). Swift certainly retains the distinction, reiterated in the fourth letter, between the native Irish and 'the true English people of Ireland' and it is clear that both he and the Drapier belong to the latter. However, the sort of point made earlier about Berkeley also applies to Swift, only with more force and plausibility. Regardless of his own conscious intentions and his own immediate concerns and goals, the logic of his principled stance was to carry him, willy-nilly, into the history of the Irish struggle for an independent identity and, in principle, into the history of every struggle against unjust dominion. Carole Fabricant has drawn attention to Swift's own condemnation of those vast numbers 'who think themselves too good to live in the Country which gave them birth, and still gives them Bread' (Swift 1948: 200; Fabricant 1982: 229). Implicitly, then, Swift considered himself to be more than just an accidental Irishman. He was, by his own acknowledgement, an Irishman by privilege and also by duty and public spirit. His duty and public spirit were expressed with such passion and principle through the persona of the liberty-loving Drapier that this persona itself floated free of the historical Swift and became 'a means by which Swift, the stranger in a strange land, became the beloved patriot and folk hero of a people who enthusiastically claimed him as their own' (Fabricant 1982: 262; see also Mahony 1995).

THE CONVERTING IMAGINATION

Swift against the moderns

Though Swift is not a philosopher or 'thinker' in the stricter senses of those terms, he is nonetheless a highly observant and critical satirist who shares with Berkeley the objective of defending orthodox Christian belief against the claims of atheists, freethinkers, and rationalists generally. His targets, in other words, are very often the irregular theological and philosophical positions of his contemporaries. Indeed, much of his satirical work cannot be fully understood unless it is read against the backdrop of the theological, scientific, and philosophical controversies of his time. His own positions are consistently antagonistic towards the new theologies of the dissenters and freethinkers and the new scientific philosophies associated with Descartes, Bacon, and Boyle. His antagonism towards the new religious and philosophical thinking is already vehemently expressed in his early satirical essay, *The Battle of the Books* (1697). This essay had its remoter origins in a controversy that had originated in France in the second half of the seventeenth century over the relative merits of ancient and modern authors, and had its more immediate origins in a local version of the controversy that had been provoked by Swift's mentor, Sir William Temple. In 'An Essay upon the Ancient and Modern Learning', first published in 1690, Temple had suggested that the ancient authors remained superior to the moderns in most areas of intellectual endeavour. Thales, Pythagoras, Democritus, Plato, and Aristotle are among those who were 'the first mighty Conquerors of Ignorance in our World, and made greater Progresses in the several Empires of Science, than any of their Successors have been since able to reach' (1705: 28). He knows of no new philosophers, 'unless Descartes and Hobbes should pretend to it' (42), who can eclipse the lustre of the ancients, even in the sciences. There is nothing new in astronomy to vie with the ancients, 'unless it be the *Copernican* system; nor in *Physick*, unless it be *Harvey's* Circulation of the Blood' (42). No sooner has he allowed for these possible exceptions than he qualifies his concession by suggesting that it is a matter of dispute whether these discoveries have been derived from older sources. In any case, the discoveries of Copernicus and Harvey had not, in Temple's opinion, brought about any significant changes in the practice of either astronomy or medicine, 'and so have been of little Use to the World, though perhaps of much Honour to the Authors' (43).

The controversy that followed Temple's essay was not prompted by his rash disparagement of modern discovery but by a specific failure of scholarship. In the course of his essay he had expressed particular admiration for Phalarais's *Epistles* and Aesop's *Fables*, both of which he believed to be very ancient and the best of their kind. On the basis of 'tasteful' stylistic analysis he found the *Epistles* to have 'more Race, more Spirit, more Force of Wit and Genius' than anything produced by the moderns (59). He noted that some critics had expressed doubts about their authenticity, attributing them to Lucian, but he dismissed such doubts, claiming that the *Epistles*, on account of their power and boldness, could only have been produced by a true tyrant and commander, such as Phalarais was, and not at all by a mere scholar and sophist, such as Lucian was. By 1697 a two-pronged attack had been launched against Temple by a brace of scholars, Sir William Wotton and Richard Bentley. Wotton had already replied to Temple in his *Reflections upon Ancient and Modern Learning* (1694) in which he had made an impressive catalogue of the achievements of the moderns, asserting their superiority in all areas except literature and the fine arts. Three years later, when Wotton published a second edition of the *Reflections*, he included in it an important paper by his friend, Richard Bentley, a respected classical scholar and the keeper of the royal library at St James's Palace (soon to become the battleground for Swift's satire on the controversy). In his *Dissertation* Bentley showed beyond all reasonable doubt that the *Epistles* of Phalarais were a forgery, full of anachronistic references to things that did not exist at the supposed time of their composition. He also showed that the *Fables* – that is, the particular collection about which Temple had written – did not constitute an ancient text, and that one half of the fables were over a thousand years more recent than the historical Aesop, the other half more recent still.

Although it is clear now that Wotton and Bentley had the better argument, this was not at all obvious to their contemporaries. To Swift in particular the method and style of the two 'modern' scholars seemed unduly pedantic and academic. Moreover, the scholars in question had overlooked the *moral* critique that Temple had made of the moderns, namely, his critique of their 'sufficiency', of their tendency to depend entirely on the powers of their own reasoning, without respectful and modest deference to tradition or to the work of those who had preceded them. According to Temple, the learning of the ancients had brought them to a sense of their own ignorance and of

the imbecility of human understanding in general, whereas the learning of the moderns had led them to the arrogant presumption that we
already know a great deal and shall know in time as much as the angels
(1705: 284). It was this critique of sufficiency and intellectual pride,
and not the scholarly dating of old texts, that lay behind Swift's own
indignant response to the claims of the moderns.

His immediate response to the controversy surrounding Temple's
essay takes the form of *The Battle of the Books*, a satirical account of a
violent 'confrontation' between the ancient and modern books
housed in St James's Library. In the satire Aesop and Phalarais are presented as two heroes of the army of ancients, an army led by Homer,
Pindar, Aristotle, Herodotus, and other illustrious figures from the
classical period. Among the leaders of the moderns are Milton,
Dryden, Bacon, Descartes, Hobbes, and a number of others whose
names are now forgotten. Although the outcome of the battle is
unknown because the conclusion of the narrative is 'lost', it is evident
from Swift's description of individual battle scenes that he is rather
passionately on the side of the ancients. In one scene, Aristotle fires
an arrow that is intended to strike down Bacon but which instead
hits Descartes in the right eye. The impact of the arrow causes
Descartes to whirl about 'till Death, like a star of superior Influence,
drew him into his own *Vortex*' (1958: 244). Homer is even more belli-
cose, dashing out the brains of two French moderns, Perrault and
Fontanelle. Perhaps the most violent fate is reserved for Wotton and
Bentley. In the closing scene of the story, Charles Boyle, represented
as an ally of the ancients because he had published an edition of
Phalarais's *Epistles*, drives a lance through the bodies of Wotton and
Bentley. The bloody-mindedness of the narrative at this point is an
indication of how savage Swift's indignation could be. We are told
that, just as a skilful cook trusses a brace of woodcocks by piercing
their tender bodies together with a single iron skewer, 'so was this
pair of Friends transfix'd, till down they fell, joyn'd in their Lives,
joyn'd in their Deaths' (258).

A key episode among the outrageous events at St James's Library is
the confrontation between the spider and the bee. The spider, because
he spins a complex structure from out of his own substance, is made to
represent the haughty sufficiency of the moderns, especially their pride
in their recent achievements in architecture and mathematics. The bee,

on the other hand, is made to represent the more modest ethos of the admirers of the ancients who do not involve themselves in dirty and poisonous schemes but instead pay due deference to the beauty and bounty of nature. The bee's achievements are won by patience and respectful investigation, eventually furnishing the world with the two noblest of things, namely, sweetness and light. The bee, in a rhetorical question to the spider, asks which of the following is the nobler: 'That which by a lazy Contemplation of four Inches round, by an over-weening Pride, which feeding and engendering on it self, turns all into Excrement and Venom; producing nothing at last, but Flybane and a Cobweb: Or that, which, by an universal Range, with long Search, much Study, true Judgment, and Distinction of Things, brings home Honey and Wax' (232).

The bee's question is Swift's question. But Swift is not simply an advocate of the humane and scholarly traditions, as if these were ends in themselves. The significance of these traditions of sweetness and light is that they are the product of the better part of the human spirit itself, especially that part of it that is capable of reasonable and moderate diligence. The critique of the moderns is primarily an ethical one, directed against the intellectual presumption of those individual reasoners who would dare to set their own philosophical systems, the creations of their own individual faculties, over against the accumulated wisdom of the past. The argument for tradition is also an argument for modesty of intellectual ambition and for collective responsibility in matters of learning and culture. It is an essentially conservative argument in that it seeks to preserve the best of the past, inviting the modern scholar to make a respectful contribution instead of attempting to provide a radical alternative.

MODERNISM AS MADNESS

The moral of the *Tale*

The critique of self-serving reasoners and schemers is developed more pointedly and more extensively in *A Tale of a Tub*, described by Swift himself as a satire on 'the numerous and gross Corruptions in Religion and Learning' (1958: 5). The main strand of the satirical allegory deals with the origin of abuses within the Christian religion, while abuses in learning and science are the subject of a series of digressions that alternate for the most part with episodes of the tale. The main narrative of the *Tale* begins like a fairy tale: 'Once upon a Time, there was a Man who had Three sons by one Wife, and all at a Birth, neither could the Mid-Wife tell certainly which was the Eldest' (1958: 73). In keeping with the sudden narrative transitions of a fairy tale, the father of the three sons dies in the second sentence, though not before he calls his young sons to his deathbed in order to present them with his legacy of three coats. These are, of course, no ordinary coats. Each coat will grow as the wearer grows, and will last as long as the wearer lives. And there are, as one would expect, certain conditions to be met. The coats are to be worn and treated in a particular way, otherwise penalties will be incurred; and the brothers are to live together in the same house, otherwise they will not prosper. For further details on how to avoid incurring the prescribed penalties, especially with regard to the wearing of the coats, the brothers are instructed to consult the terms of the will which their father presents to them along with the new coats.

For seven years the brothers do as their father instructed. They keep their coats in good order; and they have travelled through several countries, encountered 'a reasonable Quantity of Gyants', and slain certain dragons (74). With these gently but firmly mocking words, the narrative of the standard children's fairy tale is cut short. The brothers have now reached the age of maturity – 'the proper Age for producing themselves' – and a new set of challenges, much more difficult than giants and dragons, is about to be encountered. At this point, the fairy tale itself matures rapidly and disconcertingly into unsparing satire. The brothers come into town and fall in love with certain ladies, but these are no ordinary ladies – these are allegorical ladies, the Duchess d'Argent, Madame de Grands Titres, and the Countess d'Orgeuil, representing the vices of covetousness, ambition, and pride. Thus begins the downfall of the brothers, who have now themselves entered the realm of allegorical meaning. They yield to the temptations of the world, writing, singing, drinking, haunting the chocolate-houses, and running up debts. Most disastrously, they become victims of a sect that is not only fashionable but is itself a fashion sect. The sect worships a deity in the shape of a tailor, bases all its beliefs on a sartorial metaphysics, and reduces all values to sartorial ones. It holds the universe to be a large suit of clothes and man himself to be a kind of microcoat. So pervasive are the values of this sect that to be out of fashion is to be considered an inferior sort of being. This proves particularly difficult for the three brothers, who have been instructed not to alter their coats except in ways approved in their father's will. Much of the rest of the *Tale* is an account of what happens when the brothers try to interpret the will to suit themselves in their new circumstances, especially to justify making fashionable adjustments to their otherwise plain coats. One of the brothers, Peter, proves to be the most inventive in devising suitably 'worldly' interpretations of the will. When shoulder-knots become fashionable, and the anxious brothers fail to find any obvious reference to shoulder-knots in the will, it is Peter who invents a new way of reading which enables them to 'find' the word hidden in the text of the will. In his role as interpreter, Peter will prove to be as inventive as any projector or virtuoso of the Royal Society. Among his fanciful inventions will be the whispering office, a remedy for worms, an office of insurance for tobacco-pipes, and a universal pickle.

At this point in the *Tale* it is essential to know what (and who) is being targeted allegorically. These targets are usefully specified in the series of footnotes added to the fifth edition, including a number of footnotes not composed by Swift himself but mischievously extrapolated by him from a critical commentary on the *Tale* which William Wotton had included in the third edition of his *Reflections upon Ancient and Modern Learning* (1705). Peter represents the pre-reformation church which drifted from the spirit and letter of the New Testament (the father's will). Peter's ingenious interpretations and 'inventions' represent the additions to Christianity made by Roman Catholicism. Specifically, the whispering office is the confessional, the cure for worms is penance and absolution, the insurance office is the practice of offering indulgences – i.e., special remissions of punishment due to sin – and the universal pickle (or preservative) is holy water. The other brothers, Martin and Jack, come to represent the reformation church when they object to Peter's machinations and are eventually expelled from Peter's house. After this 'rupture' with Peter, but especially after perusing their copy of the will, they proceed to remove the fashionable trimmings from their coats. Jack very soon assumes the allegorical role of representing the Protestant dissenters when he tears his coat in the process of restoring it to its former simplicity, such is his zealous determination to distinguish himself from Peter. This leaves Martin to represent the more moderate or 'reasonable' Anglican tradition, steering a middle course between on the one hand the inventiveness of those who would depart from the spirit of the father's will and on the other hand the unconstrained zealotry of those who would attend fanatically and selectively to the letter of the will. Though Martin's moderate position is characterized less by what it is than by what it is not, it is clear that it represents elements of both reform and tradition. The fact that Martin removes trimmings from his coat suggests justifiable reform; but the fact that he refuses to damage his coat by tearing out all the close-worked embroidery suggests moderation and a reasonable acknowledgement and toleration of the traditions established, albeit erroneously, by Peter. The dissenting Jack not only tears his coat but falls prey to enthusiasm and fanaticism, eventually establishing a new sect, the Aeolists, who explain everything in terms of one principle, the principle of wind, and express themselves by emitting same, that is, by belching. Though the Aeolists are supposed to be a religious sect, they are described by the fictional narrator of the *Tale* (usually identified as a Grub Street hack) in terms more appropriate to a school or college of virtuosi. They have a theory of original causes, a theory of man, a theory of wind, a theory of belching, a theory of learning, a theory of inspiration, a theory of gods and devils. This overlapping of sectarian belief and scientific theorizing suggests that both have a similar origin, namely, the innovating and 'converting' imaginations of inspired or enthusiastic individuals who are forgetful of tradition and seek to 'strike all Things out of themselves, or at least, by Collision, from each other' (Swift 1958: 135).

The Aeolist section of the *Tale* is suggestively placed back to back with Sect. IX, the most important and most provocative of the digressions. In the preceding digressions Swift had returned to the theme of *The Battle of the Books*, namely, the ancient–modern debate. In Sect. V, for example, we find the narrator (who places himself among the 'modern authors') reflecting on the superiority of the moderns over the ancients. Wotton and Bentley are mentioned again, and Swift's satirical intent becomes apparent when he has the narrator praise

Wotton for his wit, his eloquence, and the great usefulness of his 'sublime Discoveries upon the Subject of *Flies* and *Spittle*' (128–9). The shallowness and modishness of the narrator's interest in knowledge is exposed when he bewails the fact that no famous modern has yet attempted 'an universal System, in a portable Volume, of all Things that are to be Known, or Believed, or Imagined, or Practised in Life' (125). His ignorance is exposed when he credits Homer with the invention of the compass, gun-powder, and the circulation of blood, but faults him for failing to give a complete account of the spleen and for the unsatisfactory nature of his dissertation on tea.

Sect. IX bears the title, '*A Digression concerning the Original, the Use and Improvement of* Madness *in a Commonwealth*'. What is most startling about the views expressed and for the most part ridiculed in the section is that they are not unlike views held in contemporary psychological and sociological thinking. The ridiculed modern narrator and theorist offers a mechanical, materialistic, 'environmental' explanation of the causes of madness, ultimately characterizing it as an untapped source of creativity and inspiration. Madness has all its negative connotations explained away, and is moreover described as a desirable state – hence the idea, suggested in the title of the section, that madness has its uses and can be pressed into service in society. The house of the mad, or Bedlam, is put on a par with a college or school in which a diversity of talent is being allowed to go to waste. Thus a mechanically causal account of madness concludes in a utilitarian policy of the most radical sort of rehabilitation. What makes the digression difficult to read for a modern reader is precisely the fact that the reader *is* modern, modern not only in a chronological sense but also in an ideological sense. That is, he or she is closer to the mindset of the implicitly ridiculed narrator than to the mindset of the author who is setting him up for ridicule. Yet the reader finds it hard to resist being drawn into the anti-modernist stance of the author, since the moral authority of the piece rests firmly with the author, Swift.

The digression is difficult to read for another reason. There is such a subtle interplay between the voice of the narrator, whose mindset is being exposed to ridicule, and the satirical intent of the author, whose judgements on religion and learning must ironically retain their moral force even as they issue from the mouth of the narrator, that the reader is not always sure when the narrator is speaking simply as a ridiculous modern and when he is giving unwitting voice to views held by Swift himself. Much of the digression turns on allowing the narrator to hoist himself by his own petard, ultimately revealing himself and other moderns to be mad by their own account. The narrator begins his digression by claiming that all those who have achieved greatness through conquest, through the advancement of new schemes in philosophy, or through the propagation of new religions have been singular individuals whose rational faculties were overturned as a result of diet, education, and temperament, 'together with the particular Influence of Air and Climate' (162). He takes it as axiomatic that there is something in the mind of every individual 'that easily kindles at the accidental Approach and Collision of certain Circumstances' (162), with the result that otherwise insignificant individuals may be the instigators of great events. The causes of great actions lie outside the individual understanding and reside in the phenomenon of vapours. The whole world is in a sense governed by vapours – mists, steam, exhalations, clouds, smoke – so it is no wonder that human understanding, seated in the brain, is under the influence of vapours ascending from the lower faculties, effectively and fruitfully 'watering' the brain's inventions. Instead of bewailing the influence of vapours we should (according to the *Tale*'s narrator) welcome it. No one in his right or normal state of mind would come up with such visions as the Epicurean theory of atoms or the Cartesian theory of the vortex. Such visions cannot be explained without recourse to the abnormal effects of the phenomenon of vapours. Indeed, given the modern definition of madness as a disturbance of the brain under the influence of certain vapours, madness may be regarded as 'the Parent of all those mighty Revolutions that have happened in *Empire*, in *Philosophy*, and in *Religion*' (171). There follows a passage in which Swift's own heartfelt views are articulated through the voice of the unsympathetic narrator:

> For, the Brain, in its natural Position and State of Serenity, disposeth its Owner to pass his Life in the common Forms without any Thought of subduing Multitudes to his own *Power*, his *Reasons* or his *Visions*; and the more he shapes his Understanding by the Pattern of Human Learning, the less he is inclined to form Parties after his particular Notions;

because that instructs him in his private Infirmities, as well as in the stubborn Ignorance of the People. But when a man's Fancy gets *astride* on his Reason, when Imagination is at Cuffs with the Senses, and common Understanding, as well as common Sense, is Kickt out of Doors; the first Proselyte he makes, is Himself, and when that is once compass'ed, the Difficulty is not so great in bringing over others.

(171)

The narrator will go on to praise madness and to recommend the proper recovery and rehabilitation of the inmates of Bedlam. He will, near the conclusion of his tale, suggest that invention (in the sense of imagination) should take priority over method and reason.

Clearly, what this crazy modern recommends Swift condemns. Swift's diagnosis of the modern malaise is that there is madness in all its methods, that there is unreason at the source of its pretended rationality, that there is derangement in all its attempts at system-building. The moderns share with the madman a penchant for abnormal self-isolation and extreme imaginary projections. The moral of the *Tale* is that extreme positions in philosophy and religion are, like madness, the products of imagination and private infirmity. Unlike the inventions of the madman, however, the theorizing and scheme-mongering of religious and philosophical extremists have a corrupting effect on society. First, the sheer diversity of theories and projects destroys the time-honoured traditions of common understanding and replaces them with individualistic and anarchic schemes. Secondly, the modern forms of explanation tend to be reductionist, mechanistic, and materialistic. They typically explain the higher in terms of the lower, and therefore systematically debase human beings, depriving them in principle of their souls and free will. (This process of theoretical debasement is best represented in the *Tale* when the narrator undertakes, after the fashion of Hobbes, to explain everything in terms of a physical mechanism, such as the phenomenon of vapours.) Thirdly, arbitrary and gratuitous speculation, whether in religion or in learning, originates in and promotes the vice identified by William Temple, namely, 'prideful self-sufficiency' (Paulson 1972: 92). The private reason of the individual thinker alone becomes the measure of what is true and certain. Descartes' philosophy perhaps best illustrates

156

this vice of intellectual sufficiency. It begins by setting aside the heritage of human wisdom, doubting everything that tradition and common sense have to offer, and basing everything ultimately on the bare methodic certainty of the most systematically egocentric, self-sufficing axiom in the history of modern philosophy, namely, *I think, therefore I am*. Despite the fact that Descartes systematically 'recovers' much that he had previously doubted, including his belief in God and in the existence of the material world, he has nonetheless given a kind of priority to his own existence, his own reason, and his own intuitions and powers of deduction. He has instigated the modern distrust of tradition and common understanding, and has in the process made an issue out of God's existence and the existence of the material world. Everything, except the existence of the thinking self, becomes in the Cartesian scheme of things a matter of argument and proof. Thus Cartesianism would be, for Swift, the very essence and exemplar of modern philosophical madness.

ABOLISHING CHRISTIANITY

Swift against the freethinkers

Where Descartes distrusts tradition and common sense, Swift distrusts the kind of argument on which Descartes and other moderns depend for their knowledge and for the validation of their beliefs. His distrust of scientific and philosophical theorizing is sometimes expressed in the form of mock-arguments, one of the most important of which is his *Argument against Abolishing Christianity in England* (1708), which may be read as a parody of rationalistic, especially deistic, 'defences' of Christianity. The proposer of the argument purports to defend Christianity as if were just another system of thought, albeit one which is now 'generally antiquated and exploded' (Swift 1957: 27). His apparently daring advocacy of the 'system of the Gospel' is conducted not in terms of faith but in terms of what may be prudently or usefully believed. He accepts that 'real' Christianity, 'such as used in primitive Times . . . to have an Influence on Men's Belief and Actions' (27), is indefensible. He therefore undertakes to defend only a nominal Christianity. Read ironically, the argument is directed for the most part against freethinkers. Without religion, the great free-thinking wits, who have a need to revile and ridicule the highest objects, would be at a loss for worthwhile targets and might turn their hostile attention to the government and the ministry. Society would be deprived of the benefit of wit itself if the freethinkers and other 'strong reasoners' did not continue to have religion as their main subject. Swift numbers John Toland among the strong reasoners who would be at a loss without the whipping-boy of religion. Who, he effectively asks through the proposer of the *Argument*, 'would ever have suspected *Asgil* for a Wit, or *Toland* for a Philosopher, if the inexhaustible Stock of Christianity had not been at hand to provide them with Materials?' (36). Later in the argument Toland is implicated in the proposer's attempt to link Roman Catholicism conspiratorially with nonconformism, suggesting that the papists are using the various shades of nonconformism for their own ends. The increase in sectarianism will lead to the collapse of the Christian religion, and this will leave the way open to unchristian forms of religion, including superstition and 'popery'. The Jesuits are already working among the Presbyterians, Anabaptists, Quakers, and other sects, and are even to be found associating with the freethinkers, 'among whom, *Toland*, the great Oracle of the *Anti-Christians*, is an *Irish* Priest, the Son of an Irish Priest' (37).

Behind Swift's ironical baiting of the faithless deistic reasoner lies his own conviction, vehemently intimated, that what must be defended is real Christianity, a Christianity of belief and action rather than a Christianity of theological arguments and proofs. His own preferred way of defending real Christianity is indirectly, through parody and satire, rather than through direct statement or argumentation, as if to suggest that the straightforward discursive methods are suspect, even when engaged in with the best of intentions. But Swift does sometimes give a more forthright, argumentative expression to his convictions. In his sermon *On the Testimony of Conscience*, for example, he reveals his thinking to be both theologically and politically conservative. Those who advocate liberty of conscience are found to be fanatics who are attempting to 'overthrow the Faith which the Laws have already established' (1948: 151). He is particularly opposed to the idea that conscience might function independently of religious belief, insisting that virtue cannot have a solid foundation except in a conscience directed by the principles of religion. A similar orthodoxy of thought is evident in his sermon *On the Trinity*, which constitutes his most explicit rebuttal of deistic reasoning. He accepts that the Trinity is a mystery, since we are asked to believe that in the divine nature there is both union and distinction, 'but what that Union, or what that Distinction is, all Mankind are equally ignorant, and must continue so, at least till the Day of Judgement, without some new Revelation' (161). It may seem strange that God would ask us to believe something we do not fully understand, or understand at all, but this is not to be wondered at, in Swift's view. He accepts the distinction between things contrary to reason and things above reason, and argues that the Trinity, like many other objects of faith, belongs to the latter category. That there are three distinct persons in the one God is above reason, but it is not contrary to either sense or reason. It is a mystery, but it is not something wholly senseless, incoherent, or unintelligible. All matters of faith must remain to some extent beyond our comprehension, since faith is not the same thing as understanding, nor does it depend on understanding. Faith is rather 'a Virtue by which any Thing commanded us by God to believe, appears evident and certain to us, although we do not see, nor can conceive it' (164). Like Peter Browne, he fully accepts that we see as in a glass darkly, that the experience of mystery is an inevitable consequence of the finite mind's attempting to grasp the divine or supernatural world. Like Berkeley, he maintains that the good of faith consists not in the effect it has upon the intellect, but 'in the Consequences it hath upon our Actions' (164). Not unlike Toland, but with an intention very different from Toland's, he underlines the limitations of human reason, even with regard to understanding the things of the visible or natural world. The commonest actions of nature – such as the growth of an animal, a plant, or the smallest seed – are ultimately a mystery to even the most knowledgeable among us. Some phenomena, such as the action of magnets on iron, could be considered contrary to reason by someone who is ignorant of the principle of magnetism. Swift advises his listeners not to lay too much weight on their own reason in matters of religion, certainly not to think something impossible or absurd just because they cannot form a concept of it. He then makes a comment which sheds some light on his view of reason and rationality: '*Reason* itself is true and just, but the *Reason* of every particular Man is weak and wavering, perpetually swayed and turned by his Interest, his Passions, and his Vices' (166). This observation could be interpreted as the theme of much of Swift's work, especially the satires. It will certainly come to our aid in dealing with some questions that have arisen around his satirical masterpiece, *Gulliver's Travels* (1726).

UNSENTIMENTAL JOURNEYS

Gulliver and the perversion of reason

In the first two books of *Gulliver's Travels*, which describe the voyages to Lilliput and Brobdingnag respectively, Gulliver is subjected to a kind of thought-experiment in which dramatic relativities of perception and value are played against each other. In the country of the Lilliputians, Gulliver finds himself a giant among diminutives. His gigantic stature gives him a perspective that is moral as well as physical, and so the pettiness of the Lilliputians, expressed in factionalism, intrigue, and civil conflict, becomes quickly apparent to him. He, on the other hand, finds himself capable of magnanimous gestures appropriate to his stature. For example, he prevents a major battle from taking place, yet refuses to destroy the enemies of the king of Lilliput. In Brobdingnag, however, the tables are turned on Gulliver. Here he finds himself in the reverse position, a diminutive among giants. The gestures of justice and beneficence that came easily to him in Lilliput are not an option here. He is belittled in every sense, and survives only through the condescension of the Brobdingnagians; he is exploited by them, sometimes indulged, but is never able to win their respect. One of the few lessons he learns is how difficult it is for a person 'to endeavour doing himself Honour among those who are out of all Degree of Equality or Comparison with him' (1995: 125). His own efforts to increase his standing with his prodigious hosts fail dismally, leaving him worse off than before. He tries in vain to attach himself to something larger and more awe-inspiring than himself by proudly relating to the king the history of England and describing its political system, but the king protests that Gulliver's historical narration is 'an Heap of Conspiracies, Rebellions, Murders, Massacres, Revolutions, Banishments' and concludes that the bulk of his countrymen seem to be 'the most pernicious Race of little odious Vermin that Nature ever suffered to crawl upon the Surface of the Earth' (132). When Gulliver, still trying to give himself an effective presence before the king, offers to teach the king's engineers how to make gun-powder and cannon, the better to destroy future enemies, the king is horrified, expressing amazement that 'so impotent and grovelling an Insect' could entertain such 'inhuman' ideas. There then follows Gulliver's ironically self-betraying reflections on the Brobdingnagian king. He faults the king for the narrowness of his concerns; for basing his system of government on common sense, reason, and justice; and for being of the opinion that 'whoever could make two Ears of Corn, or two Blades of Grass to grow upon a Spot of Ground where only one grew before; would deserve better of Mankind . . . than the whole Race of Politicians put together' (135). Gulliver, in his belittled and peevish mode, criticizes the Brobdingnagians for their pragmatism, for their determination to excel only in morality, history, poetry, and practical applications of mathematics, and for their refusal to interest themselves in abstract ideas.

The third book of the *Travels* delivers Gulliver into a world that is the cultural antithesis of Brobdingnag, a world given over to abstract ideas without application, to schemes of improvement which are not based on real needs, and to forms of enquiry which attempt to answer questions that have no origin in common experience. It is a world in which there is learning without understanding, knowledge without wisdom, rationality without reasonableness, and enquiry without responsibility. It is the world of the moderns, of a culture that reduces creation itself to the terms and the narrow schematic compass of some unbalanced individual's cranky hypothesis. It is the world of the flying island of Laputa controlled by people who are 'so wrapped in Cogitation' that they are accompanied by servants – 'flappers' – who shake a kind of rattle close to their ears in order to rouse them from their intense states of concentration. It is also the world of Balnibarbi, with its metropolis of Lagado in which is to be found the Academy of Projectors.

Swift's description of the Academy is interesting not just for what it reveals of his attitude to scientific enquiry and invention but also for what it reveals of his attitude to the uses (and misuses) of reason in general. What is significant about the projects and experiments underway at the Academy is that they have supposedly worthy or 'improving' ends. One academician – perhaps the most notorious inhabitant of Swift's fictive universe – has been working for years on a project for extracting sunbeams from cucumbers. His intention is to condense the sunbeams into phials from which they may be subsequently released during cold summers. Another has set himself the task of converting excrement back into its original foodstuffs; another is developing a new method for building a house from the roof down. Even the most speculative among them, 'the universal Artist', has spent thirty years employing his thoughts 'for the Improvement of human life' (173). His work-in-progress includes softening marble to make pillows and pincushions, seeding land with chaff, and breeding sheep without wool. Why are these schemes made to appear so absurdly impractical, despite the benefits they are supposed to bring? For one thing, they demonstrate the ignorant utopianism of the academicians, especially their contempt for natural processes and the laws of nature. Everyone who reads the account of the Academy *knows*, on the basis of common experience alone, that sunbeams cannot be extracted from cucumbers; everyone also *knows*, on the basis of common reason and a common understanding of the laws of nature, that a house cannot be built from the roof down. What the academicians lack is common sense and due respect for the stock of knowledge that human beings have derived not only from their own experience but from the accumulated wisdom of others as it is passed on through culture and tradition. But they also lack a properly comprehensive scientific understanding of nature. It should be noted that the academicians are not at all the same as the Laputans. Lord Monodi, Gulliver's host in Balnibarbi, explains that forty years previously a delegation of Balnibarbians had visited the flying island and had returned after no more than five months 'with a very little Smattering in Mathematics, but full of Volatile Spirits acquired in that Airy Region' (169). It was then that they proceeded to introduce new ways of doing things, putting the existing arts, sciences, languages, and mechanics on a new footing, soon establishing the Academy of Projectors as a means towards achieving all sorts of 'desirable' ends. Impatient, however, to arrive at worthy or improving results, they have neglected the laborious method of attaining knowledge in the arts and sciences. It is no wonder that one of the professors of speculative learning is engaged in designing a mechanical method – a kind of computer – which will enable the most ignorant person to write books in philosophy, poetry, politics, law, mathematics, and theology 'without the least Assistance from Genius or Study' (173). If the Laputans represent the absurdity of knowledge without needful application, the academicians of Lagado represent the absurdity of worthy experiments that are not based on a hard-earned and respectful understanding of nature. The impractical theorists and the ignorant experimenters are alike in their failure to provide realistic solutions to real problems. This failure is moreover an ethical failure as much as a failure of wisdom. When Gulliver refers to the Laputans as 'bad Reasoners', he is passing judgement on their characters rather than on their intellectual abilities. Instead of putting their rational faculties to the service of society, they are engaging in useless disputes among themselves. The academicians of Lagado may also be said to be bad reasoners in the same sense, because they too fail to see themselves as servants of the people, as seekers of realistic or practical solutions.

Though Swift is largely unsympathetic to the scientific modernism represented by Francis Bacon, it is worth noting a suggestive resonance between Bacon's conception of good science and Swift's critique of the goings-on in Laputa and Balnibarbi. In his *Novum organum* Bacon bemoaned the division that continued to exist between the rational and the experimental, between the men of reason and the men of experiment, and pleaded for a 'closer and purer league' between the two. He believed that the best philosophy does not rely exclusively either on the speculative powers of the mind or on mechanical experiments, but seeks instead to develop an inductive method in which observation and experiment place constructive constraints on the natural human tendencies towards speculation, superstition, and dogma. Like Swift, Bacon was dismissive of 'talkers and dreamers' who have emburdened mankind with promises, ranging from the prolongation of life and the retardation of age to 'divining things future, and bringing things distant near, and revealing things secret' (1858: IV, 85). In the course of his plea for a new method in natural philosophy, Bacon introduced an image that Swift would also use in *The Battle of the Books*, the image of the spider and the bee. Bacon writes:

The men of experiment are like the ant; they only collect and use: the reasoners resemble spiders, who make cobwebs out of their own substance. But the bee takes a middle course; it gathers its material from the flowers of the garden and of the field, but transforms and digests it by a power of its own. Not unlike this is the true business of philosophy; for it neither relies solely or chiefly on the powers of the mind, nor does it take the matter which it gathers from natural history and mechanical experiments and lay it up in the memory whole, as it finds it; but lays it up in the understanding altered and digested.

(IV, 93)

While Swift puts the spider-and-bee image to a different use, there is no reason to think that he would have rejected Bacon's analogy in this context. It is worth noting that Bacon is spared in the battle of the books – the arrow intended for him strikes down Descartes instead.

Swift's pragmatism about the pursuit of truth and knowledge is given its most startling expression in the scenarios that unfold in the fourth book of *Gulliver's Travels*. Gulliver's last voyage takes him to the strangest country of all, the land of the Houyhnhnms and Yahoos. Here our serial traveller is presented with the most radical departure from the norms that he has lived by, the most radical and ultimately maddening challenge to the ideas and assumptions inculcated in him by the human form of life. For Houyhnhnmland is governed not by human creatures, big or small, sane or crazy, but by non-humans, the speaking horses called Houyhnhnms. Among the creatures governed and indeed exploited by the horses are the Yahoos, an ugly, intractable, and contrary species of animal that happens to bear a close resemblance to human beings, albeit human beings at their worst. Such is the stupidity and depravity of the human-seeming Yahoos that the horses look upon Gulliver as a prodigy because he, an apparent Yahoo, exhibits signs of being a rational creature. The term 'rational creature' is used several times throughout the account of the sojourn in Houyhnhnmland, suggesting that the nature of rationality itself is a theme of the fourth book. The horses are represented as models of rationality, but their rationality is not the mathematical or 'Cartesian' rationality of the Laputans, nor is it the fanciful or experimental rationality of the academicians of Lagado. It is rather an ethical rationality, a form of reasonableness expressing itself in civilized behaviour, practical problem-solving, the avoidance of disputes, and a due tempering of passion and imagination. The horses are 'philosophical' but in the sense of being ethical, truthful, and reasonable, and not at all in the sense of being given to speculation or abstraction. Their goal is to cultivate reason and be governed by it, but they laugh at Gulliver's account of the systems of natural philosophy in his own country. As far as they are concerned, reason is operative only where its conclusions strike with immediate conviction, 'as it must needs do where it is not mingled, obscured, or discoloured by Passion and Interest' (1995: 242). The exercise of reason cannot consist in the proliferation of opinions, controversies, wranglings, or disputes. Such activities represent the failure or absence of reason and not its proper exercise.

The ethical basis of Houyhnhnmian reason becomes most apparent when Gulliver gives his account of the causes and methods of war at home. At first the master horse, alarmed and disturbed by this account, expresses the fear that the corruption of reason may be worse than brutality (such as the brutality of the Yahoos). But no sooner has he entertained this possibility than he seems to discount it, preferring to think that the creatures described by Gulliver were not possessed of reason at all but of some quality designed to increase their natural vices (226–7). The suggestion here is that the mental faculty in the service of vice is not reason, properly speaking, but some other unspecified faculty quite distinct from it. Gulliver's fellow countrymen are not accepted as rational creatures but as creatures pretending to reason. Pretending, of course, is alien to the rational horses. Such is their lack of imagination or capacity for speculation that they cannot accept that there is a land beyond the sea, or that there can be such a thing as a ship, since no Houyhnhnm could make such a vessel and no Yahoo could manage it. Language is used only to communicate or convey information, never to mislead or misinform. Such indeed is the intimate relationship between language and information that the horses do not have a concept of untruth, of 'the thing which is not'. Inability to lie or deceive is not their only virtue. Such is their natural disposition towards all virtues that they have difficulty in understanding Gulliver's account of life in his own country since so many of the events and institutions he describes turn on deceitful or vicious practices of which they have no conception.

Gulliver himself, in his gullibility and incorrigibility, is the butt of the balefully pessimistic concluding section of Book IV. Even the fact that he is finally impressed by the rational horses does not stand in his favour but rather serves to ring a further change on his foolishness. He believes that the virtues of the horses have enlarged his understanding, and begins to see the actions and passions of humankind in a very critical light. He learns to detest all falsehood and disguise. Truth appears so agreeable to him that he determines at last to sacrifice everything to it. But his recognition of virtue in the Houyhnhnms is not accompanied by a corresponding ability to practise such virtues in his own life. His determination to be virtuous fails to neutralize his capacity for self-delusion, and indeed leads him into a kind of madness on his return to England. When he arrives home he finds that he is no longer able to think like a human being since he has now, gullible creature that he is, begun to think like a Houyhnhnm. Of course this is laughably inappropriate in one who lacks the natural dispositions of a Houyhnhnm — in one who in fact possesses a nature that is more Yahoo-like than it is Houyhnhnm-like. The ultimate irony lies in Gulliver's intolerance of his own kind, including his immediate family — 'I began last week to permit my Wife to sit at Dinner with me, at the farthest End of a long Table' (265) — and in his absurdly proud dismissal of all those who have about them any tincture of the absurd vice of pride. The harder Gulliver tries to improve himself, the more obvious becomes his inability to rise above his imperfections. Even in his determination to practise himself in the ways of virtue, he gets it seriously wrong, failing in wisdom, modesty, and good sense.

What then is Swift's position on humanity, morality, and reason? From an early satirical sketch, *Meditations on a Broomstick*, to the concluding scenarios of *Gulliver's Travels*, Swift has remained consistently critical of perversity, excess, and individualism, of all actions that threaten social stability and harmony, of all thought that is not motivated by a desire to find useful solutions to real problems. Not only is Swift not a systematic thinker, he is in fact deeply suspicious of any form of systematic thought that is not subservient to practical purposes, and he is positively hostile to any form of thinking that merely flags itself as innovative. Edward Said has suggested that Swift is best seen as an intellectual who responded energetically to the issues of his place and time (1991: 72–89). But perhaps it is even too much to say that he is an intellectual, given his contempt for those moderns among his peers who were the forerunners of latter-day intellectuals. It is arguable that a disengaged intellectualism is precisely what he cannot tolerate, ostensibly because it is impractical, but really because it is individualistic and divisive, smacking always of free thought. The truth is that Swift is a profoundly anti-intellectual and reactionary thinker, and none the less brilliant for being so. He is so deeply conservative that he fears thought itself, reacting unreflectively, undialectically, and dogmatically to new ideas, generally having recourse to satirical genres that enable him to ridicule his opponents without waiting for an answer. It is our good fortune that he presents his satires so brilliantly that we cannot help but find him thought-provoking, more thought-provoking in fact than many of those forgotten thought-provokers whom he gleefully satirizes. His achievement is that he obliges the children of the enlightenment – that is to say, most of his readers – to realize how good and intelligent the reactionary position can be and how much the enlightened or modern thinker must remain indefinitely an 'answerer', must pay the price of his or her modernity by remaining to some extent the target of Swift's savage indignation. Swift has become, ironically and appropriately, the nagging conscience of all 'enlightened' moderns, especially those who would dare to consider themselves innovators and intellectuals.

6

AGAINST THE SELFISH PHILOSOPHERS

Francis Hutcheson, Edmund Burke, and James Usher

After the savage indignation of Jonathan Swift, the good-natured moral and political philosophy of Francis Hutcheson (1694–1746) presses itself to the mind like a healing balm. Hutcheson was born in the townland of Drumalig in Co. Down, the son of an Irish Presbyterian minister of Scottish parentage. He received his early education in a school held in a disused meeting house near Saintfield before going on to attend a dissenting academy in Killyleagh, also in Co. Down. His training at the Killyleagh academy seems to have been mainly in classics, scholastic philosophy, and theology. In 1710 he proceeded to the University of Glasgow, taking his MA degree there in 1712. The following year he enrolled in the theology department of the university, coming under the influence of the unorthodox professor of divinity, John Simpson. He completed his theology courses by 1717, and returned to Ireland in 1718 to his father's residence in Ballyrea in Co. Armagh. He entered the ministry of the local Presbyterian church a year later, licensed as a probationer by the general synod of Ulster, and apparently aligning himself with the liberal or 'New Light' tendency within the church. One of his earliest experiences of preaching was before his father's congregation in Ballyrea. The experience was not a happy one, principally because at least some members of his father's congregation were not yet ready for the exhortations of the 'New Light' philosophy. According to a story recounted by his biographer, he was judged in no uncertain terms by a forthright member of the congregation to be 'a silly loon' who had 'babbled' to them for an hour about a good and benevolent God, without a word about the old 'comfortable' doctrines of election, reprobation, original sin, and death (Scott 1900: 20–1).

In the early 1720s Hutcheson was invited to Dublin to set up and run a dissenting academy similar to the one he had himself attended in Killyleagh. This he agreed to do, eventually finding suitable premises at the intersection of Dominick Street (then being newly built) and Dorset Street (then called Drumcondra Lane). The first assistant to be employed by Hutcheson was Thomas Drennan, father of the poet and United Irishman William Drennan, whose letters and other writings would register the influence of Hutcheson. It was during this period in Dublin that Hutcheson encountered individuals who would have a lasting influence on the development of his life and thought. The most important of these was Robert Molesworth. An Irish peer, a wealthy merchant and diplomat, and a protégé of John Locke, Molesworth had gathered round himself a circle of young intellectuals with whom he discussed matters of literary and philosophical interest. Though he did not publish work in these areas he did show his mettle in his *Account of Denmark as it was in the year 1692*, a thorough and highly critical polemic in which he argued that it was a serious mistake to assume that 'the Popish religion is the only one, of all the Christian Sects, proper to introduce and establish Slavery in a Nation', suggesting that the other Christian religions, including Lutheranism, were perfectly capable of reneging on liberty and practising a doctrine of unlimited obedience (1694: 258–9). This work, inspired as it was by passionately held Whig and commonwealth principles, had brought Molesworth to the attention of Anthony Ashley Cooper, the third earl of Shaftesbury, an influential English thinker whose aesthetic and moral philosophy would form part of the ethos of the Molesworth circle and would soon inspire Hutcheson to write his own essays on aesthetics and morality. Within two years of meeting Molesworth Hutcheson had begun work on what would become his *Inquiry into the Original of our Ideas of Beauty and Virtue* (1725), and which would duly acknowledge Shaftesbury as a major influence on his thinking. During this productive period in Dublin Hutcheson would also publish his second substantial work, *An Essay on the Nature and Conduct of the Passions* (1728).

In 1729 Hutcheson accepted the offer of the professorship of moral philosophy at Glasgow University, and took up the post the following year. If his period in Dublin was his most productive from a creatively philosophical point of view, his period in Glasgow was to be his most influential from an administrative, educational, and political point of view. He played a key role in liberalizing the ethos of the university, generally acting in accordance with his 'New Light' principles, and thereby contributing substantially to the development of the Scottish enlightenment. As a teacher he was popular and inspiring. His most famous student was the economist Adam Smith, who was not only impressed by Hutcheson's teaching but was also proved receptive to his liberal, optimistic, and naturalistic approach to moral and political thought (Scott 1900: 232). As an administrator Hutcheson had a reputation for approachability and generosity, at least among students. Scott reports that he took a particular duty of care towards students coming over from Ireland, though he was also critical of their high-spirited behaviour, behaviour that would provoke fellow academic and philosopher Thomas Reid to refer to them as the 'stupid Irish teagues' (McBride 1993a: 89).

The contrast between Swift and Hutcheson, broadly hinted at already, is a very real and significant one. Where Swift was quick to see the potential for folly in most forms of human thought and beha-viour, especially in the new-fangled attempts by secular thinkers to improve by all means the human condition, Hutcheson is quick to see the potential for virtue in all human endeavour. Hutcheson indeed represents one aspect of the very style of secular thought that was firmly rejected by Swift, namely, the tendency to think that human beings are essentially good-natured rather than essentially pre-disposed to error and sin. In giving a central role to the concept of pleasure in his aesthetic and moral philosophy, he distances himself from the Platonic and ascetic traditions, and looks forward instead to the humanistic utilitarianism of Bentham and Mill. More importantly, in allowing for the possibility that human beings are good-natured, other things being equal, he distances himself from the Augustinian tradition within religious and theological thought, including Protes-tant thought. Where the Augustinian tradition emphasized the dependence of human virtue on divine grace, the modern humanistic tradition of Hutcheson and his mentor Shaftesbury considers human beings to be morally sufficient – capable, that is, of virtuous thought and action without the need of regular supernatural infusions of grace. In effect, Hutcheson will pass as severe a judgement on Augustinians like Swift as the Augustinians, especially Swift, might have passed on him.

HUTCHESON AND THE STRATAGEMS OF SELF-LOVE

One of Hutcheson's most substantial contributions to the history of thought is his detailed argument for the existence of a variety of 'internal' senses. These internal senses are very important to Hutcheson and are going to be used to rebut positions that vex him. They are used in particular to combat the unflattering psychologies and the con-comitantly unflattering moralities of Thomas Hobbes and Bernard Mandeville. Mandeville and his mentor Hobbes had argued that human beings are motivated in all their actions by nothing more noble than self-love. Not only the vices but also the virtues are said to have their origin in a natural and innate desire to protect or advance one's own existence. Even the social, other-directed virtues such as generosity and tolerance are motivated by self-love and self-interest. In the first part of his *Leviathan*, in his determination to give a scientific account of human behaviour, Hobbes pictures human beings as pri-marily natural beings who are as much under the influence of natural laws – or laws of motion – as are all other objects in nature. He characterizes the springs of human action as the various passions and appetites, and defines 'good' in terms of the realization of individual desire: 'For these words of Good, Evil, and Contemptible, are ever used with relation to the person that useth them: There being nothing simple and absolutely so; nor any common Rule of Good and Evil, to be taken from the nature of the objects themselves, but from the nature of the Person' (1651: 25).

Hobbes rejects the notion of an ultimate or 'greatest good' for human beings, insisting instead that there is in human nature a perpetual and restless desire 'of Power after power', a desire that ceases only in death (47). Even the state of apparent ease or tranquillity, when human beings are not ostensibly under threat from their fellows or neighbours, does not in itself bring happiness. Unlike the non-rational animals, who feel least threatened when they are most at ease, 'Man is . . . most troublesome when he is most at ease: for then it is that he loves to shew his Wisdome, and controule the Actions of them that governe the Common-wealth' (88). Yet Hobbes at least acknowledges – and famously so – that human beings are capable of making rational, if self-interested, choices. A commonwealth of individuals united under an originally agreed sovereign ruler or assembly is the most rational and the wisest option available to a competitive, desiring, and restless animal such as man is. The ideas of covenant and commonwealth provide him with a criterion for discriminating between actions that benefit the whole and those that do not. Isolated in the pre-societal state of nature the individual knows only competition and war, but united with others under an all-powerful ruler the same individual makes a contribution to the 'leviathan' that is organized civil society. Actions that advance the progress of this leviathan are good; those which undermine it are vicious. Indeed, Hobbes speaks so reverently of civil society that he describes it as 'that *Mortall God*, to which wee owe under the *Immortall God*, our peace and defence' (88).

Mandeville, though taking his basic philosophical cues from Hobbes, is rather less sanguine about humanity and a good deal less reverent about society than his mentor. His account of the origins of government, civic life, and morality is more cynical than anything in Hobbes. It is not by force of reason and rational self-interest that human beings have left the state of nature and subjected themselves to the curb of sovereign government. Rather, the initiative towards society comes from those who see themselves as law-givers and moralists, and who resort to devious means to achieve their apparently worthy ends. The chief ploy of these self-appointed civilizers of mankind is flattery – flattery directed at the most fundamental human passion of pride. Morality itself is formed on this unpromising base: 'Moral virtues are the Political Offspring which Flattery begot upon Pride' (Mandeville 1970: 88). The basic distinction between virtue and vice has not originated in some innate human desire for goodness and self-control, but was cynically fabricated and promulgated by the law-makers and civilizers, the better to exploit the innate desire of each human being for prideful superiority over others. The civilizers divided the human species into two classes, one of which is spoken of with approval, while the other is presented in terms of disgust and rejection. One class is supposed to consist of abject, low-minded, self-seeking people who care for nothing except the sensual pleasures, differing from animals only in their outward appearances; the other is supposed to consist of lofty, high-minded persons, free from selfishness, capable of heroic self-control, and generally given to serving the public interest. By thus dividing the species into two opposing moral classes – the essentially praiseworthy and the essentially contemptible – the original civilizers were able to introduce and exploit the distinction between virtue and vice. The virtuous are those who merit praise in terms of self-control and public service; the vicious are those who earn condemnation on account of their self-seeking and their sensuality. Because human beings are so anxious to be flattered above all else, they have warmed throughout their natural history to this new discriminatory vocabulary of praise and dispraise, of virtue and vice. They seek to make themselves virtuous, despite the fact that it goes against the grain of their sensual natures; and they purport to disdain vice at all costs, though that is often where their real interests lie, individually and collectively. The paradox of morality is that its origin lies in nothing more praiseworthy than pride. In one of his cruellest strokes, Mandeville maintains that the first moralists 'drew Men like Angels, in hopes that the Pride at least of some will put 'em copying after the beautiful Originals which they are represented to be' (88). Yet the harder that people strive to earn praise by being as good as angels the more they are victims of what Mandeville calls 'the secret Stratagems of Self-love' (240).

Mandeville blurs the distinction between virtue and vice in another way, and at the same time draws attention to another apparent paradox about morality. Despite the success of the first moralists in creating an ethos of public service, so necessary to the creation of a civil society, it remains the case that private vices – which are not eliminable anyway – continue to play an essential role in the evolution of a prosperous society. Private vices, directly and indirectly, produce public benefits. Ambition and vanity, for example, lead people to want bigger and better houses, thus creating work for builders and the related crafts; dishonesty creates the need for better security devices and systems, and for the construction of courts and prisons, thus creating work for other kinds of workers, including lawyers, gaolers, and bailiffs; snobbery creates the need for all kinds of luxury items, so essential to trade and commerce; self-indulgence in general leads to ailments for which a plethora of professional therapists are required. Private vices are, in short, the engine of social and commercial progress.

One of the targets of Mandeville's moral cynicism had been Shaftesbury, who had made a case in his *Characteristicks of Men, Manners, Opinions, Times* (1711) for the inherent goodness of human nature. In the 1723 edition of his *Fable of the Bees*, Mandeville had attacked Shaftesbury's view that human beings are 'made for society' and therefore have a natural disposition towards the civic virtues. He had pointed to relativities in both aesthetic and moral perception to show that there is no such thing as objective goodness – or 'Intrinsick Worth' – in either the natural or the social world. He queried both the claim that human beings enjoy a natural love of company and the corollary claim that this confirms humankind's social and benevolent nature. In Mandeville's view, the love of company is not at all universal and is not necessarily at its strongest in the best people. He suggested that the worst sort of people are often the most eager to find company, while the best often prefer solitude or the company of a well-chosen few. Even if it is accepted that the love of company is naturally present to some degree in the human species, it does not follow that it arises from a benevolent or civic impulse. Does not man love company, Mandeville asks, as he does everything else, 'for his own sake?' The friendly qualities that we see in social gatherings and in other forms of organization are motivated by the desire of individuals to protect, promote, or amuse themselves. They arise, in short, from the impulse towards self-preservation rather than from any innate sociability or good-naturedness. Each individual needs others, whether he likes it or not, to secure his many goals and satisfy his many wants. Whether in the wild state of nature or in the most civilized form of society, the impulse towards self-preservation remains constant, albeit expressing itself in diverse ways. In his most telling passage, Mandeville writes:

> [B]e we Savages or Politicians it is impossible that Man, mere fallen Man should act with any other View but to please himself whilst he has the use of his Organs, and the greatest

Extravagancy either of Love or Despair can have no other Centre. There is no difference between Will and Pleasure in one sense, and every Motion made in spight of them must be unnatural or convulsive.

(1970: 351)

So unnatural indeed is every move made against the self-interested impulses that civil society itself is inevitably based on hypocrisy and deceit. In civil society we pretend to care about people other than ourselves, or about matters beyond ourselves, but we only do so in order to satisfy our own wants and needs in the long run, or simply to win approval from others. Society does not exist as a result of humanity's social impulses (as Shaftesbury and the benevolists would claim). On the contrary, it arises willy-nilly out of the interaction of self-interested individuals using each other variously to achieve their particular ends. In the second half of his critique of Shaftesbury Mandeville reiterates his claim that commercial society in particular flourishes not because of the widespread practice of the self-denying virtues but, on the contrary, because of the continued and hypocritical indulgence of the self-serving vices.

THE PLEASURES OF MORALITY

It is this kind of thinking that Hutcheson sets out to rebut in his first important work, the *Inquiry into the Original of Beauty and Virtue*. Moreover, his rebuttal is stated in the language of sense and emotion rather than in the language of reason. The very faculties that were frowned upon in the rationalist and idealist traditions of the Platonists and Neoplatonists are now to be regarded as the foundation of an uncynical and optimistic account of morality. The fundamental fact of pleasure, also frowned upon in the Platonic traditions, is to be made central to this new account. In the preface to the *Inquiry* Hutcheson declares that there is 'scarcely any Object which our Mind are employ'd about, which is not thus constituted the necessary Occasion of some Pleasure or Pain' (1738: xiv). The object in question can be an object of external sense – something with physical colour, shape, movement, and so on – which registers on our physical senses of sight, hearing, and

175

so on; or, more pertinently, it can be an object of internal sense – some quality of excellence or beauty – which registers on one of our subtler, sublimer powers of perception. By internal sense Hutcheson means an ability of the human mind to discern certain properties and relationships of things which are not reducible to their physical properties or relationships. The internal senses are distinguished from the external senses in their ability to discern and react to complex forms, arrangements, or patterns, yet they are like the external senses in being primarily passive, and therefore not subject to the vagaries of individual will or social custom. The external senses passively discern and react to simple physical qualities, such as a colour, shape, sound, smell, or texture, while the internal senses passively discern and react to complex patterns of these same qualities. It is important to Hutcheson that he should be able to stress the passivity of the internal senses, since it enables him to argue that our perception of form is not a matter of calculation or choice but consists in the triggering of natural, necessary, and God-given capacities. The sense of beauty – the topic of the first part of Hutcheson's *Inquiry* – is just such an internal sense, passive in its response to certain organized features of the world, registering pleasure when those features come together in a beautiful, harmonious, or orderly way, and registering displeasure or pain if the arrangements in question are ugly, discordant, or disorderly. The pleasure that is felt is felt passively and inevitably, and is not in itself a selfish or 'interested' pleasure.

This is an important point for Hutcheson, since it is in terms of passivity and pleasure that he sets about rebutting Hobbes and Mandeville. It may look at first sight as if he is dangerously close to offering hostages to fortune, but his tactic is in fact as clever as it is subtle. The pleasure that we experience on the perception of beauty means that we have senses fitted for perceiving beauty – and the fact that this perception of beauty is immediate means that the pleasure involved 'is distinct from that Joy which arises upon Prospect of Advantage' (8). There is neither space nor time, as it were, for an egotistical act of will to enter into the relationship between perceiver and object, such is the immediacy of the response to the presence or appearance of beauty. Just as something will appear red or blue whether it is in our interest or not, so something will appear beautiful or ugly whether it is in our interest or not. Our motives and interests can cause us to seek out or to take possession of beautiful things – jewels, paintings, gardens – but while this desire presupposes the sense of beauty it is not at all the same as that sense of beauty. The sense of beauty is therefore disinterested. That is to say, the pleasure in perceiving beauty is not a pleasure to the ego or the will but is rather the direct affecting of an internal sense which is naturally disposed to discern and enjoy certain complex forms. The pleasure to be had from possessing a beautiful object, such as a painting, is of course a pleasure of the ego or will, a pleasure deriving from the successful outcome of intentional efforts and actions, but the pleasure enjoyed by the sense of beauty itself is automatic, occurring independently of ego, will, or reason. One can choose not to acquire beautiful paintings, but one cannot avoid perceiving the beauty of the painting in the first place. It is not paradoxical to say here that one perceives the beauty of an object whether one wants to or not.

Hutcheson has no difficulty in identifying other internal senses, each with its own appropriate 'object'. The most important of these is the moral sense, which is discussed in the second part of his *Inquiry*. Perhaps more controversially than in the case of aesthetic sense or the sense of beauty, a reference to pleasure is also made part of the definition of the moral sense. Immediately and passively, without calculation of advantage or interest, human beings are supposed to be capable of deriving pleasure from the perception of the morally praiseworthy qualities in people's actions or characters – and, conversely, capable of experiencing pain and displeasure on the perception of the vicious qualities. Our approval or disapproval of these qualities is simply elicited from us, and we find ourselves pleased by what merits approval, displeased by what does not. As in the case of the aesthetic sense, the moral sense is disinterested in its responses to the virtuous and vicious qualities. The disinterestedness of the moral sense is particularly important to Hutcheson, since it seems to provide him with the premises of his case against Hobbes and Mandeville. If the moral sense can be shown to be disinterested in its reactions, then there is no longer a basis for claiming that all action is motivated by self-love alone. In particular, altruistic actions will turn out to have an altruistic origin, performed for no other reason than the benevolent impulse of the agent.

Hutcheson's argument turns on both a conceptual point and a point of observation. First, no action can be considered benevolent unless it is disinterested, and no person can be considered benevolent whose actions are motivated by self-interest. We never call that person benevolent who is useful to others 'but at the same time only intends his own Interest' (88). An action is benevolent only in the measure that it is performed out of a desire to help another, without benefit or advantage to oneself. Secondly, we can learn much by observing our own response to the benevolent actions of others. The more benevolent an action or person is, the more we are pleased by that action or person. The experience of pleasure is the key to the true nature of benevolence, since the pleasure is diminished if we discover that an ulterior motive was present in an action that otherwise had the appearance of being disinterested. This may seem paradoxical, but only if we assume that pleasure is always suspect because always selfish. For Hutcheson, pleasure is not necessarily suspect or immorally selfish. On the contrary, the best sort of pleasure is elicited by the best sorts of things, namely, things that are aesthetically or morally beautiful. The point of his argument in favour of an aesthetic sense — the capacity to find pleasure in beautiful forms — was to show that we can take pleasure in things that are good because they are beautiful. The point of his argument in favour of a moral sense is to show that we can take pleasure in actions and qualities that are good just because they are so benevolent, so disinterested, so far from having an egoistic motivation. If pleasure is the litmus test for our judgement of aesthetic beauty, it is also the litmus test for our judgement of moral goodness. In a way, Hutcheson finds more faculties and sources of pleasure than Hobbes or Mandeville. Whereas the latter cannot dissociate pleasure from self-love, Hutcheson is able to make a connection between pleasure and the love of others. The pleasure is not the pleasure of flattered pride, as it is for Mandeville, but a simple, unanalysable pleasure that is immediately felt on perception of a benevolent act. To love others is not a duty imposed by God or the state; it is rather a pleasure in its own right, involving a particular faculty or sense.

Self-love, it should be noted, is not in any case regarded as vicious in Hutcheson's scheme of things. Self-love is not only natural and therefore essential to a well-adjusted life but may also be necessary to the good of the whole. Neglect of our own good may be morally evil, 'and argue a Want of Benevolence towards the Whole' (113). Many actions performed out of self-love are perfectly acceptable if they are not detrimental to others. Hutcheson concludes that preservation of the human community requires everyone to be 'innocently solicitous' about himself. However, where there arises a conflict between one's own interests and the innocent interests of others, then the interests of others may take priority, especially if a significant number of others should benefit from one's disinterested action. In his most general statement of his general criterion of benevolence, Hutcheson gives a central place to pleasure, formulating what is in effect the principle of utility that would be developed later by Bentham and Mill. That action is best, according to Hutcheson's version of this criterion, 'which procures the greatest Happiness for the greatest Numbers; and that worst, which, in like Manner, occasions Misery' (117). This criterion, as Hutcheson uses it, is not to be understood as a kind of impersonal imperative or rational principle to be dutifully applied, but rather as an instructive articulation of what has already been perceived by the moral sense. The person who acts so as to procure the pleasure of the greatest number of others will not do so out of a painful, self-denying sense of duty but will necessarily experience pleasure himself – pleasure at perceiving the pleasure accruing to others. The constitution of our moral sense is such that 'the moral Beauty of Actions, or Dispositions, increases according to the Number of Persons to whom the good Effects of them extend' (120).

In his *Essay on the Nature and Conduct of the Passions* (3rd edn, 1742) Hutcheson elaborates on his case against egoism, further loosening the links between self-love and moral action, and giving further emphasis to the principle of altruistic benevolence. He introduces two new 'senses', the public sense and the sense of honour, though they are not substantively different from the moral sense of the *Inquiry*. His definition of the public sense – 'our determination to be pleased with the *Happiness* of others, and to be uneasy at their *Misery*' – is no more than the moral sense redefined with a more explicitly altruistic bias. The sense of honour implies a recognition of the moral sense of others, and consists in a feeling of pleasure at having our benevolent actions duly acknowledged and commended by others. The sense of honour also has a corollary or counter-sense, the sense of shame, which is the unpleasant sensation caused by our realization that the moral sense of others has been offended by our behaviour.

In the first section of the *Essay* Hutcheson concerns himself at some length with the nature of the public sense. He is still bothered by the resourcefulness of the egoist who can continue to argue that all desires, including apparently altruistic or good-natured ones, originate in self-love. The egoist can claim, for example, that we only take pleasure in the happiness of others if that happiness has something in it for ourselves. We may be pleased that someone has come into a large fortune, but only because we ourselves may benefit directly or indirectly. The happiness of others in these circumstances is pleasing to us only because it is a means to our own happiness. Hutcheson's response to this sort of egoistical objection tends to rely on reflective introspections of what we feel (or do not feel) on those occasions when our public sense is aroused. Do we not find, he asks, that we often desire the happiness of others 'without any such selfish Intention?' (1742: 22). If we lacked a public sense, would we not be indifferent, at the time of our own mortal exit from the world, to the future happiness of others? But we are not so indifferent. It is certain that any good person 'would as strongly desire at his Exit the *Happiness of others*, as in any part of his Life' (23). The heroism of those who voluntarily risk their own lives for the sake of friends and country also bears witness to the real existence of a public sense, showing that we may not define this sense as merely a means to private pleasure. The kind of keen public sense that finds exceptional expression in self-endangering heroism is present to some degree in everyone, and is indeed connected with appropriate passions. If we have selfish passions for our own individual preservation, we also have public-spirited passions which lead us into 'vigorous and laborious' efforts on behalf of offspring, friends, communities, and countries. Indeed it is through the public-spirited passions and affections that each individual is made subservient to the good of the whole, such that all human beings are 'insensibly linked together, and make one great System, by an invisible Union' (180). He who voluntarily continues to contribute to this invisible union of all humankind, who takes pleasure in acting on behalf of the species as a whole, makes himself happy, while he who breaks the bonds of nature makes himself unhappy.

VICE AND CRUELTY EXPLAINED

Hutcheson's universalism presents him with two major problems: the problem of diversity and the problem of the prevalence of vice. If human beings universally and uniformly possess a variety of internal senses, including the aesthetic, moral, and public senses, why are there such great differences of judgement among people on all questions of value, moral as well as aesthetic? And if human beings are universally and uniformly capable of benevolent action, why is there so much hatred, conflict, and vice in the world? If the moral feelings are embedded in the structure of human nature, as Daniel Carey phrases it (1997a: 278), and if the moral law is inscribed in the very instincts, then how are we to account for the presence in the world of so much vice and cruelty? Hutcheson answers the first question – the question of the diversity of response and judgement – in terms of a theory of the association of ideas. This is the theory, derived from Locke, that explains false conceptions, bad intellectual habits, and irrational fears in terms of the accidental or circumstantial conjunctions of otherwise unrelated experiences and ideas. Such associations of ideas are, Hutcheson suggests, 'the one great Cause in the apparent Diversity of Fancys in the Sense of Beauty, as well as in the external Senses' (1738: 53). Some people develop an aversion to certain objects of beauty, while others develop a liking for objects that are ostensibly devoid of beauty, not because they have a perverted sense of beauty but because certain accidental associations have arisen in their experience of the objects in question. The beauty of trees, for example, consists among other things in the shady privacy or secludedness which they afford, making them an ideal retreat for those who love solitude, including those of a religious, pensive, or melancholic inclination. The 'cunning heathen priests' were among those who exploited such obscure places for their rituals and the fictitious 'appearances' of their deities. This association of trees (at least in the form of groves and woods) with shadows, obscurity, and secret rituals may cause them to acquire 'divine' or frightening associations, despite the fact that the trees themselves are innocent of such properties and associations. Such accidental or circumstantial associations may, however, cause the original beauty of the trees to be occluded. Similar sorts of association may affect the perception of other objects, depending on accidental circumstances, both natural and historical. A person raised in a wild, inhospitable landscape may come to see it as beautiful if the days of his childhood and youth were happy ones; while the same person raised unhappily in an ostensibly beautiful place may see it as repellent because of his formative experiences. But even while he acknowledges the power of such fortunate or unfortunate associations of ideas, Hutcheson still insists on the uniformity or universality of our internal sense of beauty. Despite the fact that people are subject to 'diversities of fancies', the idea of beauty remains constant. In some cases the beauty is, as it were, hidden from view by some overbearing association; but beauty is still present, though it remains unperceived. In those cases where delight is taken in an unbeautiful object, it should be pointed out that the delight is indeed a result of accidental associations and is not caused by beauty at all, though the delight may be expressed in terms of beauty. Such fanciful delights or approbations are 'remote from the Ideas of Beauty, being plainly different Ideas' (54).

The second problem – the problem of the prevalence of vice – seems more difficult to answer, and indeed Hutcheson's attempt to answer it takes him right into the vulnerable core of his benevolism. If human beings are so naturally well-disposed towards each other, if benevolence is natural to human beings, why is there so much moral evil in human society, especially evil in the form of what would now be called 'crimes against the person'? What evidence is there to support the belief in the existence of a universal disposition towards benevolence, a determination to be pleased with the happiness of others? Is there not evidence to the contrary, suggesting a capacity (in some people at least) towards malice and cruelty? The reason that this is such a hard question for Hutcheson is that his benevolism is really quite extreme. He does not accept that human beings are capable of malevolence or disinterested malice – capable, that is, of evil for its own pleasurable sake. If people take pleasure in the pain or misery of others, it is only out of self-love or self-interest, rather than out of true malice. If we are pleased to see someone made to suffer, it is because we believe that he has done evil and now deserves to have some evil done to him. Our pleasure in such a case is not in itself malicious but based on a desire for just retribution. We do not normally wish (Hutcheson thinks) to see evil-doers punished beyond all necessity of self-defence or public interest. Anger felt in the aftermath of an injury may sometimes cause us to feel a malicious hatred towards the perpetrator, 'but as soon as we reflect upon human Nature, and form just Conceptions, this unnatural Passion is allay'd' (97). Those who continue to indulge their vengeful passions are likely to be in the grip of a false opinion of human nature, believing human beings to be worse than they are. An exaggerated sense of honour may also lead to cruel and seemingly malicious acts of revenge, but the fact that cruel avengers can usually be said to have reasons or motives – no matter how misguided – for their acts of cruelty confirms Hutcheson in his belief that the pleasure derived from the suffering of others is not purely or disinterestedly malevolent. He believes that motivated or 'interested' malice is significantly less vicious than disinterested malice – that cruelty is somehow more acceptable if it is motivated by some 'furious pain' or some distorted sense of justice, honour, or self-interest. He concludes that human beings, even at their worst, are not capable of the kind of demonic, cold-blooded wickedness that might lead them to desire and enjoy the misery of others.

Hutcheson's account of the origins of ordinary vices follows a similar logic. Ordinary vices spring from a 'mistaken Self-Love, made so violent as to overcome Benevolence' (112). Self-love, it must be remembered, is not inherently immoral in Hutcheson's philosophy. To act out of self-love or self-interest is not necessarily to act immorally. It is only when people act out of self-love to the detriment of the happiness of others that their actions become viciously or immorally selfish. However, because the source of such selfishness is not essentially vicious, Hutcheson infers that ordinary vices stem not from an evil disposition *per se* but from an excess of self-love. The origins of ordinary vice, like the origins of more serious forms of cruelty, are relatively benign. If we examine the springs of human action, Hutcheson contends, 'we shall seldom find their Motives worse than *Self-Love*' (1742: 109). He suggests that it is in fact wrong to have too negative or cynical a view of human nature. By imagining others to be worse than they may be, we will induce in ourselves a temper full of suspicion, hatred, anger, and contempt (109). He recommends that we continually represent to ourselves the most favourable conceptions of others, thereby forcing our minds 'to examine the *real Springs* of the resented Actions' (191). For Hutcheson, then, the sense of evil, or of the prevalence of evil, has as much to do with a too-negative conception of human nature as it has to do with misguided self-love or a distorted sense of grievance. There is a strong suggestion that evil is to some extent in the eye of the beholder, and that it is incumbent on the morally conscientious person to think more highly — that is to say, more benevolently — of human nature. This of course begs the question of just how natively benevolent human beings really are if they have to be constantly reminded and exhorted (by moralists such as Hutcheson) to be more benevolent in their attitudes and actions.

THE POLITICS OF HAPPINESS AND THE PLEASURES OF CIVIL UNION

Hutcheson's benevolism informs his political philosophy as much as it does his ethics. His posthumously published *System of Moral Philosophy* (1755) – which may be read as an attempt to bring together his thinking on moral, theological, political, and economic questions – is unified around his sanguine assumption that human beings are designed by nature (and ultimately by God) to achieve happiness for themselves by promoting happiness in general. While the first of the three books of the *System* attempts a detailed restatement and defence of his moral sense theory, the aim of the second book is 'to enquire more particularly into the proper means of promoting the happiness of mankind by our actions' (1755: 227). To the vocabulary of virtues, passions, and affections is now added the more 'systematic' vocabulary of rights, duties, laws, and liberty. Hutcheson makes a distinction between perfect and imperfect rights. Perfect rights are those without which society cannot subsist and without which the individual cannot be happy. They include the right to life, to integrity and soundness of body, to the acquisitions of honest labour, and to natural liberty, 'of which liberty of conscience is not only an essential but an inalienable branch' (257). The perfect rights are of such a nature that force may be used to implement them. The imperfect rights are not so enforceable, and depend more on the goodwill of citizens. These include the right of the poor to relief, and of friends and benefactors 'to friendly and grateful returns' (258). He also distinguishes between alienable and inalienable rights. His conception of an inalienable right stresses autonomy, liberty of conscience, and the right of private judgement: 'Thus no man can really change his sentiments, judgments, and inward affections, at the pleasure of another; nor can it tend to any good to make him profess what is contrary to his heart' (262). The state of nature is defined as a state of natural liberty, and it always grounds the laws and institutions of civil society. In other words, the laws of nature, natural right, and natural liberty cannot be cancelled out by those of the civil state. Rather, it is the main purpose of civil laws and their sanctions to restrain people more effectively 'by visible punishments' from the infringement of natural rights or the violation of natural laws. So natural is the sense of liberty, for example, that the loss of it is always deeply resented and can only be justified where the interests of society are seriously threatened. Anticipating Mill's rejection of paternalistic legislation, Hutcheson recommends against interfering with unwise or imprudent uses of liberty as long as such uses are not injurious to others.

The right of natural liberty is not to be understood in a purely private or self-interested sense. To assert anyone's right is to assert everyone's; it is to recognize that rights are natural precisely in the measure that they belong equally to all. No endowment of any kind, whether natural or acquired, can give any individual (or group of individuals) the right to assume power over others without their consent (301). Hutcheson explicitly rejects the Aristotelian doctrine that some human beings, because of their superior wisdom and intelligence, are naturally fitted to be masters, while others, because of their irrationality or 'low genius', are naturally fitted to be slaves. Apart from the fact that Aristotle's doctrine offends our natural sense of justice and humanity, there is no historical evidence in any case for the truth of such a claim. If providence had intended some people for government, then their difference from everyone else should be perfectly obvious – as markedly obvious as the difference between human beings and beasts. But there are no such obvious marks of distinction. Even if superior wisdom and understanding were more in evidence in the countenance or behaviour of prospective rulers, this would not in itself confer a right to govern, since the intellectual virtues may be involved with corrupt and selfish motives. Moral as well as intellectual virtues would have to be guaranteed, but this is not practicable, since the worst and most ambitious individuals can pretend to the most admirable moral virtues until such time as they achieve power. To base a right of governing others on a supposed superiority of abilities, without the consent of the governed, 'must raise eternal controversies which force alone can decide' (303).

The relationship between natural and civil liberties is formally stated in the third book of the *System*, in which Hutcheson considers the origins and features of civil society. Natural liberty consists in the right that each one has to act according to his own inclination within the limits of the law of nature, while civil liberty consists in the right of acting as one inclines 'within the bounds of the civil laws, as well as those of nature' (281). The civil laws are not designed to exclude liberty but 'are its natural and surest defence' (281). The point of entering into political or civil union is to ensure and secure such defence. Hutcheson's account of the origin of political and civil union is a version of the Lockean theory of social contract, according to which numbers of individuals choose to leave the state of nature and voluntarily unite under a ruling person or council for purposes of greater self-protection and greater promotion of justice and the general good. The most potentially subversive right that Hutcheson identifies in this context is the right of resistance. Though he approaches his enunciation of this right with an earnest warning against the dangers and evils of 'violent changes' and civil war, he nonetheless asserts that when no gentler way can be found to relieve a state from the misery of a perfidious governor or administration, it is incumbent on a people 'to make all efforts to change the plan' (270). Since all civil power is constituted for the benefit of the public good and not at all for the good of the ruler or administration, it follows that whenever the civil power acts against the interests of the public good, then the original contract is broken and the people or 'subjects' in question have a right to defend themselves – and indeed have a duty to take action – against their renegade rulers. It is never the right of rulers to deny their subjects the right of resistance, since the contract between themselves and the people is always a conditional one – conditional, that is, on the determination of the polity in question to promote the general good. Not even absolute hereditary rulers can justly force their subjects to take oaths against resistance.

That Hutcheson's political writing was popular in America during the second half of the eighteenth century comes as no surprise, given the direction of his thought on the nature of civil polity in general and on the right of resistance in particular. His *Short Introduction to Moral Philosophy* (1747) was regularly imported into America until an American edition was published in 1788 (Downie 1994: xlv). Significantly, most of the text of Chapter VII of the third book of the *System* was, as Caroline Robbins has noted, reprinted in the fiftieth number of *The Massachusetts Spy* on 13 February 1772 (1968: 190). In the concluding section of the subsequent chapter Hutcheson goes on to outline explicitly the circumstance in which colonies might have legitimate claims against the mother country. He suggests, for example, that if a colony reaches the point where it has sufficient numbers to enable it to meet the good ends of a political union in its own right, then it is not bound to continue in a state of subjection to the mother-country: 'Large numbers of men cannot be bound to sacrifice their own and their posterity's liberty and happiness, to the ambitious views of their mother-country, while it can enjoy all rational happiness without subjection to it' (1755: 309).

If Hutcheson had not written his *Inquiry*, *Essay on the Passions*, and *System of Moral Philosophy* the history of modern thought would be the bleaker for their absence. Taken together, these three texts provide a powerful antidote to the moral egoism of Hobbes, the moral cynicism of Mandeville, and the moral pessimism of Swift. Their continued relevance is not easy to determine. Given the terrible and chastening wisdom that is still dawning in the aftermath of our Western wars, it is hard to see how a benevolist like Hutcheson could maintain an unflagging optimism in the face of the genocidal campaigns and the resourcefully destructive wars of the twentieth century. He could no doubt still maintain his distinction between interested and disinterested evil, but it seems hard to accept that there is any significant difference in the end between an evil act that is motivated by monstrous self-love (such as the balefully exclusionary self-love of the anti-Semite), and a similarly evil act that is motiveless to the point of being simply demonic. For a prospective victim of genocidal savagery there seems little to choose between a cruel death at the hands of a passionately motivated racist and a cruel death at the hands of a demonically motiveless executioner. Moreover, to explain such cruelty in terms of misguided self-love and wrong associations of ideas seems seriously inadequate. It would seem that self-love, if it can be said to be at the root of such acts at all, loses all trace of benignity and leaves us when all is said and done with the bleaker visions of Hobbes and Mandeville. Yet, it is significant that those who wish to ensure that the terrible sins of the past will not be repeated in the present or in the future tend to think in terms of cultivating ever more tolerant social and political philosophies, with a view to having them hard-wired into new improved constitutions and legal systems. Such an optimistic programme of enlightenment would not make sense, argu-ably, unless its advocates believed in the general capacity of human beings to form new associations of ideas and subsequently practise greater benevolence. So, while reflection on recent human history tempts one towards the worst sort of Hobbesian cynicism or Swiftian pessimism, equally necessary reflection on future social structures and value systems tempts one all the way around again, more or less hopefully, towards something like the benevolism of Hutcheson.

REFLECTION AND REACTION
The life and thought of Edmund Burke

The highly charged conservative political thought of Edmund Burke goes powerfully against the grain of the kind of radical thinking found in the work of Francis Hutcheson. Edmund Burke was born in 1729, probably in Dublin but very possibly in Co. Cork. His biographer Conor Cruise O'Brien has raised a question mark over the previous consensus that Burke was born in Dublin, recounting a local tradition in the Blackwater Valley area of Co. Cork that Burke was in fact born at Shanballymore, in the house of his maternal uncle, James Nagle (1992: 14). The main reason that Burke might have recorded a Dublin birth in the matriculation register of Trinity College, Dublin, would have been connected with the conditions of the time, specifically with the need of a prospective Trinity student to distance himself from a local habita-tion and a name – Shanballymore – that had strong Catholic and 'native' connotations. Though Burke's father was a Protestant, his mother Mary Nagle remained a Catholic, despite the fact that she 'conformed' to the Church of Ireland shortly after her marriage. The confessional ambivalence of Burke's immediate family was reflected in his early education. At the age of six he was sent to the Catholic homeland of his mother's relatives, to live with his uncle, Patrick Nagle, in Ballyduff in the middle of the Blackwater Valley. Until the age of eleven he attended a hedge school – a kind of clandestine pay school located in an improvised classroom – where he probably received instruction in the basics of Catholic belief and perhaps learnt to speak Irish. At the age of twelve he was moved, as if to introduce a measure of balance into his education, to a Protestant school in Ballitore, Co. Kildare, where he received a good classical preparation for admission to Trinity College (O'Brien 1992: 24). He duly entered Trinity in 1744, becoming involved in the establishment of a debating club (from which Trinity's College Historical Society would later claim descent) and a periodical called *The Reformer* which ran to thirteen issues. He graduated with a BA in 1748.

Two years after graduation Burke went to London to study law but failed to be called to the bar. He returned to Ireland in 1761 as private secretary to William Gerard Hamilton, the newly appointed chief secretary for Ireland. This position gave Burke his first active role, albeit a small one, in the administration of government. He resigned his post with Hamilton after two years, and returned to England to become private secretary to the new prime minister, Lord Rockingham, leader of a cohort of Whigs whose views were respected by Burke. Burke himself was elected to the British parliament, as MP for Wendover, in 1765, and already attracted attention with his first speech. From this point Burke would be drawn ever deeper into politics. He would remain active in politics and public life – and also remain an energetic maker of speeches and a tireless author of essays and pamphlets – until his death in 1797. From the beginning, his involvement in politics was marked by principled stances rather than by tactical associations or opportunistic alliances. When the Rockingham administration fell after no more than a year in power, Burke followed its members into opposition – an opposition that lasted sixteen years – despite invitations to join subsequent administrations (O'Brien 1992: 61). He was prepared to defend unpopular causes, pleading conciliation in the case of the American colonies and, despite the delicacy of his position in a non-Catholic political environment, pleading the cause of the Catholics in Ireland. Even when elected MP for Bristol, a more prestigious constituency than Wendover, he pressed ahead with his principled agenda, helping to bring about the first relaxation of the penal code against Catholics, namely, the Catholic Relief Act of 1778. His support for ostensibly Irish and 'Catholic' causes, including his advocacy of free trade for Ireland, would lose him his Bristol seat in 1780. He subsequently became MP for Malton but resigned his seat when Lord Rockingham died in 1782. His principal contribution to public life after his resignation was his involvement in the impeachment and protracted trial of Warren Hastings, the governor-general of India. In 1790 he published the work for which he is now best known, his *Reflections on the Revolution in France*, which went into many editions and provoked many replies, including Tom Paine's *Rights of Man* and Mary Wollstonecraft's *Vindication of the Rights of Men*. The *Reflections* – which cost Burke his friendship with his former Whig associates – lies at the centre of a small cluster of works that may be said to contain 'Burke's thought'. This cluster includes *A Philosophical Enquiry into the Sublime and the Beautiful* (1757), *Thoughts on the Present Discontents* (1770), *Speech on Conciliation with the Colonies* (1775), *Appeal from the New to the Old Whigs* (1791), and *A Letter to a Noble Lord* (1796).

Although Burke's thought will turn out to be substantively at odds with that of Hutcheson, the basic interests and even assumptions of both thinkers overlap to a considerable degree. Both men wrote on aesthetics before turning to more social and political themes; both believed in the universality of taste and the 'objectivity' of aesthetic judgement; both believed in the primacy and reliability of the heart's affections, assigning a more or less secondary role to the calculations of reason; both stressed the importance of social institutions and civil union; both saw a direct link between virtue and civility; both rejected idealistic or utopian visions of the human future; and both registered, albeit critically and selectively, the influence of Locke's epistemology of the senses. More specifically, Hutcheson's work made an impression on the young Burke. One of Burke's earliest compositions is a poem, an address to Hutcheson, recently published for the first time by T.O. McLoughlin and James Boulton in the first volume of a new edition of Burke's writings and speeches. Composed shortly after

Hutcheson's death, the poem makes a somewhat oblique comment on the late philosopher's theory of the passions. Though the poem, entitled 'To Dr H—N', begins with a respectful address to the philosopher, it soon turns into a dramatic account of the relationship between Samson and Delilah. Samson is presented as such a victim of the powerful passion of love that a kind of shadow is implicitly cast over Hutcheson's optimistic notions of passion, including the passion of love.

THE TASTE OF FEAR

Burke's aesthetics of sublimity

Hutcheson's aesthetic treatise *An Inquiry into the Original of our Ideas of Beauty and Virtue* seems to have had a positive influence on Burke, possibly suggesting the title of his own *Philosophical Enquiry into the Sublime and the Beautiful*. In his introductory essay on taste, Burke accepts that there is a sense or faculty of taste, and goes on to defend a position that is close to Hutcheson's. He argues for an underlying uniformity or universality of the human senses, rejecting the sceptical suggestion that the senses might present different images or impressions of the world to different perceivers. He accepts that custom may bring about apparent deviations from the natural pleasures that belong to taste, but maintains that the power of distinguishing between a natural and an acquired taste remains intact. Though some people may acquire a taste for tobacco, garlic, or 'fermented spirits', perhaps by taking them in the first instance for medicinal purposes, they will nonetheless regard these as acquired tastes, associated with pleasurable side-effects rather than with original palatability. A person may come to prefer the taste of tobacco to that of sugar, or the flavour of vinegar to that of milk, 'but this makes no confusion in Tastes, whilst he is sensible that the tobacco and vinegar are not sweet, and whilst he knows that habit alone has reconciled his palate to these alien pleasures' (1997: 199). If we should discover someone who declares that tobacco is as sweet as sugar, or who says that he cannot distinguish milk from vinegar, we should conclude that this person's organs are in fact out of order. There is no more point in

191

discussing tastes with such a person than there is in reasoning about matters of proportions and quantities with someone who denies that the sum of parts is equal to the whole. Burke concludes that the groundwork of taste is common to all, 'and therefore there is a sufficient foundation for a conclusive reasoning on these matters' (206).

Burke's enquiry, like Hutcheson's, is based then on certain Lockean assumptions about the senses, and about the importance of pleasure and pain in the life of the individual and in the formation of society. All kinds of pleasure and pain are associated with either self-preservation or the preservation of community and society, and all the passions that the human sensibility is heir to are traceable to either the 'push' of self-preservation or the 'pull' of society. Burke's originality consists in his developing a concept of delight that is not reducible to either pleasure or pain, positively understood, and also in developing a related concept of the sublime that is not explained in terms of order, harmony, or beauty. The sublime and the beautiful are in fact contrary qualities giving rise to contrary sensations, and it will transpire that delight in the sublime, as understood by Burke, is originally closer to pain than to pleasure. The qualities of the beautiful include smallness, smoothness, gradual variation, and delicacy, including delicacy of colour and texture. The beautiful is essentially pleasurable and non-threatening, far removed from the threat of pain or death. It is otherwise with the sublime. Our sense of the sublime is aroused by rather unbeautiful, potentially threatening objects and qualities, and has its origins not in our capacity to feel positive pleasure but in our capacity to experience fear or horror. When a pain or threat is removed we experience a kind of delight that is different from a positive pleasure, and it is this sort of delight that is involved in our experience of the sublime. Something that is fearful and threatening or terrible is put at a distance from us, or is represented to us in a way that does not cause, or immediately threaten, actual pain. Things that are massive, dark, vast, obscure, overwhelming, or very high or very deep, or that suggest infinity, can be sublime. A thunderstorm is sublime, unless it is literally threatening; likewise the cries of wild animals, or the intensity of a certain kind of silence, or the striking of a great clock, or the effect of 'a light now appearing, now leaving us' (252). There must be an element of fear, or an approach to fear, but it cannot be real fear, since real fear will cause us to become too preoccupied with saving ourselves, thus eliminating or at least postponing the possibility of delight.

One of the most engaging sections of the *Enquiry* deals with the experience of obscurity in both nature and language. Anything of which we cannot form a clear idea – anything which is literally obscure to us – is potentially threatening, and therefore potentially awe-inspiring or sublime, hence the likely reason that the 'heathen temples' were kept dim or dark. But it is not just physically obscure or dark places that are potentially awe-inspiring. Pictures or texts that are not perfectly clear can be more affecting to the imagination than those that are clearly pictured or grasped. Most texts, just because they are verbal and not literal representations of the objects they describe, tend to present more obscure ideas to the imagination than do pictures. This may seem to put verbal representation at a dis-advantage, but only if a clear idea or impression is what is called for. It is one thing, says Burke, to make an idea clear, 'and another to make it *affecting* to the imagination' (232). If one wants to affect the imagination rather than simply inform the understanding, then verbal description is what will best serve this end, since it will tend to raise the more obscure and imperfect idea: '[I]t is in my power to raise a stronger *emotion* by the description than I could do by the best painting' (232).

This conception of obscurity is discussed in more detail in the con-cluding section of the *Enquiry*, which deals more generally with the sublime effects of language, especially poetry. Taking his basic defini-tions from Locke, Burke develops a view of the relationship between the passions and poetic language that is reminiscent of Berkeley's posi-tion on the passions and religious language. Like Berkeley, he denies that words have meaning or effect only if they raise clear ideas in the understanding. He goes further than Berkeley, however, in suggesting that the most general effect of words does not arise from their forming pictures in the imagination of the hearer. Some words, such as 'com-pounded abstract' words, certainly produce effects on the emotions without passing through an imagistic or representational stage, but even in ordinary conversation where such words are not frequently used, it is impossible, given the rapid succession of terms and expres-sions, to keep forming representations for each word used (312). The effect of even ordinary language, then, is to stir the passions rather than create particular images in the mind. Poetic language exploits this feature of language by striving not for clear expressions (which convey themselves to the understanding alone) but for 'strong' expressions which convey themselves to the passions. While pure or 'naked' description seeks to represent a thing as it is, the more expressive or poetic use of language 'describes it as it is felt' (319). Burke concludes that poetry and rhetoric are not as successful as painting in conveying exact descriptions, but only because their business 'is to affect rather by sympathy than imitation; to display rather the effect of things on the mind of the speaker, or of others, than to present a clear idea of the things themselves' (317).

FROM THE SUBLIME TO THE POLITICAL

Burke and the philosophy of custom

Though Burke's treatise on aesthetics, following close on the heels of his satirical essay, *A Vindication of Natural Society* (1756), was considered brilliant enough and stylish enough to bring him to the attention of literary circles in London, he would not further develop his interest in that literary and 'gentlemanly' subject. After the completion of the *Philosophical Enquiry* Burke turned his attention to history, entering into a contract with his publishers to write a one-volume history of England. He also contracted, more ambitiously and with more success, to compile an annual review, the *Annual Register*, which would contain contributions on politics, history, and literature. Though he would not complete his volume on English history, his interest in history and his work for the *Annual Register* served to redirect his energies from the world of letters to the world of politics and affairs of state. This new direction received a small but crucial boost in 1759 when he was employed in a personal secretarial capacity by William Gerard Hamilton, a member of parliament for Pontefract, later becoming Hamilton's private secretary when Hamilton was appointed chief secretary for Ireland. From these early, uncertain, but formative years Burke's abiding concerns would be political rather than literary, and the bulk of his published work from this time forward is of a passionately engaged political and moral nature.

It is generally accepted that Burke did not develop a systematic political philosophy. Conor Cruise O'Brien has gone so far as to say that the various systems called 'Burke's philosophy' which pedants have extrapolated from his writings and speeches are 'sad, boring objects, not worth consideration' (1968: 70). It is certainly true that we will not find in Burke a sustained analytical, schematic, discursive treatment of concepts and definitions such as we find in Locke's *Second Treatise of Government* or Hutcheson's *System of Moral Philosophy*. It is true, and even more to the point, that Burke explicitly and forcibly rejects 'philosophical' politics – that is, the pursuit of ambitious policies and programmes that are derived from abstract, speculative, or metaphysical theories of society. A major feature of his attack on Jacobinism is precisely this rejection of radical, programmatic theorizing. Again and again he abuses the speculists and metaphysicians who would demolish an old and stable society in order to recreate everything anew according to some theoretical and untested blueprint. Like Swift, he is consistently suspicious of the innovative schemes hatched by individual reason. Some of his most heady and most inspired tirades of invective are directed against the abstract scheming of individuals or groups of individuals – 'literary caballers and intriguing philosophers' – who would put themselves forward as wholesale unravellers and reshapers of history. In his *Reflections on the Revolution in France* (1790) he writes dismissively of the shallow speculations of 'the petulant, assuming, short-sighted coxcombs of philosophy' (1989: 103), of the new age of 'sophisters, economists, and calculators' (127), of the barbarous and mechanical philosophy which is 'the offspring of cold hearts and muddy understandings', and of the 'new conquering empire of light and reason' in which all the decent drapery of life is rudely torn off (128). He characterizes the French Revolution as 'this philosophic revolution', and suggests that it has all the appearance of a process which is under the special direction of the learned academicians of Laputa and Balnibarbi (181–2). Burke's own footnote to this allusion invites the reader to consult *Gulliver's Travels* 'for the idea of countries governed by philosophers'. Similar invective against the radical schemes of innovators and reformers appears in other works in which he defends stability and tradition. In his *Appeal from the New to the Old Whigs* (1791), metaphysical abstraction is dismissed as inappropriate to matters of morality and politics. The lines of morality, we are told, are not like the ideal lines of mathematics: 'They are broad and deep as well as long. They admit of exceptions; they demand modifications' (1999: 476). Perhaps his most chillingly graphic denunciation of philosophical politics is to be found in his *Letter to a Noble Lord* (1796), an eloquently outraged piece in which he suggests a Swiftian analogy between scientific and political experiments:

> Nothing can be conceived more hard than the heart of a thoroughbred metaphysician. It comes nearer to the cold malignity of a wicked spirit than to the frailty and passion of a man. It is like that of the principle of evil himself, incorporated, pure, unmixed, dephlegmated, defecated evil. . . . The geometricians, and the chemists, bring, the one from the dry bones of their diagrams, and the other from the soot of their furnaces, dispositions that make them worse than indifferent about those feelings and habitudes, which are the support of the moral world. . . . These philosophers consider men in their experiments, no more than they do mice in an air pump, or in a recipient of mephitic gas.
>
> (1991: 176–7)

The paragraph containing this passage concludes with what must be one of the most unflattering characterizations of the speculative philosopher in modern intellectual history. Burke, having introduced a belittling comparison between the Duke of Bedford and a mouse, refers to 'that little long-tailed animal that has been long the game of the grave, demure, insidious, spring-nailed, velvet-pawed, green-eyed philosophers, whether going upon two legs, or upon four' (177).

There is no doubt then that Burke is deeply suspicious of political theorizing, not because it is ineffectual or impractical but on the contrary because it tends to raise disturbing questions over tradition and custom, creates dissatisfaction with the 'compromise and barter' of ordinary human existence, and ultimately leads to disruption and revolution. His own solutions are always sensitive to context and historical circumstance, always pragmatic and adaptive. Even when making a case for reform or repeal, as he does repeatedly on behalf of Ireland and the American colonies, he refuses to base his arguments on idealistic or 'metaphysical' distinctions, preferring to have recourse to tradition, customary practice, and even prejudice. Leave the Americans as they anciently stood, he pleads in the course of his speech on American taxation, and it will follow that they should not be burdened by new taxes (1999: 256). In his *Speech on Conciliation with the Colonies* (1775) he provides a telling example of the extent to which he wishes always to bend and bind his thought pragmatically to particular, regional, historically specific practices and institutions. Having pointed out that the American colonists are descendants of Englishmen, he infers that they are therefore devoted to liberty. He immediately qualifies this, however, by insisting that it is not abstract liberty that is at issue here but 'liberty according to English ideas and on English principles' (1999: 261). Abstract or 'extreme' liberty does not exist; liberty must have a local habitation and a name. It is not something that somehow theoretically precedes the existence of historical nations and states, but is a kind of timely discovery of particular peoples in particular places: 'Liberty inheres in some sensible object; and every nation has formed to itself some favourite point, which by way of eminence becomes the criterion of their happiness' (261). He notes that in England the great contests for freedom have always turned – and here Burke risks bathos in his determination to be particular – on the question of paying taxes. On the point of taxes, he says, 'the greatest spirits have acted and suffered' (261). His rhetorical purpose, of course, is to persuade his auditors that the resistance of the colonists to the payment of taxes should be read not as an act of rebellion to be quelled by force but as a specifically English expression of a specifically English love of liberty.

But for all his attention to the particulars of history, there are concepts submerged in Burke's work which, even when they are used negatively and unsystematically, nevertheless inform and structure his political outlook. Perhaps the most balanced account that Burke gives of his position on abstract vis-à-vis concrete thought is to be found in his 1792 speech on religious toleration in which he begins by saying that no rational person ever governs himself by 'abstractions and universals', but immediately adds that he does not put abstract ideas out of the question. Without the guidance of sound, well-understood principles, 'all reasonings in politics, as in everything else, would be only a confused jumble of particular facts and details' (1999:

117). He makes a distinction, however, between the university professor who has only a general view of society and the statesman who has to combine circumstances with those general ideas. Clearly, Burke identifies with the statesman rather than with the professor. The statesman, while never losing sight of principles, must allow himself to be guided to some extent by circumstances and must remain sensitive to 'the exigencies of the moment'. If he fails to be so guided or ceases to be so sensitive, then he is 'stark mad' and may even ruin his country forever.

One of the most important concepts negatively informing the later work of this thinking statesman is that of 'the rights of men', while the most important concept positively informing all his work is that of the venerability and 'fragility' (O'Gorman 1973: 20) of civil society and its time-honoured institutions. *Pace* Locke, Burke sees laws, constitutions, governments, and societies as the precious gifts of history, as things which cannot be theoretically justified from some position outside the framework of a particular society. Though Burke does not explicitly attack Locke's political philosophy, many of his missiles nonetheless fly in the direction of Lockean targets. The biggest of these targets is the idea of natural rights – the idea, that is, of those rights that human beings are supposed to possess prior to, or independently of, any particular form of social organization. In his *Second Treatise of Government*, Locke had appealed to the idea of an original state of nature in order to explain how a society and government can come about rightfully and lawfully and also to provide the standard against which any historical society might be judged. Significantly, Locke's hypothetical state of nature is not lawless or rightless. Human beings, just because they are essentially rational beings, are governed in their pre-societal phase by the law of nature, which is simply the law that no one ought to harm another or deprive him of liberty or possessions. People will choose to come out of the state of nature because, as rational beings, they see that their interests are best served if they desist from settling wrongs among themselves and have recourse instead to a recognized sovereign body in whom all power of redress is invested. Thus people come to organize themselves voluntarily into a civil society in which their natural rights are protected by a sovereign power, a power which derives its legitimacy from the social contract entered into by the people as a whole.

Locke's basic intuition is that civil society, through its systems of legal
justice and government, is designed to preserve already existing natural
rights and freedoms. Moreover, particular governments or forms of
government are justified only to the extent that they protect and
guarantee these natural rights. One important new right comes into
existence with the social contract, namely, the right of resistance.
This is the right through which the parties to the social contract
render the contract conditional. The most radical implication of
Lockean contractarianism is the idea that a people has the right to
resist unjust or tyrannical governors, especially if the rights which
the governors were contracted to protect are in fact being flouted by
the governors themselves. Resistance in these circumstances is simply
a restoration of natural right, a reversion to the state of nature in which
tyranny and abuse by a sovereign power are rendered untenable.

Such a scenario, as dangerous as it is abstract, is anathema to Burke.
For Burke, societies and states are not established according to some
plan or hypothetical contract, nor can they be judged in the light of
such plans or contracts; rather they emerge and evolve, and have
been emerging and evolving from time immemorial. The formation
of societies is a gradual, long-drawn-out, trial-and-error, complex
organic process requiring the input of many heads over an indefinite
period of historical time. To make his case against the contractarian
philosophy, Burke draws upon the resources of what J.G.A. Pocock
calls 'a philosophy of custom', a conception of society based on the
view that an institution may have nothing more to justify it 'than
the presumption that, being immemorial, it must on innumerable
occasions have proved satisfactory' (Pocock 1971: 133). Government
and social order are understood to be the collective and aggregate
achievement of the community of generations, and not at all the
deliberate or conscious achievement of one individual or group, or
even of one generation. The grand theories and speculations of self-
appointed reformers are no substitute for the cumulative wisdom of
the ages, the slow-but-sure processes of history and tradition. Suggesting a correspondence or 'philosophic analogy' between nature and
human history, Burke recommends that the state, despite its 'arti-
ficiality', should be understood as something that develops naturally
rather than as something that can be summarily built and rebuilt
according to the plans of 'sophisters'. Thus, 'by preserving the method

of nature in the conduct of the state, in what we improve, we are never wholly new; in what we retain, we are never wholly obsolete' (1989: 84). Through his advocacy of an organic model of social change and self-correction, Burke has effectively borrowed one of his opponents' key concepts and has beaten it into an instrument that better serves his own traditionalist position. Where his opponents use the language of nature to put forward a set of natural rights that can be used to pass judgement on all historical polities, Burke uses the language of nature to put forward instead an organic, slow-growth, conservative model of internal improvement and progress.

Similarly, Burke does not reject the concept of rights but adapts it to his own purposes, refashioning it to undermine his opponents' position. He ostensibly accepts the notion of primitive rights, or what he calls 'metaphysic rights', but immediately turns the tables on the natural-rights theorists by making a plea for tradition and history, insisting that these primitive rights undergo such 'a variety of refractions and reflections, that it becomes absurd to talk of them as if they continued in the simplicity of their original direction' (1989: 112). Human nature, complex to begin with and made more complex because of its long mediation through the institutions of society, cannot be reduced to the terms and axioms that make up the simple programmes of radical reformers. The collectively and historically achieved rights of the citizens of a state, by contrast with the simple abstract rights that exist in the declarations of theorists, are often compromises not only between conflicting conceptions of good but also between good and evil, 'and sometimes, between evil and evil' (112). For Burke, real rights are historical and social from the beginning, just as human beings themselves are always historical and social from the beginning. The 'civil social man' is essentially a creature of society and history, not of nature alone. The standards of the civil and social, moreover, cannot be judged by the supposed standards of the natural. Human beings 'cannot enjoy the rights of an uncivil and a civil state together' (110). This point is reiterated most emphatically in his *Appeal from the New to the Old Whigs*, in which he denies that 'a people' can exist in the state of nature. A collection of individuals does not in itself constitute a people. The idea of a people is already the idea of an organized unit or 'corporation', presupposing a high degree of common agreement. It is not the people who enter into, or bring about, an original contract or agreement; rather it is the original contract that constitutes, or brings into existence, the legal fiction that we call 'a people'. When a people, therefore, breaks up the original self-constituting contract or agreement, they cease to be a people. They act self-destructively, breaching the very agreement that gave them a corporate form and identity in the first place, and they become again 'a number of vague, loose individuals, and nothing more' (1999: 493). They have not merely destroyed a particular form of society but the 'legal coactive force' that has hitherto bound them together as a people. The serious consequence of such collective self-disbanding is that it will take these 'loose individuals' a very long time to form themselves again into a mass that will have 'a true politic personality' (493).

Burke, as we can see, has expropriated and converted to his own use the concept of the social contract. He acknowledges that society is indeed a contract, but insists that it is a very special kind of contract, not one that can be modelled on the conditional and frangible contracts of the marketplace. The civil state should not be regarded as nothing better than a partnership agreement in a trade of pepper and coffee 'to be taken up for a little temporary interest, and to be dissolved by the fancy of the parties' (1998: 147). There is indeed a partnership at work implicitly in society, but it is to be looked on with a special reverence. It is a partnership which creates the possibility for science, art, and virtue – a partnership not only between those who are living but also implicating those who are dead and those who are yet to be born. Each contract of each particular and historical state 'is but a clause in the great primaeval contract of eternal society, linking the lower and higher natures, connecting the visible and invisible world' (1998: 147). The contract, as Burke understands it, is a sacred, once-and-for-all sort of contract of such solemnity and enormity that it cannot be broken without great loss and disorder. Insofar as he imagines a state of nature he imagines a state of anarchy or barbarism that may come after rather than precede the formation of society, a fearful state devoid of culture, art, and law, a state in which the human commonwealth disintegrates 'into the dust and powder of individuality' (1998: 146). All due care must be taken therefore to avoid the evils of changeability, versatility, and disruption in the development and consolidation of the state and civil society. We have consecrated the state, he says, 'that no man should approach to look into its defects or corruptions but with due caution; that he should never dream of beginning its reformation by its subversion; that he should approach to the faults of the state as to the wounds of a father, with pious awe and trembling solicitude' (1998: 146).

Despite the patrician sentimentality and special pleading of many passages of rhetoric in the *Reflections* and other essays, Burke's philosophy of custom, together with his preference for 'wise prejudice' against speculative reason, remains seriously provocative. Burke's 'unsurpassed articulation' of a conservative, counter-revolutionary philosophy has been a source of inspiration for those political theorists who still wish to defend a gradualist approach to social and economic reform (Deane 1991: I, 807). But this conservative philosophy should also remain an important challenge to radical thinkers. Just as defenders of enlightenment modernism and scientism need to come to terms with the anti-intellectualism and anti-rationalism of Jonathan Swift, so defenders of social and political revolution need to answer the case made against them by Burke. While it is true that, as Michael Freeman has noted, Burke offered eighteenth-century solutions to eighteenth-century problems, it is also true that those problems 'belong to a family whose descendants are still among us' (1980: 244). No solution, moreover, can be theoretically adequate that does not fully answer Burke's critique of radicalism. Perhaps the most singularly pertinent comment on Burke was made by the great Irish historian W.E.H. Lecky, who found Burke's writings to be 'so thickly starred with thought' that their influence would be lasting. He forecast that while a time would come when Burke's works would no longer be read, there would never be a time when people would not grow the wiser by reading them (Lecky 1892: III, 382).

'SHADOWY SIMILITUDES'

James Usher on the limits of language

One of the most surprising and provocative of the minor Irish thinkers of the latter half of the eighteenth century is James Usher (1720–72). Born in Dublin and educated at local schools and at Trinity College, Dublin, he was a descendent of James Ussher, the seventeenth-century scholar and Church of Ireland archbishop of Armagh, but changed the spelling of his name to Usher after he married a Roman Catholic, Jane Fitzsimons. Some time after his conversion to Catholicism in the 1750s he moved to London, where he set up a small academy in partnership with a philologist and elocutionist, John Walker (see Barry 1987: 57). His works include *A New System of Philosophy* (1764), *An Introduction to the Theory of the Human Mind* (1771), and *Clio; or a Discourse on Taste* (1767). The latter went through a number of editions, including an edition edited and annotated by J. Mathew, published in 1803 and reprinted in 1809. Of interest also is his pamphlet, *A Free Examination of the Common Methods employed to Prevent the Growth of Popery* (1766), which went through numerous editions. The title of this work, suggesting an anti-Catholic bias, belies the fact that it is actually a criticism, expressed ironically through a freethinking persona, of the treatment of the Irish Catholic population under penal legislation. As a critically ironic work by a Catholic author, it lends, as one eighteenth-century scholar has suggested, 'a crazy kind of truth to Swift's and Berkeley's conspiracy theory that freethinkers are really disguised Popish missionaries' (Barry 1988: 119).

Usher's writings on mind and on aesthetics are markedly captious and oppositional, defining themselves over against the new materialistic tendencies in philosophy, including the philosophy of John Locke. His strong religious convictions moved him to reject in particular the views of what he calls 'the selfish philosophers', those philosophical egoists among whom he numbers not only Hobbes and Mandeville but also Locke. Like Hutcheson, he cannot accept the claim that all human action is motivated by self-interest or self-love, but goes further than Hutcheson in rejecting the determining role of pleasure and pain. Much of human behaviour, he argues, has its origin in nature-given, God-given inclinations and appetites. Hunger, for example, is not an effect of calculating self-interest but rather a natural and involuntary state occasioned by the need of human beings to preserve themselves as individuals and as a species. Pleasure generally results from the satisfaction of appetites like hunger but is not in itself the reason for the existence of the appetites. We eat to live, Usher might have said; we do not live to eat. Likewise, he might have added, we do not live to seek pleasure or avoid pain; rather we experience pleasure and pain in the course of responding to

life-preserving inclinations and appetites. What the selfish philosophers call self-interest in this context is nothing more than the ability
to make provision for the satisfaction of future needs and to engage in
actions that will 'preserve our being' (1771: 20). Such practical fore-
sight on the part of members of a living species should not be taken
to mean selfishness in any ethically significant sense, certainly not in
any sense that should make us cynical about human nature or human
motives. Usher suggests that the term 'self-love' is misused by philosophers. Strictly speaking, love implies an inclination to enjoy or
possess objects external to, or other than, ourselves. We cannot be
said to love or desire ourselves. In fact, as Usher perceptively points
out, 'mankind are so far from finding attraction . . . in themselves,
that they fly their own conversations, and industriously disengage
themselves from their own company, by plunging into amusement
and crouds' (21). Rather than constituting the fundamental core of
human motivation, self-love turns out to be a philosophical chimera.
The term 'self-love' remains a useful term in ordinary conversation
and even in philosophy, provided it is understood to refer to the natural
involuntary impulse to enjoy what is life-enhancing and avoid what is
not. Unfortunately, both *self-interest* and *self-love* have been 'wrested out
of their natural import, to make a foundation for a wretched, debasing,
and unnatural system of philosophy' (27).

Usher's close attentiveness to the received connotations of words and
his determination to set 'exact limits' to key terms is displayed to best
effect in his critique of the faulty theory of language that seems to him
to lie at the centre of the materialistic tendency in philosophy. He
suggests that materialism is based on nothing more than verbal and
conceptual confusion, on a failure to recognize metaphors for what
they are, specifically a failure to appreciate the metaphoric origins of
psychological language. We, as a talking species, have been successful
enough in establishing words for objects and events in the world,
successful enough too in establishing terms for those passions, such
as anger, grief, and joy, that are 'striking and manifest' to eye or ear.
We have been equally successful in naming those robust inclinations,
such as hunger and thirst, that cause us all to behave in readily identifiable ways. There is a difficulty, however, with 'the slighter emotions
of the mind, whose symptoms are transient and hardly discernible'

(42). To overcome the difficulty of naming the more elusive states of mind we have resourcefully exploited our 'quick sense of similitude' by discovering tenuous analogies and resemblances between certain aspects of inner psychological states and certain aspects of visible objects and events in the world. The words borrowed from the visible objects of sense will turn out to be metaphors – what Usher calls 'hieroglyphics of the internal emotions of the mind' (44). Given that this metaphoric language is mostly struck from objects of vision, motion, and light, it is understandable that much of our psychological terminology retains a physical connotation. Imagining, for example, has connotations of seeing (with the mind's eye, as it were); apprehension (or intellectual 'grasping') has a clear origin in a physical gesture; while the idea of being emotionally 'disturbed' owes much to a familiar state found among physical things. But the materialist philosophers have tended to take these physical connotations too literally. The word 'motive', for example, has connotations of motion, suggesting an analogy between the causes of human action on the one hand and the causes of physical motion on the other. But it is a mistake to assume that the same kinds of cause are in operation in the case of action as in the case of motion. There is in the end only a remote analogy between the way an idea or thought 'moves' someone to action and the way one physical object produces motion in another. The motivating idea or thought is not an object at all but merely an evanescent state of the soul. The soul, however, initiates actions in a way which is absolutely different from the way in which pieces of matter causally act upon each other.

The word 'impression' has likewise been misconstrued by the materialists, inducing them to offer a mechanistic account of the formation of ideas and knowledge. While the term is useful in identifying some of the contents of the mind and also useful in suggesting the manner in which these contents are laid down, it is a mistake to take it too literally. There is only a loose, metaphoric sense in which the objects and events of the world leave something like an impression, inscription, or imprint on the mind. Once we reflect on the true nature of mental impressions we discover that they are significantly unlike physical impressions. The mind does not retain impressions in anything like the same way that physical surfaces do. A recent

impression, for example, may vanish as new experiences present themselves, yet, though the impression is effectively wiped from consciousness, it is not necessarily wiped from the mind. Memory has the power
to bring back the impressions of once-seen objects and renew an
obliterated scene (48). The impressionability of the mind is therefore
essentially different from that of a wax tablet or a sheet of paper.
It does not support or retain impressions like a *tabula rasa*, 'but by a
law wholly peculiar to itself, that distinguishes it clearly from all
material substances' (48). What this law is, however, no philosopher
has yet succeeded in describing. This is because the mind is essentially
different from all things material and cannot therefore be understood in
terms borrowed from our descriptions of the material world. Yet it is
only by reference to material things that we are able to form any sense
of what the mind is or how it functions. Even defining the mind as a
spiritual or immaterial substance does not get us close to an understanding of what it is, since the term substance, even when applied
to the material things, is already functioning as a metaphor. To call
the mind any kind of substance is merely 'the metaphor of a metaphor',
the 'hieroglyphic of an hieroglyphic' (52), and fails to provide any real
information about its object. Once we attend to the supposed analogy
between material and mental substance, the apparent similitude
vanishes, 'and we find ourselves receding into obscurity' (53). Usher
concludes that there is a defect in the very nature of language that
prevents us from adequately forming ideas of the mind, or generally
expressing our intellectual ideas. We can at best reach for 'gleams of
likeness', for 'shadowy similitudes', for faint analogies and metaphors.
This is not to say that emotions or states of mind are inexpressible, as
if we were altogether unintelligible to each other. On the contrary,
even the slightest emotions can be expressed, albeit in the eloquently
expressive 'language' of natural signs – such as tone, gesture, and attitude – rather than in the more formal or constructed language of words
and concepts.

In a brief but highly suggestive passage on music and poetry in the
Introduction, Usher makes a virtue out of the inability of language and
other systems of artificial signs to fully express the ideas towards which
they reach. In the case of music the failure is something to be celebrated
rather than regretted. More than any other means of expression, except
perhaps poetry, music derives its effectiveness from its ability to reach

endlessly towards an unknown object that seems simultaneously 'to appear and hide' from the imagination (81). Usher makes the same sort of claim about music that Berkeley did about religious language, namely, that it moves a listener in the measure that it fails to express or communicate a clear idea – in the measure, that is, that it is not fully understood. In *Clio; or a Discourse on Taste* he describes music as 'a language directed to the passions' (1803: 156). It achieves its most sublime effects by raising a confused conception of beauty that is sufficiently perceivable to fire the imagination, 'but not clear enough to become an object of knowledge' (156). The mind strives to form a distinct idea of 'the shadowy beauty' conjured by music but inevitably fails, and this failure is part of the experience of music, as the elusive object 'sinks and escapes, like the dissolving ideas of a delightful dream, that are neither within the reach of the memory, nor yet totally fled' (156).

It is not just the object of music that is sometimes beautifully, sometimes sublimely elusive. The world itself is ultimately beyond our reach. In a sequence of passages that confusedly but brilliantly unite Locke's theory of ideas with both Burke's view of the sublime and Berkeley's theory of the divine language of vision, Usher suggests that we dwell obscurely in the world, remaining this side of an impenetrable veil that God has drawn between us and the material world. Light may come 'like an intimate acquaintance' to relieve us, but it hides more than it reveals, since the fixed parts of nature remain 'eternally entombed' beneath the light, and we see only a creation of colours. Let us leave the last word of this section with the visionary obscurantism of Usher:

> [N]othing is an object of vision but light, the picture we see is not annexed to the earth, but comes with angelic celerity to meet our eyes. That which is called body or substance, that reflects the various colours of the light, and lies hid beneath the appearance, is wrapt in impenetrable obscurity; it is fatally shut out from our eyes and imagination, and only causes in us the ideas of feeling, tasting, or smelling, which yet are not resemblances of any matter.
>
> (171)

'A BENEVOLENT CONSPIRACY'

Ireland and the thought of revolution

The French Revolution has so far figured only negatively in this chapter, principally because of the hostile response it elicited from Edmund Burke, but it did of course receive a more enthusiastic response from some Irish reformers. Though the Irish did not produce from among their number a Paine, a Godwin, or a Voltaire, the ideas of these radical thinkers circulated liberally in Ireland in the last decade of the eighteenth century, preparing the way for the rebellion of 1798. The organization largely responsible for this circulation of revolutionary ideas was the United Irishmen, a political society founded in Belfast in 1791 by a group of radical Presbyterians. The idea for such a society had originated with William Drennan, whose father had been a colleague and friend of Francis Hutcheson. Formerly a member of a Belfast Whig club, Drennan wanted to pursue something rather more ambitious than the moderate and ineffectual agenda of the Whig clubs. One of the most famous texts associated with this period in Ireland is a letter sent by Drennan to his brother-in-law, Samuel McTier, in which he argued passionately that what was now needed was 'A benevolent conspiracy – a plot for the people – no *Whig* club – no party title – the Brotherhood its name – the Rights of men and the Greatest Happiness of the Greatest Number its end – its general end Real Independence to Ireland, and Republicanism its particular purpose' (Chart 1931: 54). This short passage condenses and encapsulates not one but several lines of radical thought ranging from classical republicanism to the benevolism of Hutcheson, from Lockean natural-rights theory to conspiratorial Freemasonry (see McBride 1993b). Drennan's advocacy of secrecy did not prevent himself and the other United Irishmen from engaging in a campaign of propaganda and education, which included the publication and distribution of radical literature in a diversity of popular media. Lengthy excerpts from Paine's *Rights of Man*, for example, appeared in at least four Irish newspapers, and while the reprinting of books in this way was common practice in the late eighteenth-century press, the level of exposure to Paine's book was unprecedented (Dickson 1993: 138). The book was also issued in cheap popular editions, and it has been claimed that it achieved sales of 40,000 in Ireland 'at a time when sales in Scotland

and England combined barely came to 17,000' (Lydon 1998: 271). The reformers were not limited, however, to imported materials. They composed and circulated their own propaganda – pamphlets, broadsides, songbooks, newspapers – produced by printers and distributed by booksellers who were often United Irishman themselves, thereby creating a whole popular print culture around radical and seditious notions. Significantly, the popularity of United Irish propaganda depended on style as much as on content. Inspired by the familiar, accessible idioms of Paine's *Rights of Man*, the United Irish writers cultivated 'a plain, blunt style, whose muscular rhythms approximated the spoken voice, and which was designed to be read by the many rather than admired by the few' (Whelan 1996: 71). As well as undertaking to democratize government and state, they were also undertaking to democratize the language of politics itself, making ideas available outside the pale of educated and propertied gentlemen. They were in effect seeking to democratize and 'distribute' thought itself. This was entirely consistent with their aim, as Thomas Addis Emmet put it, of 'making every man a politician' (see Whelan 1996: 74). Official sources recognized the success of the United Irishmen's pamphlets and other publications when they noted that they were disseminated so industriously 'as to find their way into every village, fair and market' in Ireland (Lydon 1998: 267).

One of the most important and influential polemical publications from the period of popular cultural sedition leading up to the events of 1798 was Theobald Wolfe Tone's *Argument on Behalf of the Catholics of Ireland* (1791). In his pamphlet Tone makes a humanistic, populist, post-sectarian plea to his fellow Protestants on behalf of the Catholics of Ireland. He begins by noting the contrast between the physical resources of Ireland – 'abounding with all the necessary materials for unlimited commerce' – and its political status, 'unheard of and unknown, without pride, or power, or name' (1998: 279), and very quickly lays the blame at the door of government. The country, he points out, has no properly national government – that is, it has no government of its own through which the whole people can have its interests fully and properly represented. He does not accept that the existing parliament in Dublin – established in 1782 and known as 'Grattan's Parliament' – is a proper national government, so limited are its representative and legislative powers. In the era of reform ushered in by the French Revolution, the time is ripe for a new dispensation, for a reformed administration, for the extension of the elective franchise – an extension that must, in Tone's view, include the Roman Catholics. He is adamant that 'no reform can ever be obtained which shall not comprehensively embrace Irishmen of all denominations' (285). He considers and rebuts the standard objections to the inclusion of Catholics in government. It is claimed, for example, that the Catholics are ignorant and therefore incapable of liberty. But this is because the dominant Protestant minority has plunged the Catholics, by law and by statute, into circumstances which have left them in gross ignorance, 'and then we make the incapacity we have created an argument for their exclusion from the common rights of man!' (288). After setting up and knocking down some other anti-Catholic arguments he prophesies that a just and liberal government would be brought about if the odious distinction between Protestant, Presbyterian, and Catholic were abolished, 'and the three great sects blended together under the common and sacred title of Irishmen' (292). The pamphlet had an immediate impact, not only by entering what Marianne Elliott calls 'the best-seller league', but also in the response it provoked among radically minded Protestant and Catholic readers, contributing to a new 'buoyancy and optimism' among reformers of both persuasions (Elliott 1989: 133).

Another important mediator of radical ideas in Ireland was yet another United Irishman, Arthur O'Connor (1763–1852), whose substantial pamphlet *The State of Ireland* remains one of the most sophisticated productions of the revolutionary last decade of the eighteenth century. Drawing on diverse sources – on the political economy of Adam Smith as well as on the philosophies of the French and English republican thinkers – O'Connor characterizes the state of Ireland in commercial as well as political terms (see Livesey 1998). He traces the 'woeful condition' of Ireland to the venality, corruption, and tyranny that have trampled on the liberties of the country, but he is not content to wallow in abstract moralizing or hand-wringing. Instead, he identifies the precise nature of the corruption that bedevils the country – namely the squandering of the nation's 'sacred funds' – and at the same time tracks this corruption to a stark historical fact, namely, the fact of an unrepresentative foreign government and legislature. Impressed by the country's climate, soil, and other physical resources, O'Connor follows Tone in highlighting the contrast between the physical advantages of the country on the one hand and the wretchedness of the people on the other. Shall beggary and famine stalk through your country, he asks, 'so blest with a temperate climate and a fertile soil, without the strongest suspicion that the people have not been done justice?' (1998: 32). The problem lies, he argues, not with the land or with the people but with the misappropriation and misuse of the capital or 'sacred funds' that should go towards the stimulation and sustenance of native industry. Industry is identified as the key to liberty and civilization as well as to the satisfaction of human needs. The duty of good government is not merely to commit itself hopefully to principles of non-sectarian liberty and justice but to ensure the proper encouragement and funding of productive native labour, from which the civic virtues will then follow. The fair and proper use of native capital funds is, in other words, the instrument of liberty and civility in society at large, just as the unfair and improper use of such funds is the instrument of slavery and degradation. The essence of O'Connor's political philosophy is encapsulated in the following statement:

> Industry is the source of human prosperity, and the wages of industry is its excitement. In every civilized country, the wealth garnered by industry forms a fund for the employment of the industrious; and as the existence of this fund is the great discriminating mark between civilization and barbarism, so the state of this fund is what regulates the condition and character of every people upon earth.
>
> (34)

Among the potential sources of capital funding for the stimulation of national industry are, in O'Connor's survey, agriculture, fisheries, free trade, manufacturing, and savings. In Ireland, however, the proceeds from all these sources are unceasingly drained away from their proper end. The clergy, the legal profession, the exorbitant land taxes, the corrupt system of grants, and the upkeep of a foreign government are among the outlets through which moneys are massively misdirected and the national capital effectively dissipated or plundered. The net result is not just the material poverty of an underpaid and overtaxed people – a people deprived of the opportunity and reward of labour – but the thoroughgoing degradation of the national mind and spirit. The mind and spirit of a nation is debased and brutalized by 'the sacrilegious plunder of industry's holy exchequer' (62). Robbed of its proper reward, the mind of the wretched peasant or labourer sinks into lassitude and indolence; surrounded by misery, it 'flies to the oblivion of intoxication, to relieve it from the torture of thought' (63). It is not to be wondered at that the labourer, compelled by his own basic needs and those of his children, at last turns to crime out of a kind of duty.

The remedy passionately advocated by O'Connor is a revolution in the ownership of property and political representation. Tyranny, vassalage, and priesthood, supported on laws of monopoly and primo-geniture, have been the ingredients of despotic government through-out the nations of Europe. But the 'stupendous revolution' carried out by the French people has demonstrated that a corrupt court, a profligate aristocracy, and an overgrown clergy can be successfully overthrown and the monopolies of property and power abolished, to be replaced by 'a controlling representative Democracy'. Rather than confine property in a few hands, a revolutionary democratic system will acknowledge that a nation cannot arrive at a state of peace and stability 'until property has become so divided, that those who possess it shall be sufficiently numerous to ensure its protection' (96). Though not an apologist for the violence of the Jacobins, O'Connor nevertheless perceives that the time, historically speaking, is ripe for a radical and complete transition from hereditary landlordism and aristocracy to a representative democracy based on a non-elitist, non-monopolistic system of property ownership. His warning to the reactionary oppo-nents of democracy is that hereditary aristocracy can no longer be main-tained except through a violent counter-revolution that will destroy not only commerce, industry, and the press, but also 'the very mind of the world' (99). It was with eloquent protestations like this that O'Connor contributed, along with other pamphleteers, to the mood of 'buoyancy and optimism' that preceded the events of 1798.

This is not the place to recount in detail the sequence of events that led from those days of buoyancy and optimism to the deadlier days of bloody rebellion and bloodier defeat. In the summer of 1798, the militant faction among the United Irishmen went ahead with plans for revolution, despite being weakened by the severe repressive measures begun in the previous year by General Lake. These ambitious plans included the partially successful soliciting of military support from post-revolutionary France. Rebellion duly broke out in different parts of Ireland, including parts that were not well organized to make maximum use of the French forces arriving on their shores. The rebellion was crushed. The main political development in its bloody aftermath was the introduction, within an unconscionably short time, of complete legislative union between Britain and Ireland – a union that would leave Ireland without an independent parliament, providing instead for Irish representation in the British Houses of Lords and Commons. The United Kingdom of Great Britain and Ireland came formally into existence in January of 1801, heralding yet another momentous and difficult turning point in the relationship between the two countries.

7

PERIPHERAL VISIONS (1)

Irish Thought in the
Nineteenth Century

Politically, the Irish nineteenth century was marked by a growing resistance among the Catholic population to English rule and to the Anglo-Irish Protestant ascendancy. This resistance expressed itself in the successful struggle for Catholic emancipation, in the more star-crossed struggle for the repeal of the Act of Union, and in the rise during the second half of the century of a militant, conspiratorial Fenianism and a constitutional, parliamentary nationalism. The militant and parliamentary movements came together in the so-called 'new departure' of 1879, a highly effective meshing of forces that resulted in what one historian has described as 'a mass movement without precedent in Irish history' (Moody 1987: 275). A new era of concessionary English rule under the administrations of W.E. Gladstone led to the disestablishment of the Anglican Church of Ireland in 1869, a significant gesture that would be followed in subsequent decades by important measures of land reform. But the outstanding fact of nineteenth-century Ireland is a massively tragic one, an event of such proportions that it cannot be swept neatly under the category of either the political or the economic. Though the period after the famine was one of recovery and reform, the fact of the famine itself must keep making its presence felt throughout this chapter and the next, even when it does not occupy our discursive thoughts. The event itself traverses the century like a permanent scar, affecting the way we view the developments that led up to it as well as those that lead away from it, including the sometimes rarefied developments that invite attention in intellectual histories such as this. The fact of the famine inevitably sensitizes us to certain aspects of economic and social development – specifically, to issues of wealth, property, and distributive justice. It obliges us to scan even the most reflective intellectual traditions for evidence of concern and sympathy, for signs of anticipation and pre-emptive policy, for due attention to the plight of large sections of a hard-pressed population. At the very least it obliges us to step some distance back from the kinds of doctrinal, theological, and philosophical questions that dominated local intellectual traditions in the previous century, to shift our attention to questions of social justice, reform, and political economy. Hence this chapter and the following one, while not ignoring the 'purer' conceptual questions, including the ever-present theological and religious ones, will give priority to the work of political thinkers, especially the work of those reformers and campaigners who were the first to note and respond to the realities of popular suffering and grievance.

DANIEL O'CONNELL AND BENTHAMISM

Even if we failed to make the downward shift of attention advised above, we should find that, ideologically and intellectually, the first half of the nineteenth century in Britain and Ireland was in any case dominated by two newly founded 'pragmatic' schools of thought, namely, Benthamism and Malthusianism. Both schools originated in the minds of English thinkers, but soon triggered response and debate in Ireland, attracting adherents and critics. One of the most influential converts to Benthamism in pre-famine Ireland was the popular political campaigner and reformer, Daniel O'Connell (1775–1847). In his early life O'Connell had been receptive to the leading radical philosophies of the day, including the revolutionary humanism and egalitarianism of William Godwin and Mary Wollstonecraft. Most remarkably, his reading of Tom Paine's *Age of Reason* had converted him to deism, an outlook that he seems to have sustained for over a decade before rejecting it as a 'miserable philosophy' and returning to the practice of Catholicism (O'Ferrall 1981: 11). The more lasting impression on his political outlook was made by Godwin, whose work he endorses in superlative terms. Godwin's work, he says in his journal, cannot be too highly praised: 'All mankind are indebted to the author. The cause of despotism never met a more formidable adversary. He goes to the root of every evil that now plagues man and degrades him almost beneath the savage beast. He shows the source whence all the misfortunes of mankind flow. That source he demonstrates to be political government' (Houston 1906: 119–20). Despite his apparent acceptance of Godwin's anarchism, O'Connell's mature political life was motivated by the desire to reform government rather than to abolish it – and, moreover, to reform it gradually and peacefully rather than suddenly and violently. His early revolutionary fervour was modified by his conversion to the reformism of the English utilitarian thinker, Jeremy Bentham. Though Bentham had been made an honorary French citizen by the National Assembly, he had remained critical of the theory of natural rights that inspired the French revolutionaries. In his essay *Anarchical Fallacies* he had written an impassioned critique of the sentiments expressed in the Declaration of the Rights of Man, dismissing the notion of natural rights as 'nonsense upon stilts'. For Bentham, rights are necessarily legal or 'instituted' entities, presupposing government and a system of laws. The same is true of all contracts, suggesting that the notion of an original social contract is incoherent. If the concept of contract presupposes a legal framework backed by the sanctions of government, then the notion of a social contract cannot be used to explain the origin of law or government. Rather, the relationship runs in the other direction. Bentham asks impatiently and rhetorically: 'Whence is it, but from government, that contracts derive their binding force? Contracts came from government, not government from contracts' (1843: II, 502).

But if Bentham is as dismissive of the theory of natural rights as was Edmund Burke, he is not at the same time a respecter of 'ancient constitutions'. On the contrary, he is critical of the principles of English common law, and campaigned to have English law codified and assessed according to an objective criterion or 'external standard'. His life's work could indeed be viewed as one long campaign to establish an external standard in the fields of ethics and law, a principle that would enable citizens and governments to objectively determine the right courses of action in private or public life. What was required was a principle that provided 'some external consideration, as a means of warranting and guiding the internal sentiment of approbation and disapprobation' (I, 8). Bentham found his 'external consideration' in pleasure and pain, the 'two sovereign masters' that govern all human behaviour. The objective standard formally proposed by Bentham himself is none other than the principle of utility or 'the greatest happiness principle': 'By the principle of utility is meant that principle which approves or disapproves of every action whatsoever, according to the tendency which it appears to have to augment or diminish the happiness of the party whose interest is in question: or, what is the same thing in other words, to promote or to oppose that happiness' (I, 1).

It is Benthamism, considered as a philosophy of legal and constitutional reform and based on the principle of 'the greatest happiness for the greatest number', that appealed to O'Connell. A revealing correspondence between O'Connell and Bentham began in 1828 when Bentham took the initiative of writing to O'Connell after he read a newspaper report of a speech in which the Irishman had described himself as 'an humble disciple of the immortal Bentham' (Bentham 1843: X, 594). The admiration of both men for each other is reflected in the gentlemanly flatteries that they occasionally trade in their letters. If O'Connell is prepared to address Bentham as 'Dear, honest, supremely public-spirited, truly philanthropic, consistent, persevering, self-defeating Friend', Bentham is happy to return the extravagant compliment by hailing O'Connell as 'Liberator of Liberators' (XI, 12). In a subsequent letter O'Connell, as if determined to have the last word in the hyperbole of courtesy, addresses Bentham as the 'Benefactor of the Human Race' before recording his allegiance once more to Benthamism: 'I avowed myself on the hustings this day to be a "Benthamite," and explained the leading principles of your disciples – the "greatest happiness principle" – our sect will prosper' (XI, 20).

One historian has suggested that O'Connell's Benthamism is ethical rather than doctrinal, that there is much more to his philosophy of happiness than is dreamt of in Bentham's 'felicific calculus' (Lee 1984: 82). It might be better to say that his Benthamism is political rather than doctrinal. In the political context in which O'Connell encountered Bentham's ideas the principle of utility would have suggested programmes of political and legal reform benefiting the majority of the Irish population, necessarily including the Catholic majority. O'Connell makes a slight but revealing alteration to the principle of utility in the course of a letter to Bentham: 'My device is yours: – "The greatest possible good to the greatest possible number". . . . I sincerely wish I could devote the rest of my life to assist in realizing this object' (Bentham 1843: X, 597). In other words, he changed the principle of utility into a more all-purpose principle of benevolence, from a principle of happiness into a principle of good, with the emphasis on the idea of improving the conditions of the greatest possible number, which in the Irish case meant the Catholic majority.

ANTI-UNION, ANTI-CREDO, ANTI-MALTHUS

The subversive thought of George Ensor

The conversion of the principle of utility into a populist or democratic principle also explains the attractiveness of Benthamism for George Ensor (1769–1843), a mutual friend of O'Connell and Bentham, who deserves to be remembered for his contributions to ethical, religious, and political thought in the first half of the nineteenth century. Ensor was born in Dublin in 1769, educated at the Royal School of Armagh and at Trinity College, and became a prolific writer of mostly radical political pamphlets and books. O'Connell describes him in his letters to Bentham as 'a man of pure principle and excellent notions' (O'Connell 1980: 204), as having a voice in the Catholic assemblies 'although if a Christian at all certainly not a Catholic' (205), and as a radical rather than a Whig. He is mentioned several times by Bentham in his letters, both before and during the correspondence with O'Connell. In a letter to his brother's wife, Lady Bentham, in 1820 Bentham describes Ensor as 'a man of good landed property (County Armagh) in Ireland, a literary man, a philosopher, a radical, a very honest worthy man, with whom I am in intimacy, Place and Mill still more' (1989: 433). (The Mill in question is James Mill, an enthusiastic convert to Benthamism, and father of John Stuart Mill. In the letter to his sister-in-law, Bentham is reporting to her that Ensor will accompany the young John Stuart to Paris, from where he will travel on to her house in the country.) In a letter to O'Connell some years later, Bentham will be somewhat less complimentary about Ensor, praising him for his learning, wit, and satire, but expressing regret that his reasoning is not as close or as consistent as it might be (Bentham 1843: X, 603).

Much of Ensor's political writing is angrily defensive of the Irish case against England, arguing in particular against the injustice of the Act of Union, and pleading the case for 'the restoration of a native resident, radically reformed, independent Parliament' (1831: 30). His most argumentative or 'philosophical' works range over religious and economic matters as well as social and political ones, and include *The Principles of Morality* (1801), *Janus on Sion* (1816), and *An Inquiry concerning the Population of Nations* (1818). The subversive bent of his thinking is already evident in the *Principles of Morality*, where he argues that morality is independent of religion, and that the historical religions cannot be considered moral authorities since they often fail to meet the most basic moral standards. In a manner reminiscent of John Toland he is scathing about priesthoods, charging them with a range of vices, including seizure of property, attacks on the liberty of the press, persecution, fraud, and contempt for 'rational piety' and human happiness. The most mischievous teaching of priesthoods is the dogma that virtue and vice incur rewards or punishments in a future state or 'hereafter'. This dogma is objectionable, in Ensor's view, because it makes virtue a matter of fear rather than of individual or social conscience, and also because it calumniates God by casting him in the role of an all-powerful avenger whose eternal sanctions are out of proportion to the offences of his finite creatures. Ensor places himself among a cohort of thinkers including Cicero, Hobbes, Shaftesbury, Hume, Hutcheson, and Adam Smith, who have located the principles of virtue 'in the sensibilities of the soul, the judgment of the mind, and the constitution of society' (1801: 197). He prefers to think that virtue and vice receive their due reward in this life, that virtue leads to happiness, vice to misery. The sources of morality are not religious beliefs but such natural faculties as instinct, sympathy, and reason. If people are liable to vicious behaviour it is not because they are lost souls but because they have fallen foul of society's arrangements. For example, theft and crimes against property are problems created by society itself, mainly by the unequal distribution of wealth. The solution to such offences lies in 'a free circulation of wealth, and an equal distribution to children of their inheritance' (335). If such a policy were pursued, all citizens would be honest citizens.

Janus on Sion, originally published under the pseudonym Christian Emanuel (see Berman 1996: v), is perhaps Ensor's most radically discomfiting work. It is such a precociously irreverent discussion of the miracles and prophesies of the Old and New Testaments that it has been described as 'a *tour de force* of irony, rivalling some of Voltaire's best satires, a virtual textbook of irreligious subversion' (Berman 1999: 317). Ensor describes Christianity as an 'unnatural' religion because of its dependence on revelation, miracles, and mysteries, and contrasts it with natural religion which is 'taught by God's laws, manifest to all observing rational men' (1816: 57). He dismisses the fideism and mystery-mongering of Swift and others who claim that our intellects are not capable of understanding the commonest actions of nature, let alone the deeper religious mysteries. In Ensor's view, the fact that we may not understand everything about nature does not mean that we must abandon ourselves to all the dogmas or 'whimsical traditions' that run contrary to our experience or contradict the rules of reason. Even if it were the case that we are in fact wholly ignorant of the natural causes of things, it does not follow that such ignorance must lead to unrestrained credulity. How, he asks, 'is man's ignorance of what man sees, to promote man's belief in what he does not see, and cannot understand?' (112). He makes the point that the kind of wholesale credulity recommended by the fideists should lead to a general and undiscriminating acceptance of all mystery-based religions, including paganism.

Ensor's most abrasive criticisms of Christianity are contained in Chapter VI of *Janus on Sion*, where he suggests that Christians are not really serious about morality, despite their claim that the gospels offer a superior moral code, that the gospels are indeed 'the very well-head of all the virtues' (116). He is quick to find evidence of Christians not practising what they preach. It is frequently affirmed, for example, that Christianity teaches brotherly forgiveness in a manner which no philosopher ever imagined. Yet Jesus himself seemed to place a limit on forgiveness when he commanded brother to pursue brother with a stranger's vengeance if the one brother should neglect to hear the word of the church (Matt. 18). Intolerance also seems to lie behind the instruction of Jesus to his apostles: 'And whosoever shall not receive you nor hear your word, when you depart out of that house or city, shake off the dust of your feet. Verily I say unto you, it shall be more tolerable for the land of Sodom and Gomorrah in the day of judgement, than for that city' (Matt. 10). The unreceptive listeners alluded to in these verses continue to receive short shrift in the injunction that 'every soul which shall not hear that prophet, shall be destroyed among the people' (Acts 3: 23). As well as such expressions of intolerance there are other attitudes that Ensor finds unethical or unwise. He notes that an impractical improvidence is commended by the words 'take no heed of tomorrow' (Matt. 6), and thinks that a 'hideous insensibility' is inculcated by the words 'let the dead bury the dead' (Matt. 7: 61). He concludes that within the general context of Christian teaching 'morality is verbiage', that morals are effectively forgotten in the drive towards faith. Faith in Jesus and obedience to articles and priests predominate and absorb all other considerations. This amoral fideism comes to a head in the teaching of Martin Luther, who 'sturdily contemned moral conduct in comparison to faith' (1816: 122). As far as Ensor is concerned, no moral achievement can be attributed to Christianity historically, given the preparedness of its advocates to accommodate themselves to such evils as the slave trade, war, sectarian dissension, and persecution.

Ensor will not even allow that Christianity, considered simply as a faith, brings any real consolation to its believers. By placing so much emphasis on our human sinfulness, it obliges us to remain fearful of eternal damnation. Is it consolatory, Ensor asks rhetorically, to believe that on the day of judgement, we must give an account of every idle word we speak? Or to hear that 'wide is the gate and broad is the way' that leads to everlasting destruction? Or to be told that many are called but few are chosen? Or to be asked to believe that those who disobey the gospel shall be punished for eternity? He suggests that it is on the contrary 'monstrous, stupefying, maddening' to believe that even a few human beings might endure eternal agony. To imagine that oneself or one's loved ones and friends may be even now approaching such a state of 'jeopardy eternal' is a cause of despair. He concludes that Christianity wins submission to its priesthood not by the promise of consolation but by the threat of eternal vengeance. Reason, morality, liberty, and happiness are marginalized, regarded

221

as mere mundane and philosophical concepts, far from the more awful and transcendent themes of our spiritual teachers. What distinguishes Ensor's critique of Christianity is his refusal to compromise, equivocate, or offer a more constructive interpretation. He is not saying that Christianity has been corrupted by the organized churches; nor does he suggest, as John Toland had done a century earlier, that the fault lies with the interventions and additions of a self-promoting priesthood. Clearly, he has little patience with the priesthood but he seems to see it as internal rather than external to the historical identity of Christianity. It is Christianity itself, considered as both a religion of mystery and a religion of moral indoctrination, that he finds wanting on account of its unreasonableness and inconsistency. His strongest objections to Christian teaching are moralistic and humanitarian. He simply cannot accept that even the most sinful souls should spend eternity in perdition, and so he cannot accept the moral claims of a religion that would invite us to accept such a vengeful article of faith.

Ensor's humanitarianism becomes particularly obvious in his *Inquiry concerning the Population of Nations*, an angry reply to Thomas Robert Malthus's controversial *Essay on the Principle of Population*, the first version of which was published in 1798, followed by a substantially revised second edition – virtually a new work – in 1803. In his *Essay* Malthus casts a cold and critical eye on the speculative, idealistic, revolutionary utopianism of William Godwin and other thinkers who would maintain that society and the human species are radically improvable or 'perfectible'. He is particularly critical of Godwin's assumption that most human ills can be attributed to the injustices of political and social institutions, and that these ills can be cured by radically altering these institutions. In Malthus's view, human institutions are not as effective as Godwin would like to think – they are 'light and superficial in comparison with those deeper-seated causes of evil, which result from the laws of nature and the passions of mankind' (1872: 272). Godwin had argued that if all civil institutions were rearranged according to new egalitarian values, then human beings would come to live in the midst of plenty and would lose the spirit of oppression and servility. But Malthus denies that human beings can ever live in the midst of plenty, or that any society, no matter how well it organizes itself, can ever produce such plenty. Humankind may be elevated in some respects above other species, but it is just as subject to certain physical laws as the rest of living nature. It has the same creaturely capacity and impulse to reproduce itself as other species, and has at the same time the same sort of physical dependence on food and other means of subsistence. The problem is that any population, including the human population, has an inherent tendency to outstrip its means of subsistence. Population in fact tends to increase at a geometrical rate (1, 2, 4, 8, 16, 32), while the means of subsistence tend to increase at a mere arithmetical rate (1, 2, 3, 4, 5, 6). Nature's 'solution' to this problem, as identified by Malthus, is even starker and harsher than the problem itself. Nature, in its effort to maintain a viable ratio between population and means of subsistence, imposes continual 'checks' on population growth. Those 'checks' are the events, acts, or processes that tend to prematurely shorten human life or to reduce the number of births. There are two kinds of check, the positive and preventive. 'Positive' or life-shortening checks include diseases, epidemics, wars, plagues, and famines, but also 'unwholesome occupations, severe labour and exposure to the seasons, extreme poverty, bad nursing of children, large towns, excesses of all kinds' (8). The 'preventive' or birth-reducing checks include delayed marriage and the general exercise of moral restraint in matters of sexuality and procreation. Though moral restraint is presented as a third category of check in Malthus's schema, it is really an addition – albeit a very important one – to the list of preventive checks. Chastity in particular is recommended by Malthus as 'the only virtuous means of avoiding the vice and misery which result so often from the principle of population' (398).

Ensor attacks Malthus on a number of fronts, using whatever weapons come to hand, sometimes resorting to empirical data that seem to contradict Malthus, sometimes drawing attention to apparent inconsistencies in the Malthusian argument, sometimes making analytical or conceptual points that are intended to strike at his opponent's basic assumptions and premises, sometimes highlighting the inhuman or immoral implications of the Malthusian vision. He sums up his opposition to Malthus as follows: 'My objections to him arise from his want of science; his infinite contradictions; his inhumanity; his loud abuse of the people; his silence respecting the hard-heartedness of the opulent; his general indemnity for kings and ministers' (1818: 79). He finds a 'want of science' in Malthus's use of the distinction between geometrical and arithmetical ratios, suggesting that it is a 'perversion of the terms of an abstract science' (94), and also that one could just as easily suppose the opposite hypothesis, namely, that the animals which humans eat are more disposed to generate than the humans themselves, that therefore food may multiply far beyond the possible multiplication of humans. Thus, 'one extravagance may rebut another; or rather, . . . two puerile hypotheses may perish together' (96). He finds contradiction in Malthus's conception of nature. On the one hand, Malthus speaks of nature as the work of God, displaying in its operations the wisdom and providence of its divine author. On the other hand, he speaks of the deep-rooted causes of evil which flow from the selfsame laws of nature and from the passions of man. How can nature be the work of an infinitely provident deity and at the same time fail to provide adequate means of subsistence for a species that has been commanded to increase and multiply? He finds inhumanity in the Malthusian conception of human life. The human being is treated reductively, as 'an eating creature, rife to generate, who increases and hungers and ravens and famishes' (132). The progress of each human life is presented cheerlessly and degradingly in terms of want, pressure, and distress. Whether we look to the heavens or to the earth, all things form one labyrinth 'leading to one sad extremity' (135). Morality itself is turned on its head, in Ensor's view. If the principle of population is indeed an expression of natural laws and the will of God, then all kinds of evils are justified or at least naturalized. Those who torture, who break up families, who expose whole families to premature death 'are accredited agents in the prime ministry of all-reconciling nature' (144).

The mass of poor people are abused by Malthus's imputations of improvidence, as if their poverty and distress depended entirely on their own conduct. Does slavery, Ensor asks, depend on the slaves themselves? Are the Irish peasantry responsible for the fact that their proprietors are neglectful absentee landlords? Are the Catholics of Ireland responsible for the tithes they must pay to the Protestant clergy? Are the poor of England to be blamed for having to pay a salt tax that is thirty times the cost of the original article (82)? Ensor is particularly offended at Malthus's remarks on Ireland. In his *Essay* Malthus had referred briefly but grimly to the rapid increase in the Irish population, which he attributed to the extended use of potatoes. He judged that the population was being pushed beyond the resources of the country, and that consequently the lower classes were in the most impoverished and miserable state. He found that the checks on the population were chiefly of the positive kind, 'and arise from the diseases occasioned by squalid poverty, by damp and wretched cabins, by bad and insufficient clothing, and occasional want' (1872: 229). He expressed scepticism about the wisdom of introducing poor laws, on the grounds that if the people are in so degraded a state that they propagate themselves without regard to consequences 'it matters little whether they have poor-laws or not' (436).

Ensor, appalled at Malthus's apparent callousness, refuses to accept that the misery of the Irish can be attributed to populousness, to reckless propagation, or to over-dependence on the potato. He explains the causes of poverty and misery not in terms of a principle of population or the improvidence of the poor but in terms of bad government, general maladministration, and the unequal division of property. He does not accept that populousness in itself is ever a cause of misery, claiming that ill-governed nations are distressed regardless of whether they have small or large populations. Rather than accept that populousness is an evil he suggests the contrary, that populousness is good if government is good, quoting with approval David Hume's observation that 'every country will abound with people and their comforts as it is well governed' (Ensor 1818: 500). Ensor attributes the ills of Ireland to long-standing social, economic, and political iniquities, to 'strange ministers and a foreign legislature', to excessive and unfair taxation, to the great outflow of wealth from the countryside to absentee landlords, to 'the pillage of the people by middlemen, and tithe proctors and clergymen' (295). At the same time he does not go so far as to advocate populousness, and seems to make a concession to Malthus when he argues that in a well-organized, prudently governed society, 'the people will improve their intelligence; and this will regulate their number, by ascertaining their wants and conveniencies' (500). That Ensor is closer to the radical reformism of Bentham than to the revolutionary utopianism of Godwin is clear from his concluding paragraphs, in which he declares that utility should be given priority in all political concerns. But he gives Bentham's utilitarianism a resoundingly populist and democratic spin when he adds that 'utility can only be learned of the people, through the people; – the people are the eye, the light, the object, and the mirror' (501).

PRODUCING HAPPINESS

The radical utilitarianism of William Thompson

The most consistently radical or 'left-wing' version of Irish utilitarianism was developed by a Protestant landowner, William Thompson (1775–1833). Thompson inherited the family estate in West Cork on his father's death in 1814, but never identified with the interests of the economic class or social group to which he belonged. Impressed from an early age by the ideals of the French Revolution, he dedicated his life to forging an alternative to the skewed economic system that had enriched himself and his class at the expense of the productive labourer or 'primary producer'. He sympathized at every turn with the labouring poor while condemning 'the idle rich'. No disengaged theorist, he identified specifically with the economic and political status of the Catholic majority. His support for O'Connell's campaign for Catholic emancipation is evident from the fact that he chaired the inaugural meeting of the County and City of Cork Liberal Club, founded by O'Connell in August 1828 (Dooley 1996: 39). He also attempted to put his socialist and cooperative principles into action by improving the conditions of his tenants, providing proper accommodation, making generous arrangements for the leasing of land, and setting up an agricultural school for the education of tenants' children.

Like O'Connell, Thompson corresponded with Jeremy Bentham, and was indeed more profoundly influenced by Bentham's principle of utility than was O'Connell. His originality as a thinker consists in his appropriation of the greatest happiness principle as a principle of fundamental social reform. From the opening paragraphs of his *Inquiry into the Principles of the Distribution of Wealth* (1824) he makes it clear that he is going to concern himself with the everyday 'vulgar' realities of life and with 'the lowly paths of observation' (1824: iv). He rejects the approaches of both Godwin and Malthus, describing the former as an 'intellectual speculator' and the latter as a 'mechanical reasoner'.

In his view, Godwin errs by placing too much emphasis on mind and intellect, thereby failing to give due attention to physical, economic, and social life. By giving the mind priority over the body, the intellectual speculator ends up disdaining labour 'as mechanical and grovelling' (v). Malthus, on the other hand, errs by adopting the opposite extreme, treating the human being as a mechanical agent, as a spiritless piece of living machinery that can have no real control over its destiny. For Thompson, the human being is a complicated being, neither a mere machine nor a mere intellectual agent, nor some curious combination of both, but rather an integrated creature capable of observation, feeling, judgement, and reason, distinctive capacities that enable him 'to look forward into futurity, to calculate the effects of his actions, and thence to be guided by *distant* as well as immediate motives' (viii). By always keeping the complicated nature of the human being in view, Thompson hopes to work out the best sort of life that such a being could have. For a committed utilitarian like Thompson, 'best' in this context necessarily means 'happiest'. His aim is to determine what sorts of institutions and social arrangements will make for the happiest life for the greatest number of the members of a community. As a utilitarian who is at the same time interested in the practical concerns of political economists, he makes an important and suggestive link between the ethical or political question of happiness and the economic question of distribution. All moral and political wisdom, he argues, 'should tend mainly to this, the just distribution of the physical means of happiness' (xvii). He finds that the chief physical means of happiness consist in the products of human labour – that is, the variety of articles necessary for life and for the enjoyment of life. The aggregate of all such desirable articles constitutes the 'wealth' of a community. Faced with the question of how wealth should be distributed so as to ensure the greatest happiness for the greatest number Thompson bases his reply on a labour theory of value. According to this theory, what gives each article of wealth its value is the amount of labour expended in the production of it. It is labour and labour alone that converts an object of desire or necessity into an object of wealth, thus making labour the sole measure of the value of the object so converted: 'Labor is that ingredient which turns the otherwise useless materials scattered abroad by nature, into the means of happiness to man. It is labor alone that gives them their value and currency as articles of wealth' (89). While labour may not be a fixed or accurate measure, given the varying circumstances under which materials are worked up into articles, it is nevertheless the best approximation to a universal standard of value or wealth.

Having established to his satisfaction that labour is the source of value or wealth, Thompson proceeds to apply the principle of utility in a way that has radical implications. If wealth is a source of happiness, then the conditions under which wealth is produced must be included in the calculation of happiness. The happiest society will be one which is most productive of wealth and which at the same time ensures the happiness of the great majority of its members, namely, its primary producers. If we ask ourselves how best to ensure the happiness of the producers of wealth, we will find ourselves answering in terms of security – security in the whole use of the product of their labour. That labourer or producer is most happy who derives most benefit or most reward from, or has most control over, the use of the thing he has produced. Historically, the constant effort of societies has been to do the opposite – to increase the misery of the productive labourer by compelling him 'to work for *the smallest possible portion* of the produce of his own labor' (36). Those who have done the least productive labour, namely, the capitalists and the idle rich, have benefited most from the productive labour of others, while the productive labourer has benefited least. This implies a systematic preference for the happiness of one (small) class of human beings over that of the majority, a circumstance that clashes so obviously with the principle of utility that it must be condemned as cruel and unjust. If we accept that the sole aim of morality and law should be the production of the greatest quantity of human happiness, we must seek to guarantee to the primary producers the entire use of the things they produce. This means in effect that the distribution of the products of labour must be conducted in purely voluntary terms, without any degree of coercion or compulsion from non-producers. The process of distribution is, of course, as necessary for the producers themselves as it is for the whole community, including those members of the community who are non-productive. Distribution happens most efficiently through exchanges – exchanges among the producers themselves and between producers and non-producers. But these exchanges must be voluntary, involving the consent of the producer as much as that of other parties to the exchange. If the labourer's product is taken from him without his consent, the transaction is not a voluntary one but rather an act of brute force and robbery (51).

For Thompson, exchange is as much a moral as an economic transaction. When a person engages in exchange, 'giving superfluity for superfluity', receiving one object of desire for another, 'mutual satisfaction is produced, mutual sympathy is excited, pleasure is felt at the same time . . . and the discovery is made that the happiness of others is not necessarily opposed to one's own' (50). The simple, necessary, and mutually beneficial transaction of exchange calls both benevolence and production into existence at the same time. If, however, the process of exchange is not voluntary, or if the producer has his product forcefully 'abstracted' from him, then the consequences are unhappy ones, both economically and morally. The producer, deprived of the motives of enjoyment and independence, will produce grudgingly and resentfully, naturally refusing to work as productively as he might; the general production of wealth is reduced, thus reducing the general happiness of the community; an ethos of insecurity, ill-will, and injustice hangs over the lives of the producers, while a culture of secrecy and fraud is cultivated by the idle consumers or 'plunderers'. The net result of robbing the producer of the fruits of his labour is an excessive and unjustifiable inequality in economic, political, and social life. Not only is the producer made the less happy by having his product taken from him, but those who take it from him are made the less happy by falling into a life of excess, imprudence, caprice, and moral deadness, dedicating their energies and their lives to nothing more substantial than the cultivation of manners and 'mummery'.

Thompson is at his most visionary when describing the cooperative alternative to the existing organization of society. In a society in which the primary producers enjoy the full produce of their labour and in which all exchanges are voluntary, based on fair equivalents, there would reign an ethos of cooperation and benevolence. Since virtually everyone would be a primary producer, and nobody an idle plunderer, the basis for many of our current vices would be removed. There would be little or no temptation to theft, fraud, or lying. Pride, prejudice, caprice, and oppression would find no congenial soil in which to take root in a society of active, intelligent, independently productive citizens. Ignorance and superstition would be abolished and the desire for knowledge and intellectual pleasure would become a felt need throughout the community. Here is Thompson at his most emotive and prophetic: 'Kindly feelings and beneficent conduct would expand. The sphere of enjoyment, like the heat of the sun, would be multiplied a hundred fold by the reflections from the cheerful hearts and smiling countenances of encircling happiness. Virtue would consist in blessing and being blessed; and all voluntary useless mortification would be spurned as insanity' (262).

One feels that Thompson is describing a newly constituted human being as well as a newly constituted community. This becomes most apparent when he discusses objections to his vision of a mutually cooperative community. To the standard objection that human beings are too much under the influence of self-interest to become truly cooperative Thompson replies that self-interest is not the same as selfishness. It is only when self-interest is allied with ignorance that it develops into selfishness. If it is allied instead with wisdom and knowledge, then it becomes an enlightened self-interest, leading as a rule to sympathy and benevolence. He is convinced that a change of economic and social circumstances, combined with the right sort of education, will indeed bring about this new kind of human being, a being virtually incapable of selfishness, a being for whom 'disputes respecting *mine* and *thine*' would be impossible (396). In the new cooperative communities the love of wealth and power would scarcely exist, and while there would be 'minor occasional motives, such as love, hatred, jealousy, revenge, envy', these would be limited in their sphere of operation (516).

Though Thompson is not given to using terms like exploitation or alienation, there is no doubt that such concepts underlie his analysis of the relationship between producer and capitalist. It comes as no surprise therefore that his work was studied by Karl Marx, and that Marx frequently cites or quotes him in *Capital* and *The Poverty of Philosophy*. Yet the differences between Thompson and Marx are more instructive than the similarities. Thompson, unlike Marx, does not have a materialist theory of history, of class struggle, or of revolution. That history is working towards some further – and final – stage of development, or that collective relationships and actions are governed by historical laws, or that there will one day be a 'dictatorship of the proletariat' are notions that are entirely absent from Thompson's thought. Thompson is a belated enlightenment thinker who places much faith in reason and education. His belief in the improving possibilities of education is, as Dolores Dooley has suggested, at least as great as his belief in the principle of the greatest happiness (1996: 240). The way in which change will be brought about will be through the diffusion of knowledge, including moral knowledge. It is this community-wide diffusion of knowledge rather than political revolution that will bring about radical change. Reason, knowledge, changing circumstances, changing motives, and the principle of happiness are most tightly interwoven in this passage from *Labor Rewarded* (1827):

> As man's knowledge increases, he looks beyond immediate into remote consequences. Sometimes this increased knowledge, sometimes accident, leads to a change of the circumstances surrounding him. These new circumstances give rise to new motives: i.e. to modifications of the desire of happiness as supposed to arise from different sources. If Co-operative Industry tend more to human happiness than Competitive Industry, its supporters are confident it will be adopted when understood. On no other ground would they wish it to be adopted.
>
> (1827: 100)

The concluding line of this passage points to the most telling difference between Marx and Thompson. Where Marx gravitates towards economic determinism, Thompson gravitates towards economic voluntarism. For Marx there are forces at work in human history, especially in the economic sphere, that will produce the conditions for revolutionary change – conditions, in other words, that will objectively present one class (the proletariat) with the historical opportunity of bringing about a classless society. The revolutionary changes will occur, moreover, throughout the whole of a society – they will not be confined to a voluntary group or community. For Thompson, by contrast, the membership of a cooperative community must be entirely voluntary. He makes a distinction between cooperative communities and 'general society', implying that the possibility of moving back and forth between general society and the cooperative communities should remain. This suggests that if the whole of society were to be converted to the cooperative principle, such that society in general became one big cooperative, then the voluntary nature of membership of the new communities would be undermined.

HAPPINESS AND SUFFRAGE

The feminist utilitarianism of Anna Doyle Wheeler

In the course of applying the principle of the greatest happiness and the related principles of distribution and security, Thompson was led to make a case for the rights of women. He found women to occupy a position of civil and domestic slavery, and declared that the only solution to this evil was to give men and women '*equal* civil and political rights' (1824: 300). His most extended treatment of this issue was carried out under the influence of, and in collaboration with, Anna Doyle Wheeler (1785–1850). Though born into a well-to-do Protestant family, Anna Doyle, like Thompson, rejected the values of her class early in her life. Marrying at the age of fifteen, giving birth to two children by the time she was seventeen, she left her husband Francis Massy-Wheeler in 1812 and moved to the island of Guernsey where her uncle Sir John Doyle was governor. She subsequently sailed to London, where she met her godfather, Henry Grattan, whose constitutional nationalism she supported. After making arrangements for the education of her daughters, she moved to Caen in France, becoming a member of the radical Saint Simonian circle, where she was judged to be 'the most gifted woman of the age' and became known as the 'goddess of reason' (Pankhurst 1983: vi). After her husband died in 1820 she returned to London, where she soon entered into collaboration with Robert Owen, the leading English advocate of cooperativism, and also began an affectionate and mutually supportive relationship with Jeremy Bentham. She was a frequent visitor to Bentham's Westminster 'hermitage', finding in Bentham 'a receptive listener, a ready source of encouragement and a helpful critic' (Dooley 1996: 67). It was also at this time that she met Thompson, beginning a friendly collaboration that resulted in the joint authorship of *An Appeal of One Half the Human Race* (1825), the most important work on women's rights to be published between Mary Wollstonecraft's *Vindication of the Rights of Women* (1792) and John Stuart Mill's *Subjection of Women* (1869).

The occasion for the composition of *An Appeal* was a passage in James Mill's 'Article on Government' in the 1824 supplement to the *Encyclopaedia Britannica*. In the course of outlining the utilitarian case for political representation Mill had stated that all individuals whose interests were included in those of others could be denied representation 'without inconvenience'. This category of 'virtually' represented individuals comprised not only children, whose interests were involved in those of their parents, but also women, 'the interest of almost all of whom is involved either in that of their fathers or in that of their husbands' (quoted in Thompson and Wheeler 1997: 61). Thus cavalierly, write Thompson and Wheeler, 'are dealt with by this philosopher of humanity, the interests of one half the human species' (1997: 62). Having expressed their dismay at Mill's failure to apply the greatest happiness principle to men and women equally, Thompson and Wheeler subject his 'identity of interests' doctrine to a lengthy, sophisticated, and devastating critique. Rarely indeed in the history of thought has a doctrine been so thoroughly discredited.

They attack Mill's identity-of-interests doctrine by showing how it applies, or rather fails to apply, to three large groups of women – women without husbands or fathers, adult daughters in their fathers' establishments, and wives. Women who are unmarried, widowed, and who have at the same time left their fathers' houses do not obviously fit into Mill's category. That is, even if we grant Mill his assumptions, it seems that these women's interests are not directly involved in the interests of men, since they do not stand in any direct relationship to fathers or husbands. What then are their claims to representation? Either their interests are to be completely neglected or they deserve to have their interests directly represented. Given Mill's earlier claim that all those whose interests are not involved in those of others ought themselves to have votes, it follows that at least this group of 'non-identified' women should have the same political rights as men. In the case of adult daughters living in their father's establishments, there is no evidence of a real identity of interests between fathers and daughters. On the contrary, daughters are disadvantaged relative to sons, manifesting in microcosm the disadvantages of women relative to men in society at large. If fathers had taken the real interests of daughters to heart historically, and had really represented these interests in political and social life, then the unequal distribution of advantages between men and women would not exist. While social and political practice reveal a clear identity of interests between fathers and sons, they reveal the contrary in the case of daughters:

> All the numerous marts for mingled recreation, information, and discussion on politics, trade, and literature, or all but the most insignificant, such as those which merely excite the feelings but afford no scope for the judgment, are shut to daughters, while to adult sons they are as open as to fathers, and afford them a theatre for an ever-renewing interchange of emotion and interests.
>
> (84)

So divergent are the interests of daughters and fathers that the daughters are expected, as soon as they become adult, to leave behind them even their father's name and vainly hope for 'happiness without independence' in gratifying the sensuality of another man. Given the much more apparent identity of interests between fathers and sons, it would make more sense to deny direct representation to sons than to daughters. Given the real and manifest differences of interest between fathers and daughters, there is no rational basis for denying daughters the right to direct representation.

Traditional marriage, that despotic contract through which each man 'yokes a woman to his establishment' (95), is not founded on identity of interests of male and female. On the contrary, marriage is an 'ungenerous, all-corrupting, and mutually-degrading code' (100). The history of marriage is the history of a relationship in which women are so disadvantaged that they are in effect domestic and civil slaves. Wheeler and Thompson make the point most graphically in terms of the difference between a man's smile and a woman's, both before and after marriage: 'The dependence of man on the smiles of woman, is always *voluntary* on the part of man, and is limited to the short-lived moment previous to possession. The dependence of woman on the smiles of man is eternal, may be voluntary for a moment before the *contract*, but is unrelentingly *forced* during the whole remainder of life' (100). Even such an apparently natural response as smiling is affected by the custom and law of marriage, showing that the dependence of woman on man, of wife on husband, ranges all the way from the economic and social to the personal and private life. Even sexual pleasure itself, the most apparently compelling of all human and animal emotions, is subject to unequal permissions and constraints. Such is the emphasis on man's needs and man's happiness that the wife is not supposed to have similar needs, or the same capacity for happiness. In this, as in other spheres of human experience and activity, her senses, appetites, and general capabilities for enjoyment are denied by law, superstition, and opinion. At all levels, then, it is clear that the interests and happiness of wives are very certainly not involved in those of their husbands. There is such an obvious inequality of enjoyments and privations, of rights and duties, of powers and privileges, that one must conclude that there is nothing in law or custom to show that husbands are determined to represent the interests of their wives – that is to say, the interests of their wives considered as whole human beings. Given these perfectly obvious and long-standing inequalities, it is clear that wives 'are *more in need* of political rights than any other portion of human beings' (132). Ultimately, only a society founded on the mutual cooperation of large numbers of men and women can provide both men and women with the conditions of equal happiness. Such a society can only come about if all women are granted the same political rights and subsequently afforded the same opportunities as men.

As well as holding Mill's doctrine up against the harsh light of empirical reality, Thompson and Wheeler make an important general point about the notion of 'identity of interests'. They insist that there is no such thing as general happiness, that the happiness of the family or community is made up of the happiness of the individuals who compose the family or community. The vaguely gross or collective interest of any large group – family, state, nation – can be promoted at the expense of particular individuals. It is essential therefore to recognize that the calculation of happiness begins and ends with the individual, not with the group. The happiness of one individual cannot be made dependent on, or subservient to, the interests of any other individual, regardless of how benevolent that latter individual may be. It is a serious error of concept and principle to imagine that the rights or political interests of any individual can be involved in those of another.

The moment that a right or a power is given to one person at the expense of the other, then 'it is an absolute contradiction in terms to speak of identity of interest' (91). The most logical way to demonstrate and preserve identity of interests is to ensure that all individuals have the same means of happiness, the same rights, the same freedoms, the same powers of self-determination. Given the essential link between individuality and happiness, it is absurd to use the notion of identity of interests to promote the notion of non-identity of rights.

THE POWER OF CIRCUMSTANCE

The holistic philosophy of Henry MacCormac

One of the most conscientious objectors to social conditions in nineteenth-century Ireland was Henry MacCormac (1800–1886), a medical doctor and hospital administrator who wrote urgently and prolifically on a range of medical, social, political, and philosophical questions. Born in Carnan, Co. Armagh, he studied medicine in Dublin, Paris, and Edinburgh, was appointed physician to Belfast general hospital by 1830, and became physician to Belfast mental hospital in 1849. Whether dealing with physical or mental illness he improved conditions and treatments wherever he went, and was among the first to advocate that tuberculosis patients should be exposed to a regime of isolation and fresh air. So strong was his belief in the medicinal properties of fresh air that he regarded its opposite, already breathed air, as the direct cause of a range of ailments, including tuberculosis itself. When the tubercle bacillus was discovered in 1882 he persisted with his own theory, going so far as to publish a 'refutation' of Robert Koch's bacillus theory (Fraser 1968).

Though his writing makes frequent references to the deity and is often pietistic in sentiment, MacCormac does not make a virtue out of suffering or asceticism, nor does he opt for an other-worldly philosophy of life. Even in his prayerful contribution to theodicy, *The Conversation of a Soul with God* (1877), he does not allow himself to stray far from his social concerns. In one of his 'conversations' or meditations he addresses God as 'the mighty labourer' and draws an analogy between divine and human toil, the one eternal, the other ceaseless. The human worker is perceived to be 'a fellow-striver' with

God, despite the fact that this same worker, instead of occupying the lofty sphere to which he or she is entitled, is neglected and debased, 'left to grovel in the slough' (1877: 27). In another meditation he shows his sympathy with the social and economic circumstances of women, bemoaning the fact that women are often the victims of base oppression, that their divine capabilities are left 'incult and fallow' (1877: 41). His concern with the poor, whether working or un-employed, whether male or female, and regardless of religious affilia-tion, receives passionate expression in a number of pamphlets, including *A Plan for the Relief of the Unemployed Poor* (1830), *An Appeal in Behalf of the Poor* (1831), and *Moral-Sanatory Economy* (1853).

MacCormac's socialism is not at odds with his piety. Both his political and religious convictions reflect his determination to produce a radically holistic and unified philosophy in which due attention is paid to all aspects of human existence, its physical and emotional as well as its intellectual, moral, and spiritual aspects. The title and the tripartite, all-embracing structure of his main philosophical work, *The Philosophy of Human Nature*, is reminiscent of Hume's *Treatise of Human Nature*. The resonance with Hume is not entirely accidental, since MacCormac's theory of mind and human understanding is clearly influenced by the work of the empiricists. He frequently reminds him-self that all ideas have their origin in sensation, that complex ideas succeed each other in trains from the first to the last moment of consciousness, that life itself is 'a name for the three great classes of phenomena – sensations, emotions, and ideas, which are ever going on' (1837: 146). He makes very effective use of the theory of the asso-ciation of ideas, putting the same sort of radical spin on the principle of association that William Thompson put on the principle of utility. In each of the three parts of his *Philosophy of Human Nature* he discusses the good or evil associations that are produced by the different kinds of environment in which people live. In Part I, which deals with human nature in its physical form and setting, he stresses the influence of the most basic as well as the most subtle circumstances on mind and body. Material circumstances give rise to healthy or unhealthy associations and patterns of behaviour. The actions that we perform repeatedly in response to our circumstances acquire 'a singular facility of performance' (65), even though they may be detrimental to health and happiness in the long run. Disease and deprivation create the circumstances which bring about damaging and poverty-perpetuating habits and patterns of behaviour. The only way to break the vicious circle of bad associations and habits is through education, the spread of a healthy 'physical culture', and the enlightened reorganization of society. Education is necessary to teach new habits of thought and behaviour, but the material circumstances in which people live must change at the same time. The principle of reform favoured by MacCormac is similar to that advocated by Robert Owen and William Thompson, namely, cooperative labour and communal ownership of property (see Geoghegan 1993: 103–6).

In Part II of his *Philosophy of Human Nature* MacCormac returns to the theme of education, this time paying due attention to mental or intellectual culture. His values here are clearly enlightenment values, since knowledge is unquestionably preferred to ignorance. A culture of mental and moral energy can only be created through the cultivation of art, literature, and science. These different practices are not cultivated for their own sake but for the sake of strengthening and energizing the mind and intellect. The key concept once again is 'the wonder-working wand' of association. Knowledge, art, and litera-ture introduce the mind to new enlightening trains of associations, bringing about a healthy mental culture from which the evils of ignor-ance, prejudice, and superstition are eliminated. It is therefore the duty of governments, communities, and individuals to dedicate themselves to policies and practices of mental as well as physical culture, the better to create the conditions in which understanding is enlarged. These policies and practices must give due weight to the 'sublime provision' that the mind of each individual is most fully energized and developed in the course of diverse relationships with the phenomenal world and with the minds of others. The mind is dependent on these relationships for all the complex ideas, beliefs, opinions, and knowledge that enter and form it. As a species we have been 'intended for communion', impelled to depend on each other for assistance and support in all areas of life and culture, including the acquisition of knowledge (177). Nothing is given or innate; nothing comes by easy intuition; every bit of knowledge must be won or earned by effort, both the effort of governments and communities and the effort of the self-educating individual. If this effort is wanting, then ignorance, super-stition, sectarianism, prejudice, and general insensitivity will prevail.

Even that 'unhappy malady', insanity, will become rarer according as society improves and all individuals receive better physical, intellectual, and moral education (265). It is not enough for any individual to cultivate his own mind and intellect, or to possess knowledge for himself. He or she must try to inform and enlighten others, to make them knowledgeable, to bring about the conditions of their optimum mental cultivation. 'Knowledge is power,' MacCormac writes, 'but like money, it ceases to be so, when not in circulation' (274).

The belief that human beings are 'creatures of circumstances' is also central to MacCormac's concluding section on human nature and its moral relations. Moral culture consists primarily in the education of the feelings and passions, since these are understood to be the sources of good or evil action. The inferior sorts of feeling and passion are not innate or 'natural' but are induced and cultivated by circumstances. Virtue and vice, like knowledge and ignorance, 'result alike from the actions of circumstances on the common susceptibilities of our nature' (372). Conscience itself is not innate but is the product of experience, association, habit, and feeling. The destructive feelings and passions are produced by subjecting people, especially when young, to the wrong sorts of association – subjecting them, that is, to a culture of corrupt example, deficient influence, and erroneous precept. It follows that the best way to make people morally better is by reforming the circumstances in which their moral natures are formed. Here again, predictably, the need for education is made central, but it is education with a difference. Though moral truths can be taught like the truths of any discipline, the education of the intellect is not enough. It is necessary that the feelings be cultivated at the same time, and this cannot be achieved by mere instruction. What counts most are the immediate relationships into which people enter. Educators must pay greater attention to the emotional life, to internal psychological culture, the culture of the emotions. Like John Stuart Mill, MacCormac recommends art and literature as important sources of moral and emotional culture, since the painter, poet, and musician are 'in possession of a language with which the feelings are united, and by which the slumbering emotions of our nature, are indirectly aroused (438). Another source of healthy, morally invigorating associations is the material world itself, which includes not only the natural world of oceans, mountains, valleys, rivers, lakes, and the lonely forest, but also 'the crowded scenes of human existence' (444). Echoing the romantic, Wordsworthian vision of nature, MacCormac suggests that these magnificent features of the world are connected with 'deep and varied emotions in which we delight to dwell' (444).

Given his criticism of a society that fails to distribute its goods and resources equally or justly, and given his own practical contribution to improving the conditions of the ill, the exploited, and the poor, MacCormac stands alongside O'Connell, Ensor, Thompson, and Wheeler as one of the most important of the honourable, radical, and 'improving' thinkers of the nineteenth century. But Irish history was not set to take the direction that MacCormac and the other improvers had envisaged for it. The period 1845–50 is the period that confirmed the greatest fears of the reformers at the same time that it repulsed their greatest hopes. This is the period of the great famine in Ireland. The famine was not limited to a single period but was in fact a series of famines which struck the population 'for large portions of four [years], namely, 1846, 1847, 1848, and 1849' (de Vere 1897: 221). Another contemporary observer, Frances Power Cobbe, gives a chilling personal recollection of the moment when the famine struck locally. It seems appropriate that, without further comment, analysis, or narration, we should bring this chapter of radical outcry to a close with her silencing recollection:

> I happen to be able to recall precisely the day, almost the hour, when the blight fell on the potatoes and caused the great calamity. A party of us were driving to a seven o'clock dinner at the house of our neighbour. . . . As we passed a remarkably fine field of potatoes in blossom, the scent came through the open windows of the carriage and we remarked to each other how splendid was the crop. Three hours later, as we returned home in the dark, a dreadful smell came from the same field. . . . Next morning there was a wail from one end of Ireland to the other.
>
> (1894: 181–2)

8

PERIPHERAL VISIONS (2):

Irish Thought in the Nineteenth Century

The Irish system of land ownership was seen by many post-famine reformers and analysts as the main factor predisposing the country to the worst consequences of famine. It comes as no surprise, therefore, that some of the most pertinent and noteworthy thinking to take place in Ireland during the second half of the nineteenth century was concerned with 'the land question'. The demand for land reform had already been made by the Young Irelanders, a group of cultural nationalists who had joined the Repeal Association in 1841 and subsequently organized themselves around their consciousness-raising newspaper, the *Nation*. Thomas Davis, one of the leaders of the group, had attacked the landlord and tenant system, describing it as an evil legacy of 'the rank feudality' of a darker age. Over against feudal landlordism he had set udalism, an earlier and (in his view) superior form of freehold tenure based on the rights of both the community and the individual tiller. In Davis's conception of udalism, 'the soil remained the property of the tribe, though the crop was the property of the tiller' (1889: 45). On the death of the head of a family, 'his land returned into the common stock of the clan, and at the same time land was distributed in such quantity as was convenient among his children' (46). However, with the Norman invasion and subsequent English conquests, udalism gave way to feudalism and landlordism, resulting in what has now become Ireland's 'master-grievance', a grievance that Davis articulated in exclamatory italics: '*Ireland itself, belongs not to the people, is not tilled for the people*' (55).

Davis had decried not just the historical injustice of landlordism but also the demoralizing ethos it had generated among a whole nation of tenants and cultivators. Landlordism had militated against personal industry and the sense of posterity, and had encouraged only the most short-term kind of self-interest. By contrast, long-term owner-ship of land by the occupier and tiller would make him 'the friend and servant of posterity' (71–2), inducing him not only to till the land more productively but also to care for it more energetically. Though the Young Irelanders rejected political economy because it had come to be associated with the grim *laissez-faire* philosophy endorsed by the English government, there is a gesture towards an alternative political economy not only in Davis's essay on udalism but also in his review of Robert Kane's important and influential book, *The Industrial Resources of Ireland* (1844). Kane, an industrial chemist, had demonstrated by sheer dint of information and statistical analysis that Ireland had all the mechanical and physical resources – energy, minerals, land, labour, transport routes – necessary to become economically viable. The only resource lacking was, in Kane's view, 'special industrial knowledge', and he duly recommended the intro-duction of a technical and scientific curriculum into the heart of the educational system. Davis agreed with Kane's characterization of the country's economic potential, immediately grounding his own romantic nationalism in this newfound material base. He declared: 'We must know Ireland from its history to its minerals, from its tillage to its antiquities, before we shall be an Irish nation, able to rescue and keep the country. And if we are too idle, too dull, or too capricious to learn the arts of strength, wealth, and liberty, let us not murmur at being slaves' (1889: 124).

In the decades after the famine the kind of critique that Davis had initiated from a nationalist perspective would be taken up and developed in a more methodical way by a new generation of political economists – Irish political economists – who would refuse to take on board the ideological baggage of their English predecessors. The next section examines the attempt by some of the most important political economists in post-famine Ireland to give an informed and scientific account of the kinds of forces, factors, and conditions that give rise to wealth and poverty generally. The fact that their styles of thought and expression are more analytical and dispassionate than the styles of the campaigning reformers discussed in the last chapter should not be seen as inappropriate or showing a lack of concern. On the contrary, their rational styles can be interpreted as displaying the sometimes business-like, impassive formality of those whose task is to come to terms with the aftermath of catastrophe.

ENGLISH THEORY, IRISH FACTS

John Elliot Cairnes and the turn of political economy

Political economy may still be defined in Adam Smith's terms – albeit a little quaintly – as 'an inquiry into the nature and causes of the wealth of nations'. More specifically, it studies the nature of value and price, the laws of supply and demand, the relations of capital and labour, and the nature of rent and interest. The most important political economist to come out of Ireland was John Elliot Cairnes (1823–1864). Born in Castlebellingham, Co. Louth, Cairnes graduated from Trinity College Dublin in 1848, and was appointed professor of political economy there in 1856. In 1859 he was appointed to the chair of jurisprudence and political economy at Queen's College, Galway, and while still at Galway he accepted in 1866 the professorship of political economy at University College, London. His first major publication, *The Character and Logical Method of Political Economy* (1857), presents a comprehensive account of the scientific ambitions of his discipline. He takes for granted that wealth can be treated as an objective phenomenon, that it lends itself to scientific treatment, that there are laws of production and distribution which can be discovered and made to serve as the principles of subsequent deductions (1857: 7). He is adamant that political economy is a science in the same sense in which astronomy, chemistry, or physiology are sciences. What astronomy, for example, does for the phenomena of the heavens, political economy does for the phenomena of wealth. In both cases certain constant relations are identified, described, and explained in terms of causes and laws. Political economy may be as non-committal and as 'neutral' as astronomy, and may make discoveries that are independent of any particular political, economic, or social programme.

243

Despite his insistence on the objectivity and neutrality of the science of political economy, Cairnes did not think that the political economist, considered as a moral agent and a member of a community, can avoid making moral judgements or supporting political programmes. He required only that the judgements that people make and the agendas they pursue should be grounded first and foremost in the scientific findings of political economy, and that these findings should not be cut to the template of any particular moral or political code, no matter how worthy that code might appear to be. In his *Essays in Political Economy* (1873) he makes his position clearer when he declares that his argument is not with social reformers or with schemes for human improvement but with those reformers who will not submit their schemes to scientific evaluation, who think it better 'to take a leap in the dark, than to examine beforehand by the lamp of science the ground to which they invite us to commit ourselves' (1873: 262). Cairnes is effectively exhorting the reformer to look carefully before he leaps, and to use the findings of political economy to inform his judgement and to plot his trajectory to new ground.

Cairnes follows his own advice in exemplary fashion in *The Slave Power* (1862), a thoroughly informed analysis of the economics and culture of slavery. His comprehensive argument against slavery – an argument which was influential in England and America – is an impressive interweave of economic analysis and political and moral judgement. His analysis begins in the economistic mode, emphasizing the material conditions that predispose a society to a slave economy and a slave culture. Having asked himself the question: Why did slavery continue to flourish in the southern states of America after it had been abandoned in the northern states? he offers an explanation in terms of climate, soil, crop, and availability of land and labour. Given certain features of slave labour – the fact that it is given under duress, that it therefore remains unskilful and lacks versatility – it follows that the only economic advantage of such labour is its capacity for organization (1863: 47). Certain kinds of crop, such as tobacco, rice, cotton, and sugar, lend themselves to cultivation by slave labour because they lend themselves to cultivation by large numbers of unskilled labourers within a limited space (50). On the other hand, cereal crops – the kind predominantly produced in the northern states – do not need such extensive combinations of labour and are better suited to cultivation by individually motivated 'free proprietors'. But while Cairnes in his economistic mode is certain that the New Englanders 'were not withheld from employing slaves by moral scruples' (35), he does not refrain from passing severe moral judgement on slave culture. As well as condemning slavery on economic grounds – as 'absolutely incompatible with the full develop-ment of the resources of the country' (160) – he goes on to condemn it on ethical grounds also. He describes the slave culture of the southern states as a despotism 'more complete and searching' than anything else in human history (176). At the same time that institutionalized slavery does violence to a whole race of people, depriving them of 'all the rights and privileges of rational creatures' (170), it perverts the moral instincts of those who benefit from it. It has entered into the very soul of the people, 'and has generated a code of ethics and a type of Christianity adapted to its peculiar requirements' (165). In other words, the traditional sources of humane and benevolent response – ethics and religious belief – have been contaminated and poisoned by the culture of slavery. Much of the book is taken up with considera-tions of how best to end America's slave culture, and it is clear that Cairnes has no doubt that for moral as well as economic and political reasons it should be ended.

His approach to the Irish land question shows the same combination of dispassionate economic insight and passionate moral concern, and was developed in the course of correspondence with England's leading nineteenth-century political economist and philosopher, John Stuart Mill. Cairnes first met Mill at the Political Economy Club in London in 1859 and they entered into regular correspondence soon after (see Boylan and Foley 1983). Mill had become seriously interested in Irish affairs during the famine years and had contributed a series of articles, dealing primarily with the implications of the famine, to the *Morning Chronicle*. His thinking on Ireland, informed as it was by Cairnes's published writings and correspondence, culminated in the startlingly radical views expressed in the pamphlet essay, *England and Ireland* (1868), in which he proposed a new 'unEnglish' land system for Ireland and expressed sympathy with the 'embittered feelings' that lay at the root of Fenianism. He recognized Fenianism as something new in the relationship between England and Ireland, as 'rebellion for an idea – the idea of nationality' (1982: 509), and he forecast that such rebellions are unlikely to stop for any concession short of independence. While defending the continuation of union between England and Ireland, he argued that the union could only be maintained justly if the land system was changed to favour tenants and end exploitation by landlords. These relatively pro-Irish views represented a shift in what we may describe as Mill's 'Irish thought', and it has been convincingly argued elsewhere (Boylan and Foley 1983) that these views and this shift were substantively influenced by a series of articles published by Cairnes in the *Economist* in 1865. In these articles Cairnes had argued for tenant rights and for peasant ownership, and did so on the grounds that, contrary to claims by English economists, there is nothing peculiar about the Irish demand for security of tenure or for ownership by the cultivator, that this demand is well understood in the rest of the world, that it is the British theory of open competition and contract that is at odds not only with Irish facts but also with universal practice and sentiment. Cairnes based his position on an important and potentially radical distinction between land and other forms of wealth or private property. Land, unlike other commodities, is not originally produced by human industry; it is absolutely indispensable to the most urgent human needs while being at the same time absolutely limited in quantity; and, unlike other factors in the productive process, it may be greatly improved or damaged according to the treatment it receives – that is, it cannot be treated as mere capital which appreciates or depreciates according to purely commercial criteria (1865: 1238). These features of land remove it from the category of ordinary commodities – and therefore from the sphere of English economic orthodoxy. They also go a long way towards explaining and justifying popular – including Irish – sentiment about land and its ownership.

It is a measure of Cairnes's influence on Mill that Mill accepted not only Cairnes's reasoning on tenant rights and peasant proprietorship but also his argument for the removal of land from the category of ordinary capital or commercial property. He accepted likewise Cairnes's highlighting of the contrast between English theory and Irish facts, asserting even more plainly than Cairnes that the English institution which has the most direct connection with the worst practical grievances of Ireland is 'absolute property in land, the land being engrossed by a comparatively small number of families' (1982: 512).

Before the Norman and English conquests the Irish people 'knew nothing of absolute property in land' (513). The feudal idea of ownership by a landlord came in, according to Mill, with the conquest, 'was associated with foreign dominion, and has never to this day been recognised by the moral sentiments of the people' (513). He surmised that in the moral feelings of the Irish people the right to hold land goes with the right to till it, and he went on to make the case for appropriate 'revolutionary measures', including permanent possession of the land by the peasantry.

Among Cairnes's most important critics were his Irish contemporaries and fellow economists, John Kells Ingram (1823–1907) and Thomas Edward Cliffe Leslie (1825–1882). Influenced by the French positivist philosopher Auguste Comte, Ingram preferred an integrated, all-incorporating approach to the study of human society, rejecting the assumption that there existed an abstraction called 'economic man' that could be exclusively studied by political economists. The ultimate human science is the science of morality under which all other studies are subsumed. All questions of interest to human beings are moral questions, and moral questions always refer to 'the well-being of Humanity' (1901). All our duties are to the larger society – to the 'great being' that is humanity – and not to ourselves as individuals. A duty is nothing more or less than 'a useful function voluntarily discharged' (1901: 59). The only right that any individual can demand from others is that of being free to do his or her duty. Such is Ingram's emphasis on wholes or 'ensembles' that he tends to neglect the fate of individuals, even large groups of individuals. Humanity itself is raised to such a level of abstraction, and historical events are viewed from such a remote vantage point, that only the grossest patterns are visible. In his 'Considerations on the State of Ireland' (1864) he describes post-famine emigration in highly optimistic terms, seeing it as part of a pattern of progress, 'a perfectly natural consequence of economic laws acting under the new conditions of human societies' (1864: 14). The hordes of emigrants are simply moved by forces that are carrying them forward into a new, improved future. They are seen, in Terry Eagleton's apposite interpretation of Ingram, as 'merely the bearers of historical destiny' (1999: 125), and their 'movement' is no more to be regretted than the movement of water finding its own level. Ingram is particularly sanguine about emigration to America, that great republic where 'Irish blood did not prevent a Jackson from rising to the presidential chair' (1864: 16). Such is his enthusiasm for emigration that he attributes its cause not merely to the aftermath of famine but to certain progressive tendencies in Irish society itself, including improvements in education, the increasing use of English rather than Irish, reductions in the cost of travel, and a new enterprising spirit among the farming and labouring classes.

Thomas Edward Cliffe Leslie rejects the quest for universals, constants, or 'natural laws' in the study of human society and proposes a historical approach according to which the economy of every nation 'is the result of a long evolution, in which there has been both continuity and change, and of which the economical side is only a particular aspect or phase' (1888: 175). The changes that occur in human history are not just social or economic but include changes in 'feelings, desires, morals, thought and knowledge' (175). More careful than Cairnes to avoid the charge of economic determinism, he maintains that an intellectual and moral evolution is visible in the successive modes of society and that this evolution takes place alongside economic evolution. Slavery would still exist in England 'but for the co-operation of moral and political, with what are termed economical causes' (176). It is not the case, in Leslie's view, that the economic necessarily precedes and determines the intellectual or moral culture of an evolving society. Rather, every successive intellectual discovery or development, every new development of 'mental energy', has its role to play in determining the economic condition of a particular nation (177). Though anxious to avoid a crude economic determinism, Leslie is nonetheless a determinist about the individual. A range of forces, from the intellectual to the economic, determines the life of the historical individual. The individual in every society, whether primitive or modern, is moulded by the history of the community to which he or she belongs. It will not do, therefore, to appeal to such supposed psychological constants as the desire for well-being or the desire for wealth in the course of trying to describe social or economic behaviour. The individual, as understood in deductive systems like that of Cairnes, is a mere fiction, 'a personification of two abstractions, the desire of wealth and aversion to labour' (207). Leslie disagrees explicitly with Cairnes's claim that the economist starts with a knowledge of ultimate causes, such as the 'general desires' of human beings. There are no such causes and therefore there can be no such knowledge.

It has been rightly noted that Leslie's rejection of universal constants and principles makes it possible for him to reject the English land ownership system as the solution to Ireland's economic, especially agrarian, problems (see McDonough et al. 2000). In his *Land Systems and Industrial Economy* (1870) he makes a strong case for peasant proprietorship, at the same time advocating state intervention on behalf of the insecure tenant. Though a defender of the union with England and a critic of seditious Fenianism, he nonetheless acknowledges the historical and cultural difference of Ireland vis-à-vis England. He comes close to the language and sentiment of Thomas Davis when he observes that the system of land tenure in Ireland 'is admitted on all sides to be an intolerable evil', and that there exists an 'unhealthy and unnatural economy produced by the land system' (1870: 58). He comes even closer to Davis when he touches on the psychology of ownership and cultivation, arguing that 'the best security the public can obtain for the good management of land is the personal interest of its private holders' (124), that the public can only count on the agricultural tenant 'doing his best by the land, if he is sure of deriving the benefit' (126). This will mean providing the Irish tiller of Irish soil with the security necessary to induce personal interest and guarantee rightful benefit. The great aim of government ought to be to 'diffuse property in land widely throughout the nation' (84).

Leslie expresses impatience with those who would appeal at this point to the principle of *laissez faire*. Like Cairnes and Mill, he maintains that the maxim of *laissez faire* is not applicable to the necessities of life, and he proceeds to defend state intervention on two grounds. First, it is the state's business to provide security in the case of any enforceable contractual relationship between individuals or classes of individuals. Without sustained intervention by the state, the present landlord–tenant relationship could not have come into being in the first place. Securing rights for tenants, such as rent and tenure rights, is as much the business of the state as the securing of rights for landlords or entrepreneurs. Secondly, the state has already created existing problems in Ireland through a history of intervention – a history of direct and forceful intervention largely unfavourable to the tenant. The existing landholders of Ireland, he points out, are not

only the creatures of the state, 'they are the creatures of a violent interference with pre-existing rights of property' (128). The penal laws were
an additional and particularly violent intervention, expressly directed
against the industry of the majority of the people, leaving them
'even more at the mercy of the landlord than the Egyptians were at
the mercy of the Pharaoh in the famine, for their land as well as
their cattle and money were gone, and nothing remained to exchange
for bread but their bodies and their labour' (128). To make a case for
the rights of tenants in the present circumstance in Ireland is, in
Leslie's view, merely to introduce a principle of fairness into a situation
that has been created by a history of one-sided state intervention.

As if to confirm Leslie's belief in the equal importance of the intellectual, moral, political, and economic factors that shape events in a
society, Irish history itself soon came to reflect the kinds of change
he supported in principle. In response to growing political pressure,
the English administration under Gladstone introduced a series of
important land acts intended to reform the system of land tenure.
The first of these was introduced in 1870, the second and most important in 1881, the year before Leslie's death. Though these land acts did
not meet all the demands of the more radical campaigners for land
reform, they represented the beginning of the end of landlordism.
Michael Davitt, the founder of the Land League which initiated a
period of agrarian and political agitation called 'the land war', acknowledged the 'great act' of 1881 to have been semi-revolutionary in effect
and to have 'struck a mortal blow at Irish landlordism and doomed it to
abolition' (1904: 317).

RELIGION AND THE SCIENCE OF GENESIS
Darwin in Ireland

One major feature of recovery after the famine, especially under
Gladstone's liberal and concessionary administrations, was the development of a confessional political culture, specifically a growing identification of Catholicism with the nationalist cause. The conditions
for this identification had been laid down before the famine with
O'Connell's involvement of the Catholic clergy in the organization

of pro-emancipation meetings, enabling the priest to establish his position as 'a curious amalgam of spiritual leader, legal adviser and political organiser' (Ó Tuathaigh 1972: 71). By 1870, as R.F. Foster concludes, the social and religious dominance of the 'Ascendancy' outside Ulster had been effectively broken, and 'the power of Catholic nationalism was on the edge of realization' (1989: 211). The position of clerical leadership was reinforced during the final quarter of the century when Charles Stewart Parnell succeeded in winning over the Catholic church, organizationally and ideologically, to the side of the home rule campaign. This great confessional renascence was not unconnected with an event in Irish intellectual history which is at the same time an event in the history of one of the defining controversies of the nineteenth century, the controversy triggered by the publication of Charles Darwin's *Origin of Species* (1859). It is a measure of the growth of Catholic power that a rather minor decision by the Irish Catholic hierarchy should have sparked off a local version of the controversy, involving John Tyndall, the most provocative Irish supporter of Darwinism who was also the most influential physical scientist to come out of Victorian Ireland.

John Tyndall, scientific evangelist

John Tyndall (1820–1893) was born in the village of Leighlinbridge in Co. Carlow, the descendant of a family of small landowners who had come to Ireland in the seventeenth century. After receiving his primary education locally, he joined the Irish Ordnance Survey at the age of eighteen, remaining with the Survey until it concluded in 1842. He spent most of the famine years in England, working as a surveyor, draftsman, and railway engineer, and also became involved with a number of schools and colleges, including Queenswood College in Hampshire, where he took up his first teaching appointment at the age of twenty-seven. In 1848 he went to study science under Robert Bunsen and his colleagues at the University of Marburg in Germany, graduating from there with a doctorate in 1851. He returned to England, spending two further years at Queenswood before being appointed professor of natural philosophy at the Royal Institution in 1853. He soon began to earn a reputation not only as a scientist and teacher but also as an evangelist in the cause of science (Burchfield

1981: 6). It was his scientific evangelism that brought him into conflict with the changing confessional culture in Ireland in 1874. In that year Tyndall delivered to the Belfast meeting of the British Association for the Advancement of Science a controversial and challenging lecture in which he not only defended science against interference by religious authorities but also declared a state of war between the two worldviews. The occasion of his Belfast address (on Tyndall's own account) was the Catholic hierarchy's refusal to include physical science on its programme of courses at the Catholic University in Dublin, a decision which Tyndall interpreted as an attack on the freedom of scientific thought and an indefensible interference in the very practice of science itself.

In the address, Tyndall takes an adversarial rather than a conciliatory view of the different spheres of religion and science. He is uncompromising in his defence of the independence of the scientific enterprise, and begins his address by rewriting the history of Western thought from a scientific perspective. The first beneficiary of his summary reclamation is the Greek philosopher Democritus, whom he considers to have been, as Francis Bacon put it, a man of 'weightier metal' than either Plato or Aristotle. He finds the atomism of Democritus to be far more relevant to modern thought than anything in the metaphysics of the more celebrated Greek thinkers. Other additions to Tyndall's revised canon include Empedocles, Epicurus, but especially the Roman philosopher and poet Lucretius. He is particularly impressed by two Lucretian arguments – the argument that the motion of atoms is the 'all-sufficient cause of things' and the argument that nature acts through invisible particles. The first argument rightly rules out 'the meddling of the gods' or, in more modern parlance, the need to postulate an intelligent supernatural designer, while the second allows for entities and processes that are beyond the scope of the senses, thus leaving room for the projective imagination of the scientist. Tyndall cites with approval Lucretius's inspired illustration of how there can be motion in things that seem to the naked eye to be at rest. Lucretius uses the simple but effective image of a flock of sheep with skipping lambs, 'which, seen from a distance, presents simply a white patch upon the green hill, the jumping of the individual lambs being quite invisible' (Tyndall 1874: 9). It is suggested that the person who denies the existence and motion of invisible particles, such as atoms and molecules, is as unwise as the person who would deny that the motionless white patch on the green hill is in fact a lively flock of sheep and lambs.

According to Tyndall's succinct and eclectic history, nothing much of scientific interest happened for nearly two millennia after the first flourishing of ancient Greek science. The reasons for the decline of science include the fall of empire and the rise of a form of Christianity in which recourse to scripture replaced recourse to enquiry. The Middle Ages in particular witnessed a long period during which thought had become 'abject', and during which the acceptance of mere authority led to 'intellectual death' (12). The scholastic philosophy derived from the works of Aristotle was no substitute for scientific thought. Despite his reputation as a philosopher, Aristotle as physicist displayed some of the worst attributes of a scientific investigator – indistinctness of ideas and confusion of mind, for example – and was all too capable of simple errors of observation and detail. Not until the early modern period, with the emergence of such brave figures as Copernicus and Giordano Bruno, is there a return to proper scientific practice and principle. Tyndall (like John Toland before him) expresses a particular admiration for the Italian philosopher and astronomer Bruno, chiefly because of his daring to conclude that nature 'does not imitate the technic of man' (19), that the forms of nature were not imposed by an external artificer, that matter itself is 'the universal mother who brings forth all things as the fruit of her own womb' (20). Of course, the great modern exponent of this conception of matter and nature – and the thinker whom Tyndall is really most anxious to defend – is Charles Darwin, who, like Bruno, rejects the notion of direct intervention by an external creative power in his account of the origin of species. The beauty of the flower is not due to a special act of creation but to the slow method of nature itself, namely, evolution by natural selection. Even that complex organ, the eye, does not require an ingenious external designer but rather a long process of development that began as the simple action of light on surface cells and continued through the operation of 'infinite adjustments' until it eventually reached the perfection displayed in the eye of the hawk or eagle (48).

For all this antipathy to religious as distinct from scientific theorizing, Tyndall recognizes the religious impulse as natural and ineliminable. There exists, he suggests, a deep-seated feeling, a capacity for awe and reverence, that is woven into the texture of human nature and is capable of being guided towards either mischievous or noble ends. Tyndall tries to show his accommodation of the religious impulse by describing himself as a modern 'materialist' rather than a materialist in the classical sense. Classical materialism was developed by mathematicians who tended to empty it of its promise and potency. Modern 'materialism' is a naturalistic materialism that recognizes the rich possibilities of matter, and that regards the material and natural world with a virtually pantheistic respect. At the end of the Belfast address he strikes an expressly pantheistic note, reminiscent of the Neoplatonic theology of Eriugena, when he acknowledges that the human mind, 'with the yearning of a pilgrim for his distant home, will turn to the Mystery from which it has emerged, seeking to fashion it as to give unity to thought and faith' (64). He makes a case for the persistence of mystery within science itself, especially with regard to attempts to explain the nature of consciousness. We are aware of the causal dependence of mind or consciousness on the brain but the moment we try to comprehend the actual connection between brain and mind we are at a loss. His reasoning here looks ahead to the arguments of the so-called 'new mysterians' in twentieth-century philosophy who have denied the possibility of giving an objective, scientific account of the subjective reality of consciousness (see Flanagan 1992). When Tyndall declares, 'Man the *object* is separated by an impassable gulf from man the *subject*' (1874: 59), he might be summarizing the views of Thomas Nagel (1986) or Colin McGinn (1991).

Neither Tyndall's gesture towards pantheism nor his acknowledgement of the mystery of consciousness succeeded in disarming all, or many, of his opponents. One of the most resolute and comprehensive of his Irish critics was Presbyterian minister Robert Watts (1820–1895), who had been appointed to the chair of systematic theology at the general assembly's college in Belfast in 1866, and whose essays on science, religion, evolution, and atomism were collected and published in 1888 under the title *The Reign of Causality*. Watts came to public notice in the first place when he joined controversy with Tyndall in the aftermath of the 1874 address. His main objection to Tyndall was that Tyndall's form of materialism is not intellectually satisfying. No mind, he argues, 'whether scientific or theological, can

find a resting-place in the play of atoms and molecules under the operation of laws' (1888: 20). The human mind, by virtue of its constitution,
is compelled to go on asking questions that can only be satisfactorily
answered by reaching beyond the realm of physical particles to the
realm of ultimate causes. For Watts, this means that the chain of
causal questioning and reasoning leads to the idea of an 'extramundane
Intelligence' or 'intelligent Systematiser', namely, God. He is adamant
that purely atomistic or mechanical hypotheses cannot adequately
account for the emergence of life, for the development of such finely
tuned organs as the eye, for the phenomena of sensation and thought,
or for 'the facts revealed by the inextinguishable feeling of identity'
(40). His observations on personal identity are particularly poignant,
given the developments that were to take place in the next century
in the life sciences. On the question of the identity of personal
consciousness, Watts wonders how an atomist like Tyndall can explain
the continuity of memory and consciousness that constitutes the sense
of identity. What links the consciousness of the mature Tyndall with
the consciousness of the boy he once was? Given that no atom of the
student boy continues to exist in the mature, scientific president,
'how comes it that the president feels conscious that he is identified
with the boy?' (39). Watts then proceeds to ridicule Tyndall's proto-
genetic theory that the departing atoms and molecules somehow communicate the 'secret' of personal identity to the arriving atoms. This is
what Tyndall says in answer to the question of how the sense of identity
is maintained across the flight of molecules: 'Like changing sentinels,
the oxygen, hydrogen, and carbon that depart, seem to whisper their
secret to their comrades that arrive, and thus, while the Non-ego
shifts, the Ego remains the same' (1902: II, 56), and he soon adds:
'Life is a *wave* which in no two consecutive moments of its existence
is composed of the same particles' (II, 56). The constancy experienced
at the level of self-perception is explained in terms of a continuity in
the form rather than in the 'matter' of the changing molecules. In a
revealing gloss, Watts interprets Tyndall to mean that the departing
atoms and molecules give the password of identity to the new atoms
and molecules, a password 'which must embrace not simply their
own history, but the history of the antecedent elements of the organism
from the dawn of memory!' (1888: 40). Given the implausibility (as
he sees it) of such a theory, Watts concludes that the problem of the

origins of life and consciousness, and the equally important problem of the persistence of personal consciousness, are the rocks on which Tyndall's materialism, atomism, and evolutionism are bound to founder.

It is easy to concede that in his strictly scientific work, including his books intended for the general reader, Tyndall does not seem to be deeply imbued with the sense of the transcendent that he aspires to in the Belfast address. It is easy to show that he does not dwell very much on the mysterious aspects of the relationship between mind and nature, that the pantheistic leaning hinted at in the Belfast address is not much in evidence in other essays. In a series of books, including *The Forms of Water* (1872), *Sound* (1875), and *Fragments of Science* (1902) he makes a virtue of providing precise, descriptive, largely unspeculative accounts of basic forces and features of the physical world. (Still worth reading because still informative and carefully phrased are a number of essays from the various editions of the *Fragments of Science*, especially 'The Sky', 'Reflections on Prayer and Natural Law', 'Matter and Force', 'Scientific Use of the Imagination', and a curiosity entitled 'Death by Lightning' that is at once macabre and reassuring.) There is, at the same time, overwhelming evidence of his scientific materialism, a philosophy and world-outlook that is most succinctly and starkly iterated in his preface to the sixth edition of *Fragments of Science*, in which he announces: 'Holding, as I do, the nebular hypothesis, I am logically bound to deduce the life of the world from forces inherent in the nebula' (1902: 3). But it would be unfair to Tyndall to suspect him of making no more than a patronizing gesture towards the religious impulse. Apart from the Belfast address, his journals and letters reveal a sustained and serious interest in the romantic and idealist philosophies of Thomas Carlyle, Ralph Waldo Emerson, and Johann Gottlieb Fichte (see Barton 1987). Perhaps the most cogent – and most poignant – expression of his sense of the transcendent occurs in his essay 'Vitality' in which he regrets the extent to which philosophers and theologians have misrepresented and maligned matter, for, in his view, matter is, at bottom, 'essentially mystical and transcendental' (1902: II, 57). Even as the scientist finds the origins of organic life in the various compounds of inorganic matter, he must also find that this very compounding 'constitutes the mystery and the miracle of vitality' (II, 55). Of science itself Tyndall says that in one sense it knows everything, while in another sense it knows nothing. It can answer questions about 'this intermediate phase of things that we call nature' but cannot answer questions of origin or destiny. If someone wishes to know who or what bestowed on the ultimate particles of matter their wondrous power of varied interaction, then science can make no answer: 'the mystery, though pushed back, remains unaltered' (II, 57).

Three non-Darwinian evolutionists: Gerald Molloy, J.J. Murphy, and G.G. Stokes

Though Tyndall's Belfast address seems to have been delivered on the basis that attack is the best form of defence, its revisionary and confrontational mode was not typical of the stance of Victorian scientists or scientific writers. James Moore (1979) has persuasively argued that the historiography of the post-Darwinian controversy has been marred by clever but ill-chosen metaphors of polarization, including metaphors of warfare and conflict. In the course of developing his own 'non-violent' history of the debate, he tries to show that conversion, accommodation, and 'dissonance reduction' were among the bewildering range and variety of responses to Darwin's challenging theory. While Moore concentrates on the English Protestant response, it is arguable that a small number of Irish thinkers from different religious backgrounds contributed to the non-violent history of the response to evolutionary theory. This small number included Gerald Molloy, Joseph John Murphy, and George Gabriel Stokes, all three of whom may be described as evolutionists of a non-Darwinian variety.

Gerald Molloy (1834–1906), professor of theology at the Royal College of St Patrick, Maynooth, and later professor of natural philosophy at University College, Dublin, draws frequently (as did Darwin) upon the works of the English geologist Charles Lyell in the course of his attempt to harmonize the new findings of geology with the old beliefs supported by the Genesis account of creation. Molloy is in no doubt about the rightness of the geologist's views on the long formation of the crust of the earth. In his *Geology and Revelation* (1872) he presents what is in effect a detailed course in geology and fossil remains, laying emphasis on the incredibly long and gradual evolution of the surface features of the earth. His academic prose cannot fully

disguise his capacity to marvel at the antiquity of the earth's formations and deposits. In a passage on chalk rock, for example, he marvels
at the vast accumulation of shells it took to lay down such rock,
especially at how many generations of animalcules it took to pile up
in such immense thicknesses. When he muses on how many ages
were consumed in the process of accumulation, and how much time
must have elapsed, he finds that it is 'beyond the reach of science to
calculate, almost beyond the power of imagination to conceive'
(1873: 342).

On the question of fossil remains, Molloy refuses to follow the
example of those who seek to 'interpret away' the scientific record.
He expresses impatience with those who try to make the fossils part
of the act of creation, as if God might have made bones, shells, and
skeletons and then dispersed them 'up and down through his creation,
on the lofty mountains, in the hidden valleys, and in the profound
depths of the sea' (232). Molloy declares that he has no wish to limit
the power of God, since theoretically God could do such things. But
we have learned from daily experience that God is pleased to employ
the agency of 'secondary causes' such as we find at work in the ordinary
processes of growth, reproduction, and regeneration. When a traveller
in foreign parts comes upon a forest of great trees, or a herd of unknown
animals, he does not suppose that the trees and the beasts came directly
from the hand of God. Just as an individual tree or animal comes into
existence as a result of natural reproduction, so whole species and large-
scale features of the earth have been coming into being and passing
away in accordance with the laws of nature. Much of what the earth
contains was not produced in a moment by a special act of creation.
God has not directly created each existing honeycomb himself, 'but
He has taught the bee to make it' (175). Likewise, albeit on a larger
scale, the stratified rocks of which geologists speak were not the
immediate work of creation, but were slowly produced 'by a vast and
complex machinery of secondary causes' (180).

Molloy then offers two alternative ways of respectfully reinterpreting
Genesis in order to make it fit in with the scientific facts, especially to
account for the geological antiquity of the earth. One way is to 'stretch'
the time-frame of Genesis by allowing 'an interval of indefinite duration' to pass between the creation of the world – of the heavens and
the earth – and the divine work of the first Mosaic day. The biblical

text does not say that the heavens and the earth were created *on the first day*, rather that they were created *in the beginning*. This implies that by the first Mosaic day the earth had already existed for a long time in a state of waste and emptiness 'when darkness was upon the face of the deep', that the six days of creation were not six days of creation *ex nihilo* but rather six days of 'fashioning' or 'furnishing', and that therefore there could have been an indefinite lapse of time between the two great acts of divine omnipotence (356). The second alternative also involves stretching the time-frame of Genesis, this time by simply interpreting the six 'days' of creation as six periods of long and indefinite duration rather than as six solar days. Either approach is consistent with the scientific facts while at the same remaining true to the creationist spirit of the Genesis account. Although Molloy does not deal explicitly with the evolution of species – indeed, he ignores the problem as if it did not exist (see Whyte 1999: 157) – it is not too hard to see that he could, with due ingenuity, have worked biological evolution into his conciliatory schema. He could have argued that the emergence of the human and other species out of some earlier or 'primal' form of life could be attributed to the complex action of secondary causes, all in accordance with the creative will of God.

If Molloy avoided direct engagement with Darwin's theory of the origin of species, the same is not true of his contemporary, Joseph John Murphy (1827–1894), a Church of Ireland businessman who was active in Belfast's literary and scientific circles, and who produced 'the most considered and expansive appraisal of the new biology' (Livingstone 1997: 392). Murphy begins one of his books by declaring that he will not be engaging in yet another attempt at 'harmonizing Scripture with Science' (1873: 1). Suspecting that harmonization implies some degree of distortion or misrepresentation on either side, he declares that harmonization is not necessary or possible, and insists instead on the independence of both provinces of thought. The things of science and the things of faith 'have no point of contact, and have absolutely nothing to do with each other' (2). The definitive contrast between the two provinces consists in the fact that the truths of science are discovered by human effort, while the truths of religion are revealed (6). This contrast, however, does not imply a mutual antagonism, any more than the contrast between the self-evident truths of mathematics and the inductive truths of science implies an essential antagonism between those two areas of enquiry. Each province of enquiry, whether religion, science, or mathematics, has its own characteristic method and makes its own assumptions but all provinces are united in the quest for truth. The fundamental conception of both religion and science is that there exists a system of truths that human beings have not made and cannot alter, but which it is their privilege to understand. No one method has a prerogative on truth, so understood. From this 'identity of fundamental conception' it follows that the religious and scientific spirits are closely akin, and that love of truth, humility, and intellectual independence are virtues of both the religious and scientific habits of mind.

Despite his protestations to the contrary, Murphy does in effect produce an account of evolution that could easily be mistaken for an attempt at harmonization. He seems to go a long way with Darwin when he accepts that distinct species have not been separately created but have been derived by descent, with modification and variation, from a single germ or at most a small number of germs (1869: I, 205). In the case of human evolution he accepts that man has developed, like all organisms, out of a minute structureless germ 'which cannot by itself be distinguished from that which will develop into the form of any other species' (I, 330). He accepts, moreover, that there are no significant differences between the human brain and anatomy and the brain and anatomy of our nearest evolutionary ancestor, the ape. At the same time, while being prepared to accept so much of the theory of evolution, Murphy declares that he is not a believer in Darwin's version. He refuses to accept that the purely physical principle of natural selection is enough to account for the whole complex process of modification whereby highly organized forms emerge from unorganized 'germs'. He maintains that there is a guiding intelligence at work in and through the process of modification, that an 'organizing intelligence co-exists and co-operates with the unintelligent forces through all life', and that this principle of intelligence 'is most dominant in the highest life' (I, 337). He has no doubt that life, like matter or energy, had its origins in the direct action of a creative intelligence – that, while all species are descended from a few original germs, these few germs 'were originally vitalized by Creative Power' (I, 328). He is equally convinced that the spiritual nature enjoyed by human beings was also a direct result of the same creative power. His argument cleverly exploits the scientific 'fact' that there is no significant difference between the human brain and the brain of the ape. On the one hand, the human brain shows no anatomical superiority over that of the highest apes, yet there is no doubting the mental, intellectual, and spiritual superiority of the human mind over that of the apes. This strongly suggests that superior human mentality must have a source other than the purely physical process of natural selection which produces only the ape-like physical human brain. He writes: 'I do not see any improbability in the belief that the same Creative Power which at the beginning created matter, and afterwards gave it life, finally, when the action of that life had developed the bodily frame and the instinctive mental powers of man, completed the work by breathing into man a breath of higher and spiritual life' (1869: 331).

In a later book, *The Scientific Bases of Faith* (1873), he is less guarded in his statement of the creationist intuition, maintaining that the spiritual nature of human intelligence is not a mere development out of the mental nature of the lower animals, 'but has been directly imparted by the Divine Spirit' (1873: 12). He immediately adds, however, that the divine spirit, in introducing such new forces as life and mind into the universe, does not thereby alter the laws of nature or break the continuity of the formative history of the universe. By the time he comes to write *Natural Selection and Spiritual Freedom* (1893) Murphy's concerns are primarily religious. Religious language intrudes into and colours his conception of evolution. It is certain, he says, that the present divine government of both the natural and spiritual world 'has for its purpose the perfection of the elect' (1893: 79), though he is quick to add here that the creator will hereafter allow the rejected ones to realize all the possibilities that were frustrated in the natural world. He also insists that the Darwinian principle is not a moral principle – that it is in fact beneath morality (79). If the Darwinian principle were adopted in the moral domain it would condemn the weak, the infirm, and the destitute. But the highest morality must always recognize the claims of the weak and the rejected. This indeed is what morality is designed to do, namely, to protect those who fare least successfully in the competitive earthly world. Because morality has just such a role in human society it follows for Murphy that it cannot have evolved by any natural Darwinian process but must have its origin in the supernatural domain. It is to a Christian rather than a secular sense of morality that he appeals when he wishes to place an important constraint on racialist interpretations of Darwinism. Lest concepts of competition, survival, and 'the elect' be used to justify 'the distinction of races', he points to the fact that in the divine personality of Christ there is no distinction between Jew and Gentile, between Greek and barbarian, or between European and African.

George Gabriel Stokes (1819–1903), mathematician and physicist, was born in Skreen, Co. Sligo. He received his education at Bristol College and at Pembroke College, Cambridge, eventually becoming professor of mathematics at Cambridge and president of the Royal Society of London. Though best known to historians of science for his contributions to mathematics and the wave theory of light, he also contributed to the post-Darwinian debate. In the two volumes of his *Natural Theology* (1891, 1893) he wrestled with the apparent conflict between the claims of science and the claims of religious belief. Stokes makes no secret of his own religious convictions, particularly his belief in revelation as a source of truths not necessarily ascertainable by the effort of reason alone. One of his main concerns is whether the theory of evolution is more consistent with atheism than with theism – whether in fact it leads to atheism, or at least makes it more difficult to remain a believer. When he considers cosmological and geological evolution, he has no difficulty in accepting their perfect compatibility with theism. He has no difficulty, in other words, in accepting that the earth in particular and the cosmos in general have developed – gradually evolved – over long periods of time. There is no need to imagine that each stage in the natural history of cosmos and earth necessitated a special act of creation. It is enough that all these great developments took place according to natural processes governed by the laws of nature. The developments in question occur within nature or 'creation', and the laws that govern the created world are in any case divinely instituted.

Yet, Stokes is unhappy with the suggestion that we may assimilate the Almighty to those Greek gods 'who created the world, and then left it all to itself' (1893: 154). A particular problem arises with the evolutionary theory of biological life. It is not the concept of the evolution of species that bothers Stokes here, but rather the problem of how life got started in the first place. While some evolutionists seem to believe that life spontaneously emerged out of inorganic matter, Stokes prefers to think that life appeared in the first instance as a result of 'a special exertion of Divine energy' (151). He has scientific as well as religious reasons for saying this. There is, he thinks, no evidence that spontaneous generation has ever taken place in the past; and no experiment has ever shown that it can occur in principle. Nor does there exist any natural process that might be considered analogous to that of spontaneous generation. Is there, he asks, something that we can scientifically examine 'that seems so far akin to the origination of living from dead matter as to raise some degree of probability that such a thing is possible by mere natural causes?' (1891: 170). He thinks not, and argues that whereas observable natural processes suggest the plausibility of cosmological and geological evolution, there is no equivalent observable event that does the same for spontaneous genera-tion. The phenomena of life are so utterly unlike anything that we witness in lifeless matter, 'that it would require the strongest experi-mental evidence to lead us to accept the possibility of spontaneous generation' (1893: 148). It is an expression of animus towards the idea of creation to dogmatically assume that spontaneous generation *must* have occurred, as if the notion of divine intervention must be excluded at all costs from the scientific account of the origins of life. To avoid the charge of animus scientists should remain open to the possibility of divine intervention, given the absence of conclusive evidence to the contrary.

Stokes should have been reassured to some extent by the closing pages of *The Origin of Species* where Darwin allowed in principle for the possibility that the first forms of life were brought about by special divine intervention. In these closing pages Darwin has begun to address the question of the 'religious feelings' of his readers by quoting a passage from a letter sent to him by the English clergyman Charles Kingsley. The passage from the original letter, which was slightly altered in the course of quotation by Darwin, is as follows:

> I have gradually learnt that it is just as noble a conception of Deity, to believe that He created primal forms capable of self-development into all forms needful *pro tempore* and *pro loco* as to

believe that He required a fresh act of intervention to supply the *lacunas* which He Himself had made. I question whether the former be not the loftier thought.

(Darwin 1959: II, 82)

Darwin endorses Kingsley's sentiment and duly concludes *The Origin* by declaring that there is indeed a 'grandeur' in the new evolutionary idea of life, specifically in the idea of life having been 'originally breathed by the Creator into a few forms or into one', perhaps into a single progenitor from which 'endless forms most beautiful and most wonderful have been, and are being evolved' (1885: 429).

Religion, rivalry, and progress: the social Darwinism of Benjamin Kidd

Born near Bandon, Co. Cork, Benjamin Kidd (1858–1916) spent his early life in Ireland before moving to London in 1877 after accepting a post in the British civil service. An admirer of Darwin and an enthusiastic amateur naturalist, he wrote articles on birds, bees, flowers, and other species before publishing his most successful book, *Social Evolution*, in 1894. The book was such an immediate success that its author was to be remembered as 'the man who made his name in a day and with a single book' (Crook 1984: 52). The popularity of the book can be attributed partly to the central role that Kidd found for religion in his highly Darwinian account of struggle and rivalry in human life and human history.

Like other social Darwinists Kidd believes that progress in human history and in particular societies can be understood as the outcome of an unavoidable and never-ending process of competition, selection, and rejection. There is progress because there is struggle followed by victory and advancement. Individuals, cultures, societies, nations, civilizations, and 'races' make progress according as they succeed in overcoming the challenges of their circumstances. The motor of survival and advancement, however, is not just a desire to succeed but a preparedness to compete. Rivalry must exist at all levels of existence. The orderly and beautiful world that we see around us is the scene of incessant rivalry conducted not only between species but also between members of the same species. Even the plants in the green-sward beneath our feet are engaged in silent rivalry with each other, a rivalry that will result in some surviving and flourishing, others not. And what is true of the plants is true of all forms of life, including human life. Each human society can be viewed as an organism, and each member of each society – as the term 'member' already suggests – as a functioning part of that organism. Each organic society depends for its survival and advancement on the efficient integration of its constituent members. This means that the development of human beings as unique individuals is less important than their development as 'social creatures'. While the interests of individuals will remain all-important to themselves, no society will continue to be progressive unless it is able to subordinate the self-assertive interests of its members to its own larger interests. Historically, the most efficient way of achieving the necessary level of subordination is through religious belief and practice. The important cohesive feature of religious belief is the fact that it is super-rational, that it appeals not to the reason of the individual but to something beyond individual reason, namely, the collective heart of the social mass. Whereas reason tends to serve the private interests of the individual, religion tends to serve the collective interests of the larger society. Whereas private reason is a 'disintegrating principle', religious belief is the supreme 'integrating principle' that provides the most effective sanction for social conduct. Religion, as a super-rational principle of collective thought and action, is the best means of giving expression to 'the profound social instincts of the masses of the people' (1895: 162). Given the fact that religion is the key to social progress, it follows for Kidd that the strongest and most long-lasting societies will be the most religious ones. The human species itself, in order to ensure its survival as a species, 'must continue to grow ever more and more religious' (263).

A paradoxical element in Kidd's thinking lies in his startling conception of altruism and humanitarianism. He finds that the most successful religions are the most altruistic ones, precisely because they are the most efficient at encouraging and promoting the subordination of private self-interest to the social process. If this seems to contradict his emphasis elsewhere on competitiveness and rivalry, his response is that an altruistic religion (such as Christianity) leads to greater inclusiveness, to more accessible and democratic institutions, to greater equalities of opportunity. This means that more people are brought into the competitive arena, thus ensuring that the best individuals are given an opportunity to compete and are subsequently enabled to make their contribution to social progress. The spread of humanitarian ideals, the 'deepening and softening of character', has made possible 'that developmental movement whereby all the people are being slowly brought into the rivalry of life on equal conditions' (177). The reason that Christianity has tended to raise the Christian nations to their commanding place in the world is because it has contributed so much to the widespread equalizing of the conditions of rivalry and subsequent progress.

Despite his best efforts, Kidd cannot escape paradox and incoherence. The altruism that is supposed to bring more people into the arena of opportunity and rivalry is surely cancelled out by the competitive and selective ethos of that arena. Greater inclusiveness in this context is no more a mark of altruism than is, say, increasing the number of Christians to be thrown to the lions, or increasing the number of people to be pushed off the raft. There is certainly little evidence of altruism or humanitarianism in Kidd's own references to higher and lower types of humanity, to superior and inferior races, and to what he calls 'racial ascendancy'. Though he does not define superiority or ascendancy in terms of intellectual ability, it is not easy to find altruism or humanitarianism in any philosophy or ideology that explains progress in terms of the inevitable defeat and decline of less 'efficient' societies, nations, or cultures. Perhaps Kidd's most usefully provocative comment – made in the course of describing the effects of Western culture on conquered peoples – is that we, the conquerors, are too quick to assume that it is only our vices that have had a destructive effect on native or aboriginal peoples: 'the truth is that what may be called the virtues of our civilization are scarcely less fatal than its vices' (51). He complicates and spreads the responsibility for Western progress when he notes that the modern Anglo-Saxon may look forward to the time when wars will cease, and he may cheerfully set about beating his swords into ploughshares, 'but in his hands the implements of industry prove even more effective and deadly than the swords' (62).

Ethics and the primal nebula: Frances Power Cobbe

Not all difficulties with Darwinism were prompted by disparities between scientific theory and religious belief. A critique of Darwinism by Frances Power Cobbe (1822–1904) is noteworthy for the reason that it is made from an ethical rather than from a religious point of view. Described recently as one of 'the unsung heroines of the Victorian women's movement' (Raftery 1995: 91), Cobbe was an all-purpose philanthropist, active in the causes of animal as well as human rights. She was passionately and productively engaged with many of the defining intellectual issues of the Victorian era, and when she moved to London in the 1860s she took an active part in Victorian cultural life, becoming friendly with Mill, Tyndall, Cairnes, Matthew Arnold, and Darwin. Her thought is dominated by her moral convictions, and her objections to Darwinism and to 'the scientific spirit' generally are motivated by those convictions. A story which she tells of a conversation and later correspondence with Darwin is illustrative of her categorically moralistic stance. She recounts that while Darwin was working on *The Descent of Man* he happened to mention to her that he was trying to formulate a position on the moral sense in the human species. She immediately advised him to read Kant's *Groundwork of Morals*, and despite his apparent lack of interest sent him a copy of the book shortly after their conversation. On returning the book some time later, Darwin pointed to the contrast between Kant and himself, 'the one man a great philosopher looking exclusively into his own mind, the other a degraded wretch looking from the outside through apes and savages at the moral sense of mankind' (Cobbe 1894: 125–6). Cobbe usefully exploits Darwin's self-deprecatory distinction in order to identify two great and mutually antagonistic schools of thinkers – those who study human beings from the 'inside' and those who study them from the 'outside'. She opts for the former school, insisting that a philosophy that dwells exclusively on the outer facts of anthropology, regardless of human consciousness, 'must be worse than imperfect and incomplete. It resembles a treatise on the Solar System which should omit to notice the Sun' (126). For her, human consciousness is not merely a fact in the world but the greatest and most defining fact about human nature, one which it is morally irresponsible to ignore or belittle.

That Cobbe's objections to Darwinism are ethical rather than theological is apparent in her essay 'Darwinism in Morals' (1872) in
which she not only shows a preparedness to accept Darwin's 'fairytale
of science' but also expresses a degree of intellectual pleasure in its
novelty and originality. Responding specifically to *The Descent of
Man* she wonders why any 'free mind' should have purely religious
objections to Darwin's views, and suggests that when the orthodox
creationist account is compared with that of the slow evolution of
order, life, and intelligence from 'the immeasurable past of the
primal nebula's "fiery cloud," we have no language to express how
infinitely more religious is the story of modern science than that of
ancient tradition' (1872: 2–3). Nevertheless, she finds that Darwin's
doctrines, considered from the ethical point of view, are 'the most
dangerous which have ever been set forth since the days of Mandeville'
(11). Darwin's reduction of the moral sense to the level of social or sympathetic instincts fails to do justice to the fundamental and principled
requirements of morality. The physiology of instincts cannot begin to
'explain' the awful imperatives of conscience or the tremendous sentiments of repentance and remorse. The idea of right – what she calls 'the
sacred obligation of Rightfulness' – belongs to a category wholly
distinct from that of either social utility or animal instinct. The
moral sense is intuitive, a natural and innate element of human consciousness, not something derived from the accumulated experiences
of earlier generations. At the same time, while asserting that moral
sense is innate, Cobbe does not want it to be confused with the instinctive social behaviour among the lower animals. Repentance and
remorse have no ancestral precursor in the behaviour of even the
higher animals, nor do they serve any purely utilitarian origin or purpose. The transition from a sense of utility to a sense of moral obligation does not have a natural or evolutionary history. Her commitment
to moral intuitionism is such that, despite her own religious beliefs,
she does not require morality to have a religious origin. Her position
is encapsulated in her claim that the sentiment of remorse, 'though
it allies itself with religious fears, seems to me not so much to be
derived from religious considerations as to be in itself one of the
roots of religion' (23).

In a later essay on 'the scientific spirit' Cobbe is more astringent in
her criticism of Darwinism and of the scientific mindset in general.

She rejects without reservation John Tyndall's boast that science is 'the noblest growth of modern times' (Tyndall 1865: x), and enters into a pessimistic reflection on the destructive capacity of science. She objects in particular to the intrusiveness and oppressiveness of the scientific spirit 'in regions where it has no proper work' (1888: 7), and detects everywhere 'a materialising tendency' that proposes to explain everything in terms of physical processes. The student of science will view his mother's tears not as expressions of her sorrow, 'but as solutions of muriates and carbonates of soda, and of phosphates of lime', and he will conclude that the tears were caused not by his own heartlessness 'but by cerebral pressure on her lachrymal glands' (12). The scientific spirit, in her view, is a callous and irreverent spirit, and has 'sprung a mine under the deepest foundations of Morality' (23). In particular, the loftier ideals of duty and goodness are being replaced by the Darwinian notion of instincts, all of which will lead to a lowering of the standards of human behaviour. The expression 'the descent of man', normally uttered in the scientific context of evolutionary theory, has for Cobbe a tellingly moral connotation.

VARIETIES OF IRISH IDEALISM

From William Rowan Hamilton to Oscar Wilde

Idealism in the broadest sense may be understood as a philosophical outlook that tends to emphasize the formative activity of the mind in the perception and understanding of the world, as if to say that the mind meets the world more than half-way. Reality as we perceive it is supposed to reflect the projections and structures of the mind itself, and is therefore in some sense mind-dependent, at least for some of the features it appears to have. In its more extreme or metaphysical form idealism regards mind, self, or ideas as having more reality than the material world. A strong metaphysical idealism may so compromise the 'externality' of the material world that the world loses its very objectivity. Berkeley was an idealist in this strong metaphysical sense, since he rejected the very idea of matter and made mind or spirit the be-all and end-all of existence. A more moderate or 'compromised' form of idealism – which may be called critical or transcendental idealism – can be extrapolated from the work of the influential eighteenth-century German philosopher Immanuel Kant, who made a distinction between, on the one hand, the world as it appears to the internal faculties and structures of our minds and, on the other hand, the world of things-in-themselves which exists beyond the reach of our knowing faculties. Kant's special brand of transcendental idealism began to have an appreciable influence in Britain and Ireland towards the middle of the nineteenth century. The most significant date in this context is 1838, the year of publication of the first complete English translation (by Francis Haywood) of Kant's *Critique of Pure Reason*. By the second half of the nineteenth century this interest was also manifesting itself in Ireland. In the preface to his *Immanuel Kant in England* René Wellek refers to an 'Irish group' of Kantian scholars who contributed substantially to the development of interest in Kant and Kantianism. This group would have included J.P. Mahaffy (1839–1919), W.H.S. Monck (1839–1915), Thomas Kingsmill Abbott (1829–1913), and J.H. Bernard (1860–1927), all of whom translated works by Kant, or gave courses on his thought, or published commentaries on him (see Furlong 1973). Mahaffy, for example, published a commentary on the *Critique of Pure Reason* in 1866, while Monck's introduction to Kant's philosophy appeared in 1872. Abbott's translation of the *Critique of Practical Reason*, first published in 1873, remained the standard English translation until well into the next century.

However, prior to the formation of this identifiable group of Kantian academics the German philosopher had found at least two disciples among Irish thinkers. One of the earliest accounts in English of Kant's philosophy was contained in a short work by J.A. O'Keeffe, a young Irishman about whom little is known other than that he studied medicine in Leipzig before moving to London, where his *Essay on the Progress of Human Understanding* was published in the autumn of 1795 (see Wellek 1931: 6–7; Micheli 1993: 35–9). The *Essay* aroused only a short-lived and mostly critical response in England, partly because it presented Kant as a radical secular, anti-clerical, humanist thinker. O'Keeffe signals his own radicalism by including Montaigne, Locke, Shaftesbury, and Hutcheson on his list of 'the best writers on moral philosophy'. He puts himself firmly on the side of a militant enlightenment republicanism by blaming the English civil war on 'priest-craft and priest-jealousies', at the same time commending Oliver Cromwell for rendering the people of England 'respectable and awful in the eyes of kings' (1795: 36). The only fault he finds in Cromwell is that he was 'too enlightened for his times' (35). A letter-writer to *The English Review*, clearly upset by the subversive tenor of O'Keeffe's pamphlet, upbraided the journal's editor for reviewing 'with seeming approbation, such poisonous trash as Dr. O'Keeffe's essay, and Kant's philosophy' (Micheli 1993: 47). The small historical importance of O'Keeffe's essay lies not in its advocacy of Kant but in the fact that O'Keeffe includes in the body of the essay the first English translation of a Kantian text, in this case the opening paragraphs of the introduction to the second edition of *The Critique of Pure Reason* (see Wellek 1931: 6–7). The first paragraph of the Irish doctor's ground-breaking translation is as follows:

> It is not at all to be doubted that our knowledge arises from experience. In what other manner, else, should our mental faculty of knowing things be awakened to its duty? Is this not performed by objects that strike our senses, and effectuate representations, partly of themselves, partly by exciting the industry of our understanding, in order to compare, link, or sever them; and work up, in this manner, the raw stuff of sensual impressions to the knowledge of objects? The know-ing of this object is called experience. If we measure our actions with time, no kind of knowledge can arise in us prior to experience, because all things begin with it; but even allowing all our knowledge to begin with experience that is no reason that all of it should derive from the same source; because it can be very possible, that the knowledge acquired by experience forms a composition of what is conveyed to the mind by impression, together with what the capacity of our own knowledge, when excited by sensible impressions, can produce of itself.
>
> (O'Keeffe 1795: 47–8)

Before the complete Haywood translation of the *Critique* appeared in 1838, Kant's thought had already found another eager disciple in one of Ireland's greatest and most original mathematicians, William

Rowan Hamilton (1805–1865). Hamilton, whose work on the algebra of quaternions has ensured him a place in the history of mathematical discovery, was born in Dublin. He received his early education, mainly in classics and languages, from his uncle in Trim, Co. Meath, but was largely self-taught in mathematics. It seems that he had thoroughly mastered Newton's *Principia* before he entered Trinity College in 1823. While at Trinity he so impressed his tutors that he was appointed professor of astronomy in 1827, a post which at the same time made him director of the observatory at Dunsink. Alongside his study of languages and mathematics Hamilton also cultivated an interest in poetry, including poetic composition. His biographer Thomas Hankins suggests that Hamilton's enthusiasm for poetry preceded his enthusiasm for mathematics, and that 'his love of the ideal and abstract was confirmed in his poetry before it was confirmed in his science' (1980: 386). Such was his passion for poetry and his desire to excel in the art and craft of composition that he made the acquaintance of Wordsworth during a visit to the Lake District in the autumn of 1827. Through Wordsworth he came to meet Coleridge, but even before this face-to-face meeting he had studied Coleridge's speculative writing and had found there a form of idealist thinking that appealed to his own developing intuitions about the nature of reason, ideas, and knowledge. Central to Coleridge's philosophy – which is derived largely from Kant – is the belief that what takes priority in the quest for truth is not experience or empirical content but valid deductions from intuitively grounded ideas or principles. This romantic emphasis on the illuminative, truth-seeking, form-finding power of the mind greatly appealed to Hamilton. His idealism is perhaps more truly Kantian than that of Coleridge, tempered as it is by an anxiety to acknowledge the limits as well as the power of the mind. In a memorandum towards an essay on the philosophy of astronomy he begins by drawing attention to the transcendental dimension of astronomy – that is, to those elements of it that are *a priori*, that precede observation and make such observation possible. He notes that every treatise on astronomy employs mathematical conceptions and has recourse to exact reasoning, all of which constitute the purely mental or intellectual input of the science. Astronomy, as a transcendental system as well as a science of observation, 'should seek its unity *within*, rather than without; in consciousness rather than in observation; should ever and anon return to the mind as centre, rather than remain long in the external world of things' (Graves 1885: II, 304). At the same time he warns that it is not acceptable 'that the *a priori* power should usurp the province which belongs to the *a posteriori*' (II, 305). In other words, while the mind and its internal structures bring form to astronomy, experience and observation deliver the matter or content of it.

That Hamilton carried his idealism into his everyday life – that he was somewhat disengaged from practical realities – is suggested by the invitation that closes a letter to him from the novelist Maria Edgeworth: 'Take your head from the stars or from transcendental mathematics, and come and enjoy folly and friendship with yours affectionately, Maria Edgeworth' (Graves 1885: II, 384). A more questionable level of disengagement is suggested by the virtual absence from his letters of expressions of concern for the victims of the great famine. His first biographer Robert Percival Graves excuses him by reminding us of the absorbing nature of his studies before assuring us that he was in any case a most considerate and passionate neighbour, 'thinking no small act of kindness beneath him' (1885: II, 556). Yet there is a note of reproach in a letter from his friend, Aubrey de Vere, dated 3 February 1847. After mentioning his involvement with the organizing of relief committees, soup kitchens, and agricultural societies, de Vere continues:

> While you are ranging beyond the visible bounds of the universe in mathematical poetry, or 'sounding on a dim and perilous way' in regions where few can follow you . . . my time is all taken up with details which would be insignificant, if they were not just now so nearly connected with some of the humblest yet some of the closest ties of our humanity.
>
> (Graves 1885: II, 556)

In his surprising reply, sent from Dunsink Observatory a few days later, Hamilton seems to confirm his distance from de Vere and his charitable concerns when he says that he does not wonder at his correspondent's time being taken up with 'the relief of the temporal wants of our poor fellow-countrymen'. He then makes an honest, if disconcertingly high-minded, declaration of how he perceives his patriotic duty at this time. As he sees it, his best hope of being useful to Ireland lies in the pursuit of 'those abstract and seemingly unpractical contemplations to which my nature has so strong a bent', and adds:

> If the fame of our country shall be in any degree raised thereby, and if the industry of a particular kind thus shown shall tend to remove the prejudice which supposes Irishmen to be incapable of perseverance, some step, however slight, may be thereby made towards the establishment of an intellectual confidence which cannot be, in the long run, unproductive of temporal and material benefits also to this unhappy but deeply interesting island and its inhabitants.
>
> (Graves 1885: II, 558)

The influence of idealist thinking in the later decades of the nineteenth century was not derived from Kant alone. The most passionate advocate of idealism during this period is William Graham (1839–1911), who found his inspiration in a variety of sources. Born in Saintfield, Co. Down, Graham had an intellectually ecumenical career, even by nineteenth-century standards. Graduating from Trinity College in mathematics and physics, he earned academic prizes in logic, ethics, metaphysics, and English composition, before he eventually became professor of jurisprudence and political economy at Queen's College, Belfast. His publications range from an essay on science to a treatise on socialism and another on free trade, but of most interest in this context is his earliest and most provocative work, *Idealism: An Essay* (1872), in which he sets himself the task of defending and promoting the extreme metaphysical visions of Berkeley and Hegel. Though prepared to concede that his favourite idealists have not achieved perfect systems, he is happy to fire over their heads the better to let their full philosophical resources be deployed against the twin evils of materialism and positivism (or scientism). Both of these perspectives are condemned because they 'proceed from a false and shallow estimate of Human Nature' (1872: xvii). Berkeley and Hegel are 'the only hope' for the future spiritual life of humanity because they offer the most complete antidote to these new theoretical debasers of the human spirit. Materialism debases the human spirit because it makes thought itself a function of the brain and treats the human being as nothing more than a highly elaborated physical organism. Darwinism is the most recent variety of materialism, since it tries to trace an unbroken continuity from protoplasm to man, from chemical action to the energy of the soul, even filling up the gap that was assumed to exist between vegetable and animal life. Positivism has an equally debasing effect when it bids the human soul 'to dream only of material comforts', tempting it to look no further than the reality of 'perishing phenomena' for its enlightenment (xx).

In Graham's view, a spiritual life worthy of the name cannot flourish in a materialistic ethos. For the idealist it is not physical matter but consciousness that is the deepest thing in the world. Berkeley's uplift-ing and 'spiritualizing' intuition is that consciousness is the first and only reality, that everything else is real only in the measure that it appears to consciousness, that matter per se does not exist. Hegel's equally uplifting intuition is that thought or reason is the only reality. Hegel's reason is like 'a lamp that sheds a sphere of light around itself', a sphere of light which is the universe itself, the whole of intelligible existence (67). Graham seems to prefer Berkeley's subjective or theo-logical idealism since it is more thoroughgoing in its claim that nothing exists apart from consciousness. Berkeley affirms more emphatically than any other thinker that, apart from mind, things and relationships have no independent existence. These are made by the mind, 'address themselves to a Mind, have no meaning but for a Mind, and cease to exist with the cessation of Consciousness or Mind' (50–1). Hegel, on the other hand, allows for the existence of 'a shadowy universal' called reason, a mode of rational existence that is not always or necessarily conscious. For a true Berkeleian such an abstraction is as much a philosophical fiction as matter. For Berkeley, conscious intelligence, either subjective or divine, 'was from the begin-ning, is, and ever must be, the Universe' (51). No logical space is left for the existence of anything apart from, or prior to, consciousness, not even for the unconscious rational thought of Hegel.

There is a patriotic dimension to Graham's preference for Berkeley's idealism. Just as some English historians have found Locke to be central to the literary inheritance of England, so we may say of Berkeley that 'his name is one which as Irishmen we cannot now, after History has produced her verdict, suffer to be depreciated' (130). The Scots likewise would be justified in laying claim to the centrality of

Hume. He adds that these three thinkers – Locke, Berkeley, and Hume – not only represent their respective nations in European philosophy but also represent three great schools of philosophy, namely, realism, idealism, and scepticism. There is a suggestion here that idealism, especially in the radical version defended by Berkeley, is a distinctly Irish philosophy and is therefore entitled to particularly sympathetic attention from the Irish. His patriotic defensiveness about Berkeley's philosophy may account for his dismissive treatment of Thomas Kingsmill Abbott's critique of Berkeley. In his *Sight and Touch* (1864) Abbott had attempted a rebuttal of Berkeley's theory of vision and by implication of his idealism. He set out to show that distance in particular is not, as Berkeley had claimed, a matter of judgement based on learnt associations and visual cues but is revealed directly to the eye, that the eye is designed by nature to register extension, space, and distance, and is indeed so good at its task that it can 'receive impressions at once from objects within a finger-breadth and as remote as the stars' (1864: 177). He pointed to the predominance of sight as a means of survival in the animal world, suggesting that both animals and human beings 'would be ill provided indeed if brightness and visible magnitude were the only means of perceiving distance' (171). His solution to 'Molyneux's problem' was that the man born blind and subsequently made to see would in fact be competent to name correctly the globe and cube which he had previously only experienced by touch. Because he assumed that Berkeley's idealism turns on a particular theory of vision, Abbott seemed to think that by demonstrating the visible distance and 'externality' of objects he had thereby undermined Berkeley's case for idealism. Graham, however, simply rejects the claim that idealism rests on a particular theory of vision, insisting that the idealist can accept either Berkeley's or Abbott's solution to the question of how distance is really perceived. His argument is brief. Whether 'externality' is revealed by touch or by vision, it is in any case something which exists in and through consciousness, and is therefore 'internal' in the idealist's special sense of the term. In other words, distant objects revealed to sight are no more external to consciousness than nearby objects revealed to touch. Both sight and touch are modes of conscious experience; and their objects, whether seen or felt, whether near or remote, are equally objects of consciousness and therefore internal to it. Given the impeccable Berkeleian logic of Graham's position, it is difficult to avoid exclaiming 'Touché' on his behalf.

One of the best contributions to the history of modern philosophy published in Ireland in the nineteenth century is Thomas Ebenezer Webb's *The Veil of Isis* (1885), a series of substantial essays on modern idealism. Though serving as county court judge in Donegal at the time of the book's publication, Webb had served stints as an academic at Trinity College, Dublin, first as professor of moral philosophy and later as regius professor of laws. His loyalty to Trinity is reflected in the central position he gives to the college in the course of his 'nationalistic' advocacy of Irish thought. He agrees that the Irish are 'naturally borne to dialectics', as evidenced by their reputation abroad 'as able logicians and metaphysicians' (1885: 1–2), and is duly pleased to observe that Trinity has from the beginning accommodated itself to the national bent. The college gave a prominent place in its curriculum to mental science and to public discussion of classical philosophical texts. At the same time, it was not slow to recognize new genius and was ahead of other reputable institutions, including Oxford and Cambridge, in appreciating the worth of Locke's *Essay concerning Human Understanding*, which was from an early stage 'the recognized text-book of the schools at Dublin' (3). The college produced graduates as distinguished as Peter Browne, William King, Edmund Burke, W.E.H. Lecky, and of course George Berkeley. Webb, having begun his essay on Berkeley with a celebration of the Irish contribution to the history of thought, goes so far as to declare that Ireland may claim the distinction of having produced three great philosophers, each of whom founded an epoch in the history of thought. Eriugena may be considered the father of the scholastic system, Hutcheson the founder of the modern school of speculative Scottish philosophy, and Berkeley the first to explicitly maintain a theory of absolute idealism (1).

In *The Veil of Isis*, Webb gives a thorough and sympathetic, though finally critical account, of six idealist systems, including not only the systems of Berkeley, Kant, and Hegel, but also the 'problematical' idealism of David Hume and the 'cosmothetical' idealism of another Scottish philosopher, Thomas Reid. When he reflects on the experience of engaging with such a variety of 'shadowy and shifting systems' he feels that he has scaled the lofty peaks of thought only to find himself giddy and wrapped in a swirling mist (329). Yet he believes that something has been gained, that it is something to have climbed the mountain and seen the mists. He finds that he has after all learned a salutary lesson, even if it is for the most part a negative one, an experience of loss. What he has lost is the desire for dogmatic certainty, even with regard to fundamental matters. He is happy to learn that it is as impossible to prove thought to be a function of matter as it is to prove matter to be a function of thought (330). Instead of regretting this newfound uncertainty or agnosticism he welcomes it and sees it as rendering a service to religion, as indeed extending the boundaries of faith. Even in the most ordinary events of life we live by a kind of faith and not by certainty, for 'the whole universe is concealed from us by the veil of our ideas' (332). It is just this sense of concealment that should induce a sense of awe or mystery. The human intellect cannot help but wonder what exists beyond the veil, despite the fact that, as Kant pointed out, it cannot provide an answer. The human mind is therefore meaningfully haunted by the supposition of something beyond the scope of what it can know. This sense of the unknown, always understood as the source of religion, may also be considered the source of all philosophy. The different idealist thinkers may not be able to convert us to any particular system but taken together they induce in us the mental state of the ancient Egyptian who once bowed before the veiled statue of Isis and worshipped it as the symbol of the unknown God (332).

The life and thought of Thomas Maguire (1831–1889) present us with a dramatic example of the chasm that can open up between the high-minded aspirations of an individual's speculative reflections and the more low-thinking compromises of the lived historical life. Maguire was born in Dublin into a Catholic merchant family. He entered Trinity College in 1851, graduating in 1855, and began an academic career that included a stint as professor of Latin at Queen's College, Galway. In 1880 he had the distinction of being the first Catholic to be elected to a fellowship in Trinity after Fawcett's Act of 1873 had removed 'religious disabilities' at the traditionally Protestant institution. He was appointed to the professorship of moral philosophy there in 1882. During his time as an academic Maguire would lead a kind of double life. As an academic philosopher, his sympathies lay in the direction of idealism. He was not only an expositor and interpreter of the metaphysics of Plato but also wrote defensively about other forms of idealism, including the transcendentalism of Kant. He concludes his lively pamphlet *Mr. Balfour on Kant and Transcendentalism* (1889) with the declaration that best encapsulates his point of view, that 'there is in human experience an element which is not of experience, and this is the basis of all philosophy, and of all religion' (1889: 39).

It is Maguire's advocacy of idealism that makes it difficult to understand his direct personal and material involvement in one of the most notorious conspiracies in Irish history (see Foley 1994). If Maguire is known at all to historians of nineteenth-century Ireland it is not for his scholarly treatises on Plato but for his role in the scandal of the Parnell forgeries. The sorry story of the forgeries began in 1887 when the London *Times* published a series of articles entitled 'Parnellism and Crime', purporting to show that Charles Stewart Parnell and members of the Irish Parliamentary Party had supported criminal conspiracy and violence during the Land War. In one article it was alleged that Parnell had expressed approval of the so-called 'Phoenix Park Murders', the assassination in Phoenix Park on 6 May 1882 of two high-ranking government officials, Lord Frederick Cavendish and T.H. Burke. A special commission was set up to investigate these charges against Parnell, and it soon emerged that the incriminating letters were supplied by Edward Caulfield Houston, the secretary of the Irish Loyal and Patriotic Union, a unionist association that had been founded in 1885 to oppose home rule. It was also revealed that Houston had in turn received the letters from a journalist by the name of Richard Pigott, that Pigott had sought and been paid money for the letters – and that much of this money had been provided by Thomas Maguire. During the investigation by the special commission, Pigott confessed that the incriminating letters were in fact forgeries. Shortly after making this confession he fled to Paris, and then to Madrid. On 1 March, in Madrid, just as he was about to be confronted by British policemen, Pigott shot and killed himself. By this date also, as if by some kind of fateful coincidence, Thomas Maguire himself was already dead. In fact, on the day that Pigott fled to Paris, Maguire was found dead in his rooms in London. And so ended, in sad and compromised circumstances, the life of one Irish idealist. Newspaper reports at the time of his death made a point of noting the contrast between Maguire's exalted vocation and his involvement in the Pigott scandal. 'Tis a thousand pities,' lamented an editorial in the *County Gentleman*, 'that this most eminent of English Platonists should have been drawn into the toils' (Foley 1994: 188).

All the idealisms so far discussed have been of the metaphysical or transcendental variety. But idealism can also refer to any approach or methodology that invests ideas with the power to make things happen, especially the power to bring about, shape, and 'explain' the events of human history. This form of idealism we may designate historical idealism to distinguish it from historical materialism, an opposing approach which emphasizes the economic rather than 'mental' determinants of collective human action. Ireland's greatest nineteenth-century historian, W.E.H. Lecky (1838–1903), is an historical idealist in this sense. His idealism is most evident in his *History of the Rise and Influence of the Spirit of Rationalism in Europe* (1865) in which he tracks the decline of the supernaturalist mode of thought and its replacement by the secular and rationalistic ethos that now characterizes modern European culture. Though Lecky is a long way from endorsing the metaphysical system of Hegel, there are glancing touches of the Hegelian sense of history in the trajectory he traces for the rise of the spirit of rationalism. Every turn away from tradition and towards modernity, every step away from barbarism and towards civilization, every diminution in superstition, every increase in knowledge is taken to represent the advancement of the rationalistic spirit. Religion is taken to be the main site of the advancement of the rationalist mode of thought. In its formative period religion is characterized by credulity, superstition, and dogmatism, by magical thinking and the practice of witchcraft, and by widespread belief in miraculous events and miraculous powers. This is as true of Christianity as it is of the pagan religions. The history of pre-modern Christianity is a history of credulous, magical, and miraculous thinking, culminating in a vivid and pervasive sense of malevolent Satanic presence – a sense that extended well into the period of the reformation. That even the early reformers were still in the grip of this sense is illustrated by the story of Luther who, while living in the monastery of Wittenberg, constantly heard the devil making noises in the cloisters, eventually becoming so accustomed to these noises that, 'on one occasion, having been awakened by the sound, he perceived that it was *only* the Devil, and accordingly went to sleep again' (Lecky 1910: I, 60).

This persistence of the sense of Satanic presence is not interpreted by Lecky as a mark against the progressive credentials of the reformation but rather as proof that change comes about slowly and unevenly, and is often dependent on the thoughts and actions of an initially small group of individuals. There was inherent in reformation theology a pre-disposition towards progress, expressed in a certain scepticism about the kinds of miracle-working and magical thinking that were a feature of the unreformed church. This scepticism would eventually materialize as Protestant rationalism, but first the input of some individual sceptical minds was necessary, especially the input of secular minds that had managed to escape the influence of religious indoctrination. One such mind was that of the sixteenth-century French essayist Michel de Montaigne, who applied to every question 'a judgement entirely unclouded by the imaginations of theologians' (Lecky 1910: I, 92). Montaigne's originality lay not in the quality of his arguments but 'in the general tone and character of his mind' (I, 93). He dared to examine all questions in the light of humane common sense, 'by a measure of probability which is furnished by daily experience' (I, 93). His sense of the fallibility of the human intellect and human institutions led him to suspect that witchcraft, for example, might simply be a delusion. His sensible and secular reflections contributed to the destruction of the practice of witchcraft, not by logically and systematically refuting the arguments of believers in the practice, but by making the public 'more and more sensible of its intrinsic absurdity' (I, 95).

For Lecky, then, progress is a matter of new attitudes, new mindsets, new gestures, new tones of voice, new barely spoken assumptions about how the world works. Even when discussing what he calls 'the industrial history of rationalism' he still speaks in terms of character, spirit, and modes of thought. In the course of expressing admiration for the discoveries of political economy, he makes a distinction between the two great philosophies that have been at loggerheads historically, namely, the ascetic and industrial philosophies. Whereas the watchword of the first is mortification and self-sacrifice, the watchword of the second is development; whereas the first seeks to diminish, constrain, and deny desires, the second seeks to stimulate, multiply, and satisfy those same desires. Modern civilization is characterized by the triumph of the latter, by the rise of the industrial spirit, the spirit of self-interest, of utility, of satisfaction, and ultimately of materialism. In a long two-volume work that largely highlights the virtues of modernity and progress, Lecky waits until the last paragraph of the second volume to admit that there is a shadow resting upon the 'otherwise brilliant picture' that he has painted of the history of rationalism. He rehearses briefly what has been achieved – the destruction of witchcraft, the decline of religious persecution, the emancipation of suffering nationalities – but then acknowledges that, because the heroic spirit of self-sacrifice has indeed been replaced by the spirit of industry, 'it is impossible to deny that we have lost something in our progress' (1910: II, 375).

We should leave the last words of this chapter to the most charming and sanguine of nineteenth-century Irish idealists, namely, Oscar Wilde (1854–1900), the Dublin-born playwright, poet, novelist, fairy tale writer, and essayist whose life ended as the new century began. Wilde's idealistic, utopian vision of a future society is contained in his exceptional essay 'The Soul of Man under Socialism', first published in *The Fortnightly Review* in 1891, and subsequently published in book form in 1895, shortly after his conviction and imprisonment for homosexual offences. Defiantly rejecting the conception of socialism as a new kind of despotism, Wilde argued, without any hint of paradox, for a version of socialism that should be of value 'simply because it will lead to Individualism' (1994: 1175). By getting rid of private property, socialism will liberate individuals from economic tyranny and enable them to fully realize the personality and perfection that is in them. Since the true perfection of humankind lies not in what an individual has but in what he or she is, it follows that, with the abolition of private property, 'we shall have true, beautiful, healthy Individualism. Nobody will waste his time in accumulating things and the symbols of things. One will live' (1178). Who then will perform all the tedious and unfulfilling work that needs to be done? Machines, according to Wilde. He is close to Marx in his vision of the role of machinery. Under our present property system, human beings are the slaves of machinery, and machinery competes against man, but under proper conditions, machinery will serve man. The task of the socialist state will be to organize industry in such a way that all dull, dirty, and dreadful work is done by machines: 'The State is to make what is useful. The individual is to make what is beautiful' (1183).

Lest it be assumed that Wilde's essay is too light or idiosyncratic to be taken seriously, it should be noted that it contains deep and resonant echoes of the ideas of other reformist or idealistic thinkers. As well as the echo of Marx mentioned above, there are echoes of William Thompson, John Stuart Mill, and even Lecky. Like Thompson, Wilde conceives of the best society as a voluntary one, declaring that 'all association must be quite voluntary. It is only in voluntary associations that man is fine' (1175). Like Mill and the utilitarians, he declares that pleasure or happiness is nature's test: 'When man is happy, he is in harmony with himself and his environment' (1197). Again like Mill he refuses to equate individualism with egotism or selfishness. Selfishness is not living as one wishes to live, 'it is asking others to live as one wishes to live' (1194). Individualism, by contrast, proceeds according to the unselfish principle of live and let live, acknowledging the infinite variety of human types as a delightful thing. Like Lecky, Wilde accepts that society evolves and that certain phases of belief and behaviour are necessary or inevitable, given the circumstances in which people find themselves. While lamenting the capacity of human beings to cause suffering, and even to make a virtue of it in the form of self-torture and self-sacrifice, he nonetheless accepts it as historically inevitable that pain should be put forward as a mode of self-realization. He acknowledges that no one who lived in modern Russia – the Russia of the closing decades of the nineteenth century – could possibly realize his perfection except by pain and sacrifice (1196). But Wilde also wants to insist, like Lecky, that such conditions are historical ones, and should not be mistaken for the universal human condition. Pain is not the ultimate mode of human perfection – it is merely a provisional protest, a symptom of what is wrong, unhealthy, and unjust. Since the dawn of the renaissance in Europe with its new ideals of beauty, the modern world has been turning away from the medieval Christian worship of pain and sacrifice, and has been turning instead towards science and socialism as ways of eliminating poverty, injustice, and suffering. The modern world aims at an individualism 'expressing itself through joy' (1197); and this new individualism will achieve what the Greeks sought for but could not realize except in thought, and what the renaissance also sought for but could not completely realize except in art (1197).

Such thinking is, of course, utopian, but Wilde implicitly refuses to accept that *utopian* means *irrelevant*, *quixotic*, or *impractical*. The following quotation, asserted with defiant and commendable flair, has a poignancy for modern readers that it did not have for Wilde himself, who was too trustful and too hopeful to have foreseen a century of war, holocaust, and tyranny in Europe, much of it perpetrated in the name of the new society or the new humanity: 'A map of the world that does not include Utopia is not worth even glancing at, for it leaves out the one country at which Humanity is always landing. And when Humanity lands there, it looks out, and, seeing a better country, sets sail. Progress is the realisation of Utopias' (1184).

9

BETWEEN EXTREMITIES

Irish Thought in the Twentieth Century

The kind of thought that we have been examining throughout most of the foregoing chapters – passionate, engaged, public-spirited thought – almost ceases to exist in the course of the twentieth century. The reasons for this decline have to do in large part with the decline in popular sectarian theological controversy. When thought is predominantly theological, as it was during much of the early modern period, it is available to any believer who has an informed and intelligent grasp of the central religious concepts on which debate and controversy rest. In other words, theological thought, no matter how serious or 'difficult' it is, has the potential to become controversial and 'popular', in the sense that it can become widely available to people who are not themselves theologians. Moreover, when theological thought in a religious age is primed and fuelled by change, reformation, and division within established churches, it achieves a level of controversy that embraces all those who have a spiritually vested interest in either conserving the old beliefs or switching to the new improved varieties. But the cultural ethos of contemporary European and Western cultural life is not as religious as it once was. The period of profound and turbulent theological controversy has ended for sure. Not only have the reformed churches become established in the aftermath of earlier controversies, they have become established within the context of liberal-democratic states in which all controversy is governed (for the most part) by the official Queensbury rules of tolerance and freedom of conscience. When

P.J. McGrath published his *Believing in God* in 1995 there was no question of its receiving the same incendiary treatment that John Toland's *Christianity not Mysterious* did three centuries earlier, despite the fact that the more recent book is a serious critique of the standard arguments for the existence of God. At one level this latter-day restraint may be considered a sign of cultural maturity, but at another level it is a sign of cultural indifference. The arena for fascinating, sometimes profound, often divisive theological debate has been reduced to the size of a side-show peopled mainly by disengaged cranks and transient cult-figures, providing only an occasional pitch for a serious theological thinker like McGrath. Without an overarching religious ethos, the most serious attempts at theological controversy are largely unsuccessful and unpopular, while the contributions from the more cranky sorts of controversialist rarely merit serious or sustained attention. The decline of the religious ethos and the disappearance of the golden age of theological controversy have reduced the opportunity for the kind of complex but still accessible thought that was such a feature of the seventeenth, the eighteenth, and (to a diminishing extent) the nineteenth century.

There are other reasons for the decline in profound and accessible forms of thought. As well as the decline in theological controversy there has occurred a stagnation, even a deterioration, in political and ideological controversy. There has been a particularly marked decline in the depth and resourcefulness of conservative or 'counter-enlightenment' thinking. Intelligent and well-meaning conservatism – a form of conscientious objection to the dominantly progressive modes of thought – should not only make its own contribution to the thought of an era, but, more importantly, should serve to stimulate intelligent and resourceful responses from the ruling advocates of progressive, technocratic, liberal-democratic culture. The paradox of the dominant culture is that, while formally allowing for the expression of oppositional opinion, it has not been very good at drawing out intelligent conservative opinion and, as a consequence, has not been able to reap the benefit of continually answering the challenge of such opinion. Such has been the success of liberal-democratic culture that the best conservatives have become more accepting than their alarmed predecessors of the practices and institutions of liberal democracy, including secular and utilitarian values in legislation, and populist values in education. It is unthinkable that the late twentieth century could have produced gifted reactionaries like Burke or Swift. It is impossible to imagine a platform for a Burkean-style defender of traditional values or a Swiftian-style opponent of modern technocratic values. The old values that required all the resources of Burke's rhetoric to defend have been indefensible for a long time; and the projectors of Lagado have united so successfully with the speculators of Laputa that they have long ago met Swift's challenge of doubling the blades of grass on a spot of ground.

Whatever the cause for the decline of wise or intelligent conservatism, the absence of a serious intellectual challenge from that quarter has led to the frequently complacent and unreflective reiteration of standard liberal and radical philosophies. Contemporary liberal, radical, or emancipative thought has not advanced far beyond the nineteenth-century premises and intuitions of Mill or Marx. If there have been 'developments', they have occurred either within the departments of universities or within the editorial policies of small-circulation political journals, and have hardly entered the arena of sustainable public controversy. If the names of some innovative thinkers (Lacan, Foucault, Derrida) are known to the public at large it is mainly because of the reported eccentricity or obscurity of their published work, or because of the cultic posturing of their followers and interpreters, and not because of a widespread appreciation of the substance of their thought. Indeed, the very notoriety of these thinkers turns on their strangeness, their unavailability to the public. Of course, there continues to be public debate and controversy, especially in matters of political decision-making, but much of it comes from journalists, activists, campaigners, and political party representatives, little of it generated by local independent thinkers of genius or talent. Outside the academy and some fields of journalism (including what may be called 'activist' or 'advocacy' journalism) there is a lack of sustained, non-trivial public interest in the *arguments* for liberty, equality, or justice. This is not necessarily due to apathy, cynicism, anti-intellectualism, or idea fatigue on the part of the public, but rather to a pervasive and questionable assumption that the basic arguments have been won, even if it is at the same time acknowledged that governments and societies have yet to deliver the goods. It is assumed, even if very vaguely, that the fundamental questions of principle have been settled – and this in itself leads to a decline in controversial thought, since it is issues of principle that trigger and sustain the best and most challenging kinds of thought.

It might be imagined that the first decades of the Irish twentieth century, because they were a time of nationalist cultural revival, must also have produced an estimable revivalist philosophy or a note-worthy revivalist thinker. But this they did not do. The defensive cultural nationalism of the early decades was deliberately inward-looking and retrospective, valuing predominantly those cultural activities and practices that were supposed to manifest the imaginative genius of the ancient, pre-invasion, legendary Gael. The revivalist movement was much more concerned with the encouragement of 'authentic', nationally distinctive forms of sport, song, dance, and literature than with the stimulation of suspiciously abstract or univer-salizing modes of enquiry. Authenticity is more likely to be found in the expressive arts, it seems, than in the more abstract modes of thought that look to the universals of logic rather than to the par-ticulars of native mentality. Even Sophie Bryant, one of the most sophisticated and perceptive of the revivalist thinkers, was determined to find the sources of 'the Irish modern movement . . . in the deep instincts begotten of the dim historic past' (1913: 161). She found, for example, that the distinctive racial gifts of the Irish included a concrete imaginativeness that always 'lies in wait on abstract thought, with all the eyes of the senses open, ready to dash in the colours of reality' (74). While she detected a certain commendable 'boldness of speculation' in the thought of Eriugena and Berkeley, she seemed to value both thinkers not because of the logical or argumentative quali-ties of their philosophies but because they both displayed 'the same Irish touch' (74). The Irish touch, moreover, is the touch of the past, the touch of ancient ancestral mentors who had already achieved a spiritual reality – 'a grip on the eternal truth of real civilization' (287) – long before the first Norman set foot on Irish soil. This defer-ence of the revivalist thinkers towards the ideas and institutions of the past is perhaps best exemplified in Patrick Pearse's revealing essay, 'Ghosts', in which he represented himself as a kind of medium through which the past masters of nationalist thought might speak. Self-sacrificially reneging on any original spark in himself he chose to cite and quote uncritically – and even without comment – the words of the founding fathers of the separatist faith, the 'four master minds' of Wolfe Tone, Thomas Davis, James Fintan Lalor, and John Mitchel (1916: 227). He acknowledged, significantly, that there had been greater thinkers than these four, immediately naming Berkeley, Swift, and Burke as the great political thinkers of Anglo-Ireland before Tone. He even conceded that he could have constructed the case for nationalism from the work of these three, but decided that such an exercise was irrelevant to his purpose – irrelevant, because he was not in search of those who have 'thought most wisely about Ireland, but those who have thought most authentically for Ireland, the voices that have come out of the Irish struggle itself' (246).

Two of the strongest Irish voices to be raised during the first decades of the twentieth century were radical rather than revivalist voices, the voices of George Bernard Shaw (1856–1950) and James Connolly (1868–1916), one a Fabian, the other a republican socialist. Shaw was, along with Sidney Webb, one of the leading exponents of Fabian socialism, a brand of socialist theory and practice that advocated a gradualist, interventionist, 'lobbying' approach to social reform, thus distinguishing it from the more confrontational Marxist approaches. It also distinguished itself from revolutionary Marxism by working with a 'top down' rather than a 'bottom up' model of strategic action. In other words, its first appeal was to well-placed, influential, middle-class individuals and groups rather than to a prospectively revolutionary proletariat. The aim of the Fabian groups was not to take up arms but to 'permeate' established organizations, institutions, and political parties with a view to influencing policy and decision-making. The non-revolutionary nature of Fabian strategy does not imply a complaisant vision of the future society, certainly not as far as the role of the state is concerned. The Fabians were in a sense more committed than the early Marxists – certainly more committed than Marx himself – to the idea of state socialism. Unlike Marx, who looked forward to the eventual 'withering away' of the state, the Fabians had no such anarchistic vision. Indeed, so fundamental was the idea of the strong centralized state to their thinking that the guiding maxim of their strategy and political philosophy might well have been, as Gareth Griffith puts it, 'If the state did not exist it would have been necessary to invent it' (1993: 72).

In his political essays Shaw demonstrated just how tough the Fabians could be, especially in their defensive reflections on the new Soviet state. In his *Intelligent Woman's Guide to Socialism and Capitalism* (1928) Shaw expresses admiration for the minority of 'devoted Marxists' who are maintaining by sheer force 'such government as is possible in the teeth of an intensely recalcitrant peasantry' (318). He also defends coercive agricultural policy, explaining that the Soviet government had to get rid of peasant proprietors in order to create collective farms and garden cities, and declares that there is now 'no excuse for persistence in the old plan of leaving our agriculture in the hands of uneducated peasants and miseducated country gentlemen' (1944: 19). But there is tougher to come. In a chapter on sanctions and coercion in *Everybody's Political What's What* (1944) he makes a general case for the relationship between coercion and civilization, proposing the future establishment of a kind of inquisitorial board or court that would be empowered to call before it any citizen whose 'fitness to live' might be in question. By fitness to live he means not physical fitness but social fitness, a form of fitness that would express itself in the regular fulfilment of civic duty and social contribution. Dismissing all notions of natural liberty, including the kinds of liberties identified in the American declaration of independence, Shaw would assign to his hypothetical court the power to determine 'how much liberty a citizen can be entrusted with if he is to be let live at all in a civilized society' (284). Though he rejected Fascism as no more than a form of state capitalism, he retained a tell-tale regard for what Gareth Griffith calls 'the collectivist lawmaker', and was never wholehearted in his criticism of Hitler and Mussolini. In 1942 he could refer to Hitler as 'the greatest living Tory' (quoted in Griffith 1993: 272), while in a disturbing chapter entitled 'The Genetic State' in *Everybody's Political What's What* he hoped that a defeated Hitler might escape his enemies 'to enjoy a comfortable retirement in Ireland or some other neutral country, as Louis Napoleon did at Chislehurst and the Kaiser at Doorn' (1944: 249). Such sentiments as these, despite Shaw's erstwhile anti-establishment stance, have rendered much of the Shavian outlook passé and contemptible.

There is a kind of irony in the fact that the thought of a more revolutionary socialist, James Connolly, should remain more presentable than the reformist gradualism of Bernard Shaw. An activist and an organizer rather than a theoretician or an ideologue, Connolly specialized in writing brief, passionate, on-the-spot responses to the political events of his day. His political philosophy is a pragmatically radical one, an eclectic and sometimes accommodating mix of socialist, republican, and feminist ideas applied to local conditions. His thought is nearly always a response to developing circumstances rather than to theoretically dogmatic or discursive concerns. Indeed, Connolly's originality consists precisely in this preparedness to be eclectic and adaptable in his response to local events and conditions, particularly in his avoidance of dogmatic or schematic applications. His pragmatic radicalism is seen at its best in his lengthy reply to the Jesuit priest, Fr. Kane, who had attacked socialism in his Lenten sermons, arguing that it was at all points incompatible with Catholic belief. In the course of his defence of socialism, Connolly gives a lively, indignant, and 'sensible' account of the different claims of socialist and Marxist theory, sometimes demurring from a too-doctrinaire interpretation or application of them. While giving a cogent account of Marx's economic determinism, for example, he insists at the same time that one may be a socialist without accepting such a specific doctrine. He is unreservedly defensive, however, in his account of the labour theory of value, and mocks Fr. Kane's failure to grasp and deal adequately with it. The spirit of Connolly's socialism is encapsulated in the closing aspirational sentences of *Labour, Nationality and Religion* (1910), the pamphlet in which he replies to Fr. Kane: 'Socialism is neither Protestant nor Catholic, Christian nor Freethinker, Buddhist, Mahometan, nor Jew; is only HUMAN. *We of the socialist working class realize that as we suffer together we must work together that we may enjoy together*. We reject the firebrand of capitalist warfare and offer you the olive leaf of brotherhood and justice to and for all' (1988: 117). Like Pearse, Connolly is a highly committed activist, albeit on the basis of principles and ideals that are very different from those of Pearse. And perhaps because he is a highly committed activist, he is also at the same time a highly 'occasional' thinker, with the consequence that his thought, like the thought of Pearse, belongs ultimately to Irish political history rather than to Irish intellectual history.

If the nationalist and socialist movements failed to produce many noteworthy thinkers during the first half of the twentieth century, the newly instituted national university failed to produce many such thinkers during the second half of the century. This is not because the modern Irish university is very different from universities elsewhere but rather because it is very much the same. The specialized ethos of the modern university generally is one of the main reasons for the decline of original, engaging, public-spirited thought. The modern university, though often perceived to be a resourceful 'think-tank', is really just a highly specialized workplace, reflecting the extreme division of labour in society at large. Although the wholesale academicization of thought began in the nineteenth century, there still existed opportunities for the informed amateur or all-rounder. Even specialists were happy to 'specialize' in more than one field, often cheerfully combining literary, scientific, and theological interests. Most importantly, the preparedness of a number of 'gentlemanly' or 'gentlewomanly' amateurs to engage with the experts meant that lively debates could still occur. Frances Power Cobbe, as we saw in the last chapter, was happy to engage with Darwin from a purely ethical point of view. And, just as significantly, Darwin was pleased to debate and correspond with his ethically minded friend, if only to pass judgement on a book she had pressed upon him or to respond to her views on the consciousness of dogs. Such interactions are scarcely imaginable in the twentieth century, especially in the second half of the century, since this becomes the era of rampant academicization and specialization. Thought – in the sense of speculative, explanatory, systematic thought – has been professionalized and commodified by the modern academy, and is therefore available only at a price, ranging from the price of a university course to the much greater price of a lifetime dedicated to the pursuit of some narrow and technical line of enquiry. This technicalization has affected all areas of thought, including the humanities, where it has become increasingly difficult for any but the most inspired and determined communicators to transcend the confines of their disciplines. The net result of the process of academicization and technicalization in the humanities has been the extraction of potentially strong individual thinkers from the public domain, and the concomitant ejection of the public domain from among the concerns of such thinkers. Too often these potentially strong thinkers succumb to the internal demands of the academy, producing lines of thought that are no more than modish syntheses of elements of some newly canonical ideology, such as Marxism or feminism, shaken together with elements of some recent development in an academic discipline – structuralism, post-structuralism, linguistic analysis, semiology – and then presented as an original-seeming cocktail to a generation of university students. The wider public again remains largely unacquainted with these syntheses and 'developments', and is rarely impressed by the little it learns of them.

The twentieth century, then, cannot be expected to present us with anything like the theological controversies of the seventeenth or eighteenth century, or the equivalent of the Darwinian controversy of the nineteenth. As far as Irish intellectual history is concerned, the twentieth century cannot be expected to produce a radical political thinker of the importance of William Thompson (though it did, as we have seen, produce a more radical activist in the form of James Connolly), nor can it be expected to produce a great scientific communicator like John Tyndall (though it did produce at least as great a scientist in the form of Nobel prizewinner Ernest Walton). Nonetheless, there are still individual thinkers – albeit a small number of them – who have responded individually, unpredictably, and provocatively to the ebb and flow of modern ideas, and have at the same time managed to elude the clutches of specialization. In a series of sections below, we will look at the work of a selection of Irish thinkers who have made contributions to psychoanalytic theory, to philosophy, and to ethical and political thought. The first section, however, will examine the perfectly unclassifiable thought of William Butler Yeats. While Yeats's thought is not of the same order as his poetry, it is nonetheless the product of one person's earnest and sustained effort to come to terms with crucial questions of identity, personality, and history. Unlike the other great literary figures of the twentieth century, James Joyce and Samuel Beckett, Yeats did not just use or exploit ideas and philosophies but also directly engaged some of the ideas and philosophies that he found intellectually as well as imaginatively congenial. Whereas Joyce and Beckett appropriated the ideas of certain philosophers – Aquinas and Bruno in the case of Joyce, Descartes and Berkeley in the case of Beckett (see Hederman 1985 and Kearney 1985b) – and converted them into the substance of their own creative imaginations, Yeats took certain ideas seriously and more or less on their own terms, and produced a reflective, if idiosyncratic, response to them.

BETWEEN SELF AND ANTI-SELF

The visionary idealism of W.B. Yeats

William Butler Yeats (1865–1939) was born in Dublin, but while still a young child he accompanied his mother to London where his father, John Butler Yeats, had gone to train as an artist. This was to be the first in a series of journeys between Ireland and London, with the result that the young Yeats received his early education at English and Irish schools, at the Godolphin School in Hammersmith and the Erasmus Smith High School in Harcourt Street in Dublin. On leaving school he went to the Metropolitan School of Art but soon discovered that his interest lay in writing rather than in painting or drawing. His life as a poet began in 1885 when his first poems appeared in the *Dublin University Review*. Significantly, the July issue of the review referred in its 'Notes and News' section to Yeats's involvement in the establishment of the Dublin Hermetic Society, a fact that heralded the poet's lifelong interest in occult systems and experiments, including theosophy and psychical research (Alldritt 1997: 42). Barely out of his teenage years he had signalled his opposition to his father's rationalism, and was already making connections between poetry and religion. In his *Reveries over Childhood and Youth* he records his proposal to the Hermetic Society that 'whatever the great poets had affirmed in their finest moments was the nearest we could come to an authoritative religion' (1955: 90). He also recalls that he used to vex his father by defining truth as 'the dramatically appropriate utterance of the highest man' (90).

Yeats's preparedness to vex his father suggests that he was fearless, even confrontational, in the pursuit of his nascent anti-rationalist beliefs. He begins his *Autobiography* with an account of two violent or near-violent exchanges between himself and his father. His father, whose thinking had been much influenced by the utilitarian philosophy of John Stuart Mill, disapproved strongly of his son's interest in psychical research and in the work of the anti-modernist utopian writer and art-critic, John Ruskin. One night a quarrel with his father about Ruskin came to such a height that (recounts Yeats) 'in putting me out of the room he broke the glass in a picture with the back of my head' (1972: 19). On another occasion, after yet another

argument, Yeats's father squared up to him, inviting him to fight –
an invitation which the son declined. These vehement exchanges
reveal Yeats's antipathy towards the kind of empirical, utilitarian
thinking that had appealed to his father. He disliked it because it
seemed to him to cast the human mind in a passive, representational,
almost mechanical role, effectively belittling the mind's active, imaginative, visionary side. He agreed with Coleridge that the empiricist
philosophers have 'turned the mind into the quicksilver at the back
of a mirror' (1955: 358). The scientific philosophers like Locke and
Newton are found guilty of failure of vision and imagination, specifically for failing to see the world as more than a physical machine. The
utilitarian, scientific mind is, like the Whiggery defined by the Sixth
Sage in the poem 'The Seven Sages', a 'leveling, rancorous, rational sort
of mind' that never looked out of the eye of a saint or a drunkard (1994:
291). The short poem 'Fragments' is a succinct summation of Yeats's
antipathy to a narrow-minded empirical, utilitarian philosophy: 'Locke
sank into a swoon; / The Garden died; / God took the spinning-jenny /
Out of his side' (1994: 260). These lines suggest a kind of nightmare
vision in which Adam is replaced by Locke, and Eve by the spinning-
jenny, a symbol of materialism, mechanization, and soul-destroying
industrial capitalism. The great, expansive, and sanguine story of
genesis and creation is summarily displaced by a bleak, curt little story
of nemesis and destruction.

Yeats's study of psychical research and idealist or mystical philosophy enabled him to align himself defiantly with those to whom it
does not matter whether the earth goes round the sun or the sun
round the earth (1955: 89). His obvious preference is for a worldview
that is visionary, that acknowledges the power of the human mind in
its more dream-like, imaginative, symbolizing, non-rational modes. As
a poet his preference is for an art that can, like Shelley's, escape from
'the barrenness and shallowness of a too conscious arrangement, into
the abundance and depth of Nature' (1968: 82). In an essay on William
Blake he recognizes and celebrates an important difference between
reason and imagination. Reason divides us from each other by showing
us our conflicting interests, while imagination 'binds us to each other
by opening the secret doors of all hearts' (112). Turning away from
what he calls 'the scientific movement' in literature, he orients himself
towards those things that natural science chooses to ignore or despise,

including such 'unbelievable' phenomena as telepathic communication, foreknowledge through dreams and visions, and the return of the spirits of the dead. This 'love of the Unseen life' (204) is as much a gesture of cultural mutiny – a defiant gesture towards the encroachments of science – as it is an article of faith. His approach to idealism and occultism is in some respects indiscriminate, as if he is prepared to be defensive on behalf of any system of thought that issues more from imagination than from rational calculation. Occultism and philosophy are equally agreeable as long as they stimulate imagination and concern themselves with more or less transcendent realities. What attracts him to the development in philosophy from Spinoza to Hegel, causing him to describe it as 'the greatest of all works of intellect', is the fact that it represents the resurgence of imagination, that imagination that sank after the death of Shakespeare (396). It is the exercise of this same imagination that he finds in Berkeley, at the centre of whose philosophy he is pleased to find 'some always undefined apprehension of spirits and their relations' (410).

Yet, for all his interest in Plato, Plotinus, Berkeley and other idealist thinkers, Yeats was too impressed by, and too responsive to, the material particularities of life and reality to be an uncomplicated, full-dress idealist. While endorsing the primacy of mind and imagination, he did not consistently disown the world of the body, sensation, and passion. Yeats's prose essays contain explicit endorsements of the worldview put forward by Plato and others, but his poetry is 'much more ambivalent, accepting, rejecting, modifying, vacillating' (Arkins 1990: 48). Yeats is at his most ambivalent and vacillating in his use of the classical idealists in his complex poem, 'The Tower'. In the first part of the poem, keenly aware of advancing age, he thinks ruefully that the only companions he is fit for now are Plato and Plotinus, and that these will remain with him 'Until imagination, ear and eye, / Can be content with argument and deal / In abstract things' (1994: 240). It seems at first reflection that abstract ideas and abstract things are the more suitable sorts of preoccupation for someone of his age, despite the fact that he has found his imagination to be more 'excited, passionate, and fantastical' than it was in childhood or youth. No sooner does this rueful thought occur to him than he finds himself turning to his imagination, calling up images and memories, some violent, all very particular, all filling his mind more movingly than any Platonic abstraction could. Instead of resisting the temptation to indulge memory and imagination he yields to it, and in the third part of the poem he declares his faith, famously: 'I mock Plotinus' thought / And cry in Plato's teeth, / Death and life were not / Till man made up the whole, / Made lock, stock and barrel / Out of his bitter soul' (244). These lines suggest that it is not from a lofty, remote, transcendent perspective that human beings create the world of their imaginations but out of positions of human frailty, out of desperation, out of bitterness, out of immersion in the memorable details of life as it is passionately lived in the mortal world. Only those who can die, or who are dead, can 'rise / Dream and so create / Translunar Paradise' (244). It is out of raw living mortal materials, out of experience and memory, that imaginative and yearning human beings manage to make 'a superhuman / Mirror-resembling dream' (245). Thus the poem becomes what Richard Ellmann has called 'a defiant, Faustian cry of the infinite power of the mind of man' (1979: 254).

A less Faustian reflection on age, imagination, life, and art emerges from his poem 'Among School Children'. As he, a 'sixty-year-old smiling public man', moves among the children he is overcome by dream-like memories of a young woman he once knew. The sense of the past and of loss leads him to realize the contrast between the immortal ideas of the Greek thinkers (especially Plato, who 'thought nature but a spume that plays / Upon a ghostly paradigm of things') and the stark fact that the very transient spume of temporal reality finally reduced all these great thinkers to 'Old clothes upon old sticks to scare a bird' (1994: 262–3). Only images, symbols, 'presences' manage to survive, mocking human frailty as they float free of the mortal imaginations that produced them. Though these images emerged in the first place out of normal experience, they do not remain there but become alienated, virtually self-subsisting abstractions (see Snukal 1973: 213–14). In the final stanza the poet turns to something that is alive, yet at the same time objective and invulnerable. The chestnut tree, though it is a living thing, is nonetheless so unified in its being that, blossoming and dancing as it does, one cannot 'know the dancer from the dance'. Being mindless and soulless, the great tree does not yearn, does not have to bruise its body to pleasure its soul. And yet, poignantly, in the very act of reaching out towards this enviable reality of the tree, so simple and unified in its inhuman perfection, Yeats only succeeds in discovering the futility of his idealistic yearning. No sooner has he discovered in the tree an impressive epitome of self-transcendence and unity of being than he has begun to beset it with images that are essentially images of human expression, yearning, and transience – images of music, glancing, and dancing. The imagery of transcendence, as soon as it forms, resolves itself into the imagery of transience. Yearning and disappointment are expressed together in the plaintive, exclamatory language of the closing lines of the poem.

Yeats is at his most 'philosophical' in his exploratory reflections on the notions of self and anti-self. Despite his expression of admiration for Berkeley's idealist project, Yeats's theory of self and anti-self is some distance from the idealist philosopher's narrowly defined notion of the self – that is, the notion of the self as a spirit whose essence is simply to perceive. For Yeats the real or true self is not some God-given or nature-given primary self but the achieved self, that 'theatrical' second self that is deliberately and artfully fashioned in the course of a disciplined productive life. It is a condition of living an 'arduous full life' that one should embrace an anti-self – in other words, that one should imagine oneself utterly different from what one now is and strive to assume the identity of this other, contrary self. This achievement of a second self he regards as a kind of ethical imperative, as the mark of an actively virtuous personality. While conventional morality associates the wearing of a mask with disguise and duplicity, Yeats sees the attempt to grow into a mask as a virtuous act, an expression of strength, creativity, and discipline. The forging of an anti-self is analogous to a rebirth, a remaking or 'making new' of oneself. He writes: 'If we cannot imagine ourselves as different from what we are and assume that second self, we cannot impose a discipline upon ourselves, though we may accept one from others. Active virtue as distinguished from the passive acceptance of a current code is therefore theatrical, consciously dramatic, the wearing of a mask' (1955: 469). It is tempting to conceive of Yeats's anti-self or mask as a variation on the idea of a social or public persona, but his sense of the mask is more subtle than that. For one thing, a public persona is something elicited from outside, something demanded from us by society, whereas the Yeatsian anti-self is forged from within by oneself, perhaps over against what society demands or expects. Moreover, the anti-self requires the perpetual transcending of old selves, the restless reaching forward into newer and ever more characterful formations of oneself that are always the antithesis of what went before. But perhaps the most subtle aspect of Yeats's theory is that each person's ultimate identity is neither the primary self nor its antithesis but the complex dynamic balance that is achieved between the two.

The notions of mask and anti-self take on a dramatically more radical and more obscure form in *A Vision* (1937), the work in which Yeats advances a theory of personality and history. The book is in fact a curiously daunting mixture of mystical and quasi-astrological thinking, made all the more curious and challenging by Yeats's claim that the contents were presented to him by 'instructors' speaking through the medium of his sleeping wife. The instructors can perhaps be blamed for the fact that *A Vision* relies more on symbolism than on logically sequenced propositions or arguments. If any clear or coherent idea can be extrapolated from the theoretical machinery of gyres, lunar phases, and turnings of the Great Wheel, it is the idea that an individual personality, or an individual human life, or the span of human history itself, must move in cycles, running the whole gamut of conflicts and reversals, shuttling back and forth between contraries, between subjectivity and objectivity, between will and fate, between chance and choice, between thought and passion. Different combinations and permutations of faculties, impulses, tendencies, and circumstances bring about particular phases of history and particular kinds of personalities. Phase Eighteen, for example, on the Great Wheel of cyclical evolution brings around the emotional man whose 'true mask' is emotional intensity and whose 'body of fate' (his inheritance from the past) is 'empowered disillusionment' (1937: 145). The same categories applied to history suggest that Christ lived and taught during a phase of rising objectivity when the self was struggling to escape from personality – to be lost in 'otherness', as Richard Ellman puts it – while at the time of the renaissance subjectivity was to the fore once more, 'and great personalities were everywhere realizing themselves to the utmost' (Ellmann 1979: 232).

Despite its oddness and indeed its downright repugnance to practically all styles of traditional philosophical thinking, the Yeatsian system is important insofar as it offers an antidote to modern analytical, critical, rationalistic, materialist, progressivist theories and phil-osophies. It is in the end provocatively anti-philosophical and anti-discursive, offering high-density synthesis rather than protracted analysis, turning on symbol and image rather than on concept and argument, appealing to the less conscious areas of mind, memory, and imagination. The kind of visionary thinking championed and prac-tised by Yeats continues to find adherents and exponents in contempor-ary Irish thought. Recent examples include the popular exhortatory spiritualism of John O'Donoghue, as presented in his *Anam Chara* (1997), and the less popular but even more visionary work of John Moriarty as presented in his *Dreamtime* (1994) and in his trilogy *Turtle Was Gone a Long Time* (1996; 1997; 1998). The work of neither author lends itself easily to summation or discussion, mainly because neither author engages in conventional, sequential, systematic argu-mentation. Both writers are in any case determined to inspire rather than inform, to deepen awareness rather than add to the sum of knowl-edge. Their books are clarion calls to wisdom rather than attempts at the logical fine-tuning of our existing conceptual frameworks. As texts, these books are meant to be experienced in their totality rather than analytically dismantled and reassembled, and it is arguable that this is at once their strength and their limitation, since they demand a high degree of uncritical, unanalytical, thrilled co-operation from the reader. In Moriarty's case, the extensively eclectic nature of his writing is an important part of his 'message'. That is to say, he is determined to play creative havoc with all the conventional boundaries of composition, whether these be the supposed boundaries between Western and Eastern thought, between prose and poetry, between conversation and liturgy, between old thought and new thought, or between the thought of Bishop Berkeley and the thought of Black Elk. An all-embracing synthesizer rather than a fault-seeking analyst, Moriarty's ambition is to draw cheerfully, even wildly, on the many-splendoured resources of human culture, regardless of time or place, form or genre. At the risk of giving an inadequate impression of his work, let us conclude this section on Yeats and the contem-porary visionary tradition with an exemplary observation from Moriarty:

We most certainly have come up out of the commonage consciousness of Altamira and Lascaux into a great and terrible *res extensa* desert of Cartesian clarities. This place we are in, it is no place of Earth oracles, of God-haunted gorges, of holy wells, of Paps Mountains, of Uffington horses, neither, on Halloween night, do we leave our doors on the latch.

(1994: 33)

THE DREAMS OF REASON

J.O. Wisdom on the unconscious origins of thought

John Oulton Wisdom was born in Dublin in 1908. He graduated from Trinity College, Dublin, in 1931, continuing his postgraduate studies until 1933 when he received a doctoral degree for a thesis on Hegel. He then moved to Cambridge where he encountered the analytical philosophy of G.E. Moore and Ludwig Wittgenstein. His first teaching post was in Cairo, where he published *The Metamorphosis of Philosophy* in 1947. In 1948 he was appointed to the staff of the London School of Economics, where he became acquainted with Karl Popper, best known for his influential contributions to political philosophy and the philosophy of science. In the 1960s he moved to North America and taught at several universities there before finally moving to Canada and to a professorship in philosophy and social science at York University, Toronto, where he remained until his retirement in 1979. He died at his home in Castlebridge, Co. Wexford, in 1993.

In the preface to his early work, *The Metamorphosis of Philosophy* (1947), Wisdom thanks G.E. Moore for explaining to him the intricacies of logical analysis. More significantly, he also thanks Ernest Jones, the president of the International Psycho-Analytical Association, for convincing him of the importance of unconscious mental activity. The quite diverse influences of Moore and Jones, representing two different kinds of 'analysis', are evident in Wisdom's work, and indeed the originality of his own thought consists in his attempt to provide a constructive psychoanalytical response to the central claims of logical analysis (more commonly called logical positivism). The central argument of logical analysts is that all statements or theories that are not verifiable in experience are, strictly speaking, meaningless.

Statements about transcendental realities – about realities that are beyond the reach of the senses – are just a kind of nonsense because there is no possibility of establishing their truth or falsity. Yet, while accepting that such metaphysical statements are indeed nonsense, *strictly* speaking, Wisdom is unhappy with the claim that they are altogether meaningless. For one thing, people who make such statements seem to speak intelligibly to each other, seem to understand each other perfectly well, and generally behave like people engaged in significant conversation or discussion. Wisdom contends that speculative philosophies, just like dreams, myths, literature, and art, arise out of deep emotional needs that are not always apparent at the level of conscious thought itself. People have not only an intellectual need but also an emotional need to speculate about their place in the universe, about the origins of that universe, about the persistence of order in nature, about the possibility of life after death, about deity, about the possible existence of things unavailable to sense or reason. Telling people, as the logical analysts do, that their metaphysical beliefs are nonsense is not much more helpful than telling them that their dreams are nonsense. As far as the psychoanalyst is concerned, there is a lot more to be said about both dreams and metaphysics, since both are creations or expressions of the complex human psyche and can be understood, albeit not in the same way that other expressions are understood. The fact that the speculative thinker is more 'awake' than the dreamer does not mean that he is completely disengaged from his unconscious, or that unconscious needs do not find their way into his speculations.

The analogy can be taken further. Dreams, considered rationally, are indeed nonsensical; but considered symptomatically, as expressions of unconscious wishes, impulses, or conflicts, they soon become more meaningful than many orderly sequences of well-framed propositions. Analogously, the 'nonsensical' theories of speculative philosophy may, when considered symptomatically, prove meaningful to the psychoanalyst who knows what to look for. If one merely looks at what the sentences of metaphysical philosophy directly or literally express, then it may be true that they do not make sense from the point of view of logical analysis. But if one looks at those same sentences from the point of view of what they express symptomatically, then it may be possible to find meaning among them. For the psychoanalyst, speculative philosophy is always about its authors in much the same way that dreams are always about the dreamer. In a sense, therefore, 'the history of philosophy consists of important autobiographies' (1947: 166). People other than psychoanalysts may derive satisfaction from reading speculative philosophy if they can 'attune' their emotions or frame of mind to that of the philosopher. This attunement, however, has more to do with unconscious resonances that have been aroused by the rhetorical devices of the writer than with the literal, rational claims of the text itself. Sympathetic readers of a philosopher such as Hegel are responding not to the power of his reasoning but to the powerful rhythms of an unconscious emotional structure working itself out at an extraordinarily abstract level. The effect of the 'hidden' text of speculative philosophy is to some extent like the effect of a certain kind of poetry where emotive, rhetorical devices are more important than any statement that the poet makes.

Wisdom offers his most ambitious 'psychoanalysis' of a speculative philosopher in his *Unconscious Origin of Berkeley's Philosophy* (1953), an analysis which reveals the strengths and weaknesses of his approach. Having scanned Berkeley's biography for signs of neurosis, he concludes that he suffered from hypochondria – that is, from a morbid anxiety about his health. His fascination with tar-water (a dilution of conifer resin) as a cure-all for a whole range of ailments can be understood as a fairly obvious symptom of this neurosis. Particularly significant is Berkeley's conception of tar-water as a cleanser or purifier. Its function in his scheme of things is to clear all kinds of impurities from the body and thereby improve the health of the patient. According to Wisdom there is evidence in *Siris* (Berkeley's essay on the medicinal powers of tar-water) that he frequently felt poisoned and defiled, believing that he had 'some bad, harmful, or persecuting stuff inside him, possessed of physical and psychical powers, such as only . . . a magical purifier would dispel' (1953: 141). Wisdom interprets this sense of a clogging internal poison as a variation on the theme of Berkeley's philosophy of perception. In his philosophy of perception Berkeley's neurosis expressed itself as a fear or horror of matter, and impelled him to set about cleansing the world of matter by putting forward his famous idealist formula, namely, that the existence of things consists in their being perceived. Matter, because it is the basis of materialism, threatens religious belief, and therefore works its way into human thinking as a kind of intellectual and cultural poison, challenging philosophers like himself to develop an anti-materialist antidote. The idealist formula functions as just such an antidote, as a metaphysical equivalent of tar-water, as a universal panacea or principle of intellectual purification. It does this by denying reality to matter and equating reality instead with the perceptions of either the human mind or the mind of God. As tar-water serves to expurgate the internal poisons, so the *esse-percipi* principle serves to expurgate the 'external' poison that is matter, making the world safe for true and purified believers.

A major problem with this way of interpreting a philosopher's work is that it seems to fall foul of the genetic fallacy. The genetic fallacy is a logician's label for the erroneous assumption that we can evaluate a theory or belief by tracing it to the ulterior motives or unconscious goals of the person who is its source or 'genesis'. Logicians will point out that a theory cannot be validated or invalidated in this way, and will insist that every theory must be assessed according to the appropriate logical and empirical criteria of consistency and truthfulness. In his later book, *Philosophy and Its Place in Our Culture* (1975), Wisdom tries to take the sting out of the genetic-fallacy charge by suggesting that too much anxiety about the fallacy can lead to a one-sided assessment of theories and beliefs. He reiterates his conviction that it is not the business of the psychoanalyst to pass judgement on the truth or validity of theories or philosophies, only to add to our biographical understanding of the people who produce the theories and philosophies. A false theory can be as insightful in this respect as a true one, just as a bad novel can tell the analyst as much about the author as a good one. At the same time, Wisdom presents a much more expansive conception of philosophy than he did in his early work. He has less respect now for logical analysis or logical positivism. He now thinks that philosophy is a major contributor to the formation of the dominant worldview (or *Weltanschauung*) according to which people 'justify' the way they live in a particular place at a particular time. A personal philosophy and a social *Weltanschauung* share similar features in that neither is in itself provable or disprovable, yet people's minds and lives are governed by them. Personal philosophies and worldviews feed off each other, and their rise and fall has a lot to do with developments taking place outside themselves. The modern

Weltanschauung is one of diversity and uncertainty, a fact that is reflected in the almost anarchic diversity of philosophical methods, arguments, and systems. This diversity of systems may suggest a failure on the part of philosophers to find the one true method that would enable them to resolve their differences and disagreements, but in reality it represents the susceptibility of philosophy to the culture in which it finds itself and to which it duly gives expression. If the culture is diverse, then philosophy will reflect and contribute to that diversity. In that case, systematic diversity is not a failure but a kind of success.

AGAINST METHOD

M. O'C. Drury on the imprisoned mind

Maurice O'Connor Drury (1907–1976) was born in Exeter of Irish parents. While at Trinity College, Cambridge, he met the enigmatic but highly influential German-born philosopher Ludwig Wittgenstein, with whom he formed a relationship that lasted until Wittgenstein's death in 1951 (see Hayes 1996). Wittgenstein's influence on Drury was strong enough to warrant his being called Drury's mentor. He encouraged Drury not to take up an academic career in philosophy but to try instead a career in medicine and psychiatry. This Drury eventually did. Even his decision to study medicine at Trinity College, Dublin, was arrived at in consultation with Wittgenstein. In 1947 Drury was appointed resident psychiatrist at St Patrick's Hospital in Dublin, becoming consultant psychiatrist there in 1969. He also gave lectures in psychology to medical students at Trinity College and at the Royal College of Surgeons.

Drury's most important work, *The Danger of Words*, was published in 1973, and is concerned mainly with the possibility of mental science or scientific psychology. His guiding intuition is that psychology, understood as a discipline intended to provide useful insights into the human personality and psyche, is not and cannot be a science like physics or chemistry. Those areas or aspects of experience that lend themselves to measurement are not going to tell us much about the unique interior lives of individuals. Those areas and aspects of experience that make up the life of an individual are not available for exact observation or observation of any kind. Psychology and psychiatry, insofar as they purport to treat the individual in all her uniqueness and peculiarity, cannot hope to arrive at a universal method, since such a method is not designed to detect or register those very features that make individuals peculiarly themselves. The more one attempts to apply general categories – such as 'introvert' or 'extrovert' – to human beings, the more their individuality is ignored and diminished. What is of the deepest concern to the therapist is not universals but particulars – not general categories of classification but particular persons with particular personalities and particular problems arising out of particular circumstances (1973: 35). The closer the therapist gets to the person-as-patient the less 'scientific' will be her understanding of him. The more indeed she will tend to find the patient to be enigmatic and in a certain sense 'un-understandable'. This sense of the 'un-understandable' does not represent some kind of failure on the part of the therapist but rather a kind of success – an effective recognition and appreciation of the irreducible and inalienable individuality of the patient-as-person. The mentally ill person is even more of an enigma than the 'normal' individual. No advance in treatment or theory can alter the fact that there will always be a mystery about mental ill-health that will make it different from any disease of the body (89). A kind of 'hidden inwardness' is the rock on which a scientific and objective psychology will come to grief: 'The truth is that we human beings are not meant to study each other as objects of scientific scrutiny, but to see each other as an individual subject that evolves according to its own laws' (43). If a scientific approach cannot enable us to 'know' each other when we are in good mental health, neither can it help us to 'know' each other when mental ill-health befalls one or other of us. Every mentally ill person is an 'individual enigma', and should not be approached as anything less. In other words, he or she should not be approached with a reductive, objectifying, depersonalizing technical terminology. One of the dangers of words, especially technical, objective words, is that they can all too easily be pressed into service as handy labels that cover over the peculiarities they are supposed to explain.

Drury discusses the relationship between mind and body as an ethical rather than a metaphysical or scientific question. To make mind too understandable or too transparent, as if it could be 'read off' from physical behaviour or brain activity, is a morally suspect move. It is to play into the hands of those who would generally wish to objectify human beings and calculate their ratio or degree of 'humanity'. Morally preferable is the Socratic view that the soul is imprisoned within the body and that the mental life is therefore never fully available to observers. In particular, the Socratic view of those whose brains have been damaged should be that 'they are shut off from us by barriers that neither we nor they can break' (88). Drury presents the Socratic picture of the mentally disabled person not as an hypothesis 'but as a decision of the will, a decision of ethics where neither physiology nor any other science can come to our aid' (89). Even to say that someone is *mentally* disabled becomes problematic on such a view. The leap from the physical to the mental will always remain – should always remain – a leap into the realm of the enigmatic, the irreducible, the inexplicable.

The most radical expression of Drury's determination to respect the humanity and integrity of the mentally ill is contained in his concluding chapter on madness and religion. The dilemma is this: when to say, 'This man is mad and we must put a stop to his raving' and when to say, 'Touch not mine annointed and do my prophet no harm' (129). After discussing some possible criteria for distinguishing morbidity from spirituality, Drury concludes first, that there are no reliable criteria in this context, and second, that the quest for criteria is mistaken anyway. The idea that there might be well-defined distinguishing criteria here is a product of 'a cool hour', a presumption that it is possible to be both wise and detached at the same time. This presumption marks a failure to realize that 'our own life is intimately involved in the settlement of this question' (133). The absence of criteria is not, moreover, a problem but the makings of a kind of solution. Every illness can in principle bring the sufferer to the threshold of something like a religious experience; every religious experience can in principle feel like madness even to those whose belief is deep and sincere. This acknowledgement has the effect of validating mental illness, at least in the context of a culture that recognizes and values religious experience. While accepting that the therapist must treat a mentally ill person as well as current knowledge will allow, Drury concludes by suggesting that the therapist should at the same time never forget that good physical and mental health are not absolute goods, that they 'can be lost and yet nothing be lost' (137).

'UNUTTERABLE PARTICULARITIES'

Iris Murdoch on the ethics of attention

The inscrutable reality of the interior life of others is also a dominant idea in the literary and philosophical writing of Iris Murdoch. Born in Dublin in 1919, educated at Badminton School, Bristol, and at Somerville College, Oxford, Murdoch spent most of her life in England, returning to Ireland only during holiday periods in childhood and to visit relatives and friends during her adult life. Her early departure from Ireland did not, however, remove the country from her imaginative or emotional frame of reference. Her Irish historical novel *The Red and the Green* (1965), and the continual appearance of Irish characters in *The Time of the Angels* (1966) and other novels, reveal the persistence of her Irish background and what Donna Gerstenberger calls her 'consciousness of national materials' (1975: 70). In *The Red and the Green* she sets a complex story of relationships, misunderstandings, failures of perception, and ultimate self-discovery in the days leading up to the Easter rising of 1916. The narrative includes frequent references to the principal historical figures of the time, including Patrick Pearse and James Connolly, but these figures do not 'enter' the fictional world of the novel. The fictional characters occasionally come very close to the historical ones – close enough, for example, to hear the voice (but not the words) of Pearse as he proclaims the existence of the sovereign Irish Republic from the steps of the General Post Office, or close enough to see 'an appalled shocked grief' on the face of James Connolly shortly before the events of the rising – but they remain imaginatively quarantined in their own fictional space. When one of the fictional characters enters the General Post Office on Easter Monday, the narrative does not follow him there. By remaining sealed off from the larger characters and the larger events of a historical period, the novel is better able to 'represent' the troubled, uncertain, elusive psychological and interpersonal world of those whose lives are more important to themselves or to one or two other people than to the march of history, even while they are caught up in and carried along by that larger process. It is not an oversight by the author that one of the main Anglo-Irish characters does not *see* himself as a British officer in uniform until very late in the novel, just hours before the dramatic events of the rising. The mundane historical reason for his lack of self-awareness is the fact that the 'break' between nationalist and unionist sympathizers has not yet been completed. But the more dramatic literary reason is that this character, like many of the others, has been hitherto embroiled in the general confusion of 'half-guilty half-frantic human beings caught up together like carriage horses in an accident' (1965: 294). What has mattered most to him up to that point of self-discovery was not the rights and wrongs of England's fraught relationship with Ireland but the rights and wrongs of his own fraught relationship with the other characters placed nearest to him in the landscape of the novel.

Murdoch exploits one of the conventions of the traditional novel for ethical as much as for artistic reasons. The convention of multiple viewpoints enables her to dramatize what is for her a very important feature of personal and interpersonal life. A particular character, viewed through the eyes of others, may appear clownish, inept, and thoughtless, but when the narrative shifts to his consciousness there may be revealed an inner life (or a suppressed past life) that is not detectable in current words and actions. One of the principal characters in *The Red and the Green* is presented in this way, and is subsequently revealed to be quite other than he appears to be. A particularly misunderstood and 'misperceived' character, he is found to have an incommunicable emotional life – to have, indeed, such an unutterable regard for his stepchildren that 'no touch, no look, no gesture, no tone of voice could give expression to it' (1965: 148). The imaginative insight expressed through the 'multiple viewpoints' convention in the fictional work is developed into a subtle ethical position in Murdoch's philosophical work. In *The Sovereignty of Good* (1970), in the course of developing a passionate rebuttal of behaviourism, she argues that morality is more a matter of vision or attention than of public behaviour, that the most important struggles occur at the level of thought and perception rather than at the level of action, and that these internal struggles may indeed never be apparent to an observer. To illustrate her case against the behaviouristic conception of human psychology and morality, she tells a kind of philosophical fable about a mother-in-law who feels hostility and contempt towards the young woman her son has just married. Because the mother-in-law is a polite and 'correct' person, she behaves beautifully towards the young woman from the beginning; and because she is also a well-meaning and conscientious person the woman struggles inwardly to change her attitude to her daughter-in-law. Eventually her perception of the young woman alters to such an extent that she begins to *see* her differently. Where before she saw someone who was vulgar, undignified, and juvenile, she now sees someone who is refreshingly direct, spontaneous, and youthful. An inner revolution in perception and attitude, the result of sustained and well-meant attention, has taken place, despite the fact that it is not registered in overt behaviour. In other words, there is no outward alteration to correspond to either the internal struggle or the eventual revolution in perception.

Murdoch's conclusion is that the proper mark of the active moral agent is the ability to hold another individual – or indeed another reality – in 'a just and loving gaze' (1970: 34). Gazing or 'seeing' in this context has a moral significance, implying clear vision as a result of imaginative and moral effort. Clarity of vision also implies a determination to overcome the various forms of prejudice, self-deception, or self-centredness that may distort or cloud the proper perception of particular persons, places, or things. Virtue and reality are so closely linked that the task of seeing or otherwise perceiving any particular thing is first and foremost a moral one. But a task it is in any case, the task of struggling to see the world as it is. The ever-present difficulty is not only to keep attention fixed on a real situation but also to prevent such attention 'from returning surreptitiously to the self with consolations of self-pity, resentment, fantasy and despair' (91). Much of Murdoch's fiction is concerned with the ways in which the task of 'really looking' is distracted, misdirected, and sometimes made to seem impossible in certain circumstances.

She returns to the themes of privacy, internal struggle, and moral perception in her last substantial philosophical work, *Metaphysics as a Guide to Morals* (1992). Clearly impressed by the work of thinkers as diverse as Wittgenstein and Jacques Derrida, she nonetheless sets herself to defend many of the concepts and assumptions that 'embarrass' both thinkers. She defends experience and intuition but especially the 'intense lively privacy' of the internal mental lives of individuals. She finds that our whole busy moral and psychological lives abound in 'private insoluble difficulties, mysterious half-understood mental configurations' (1992: 280). While acknowledging the importance of the modern emphasis on the social, cultural, linguistic, and environmental factors that shape our minds and personalities, she also wants to retain a sense of that private 'thought-being' that is so different from our lived outer life. An anti-modernist thinker who is fascinated by the arguments of the modernists and post-modernists, Murdoch sets herself to recover what has been lost to the encroachment of environmental and deterministic theorizing, specifically 'our dense familiar inner stuff, private and personal, with a quality and a value of its own, something which we can scrutinize and control' (153). In her view, the ultimate effect of the different 'environmentalisms' of Hegel, Marx, Wittgenstein, Heidegger, and Derrida is to remove personality, value, and morality from the scheme of things. These thinkers, concerned as they are with structures or systems larger than the individual, present new determinisms, new and ever more elaborate pretexts for 'giving up', for getting rid of freedom, responsibility, remorse, 'and all sorts of personal individual unease' (190).

BEING IN THE MIDDLE

William Desmond on tragedy, 'idiocy', and intimacy

The 'extremities' that inspired the poetry and visionary prose of Yeats, and the 'unutterable particularities' that are celebrated in the novels and philosophy of Iris Murdoch, are also recurring themes in the work of William Desmond. Born in Co. Cork in 1951 and educated at University College, Cork, Desmond has spent most of his professional life outside Ireland in universities in America and Europe. The influences to which he has been most responsive are those of post-Hegelian European philosophy. He begins his keynote work, *Perplexity and Ultimacy* (1995), with a frankly autobiographical chapter that tells the reader who he is, where he has come from, where he has been, and how he continues to find himself 'in the middle of things'.

This idea of being in the middle or 'being between', of vacillating between different sets of extremities – between countries (Ireland and America), between religion and science, between philosophy and poetry, between knowledge and perplexity, between the particulars of reality and the universals of thought, between receding youth and approaching age – is a constant motif throughout his work. Among the conceptual extremities that he is most determined to avoid are atomistic individualism and 'social relationism'. The former is objectionable because it privatizes the self, setting the individual over against society, allowing that the individual enjoys social relationships only for self-interested, self-gratifying reasons. The latter is objectionable because it 'publicizes' the self, reducing the person to a mere construct or expression of social relations, so that the self becomes virtually nothing 'and its intimate singularity vanishes in a tissue of larger public forces' (1995a: 56).

Because he is sometimes taking risks with language, sometimes pushing it to the limits of intelligibility in the course of attempting to say what is well-nigh unsayable, he is not always easy to understand. But there are numerous oases of illumination throughout even his most difficult works – oases that are the more welcome and refreshing on account of the difficulty of the thinking that may have preceded them. Among his most original illuminations are his reflections on tragedy (or 'being at a loss'), idiocy (in the original Greek sense of the term), and intimacy. The argument of *Perplexity and Ultimacy* begins with a sequence of quizzical reflections on what he calls the Howl – the howl of loss and grief, the howl of tragedy, the howl of King Lear coming on stage cradling the dead body of his daughter Cordelia. This howl of loss finds no place in Aristotle's list of the categories of reality or in Kant's list of the categories of understanding. The traditional philosopher, dedicated to reasoning and knowing, has no category under which to gather the overwhelming, overflowing experience of loss. Even recent philosophers (for example, Rorty 1980) who define philosophy as the 'conversation of mankind' cannot give a voice to the inarticulable howl of loss. This howl transcends reason, silences conversation, defies logic and language. Nevertheless, the philosopher should not altogether despair of coming to terms with the Howl. As a human practice that gives expression to mindfulness, philosophy reneges on its responsibility if it fails to somehow

acknowledge the uncontainable reality of loss and duly revise its traditionally rationalistic and tidy definitions of what it is to be human.
Philosophy needs to acknowledge that we are metaphysical beings
'in the measure that the tragic breaks through, in the measure that
we know our being to be one that loses itself, that loses its way'
(Desmond 1995a: 33).

A profound and humanizing effect of the experience of tragedy is that
it brings home to us the ungainsayable fact that every thing, especially
every valuable thing, is singular, unique, unrepeatable, irreplaceable,
existing like the events of a fairy tale, once upon a time and never
again. The particularity and uniqueness of each human being can
also be compared to that of an ocean wave that forms for a brief
time, only to be 'othered' by the undying energy of the sea (46). As
a creature of time, the human being is 'the glint that mindfully
arises and vanishes on the maternal sea of being' (47). Loss is bound
to be intrinsic to the existence of such a transient being who lives in
the midst of other transient beings and transient things. Tragedy
keeps before us the fundamental fact that our life is permeated by
the liability to loss: 'to be is to be at a loss' (49). The price of anything's
being singular and unique is that its eventual loss will be absolute; and
it is this sense of absolute loss that prompts Lear's howl, that cannot be
rationalized or talked away, that can only be acknowledged with awe.

The self of each unique individual is both vulnerable and 'idiotic'.
Here Desmond exploits the connotations of the original Greek term
idios which meant private – private in the sense of being removed
from the public domain, the domain of education and civility. The
idiot as private person was someone who remained naive, uncouth,
'uncivilized', ignorant of the social skills that would enable him or
her to move about competently in the public sphere. The idiot self,
in Desmond's recovered sense, is not the privately sufficient self of
Cartesian philosophy or of classical liberalism but the original,
primal, or elemental self that is present in everyone and that predates
the civilized public self. The more status or recognition that the public
self accumulates, the greater the distance that may open up between the
'inside' and the 'outside' of any particular human being. An emperor,
king, ruler, or president is required to present his public self as
great, powerful, masterful. He is Alexander, Caesar, Lear, Stalin. Yet
when this mighty public persona lies down to rest at night, he is

stripped – strips himself – of the trappings of that persona. In the night the private or idiot self re-emerges in the darkness. When the determinations of the day recede, one has retreated from the public arena and is as nothing as far as the public world is concerned. One returns to being simply a centre of longing, of envy, of regret and recrimination. One remembers sunshine in a meadow and is 'shaken to the roots by the memory' (74). If in the determinations of the day the idiot self is forgotten, then in the indeterminations of the night this self returns with a vengeance, making its presence sometimes painfully felt.

The idiot self is a needy self. One of its deepest needs is the need to 'be with' other people. This need for intimacy or community, however, is easily corrupted or deformed. Lacking a certain 'finesse of spirit', a person responding to the primal, idiotic need for community may be dissolved into destructive forms of community or togetherness. Even the space in which intimacy or togetherness takes place may be enough to lead to the deformation and corruption of the idiot self. Desmond contrasts the monstrous spaces in which Nazi rallies took place with the intimate spaces created within a medieval cathedral. The monstrous immensity of the political rally effectively dissolved the singularity of each self in a 'visceral surge of togetherness', a collective impulse that operated at a level below mindful discrimination (84). The Nazi public space, centred on the figure of the Führer, brought to the surface the darker side of the idiot self, and created a virulent form of 'dark togetherness' (84). By contrast, the architectural space of the cathedral induces a sense of transcendence, as the self is 'drawn out of itself by the movement of the space upwards, vertically' (84). The singular idiotic self is not dissolved but raised up out of itself, at the same time joining communally with others in a spirit of repose and self-recollection. Any genuinely non-exploitative public arena should, like the cathedral, elicit a similar response, creating a space in which the self, 'even in the idiocy of its singularity, feels it can be . . . at home with the other' (85).

Other oases of illumination are to be found in Desmond's reflections on the effects of sunlight (1990: 267–9), song and singing (269–70), smiling in the city (273), the need for sleep (284–7), nostalgia (298–300), festivity (300–3), metaphor (1995b: 209–12), the presence of 'things' (300–11), nature and the wild environment (418–26), and 'the community of distracted desire' (434–8). Here, to conclude this section, is what he has to say about singing:

> Singing is an event of the highest interest. Compare a singing being with something inanimate. The wind blows around a bush and makes a whir or low burr, but neither the wind or bush properly sings. But a bird chirps, a thrush sings out again and again a line of lush notes, and we sense a presence there that was not manifest before. Something is coming awake in singing life.
>
> (1990: 269)

'A VISION OF BEING FREE'

Philip Pettit on mind, society, and the *res publica*

In one of his critical asides on analytical philosophy William Desmond suggests that there is something objectionable about thinkers who insist on sharpening their analytical tools 'while the earth is on fire' (1995a: 223). Philip Pettit cannot be accused of such Nero-like activity. Though working more or less within the analytical tradition in philosophy, he is as concerned about the burning earth as he is about the clarity, consistency, and accuracy of the language he uses. Born in Ballygar, Co. Galway, in 1945, Pettit was educated locally, graduating from the National University of Ireland, Maynooth, before going on to complete a doctoral degree at Queen's University, Belfast. He worked in a series of teaching posts at different universities in Ireland and Britain before joining, in 1983, the research school of social sciences at the Australian National University, Canberra. In 2002 he moved to Princeton University.

Like Desmond, but with recourse to a very different vocabulary and style of thought, Pettit sets out to construct a theory of human action that will avoid an atomistic individualism on one side and a holistic collectivism on the other. He first addresses the difficult problem of the nature of mind, and, after a sustained engagement with the sometimes difficult arguments of contemporary academic philosophers, he concludes that the concept of mind needs to be rescued from two kinds of threat, one from 'below', the other from 'above'. The threat from below comes from those materialists who would eliminate the concept of mind on the basis that all behaviour can be explained in terms of microphysical events taking place in the neural system. Against these eliminativists he argues that intentional (or mental) states, though dependent ultimately on processes occurring at the microphysical level, are nonetheless real and causally effective. (A decision, for example, is identifiable as a mental as well as a physical event, and any adequate account of why someone did one thing rather than another will have to make reference to that mental event, since it is part of the causal process that led to a particular action.) Many of the things we need to be able to say about human beings – about their motivations, desires, wants, beliefs – could not be said unless intentional states could be meaningfully and truthfully ascribed to them. We would not know what to say about ourselves if we were not able to conceive of ourselves as mindful agents acting intentionally on each other and on a shared environment. Mental events, moreover, are not just connected to behaviour – they are also, and more problematically, connected to neural events going on at the microphysical level. In Pettit's view, the intentional account is more or less compatible with the neural account. Eliminative materialists are mistaken in their claim that the scientific neural account provides the only true causal account, insisting as they do that there is no explanatory work left for the intentional terminology to do. Against the eliminativists Pettit maintains that intentional states *are* causally relevant in so far as they 'program' or 'arrange' for neural states sufficient to produce an action. A question about why any particular action took place can only be properly answered if some account is given of the mental or psychological processes that were occurring at the same time. To leave such processes out of the account is to leave gaps in the complete causal story. As far as Pettit can see, no scientific discovery about the physical make-up of human beings can lead us to deny the existence of intentionality or mentality. To be persuaded by neurophysiology that we are not intentional agents would be as mistaken as coming to be persuaded by atomic physicists that one's desktop is not solid after all (1993: 86).

The second threat to the reality and autonomy of mind – which is also a threat to the reality and autonomy of the individual personality

– comes from above, from collectivist views of the relationship between the individual and society. Pettit does not have a difficulty with theories that emphasize the formative importance of social relationships. Indeed, he wishes to be associated with theories that maintain just such an emphasis. He accepts that most human activities would be impossible without the existence of certain social, cultural, and linguistic practices through which individuals are not just socialized or civilized but effectively 'humanized' in the course of meaningful interaction with others. The full story of any individual's mental life is an expressive-corrective story, a story that implies the 'other-directedness' of the mental life of individuals, a story that presupposes such fundamentally public or social activities as following rules, including the sort of rules that are involved in expressing oneself in a particular language. Rules are learnt from others, corrected by others, applied with a view to having some meaningful effect on others. The complex language in which the most 'private' thoughts are articulated is first learnt in public contexts and only later used to think to oneself. There is a danger, however, that we may now begin to reach here for deterministic metaphors – that we will begin to say that each self or person is essentially a 'product' or creature of social relationships and structures. The collectivist, in claiming that social regularities override intentional ones, is eliminating or displacing individual psychology as effectively as the materialist who refuses to allow an explanatory role to intentional concepts. Pettit finds both versions of eliminativism equally unacceptable, since individual psychology represents 'one of the best-tested programs of understanding that has been devised by human kind' (1996: 144). He rejects collectivism in favour of a picture under which there are many explanatory levels – each autonomous in an important sense – with features at higher levels programming for effects that may be produced by features at the lower. All of these levels rest on a physical or microphysical foundation.

Though drawing upon a more austere vocabulary than Drury, Murdoch, or Desmond, Pettit is just as defensive as they are about the relative autonomy of individuals. His defensiveness takes its most political and challenging form in his *Republicanism: A Theory of Freedom and Government* (1997), a thoroughly analytical but accessible work in which he explores the resources of classical republican philosophy in order to develop 'a vision of being free'. Situating himself within a tradition of political thinking that extends from Cicero, through James Harrington and the English commonwealthmen, to the radical thinkers of eighteenth-century America and France, he presents a defence of republican philosophy that is intended to challenge classical liberalism by offering a more complex and far-reaching conception of liberty. Whereas liberalism tends to define liberty as non-interference (the non-interference by the state in lives of individual citizens), classical republicanism tends to define liberty as non-domination by others, as non-vulnerability to the will of others. The central grievance addressed by republicanism is that of having to live at the mercy of another, having to live in circumstances that leave one vulnerable to the arbitrary decisions or impositions of another person or persons (1997: 5). The dominated person is unfree because he or she lives in the shadow of another's more powerful presence, 'even if no arm is raised against them' (5). This last phrase has a crucial resonance for Pettit, indicating to him the main difference between the liberal and republican conceptions of personal freedom. The liberal is happy to bring about a state which guarantees that each citizen, other things being equal, will be free from arbitrary interference. This allows for the possibility, however, that others retain the power to interfere, that the law is not there to undermine this power but simply to reduce the probability that it will be exercised in certain ways. In other words, the liberal principle of non-interference can cheerfully co-exist with institutions of power and domination that are themselves left intact and unchallenged. In the republican tradition, however, the continued existence of institutions of power and domination means that freedom is always systematically compromised. For classical republicans, freedom implies emancipation from domination, from dependency, from the power (as well as from the fact) of arbitrary interference. It is not enough therefore to introduce and enforce laws against arbitrary interference; it is necessary to go further and introduce laws against the sorts of institution and practice that make such interference possible in the first place. Whereas the liberal tradition allows for the continued flourishing of the non-interfering masters, the republican tradition seeks to place systematic limits on the structures of mastery.

Pettit defines domination in terms of the power of arbitrary interference. Someone has dominion or power over another to the extent that he has the capacity to interfere in an arbitrary way in certain choices that the dominated person may make (52). Interference can include coercion of the body or of the will, or it can take the form of manipulation. All such coercion tends to worsen the situation of the dominated person, especially by limiting, controlling, or preventing the making of choices. Even where the coercion is not actually exercised, an ethos or culture of vulnerability can obtain. A culture of liability to domination and arbitrary interference is an unfree culture, a deferential culture, a culture of 'bowings and cringings' (as John Milton put it), of currying favour with the powers that be, of self-watchfulness, of strategic second-guessing, of having always to keep 'a weather-eye open for the other's moods' (5). In order to make every citizen a free person in his or her own right, it is necessary that each citizen be able to 'look the other in the eye'. A constitution or legal system based on republican principles will address the sources and sites of arbitrary interference as well as the fact of interference itself. This would mean 'republicanizing' all grievances, identifying existing and potential sources of domination, and, where possible, imposing whatever constraints are necessary to reduce or eliminate the power of arbitrary interference. The grievances in question are not just those that arise out of the relationships among the larger political entities, such as the relationship between the state and its citizenry. The grievances can be 'private', domestic, social, or cultural, such as the grievances that women have against practices or customs that leave them vulnerable and dependent; or the grievances that workers have against an economic system that requires them to constantly 'court paths of caution and deference' in their dealings with employers; or the grievances that minorities have against the pressures of democratic majoritarian rule.

Whether one looks to the claims of environmentalism, feminism, socialism, or multiculturalism, it is possible and desirable to make those claims in terms of republican philosophy – in terms, that is, of the variety of ways in which individuals, groups, and communities can achieve freedom from domination and arbitrary interference. These different movements, inspired by different clusters of grievances, should be enriched by republicanizing the language of their objectives; and republicanism, classically understood, should be enriched by drawing to itself the particular energies and concerns of those who make up these modern movements. Though Pettit's argument raises many questions that cannot be addressed here, including questions about the concentration or distribution of power in the republican state, his book deserves to be studied everywhere but especially in Ireland, where the classical republican ideal has been disowned by an imperious liberalism and where it has been too exclusively associated with a militant nationalism.

BIBLIOGRAPHY

Abbott, Thomas K. (1864) *Sight and Touch: An Attempt to Disprove the Received (or Berkleian) Theory of Vision*, London: Longman, Green, Longman, Roberts, & Green.

Alexander, Peter (1985) *Ideas, Qualities and Corpuscles: Locke and Boyle on the External World*, Cambridge: Cambridge University Press.

Alldritt, Keith (1997) *W.B. Yeats: The Man and the Milieu*, London: John Murray.

Anderson, Carol Susan (1982) 'Divine Governance, Miracles, and Laws of Nature in the Early Middle Ages: The *De mirabilibus sacrae scripturae*', unpub. D.Phil. thesis, University of California.

Anstey, Peter R. (2000) *The Philosophy of Robert Boyle*, London: Routledge.

Arkins, Brian (1990) *Builders of My Soul: Greek and Roman Themes in Yeats*, Savage, MD: Barnes & Noble.

Armstrong, D.M. (1960) *Berkeley's Theory of Vision*, Melbourne: Melbourne University Press.

Arnold, Bruce (1999) *Swift: An Illustrated Life*, Dublin: Lilliput Press.

Atherton, Margaret (1990) *Berkeley's Revolution in Vision*, Ithaca, NY: Cornell University Press.

Attis, David (1997) 'The Social Context of W.R. Hamilton's Prediction of Conical Refraction', in Peter J. Bowler and Nicholas Whyte (eds) *Science and Society in Ireland, 1800–1950*, Belfast: Institute of Irish Studies.

Augustine of Hippo, St (1982) *The Literal Meaning of Genesis*, trans. John Hammond Taylor, New York: Paulist Press.

—— (1998) *The City of God against the Pagans*, trans. R.W. Dyson, Cambridge: Cambridge University Press.

Augustine, the Irish (1844–64) *Patrologia Latina*, ed. J.-P. Migne, vol. 35, cols 2149–2200, Paris.

—— (1971) 'The Treatise *De mirabilibus sacrae scripturae*: Critical Edition, with Introduction, English Translation of the Long Rescension and Some Notes', ed. and trans. Francis P. MacGinty, unpub. Ph.D. thesis, National University of Ireland, Dublin.

Ayling, Stanley (1988) *Edmund Burke: His Life and Opinions*, London: John Murray.

Bacon, Francis (1857) *The Works of Francis Bacon*, ed. James Spedding, Robert Leslie Ellis, and Douglas Denon Heath, vol. III, London: Longman & Co.

—— (1858) *The Works of Francis Bacon*, ed. James Spedding, Robert Leslie Ellis, and Douglas Denon Heath, vol. IV, London: Longman & Co.

Barnard, T.C. (1975) *Cromwellian Ireland*, Oxford: Clarendon Press.

Barry, Kevin (1987) *Language, Music, and the Sign*, Cambridge: Cambridge University Press.

—— (1988) 'James Usher and the Irish Enlightenment', *Eighteenth-Century Ireland* 3: 115–22.

Bartlett, Thomas (ed.) (1998) *Life of Theobald Wolfe Tone*, Dublin: Lilliput Press.

Barton, Ruth (1987) 'John Tyndall, Pantheist: A Rereading of the Belfast Address', *Osiris* (2nd ser.) 3: 111–34.

Beckett, J.C. (1966) *The Making of Modern Ireland 1603–1923*, London: Faber & Faber.

—— (1971) 'Swift and the Anglo-Irish Tradition', in C.J. Rawson (ed.) *Focus: Swift*, London: Sphere.

—— (1976) *The Anglo-Irish Tradition*, London: Faber & Faber.

Bentham, Jeremy (1843) *The Works of Jeremy Bentham*, 11 vols, ed. John Bowring, Edinburgh: William Tait.

—— (1989) *The Correspondence of Jeremy Bentham*, vol. 9, ed. Stephen Conway, Oxford: Clarendon Press.

Bentley, Richard (1705) *A Dissertation upon the Epistles of Themistocles, Socrates, Euripides, and Others; and the Fables of Aesop*, published with William Wotton, *Reflections upon Ancient and Modern Learning*, London.

Berkeley, George (1948–57) *The Works of George Berkeley, Bishop of Cloyne*, 9 vols, ed. A.A. Luce and T.E. Jessop, London: Thomas Nelson & Sons.

Berman, David (1971) 'Berkeley, Clayton, and *An Essay on Spirit*', *Journal of the History of Ideas* 32: 367–78.

—— (1982) 'Enlightenment and Counter-Enlightenment in Irish Philosophy', *Archiv für Geschichte der Philosophie* 64: 148–65; 'The Culmination and Causation of Irish Philosophy', *Archiv für Geschichte der Philosophie* 64: 257–79.

—— (1985) 'The Irish Counter-Enlightenment', in Richard Kearney (ed.) *The Irish Mind*, Dublin: Wolfhound Press.

—— (1988) *A History of Atheism in Britain: From Hobbes to Russell*, London: Croom Helm.

—— (ed.) (1991) 'Eighteenth-Century Irish Philosophy', in Seamus Deane (ed.) *The Field Day Anthology of Irish Writing*, vol. 1, Derry: Field Day Publications.

—— (1992) 'Disclaimers as Offence Mechanisms in Charles Blount and John Toland', in Michael Hunter and David Wooton (eds) *Atheism from the Reformation to the Enlightenment*, Oxford: Clarendon Press.

—— (ed.) (1993) *George Berkeley: Alciphron in Focus*, London: Routledge.

—— (1994) *George Berkeley: Idealism and the Man*, Oxford: Clarendon Press.

—— (ed.) (1996) *Atheism in Britain*, vol. IV, Bristol: Thoemmes Press.

—— (1999) 'George Ensor', in J. Yolton, J.V. Price, and J. Stephens (eds) *Dictionary of Eighteenth-Century British Philosophers*, Bristol: Thoemmes Press.

Bethell, Denis (1971) 'English Monks and Irish Reform in the 11th and 12th Centuries', *Historical Studies* 8: 117–18, 125–6.

Bieler, Ludwig (1966) *Ireland, Harbinger of the Middle Ages*, London: Oxford University Press.

Blakemore, Stephen (ed.) (1992) *Burke and the French Revolution*, Athens: University of Georgia Press.

Boas, Marie (1952) 'The Mechanical Philosophy', *Osiris* 10: 412–541.

Bowler, Peter J. and Whyte, Nicholas (eds) (1997) *Science and Society in Ireland, 1800–1950*, Belfast: Institute of Irish Studies.

Boyce, D. George (1991) *Nineteenth-Century Ireland: The Search for Stability*, Savage, MD: Barnes & Noble.

Boyce, D.G., Eccleshall, R. and Geoghegan, V. (eds) (1993) *Political Thought in Ireland Since the Seventeenth Century*, London: Routledge.

Boylan, T.A. and Foley, T.P. (1983) 'John Elliot Cairnes, John Stuart Mill and Ireland: Some Problems for Political Economy', *Hermathena* 135: 96–118.

—— (1992) *Political Economy and Colonial Ireland*, London: Routledge.

Boyle, Frank T. (1988) 'Profane and Debauched Deist: Swift in the Contemporary Response to *A Tale of a Tub*', *Eighteenth-Century Ireland* 3: 25–38.

Boyle, Patrick (1916) 'Dr. Michael Moore', *Archivium Hibernicum* 5: 7–16.

Boyle, Robert (1772) *The Works of the Honourable Robert Boyle*, 6 vols, ed. Thomas Birch, Bristol: Thoemmes Press.

—— (1991) *Selected Philosophical Papers of Robert Boyle*, ed. M.A. Stewart, Indianapolis: Hackett.

—— (1996) *A Free Enquiry into the Vulgarly Received Notion of Nature*, ed. Edward B. Davis and Michael Hunter, Cambridge: Cambridge University Press.

—— (1999) *The Works of Robert Boyle*, vols 1–7, ed. Michael Hunter and Edward B. Davis, London: Pickering & Chatto.

Bracken, H.M. (1965) *The Early Reception of Berkeley's Immaterialism 1710–1733*, The Hague: Martinus Nijhoff.

—— (1974) *Berkeley*, London: Macmillan.

Bradshaw, Brendan (1979) *The Irish Constitutional Revolution of the Sixteenth Century*, Cambridge: Cambridge University Press.

—— (1993) 'Geoffrey Keating: Apologist of Irish Ireland', in B. Bradshaw, A. Hadfield, and W. Maley (eds) *Representing Ireland: Literature and the Origins of Conflict, 1534–1660*, Cambridge: Cambridge University Press.

Brady, Ciaran and Gillespie, Raymond (eds) (1986) *Natives and Newcomers: The Making of Irish Colonial Society 1534–1641*, Dublin: Irish Academic Press.

Bredvold, Louis I. and Ross, Ralph G. (eds) (1967) *The Philosophy of Edmund Burke*, Ann Arbor: University of Michigan Press.

Brock, W.H., McMillan, N.D., and Mollan, R.C. (eds) (1981) *John Tyndall: Essays on a Natural Philosopher*, Dublin: Royal Dublin Society.

Brockliss, L.W.B. (1981) 'Aristotle, Descartes and the New Science: Natural Philosophy at the University of Paris, 1600–1740', *Annals of Science* 38: 33–69.

Brown, Michael (1999) 'Francis Hutcheson and the Molesworth Connection', *Eighteenth-Century Ireland* 14: 62–76.

Brown, Terence (1981) *Ireland: A Social and Cultural History*, London: Fontana.

Browne, Peter (1697) *A Letter in Answer to a Book entitled Christianity Not Mysterious*, Dublin.

—— (1728) *The Procedure, Extent and Limits of Human Understanding*, London.

—— (1733) *Things Divine and Supernatural conceived by Analogy with Things Natural and Human*, London.

Bryant, Sophie (1913) *The Genius of the Gael: A Study in Celtic Psychology*, London: T. Fisher Unwin.

Burchfield, J.D. (1981) 'John Tyndall: A Biographical Sketch', in W.H. Brock, N.D. McMillan, and R.C. Mollan (eds) *John Tyndall: Essays on a Natural Philosopher*, Dublin: Royal Dublin Society.

Burke, Edmund (1968) *Reflections on the Revolution in France*, ed. Conor Cruise O'Brien, Harmondsworth: Pelican.

—— (1987) *Reflections on the Revolution in France*, ed. J.G.A. Pocock, Indianapolis: Hackett.

—— (1989) *The Writings and Speeches of Edmund Burke*, vol. VIII, ed. L.G. Mitchell, Oxford: Clarendon Press.

—— (1991) *The Writings and Speeches of Edmund Burke*, vol. IX, ed. R.B. McDowell, Oxford: Clarendon Press.

—— (1997) *The Writings and Speeches of Edmund Burke*, vol. I, ed. T.O. McLoughlin and James T. Boulton, Oxford: Clarendon Press.

—— (1999) *The Portable Edmund Burke*, ed. Isaac Kramnick, Harmondsworth: Penguin.

Butler, Marilyn (1984) *Burke, Paine, Godwin, and the Revolution Controversy*, Cambridge: Cambridge University Press.

Caball, Marc (1998) *Poets and Politics: Reaction and Continuity in Irish Poetry, 1558–1625*, Cork: Cork University Press.

Cairnes, J.E. (1857) *The Character and Logical Method of Political Economy*, London: Macmillan & Co.

—— (1863) *The Slave Power*, 2nd edn, London: Macmillan & Co.

—— (1865) 'Ireland in Transition: Land Tenure', *Economist* 14 Oct.: 1238–9.

—— (1873) *Essays in Political Economy: Theoretical and Applied*, London: Macmillan & Co.

—— (1874) *Some Leading Principles of Political Economy Newly Expounded*, New York: Harper & Brothers.

Canavan, F.P. (1960) *The Political Reason of Edmund Burke*, Durham, NC: Duke University Press.

Canny, Nicholas (1982a) *The Upstart Earl*, Cambridge: Cambridge University Press.

—— (1982b) 'The Formation of the Irish Mind: Religion, Politics and Gaelic Irish Literature 1580–1750', *Past and Present* 95: 91–116.

—— (1987) 'Identity Formation in Ireland: The Emergence of the Anglo-Irish', in Nicholas Canny and Anthony Pagden (eds) *Colonial Identity in the Atlantic World, 1500–1800*, Princeton: Princeton University Press.

—— (1989) 'Early Modern Ireland, *c.* 1500–1700', in R.F. Foster (ed.) *The Oxford Illustrated History of Ireland*, Oxford: Oxford University Press.

—— (2001) *Making Ireland British*, Oxford: Oxford University Press.

Cappuyns, Maïeul (1933) *Jean Scot Erigène: Sa vie, son oeuvre, sa pensée*, Louvain: Abbaye de Mont César.

Carabelli, Giancarlo (1975) *Tolandiana: materiali bibliografici per lo studio dell'opera e della fortuna di John Toland (1690–1722)*, Florence: La Nuova Italia.

Carey, Daniel (1997a) 'Method, Moral Sense, and the Problem of Diversity: Francis Hutcheson and the Scottish Enlightenment', *British Journal for the History of Philosophy* 5, 2: 275–96.

—— (1997b) 'Swift Among the Freethinkers', *Eighteenth-Century Ireland* 12: 89–99.

Carnochan, W.B. (1968) *Lemuel Gulliver's Mirror for Man*, Berkeley and Los Angeles: University of California Press.

Carpenter, Andrew and Deane, Seamus (eds) (1991) 'The Shifting Perspective', in Seamus Deane (ed.) *The Field Day Anthology of Irish Writing*, vol. I, Derry: Field Day Publications.

Chambers, Liam (2000) 'Defying Descartes: Michael Moore (1639–1726) and Aristotelian Philosophy in France and Ireland', in Michael Brown and Stephen Harrison (eds) *The Medieval World and the Modern Mind*, Dublin: Four Courts Press.

Champion, J.A.I. (1992) *The Pillars of Priestcraft Shaken: The Church of England and its Enemies, 1660–1730*, Cambridge: Cambridge University Press.

—— (1999) '"Manuscripts of Mine Abroad": John Toland and the Circulation of Ideas, *c.* 1700–1722', *Eighteenth-Century Ireland* 14: 9–36.

Chart, D.A. (ed.) (1931) *The Drennan Letters*, Belfast: His Majesty's Stationery Office.

Clarke, Desmond M. (1997) 'Toland on Faith and Reason', in P. McGuinness, A. Harrison, and R. Kearney (eds) *John Toland's Christianity not Mysterious*, Dublin: Lilliput Press.

Clayton, Robert (1752a) *An Essay on Spirit*, 4th edn, London and Dublin.

—— (1752b) *The Genuine Sequel to the Essay on Spirit*, Dublin and London.

—— (1753) *A Defence of the Essay on Spirit*, London.

—— (1754) *Some Remarks on Dr. McDonnell's Essay towards an Answer to the Essay on Spirit*, Dublin.

—— (1763) *Some thoughts on self love, innate-ideas, free-will, taste, sentiments, liberty, and necessity, etc., occasioned by reading Mr. Hume's works*, Dublin.

Cobban, Alfred (1960) *Edmund Burke and the Revolt against the Eighteenth Century*, 2nd edn, London: George Allen & Unwin.

Cobbe, Frances P. (1869) 'The Final Cause of Women', in Josephine Butler (ed.) *Women's Work and Women's Culture*, London: Macmillan & Co.

—— (1872) *Darwinism in Morals and Other Essays*, London: Williams & Norgate.

—— (1888) *The Scientific Spirit of the Age*, London: Smith, Elder & Co.

—— (1894) *Life of Frances Power Cobbe by Herself*, 2nd edn, London: Richard Bentley & Son.

Cohn, Norman (1970) *The Pursuit of the Millennium*, rev. edn, Oxford: Oxford University Press.

Connellan, Colm (1992) 'Michael Moore (1640–1726)', in F. O'Rourke (ed.) *At the Heart of the Real*, Dublin: Irish Academic Press.

Connolly, James (1988) *James Connolly: Selected Writings*, ed. P. Berresford Ellis, London: Pluto Press.

Connolly, S.J. (1998) 'Swift and Protestant Ireland', in A. Douglas, P. Kelly, and I.C. Ross (eds) (1998) *Locating Swift*, Dublin: Four Courts Press.

—— (ed.) (2000) *Political Ideas in Eighteenth-Century Ireland*, Dublin: Four Courts Press.

Cosslett, T. (ed.) (1984) *Science and Religion in the Nineteenth Century*, Cambridge: Cambridge University Press.

Coughlan, Patricia (1989) '"Some secret scourge which shall by her come unto England": Ireland and Incivility in Spenser', in Patricia Coughlan (ed.) *Spenser and Ireland*, Cork: Cork University Press.

Crane, R.S. (1971) 'The Houyhnhnms, the Yahoos, and the History of Ideas', in D. Donoghue (ed.) *Jonathan Swift: A Critical Anthology*, Harmondsworth: Penguin.

Craven, Kenneth (1986) '*A Tale of a Tub* and the 1697 Dublin Controversy', *Eighteenth-Century Ireland* 1: 97–110.

Crook, D.P. (1984) *Benjamin Kidd: Portrait of a Social Darwinist*, Cambridge: Cambridge University Press.

Crowe, M.B. (1956) 'Peter of Ireland: Teacher of St Thomas Aquinas', *Studies* 45: 443–56.

—— (1963) 'Peter of Ireland's Approach to Metaphysics', *Miscellanea Medievalia* 2: 154–60.

Cullingford, Elizabeth (1985) 'The Unknown Thought of W.B. Yeats', in Richard Kearney (ed.) *The Irish Mind*, Dublin: Wolfhound Press.

Daly, Mary E. (1986) *The Famine in Ireland*, Dublin: Dublin Historical Association.

Daniel, Stephen H. (1984) *John Toland: His Methods, Manners, and Mind*, Kingston: McGill-Queen's University Press.

—— (1997) 'Toland's Semantic Pantheism', in P. McGuinness, A. Harrison, and R. Kearney (eds) *John Toland's Christianity not Mysterious: Text, Associated Works and Critical Essays*, Dublin: Lilliput Press.

D'Arcy, Frank (2001) *Wild Geese and Travelling Scholars*, Cork: Mercier Press.

Darwin, Charles (1885) *Origin of Species by Means of Natural Selection*, 6th edn, London: John Murray.

Darwin, Francis (ed.) (1959) *The Life and Letters of Charles Darwin*, 2 vols, New York: Basic Books.

Davie, Donald A. (1952) 'Irony and Conciseness in Berkeley and in Swift', *Dublin Magazine* (Oct.–Dec.): 20–9.

Davis, Richard (1987) *The Young Ireland Movement*, Dublin: Gill & Macmillan.

Davis, Thomas (1889) *Prose Writings of Thomas Davis*, ed. T.W. Rolleston, London: Walter Scott.

Davitt, Michael (1904) *The Fall of Feudalism in Ireland*, London: Harper & Brothers.

Deane, Seamus (1985a) *Celtic Revivals*, London: Faber & Faber.

—— (1985b) 'Edmund Burke and the Ideology of Irish Liberalism', in Richard Kearney (ed.) *The Irish Mind*, Dublin: Wolfhound Press.

—— (ed.) (1991) 'Edmund Burke', in Seamus Deane (ed.) *The Field Day Anthology of Irish Writing*, vol. I, Derry: Field Day Publications.

—— (1999) *Strange Country: Ireland, Modernity and Nationhood 1790–1970*, Oxford: Clarendon Press.

De Paor, Liam (1985) 'The Rebel Mind: Republican and Loyalist', in Richard Kearney (ed.) *The Irish Mind*, Dublin: Wolfhound Press.

DePorte, Michael (1974) *Nightmares and Hobbyhorses: Swift, Sterne, and Augustan Ideas of Madness*, San Marino: Huntington Library.

Descartes, René (1970) *Philosophical Writings*, trans. Elizabeth Anscombe and Peter Geach, rev'd ed., Wokingham: Van Nostrand Reinhold.

Desmond, William (1987) *Desire, Dialectic, and Otherness: An Essay on Origins*, New Haven: Yale University Press.

—— (1989) *Hegel and his Critics*, Albany: SUNY Press.

—— (1990) *Philosophy and its Others: Ways of Being and Mind*, Albany: SUNY Press.

—— (1995a) *Perplexity and Ultimacy*, Albany: SUNY Press.

—— (1995b) *Being and the Between*, Albany: SUNY Press.

de Vere, Aubrey (1897) *Recollections of Aubrey de Vere*, 2nd edn, London: Edward Arnold.

Dickson, David (1993) 'Paine and Ireland', in D. Dickson, D. Keogh, and K. Whelan, (eds) *The United Irishmen*, Cork: Cork University Press.

—— (2000) *New Foundations: Ireland 1660–1800*, 2nd edn, Dublin: Irish Academic Press.

Dillon, Myles and Chadwick, Nora (2000) *The Celtic Realms*, London: Phoenix Press.

Donoghue, Denis (ed.) (1968) *Swift Revisited*, Cork: Mercier Press.

—— (ed.) (1971) *Jonathan Swift*, Harmondsworth: Penguin.

—— (1986) *We Irish*, Berkeley and Los Angeles: University of California Press.

Doody, Margaret Ann (1995) 'Swift and Romance', in C. Fox and B. Tooley (eds) *Walking Naboth's Vineyard*, Notre Dame: University of Notre Dame Press.

—— (1998) 'Swift and the Mess of Narrative', in A. Douglas, P. Kelly, and I.C. Ross (eds) (1998) *Locating Swift*, Dublin: Four Courts Press.

Dooley, Dolores (1996) *Equality in Community: Sexual Equality in the Writings of William Thompson and Anna Doyle Wheeler*, Cork: Cork University Press.

Douglas, A., Kelly, P., and Ross, I.C. (eds) (1998) *Locating Swift*, Dublin: Four Courts Press.

Downie, R.S. (ed.) (1994) *Francis Hutcheson: Philosophical Writings*, London: J.M. Dent.

Drury, M. O'C. (1973) *The Danger of Words*, London: Routledge & Kegan Paul.

—— (1996) *The Danger of Words and Writings on Wittgenstein*, eds D. Berman, M. Fitzgerald, and J. Hayes, Bristol: Thoemmes Press.

Duddy, Thomas (1998) 'The Peculiar Opinions of an Irish Platonist: The Life and Thought of Thomas Maguire', in Tadhg Foley and Séan Ryder (eds) *Ideology and Ireland in the Nineteenth Century*, Dublin: Four Courts Press.

—— (1999) 'Toland, Berkeley, and the Irrational Hypothesis', *Eighteenth-Century Ireland* 14: 49–61.

Dunne, Michael (1992) 'Petrus de Hibernia: A Thirteenth-Century Irish Philosopher', *Philosophical Studies* 33: 201–30.

—— (ed.) (1993) *Magistri Petri de Ybernia: Expositio et Quaestiones in Aristotelis Librum de Longitudine et Brevitate Vitae*, Louvain: Editions Peeters.

—— (ed.) (1996) *Magistri Petri de Ybernia: Expositio et Quaestiones in Librum Aristotelis Peryermenias seu De Interpretatione*, Louvain: Editions Peeters.

Eagleton, Terry (1995) *Heathcliff and the Great Hunger: Studies in Irish Culture*, London: Verso.

—— (1998) *Crazy John and the Bishop*, Cork: Cork University Press.

—— (1999) *Scholars and Rebels in Nineteenth-Century Ireland*, Oxford: Blackwell.

Edwards, Ruth Dudley (1977) *Patrick Pearse: The Triumph of Failure*, London: Victor Gollancz.

Ehrenpries, Irwin (1962; 1967; 1983) *Swift: The Man, his Works, and the Age*, 3 vols, London: Methuen.

Elliott, Marianne (1989) *Wolfe Tone: Prophet of Independence*, New Haven: Yale University Press.

Ellis, Steven G. (1985) *Tudor Ireland: Crown, Community and the Conflict of Cultures 1470–1603*, London: Longmans.

Ellmann, Richard (1979) *Yeats: The Man and the Masks*, Harmondsworth: Penguin.

Ensor, George (1801) *The Principles of Morality*, London.

—— (1816) *Janus on Sion, or Past and to Come*, London.

—— (1818) *An Inquiry concerning the Population of Nations*, London.

—— (1831) *Anti-Union: Ireland as She Ought to Be*, Dublin.

Eriugena, John Scottus (1968; 1972; 1981; 1983) *Periphyseon*, vols I–III, trans. I.P. Sheldon-Williams, Dublin: Dublin Institute for Advanced Studies.

—— (1995) *Periphyseon*, vol. IV, trans. J.J. O'Meara, Dublin: Dublin Institute for Advanced Studies.

—— (1998) *Treatise on Divine Predestination*, trans. Mary Brennan, Notre Dame: University of Notre Dame Press.

Esposito, M. (1919) 'On the Pseudo-Augustinian Treatise, "De mirabilibus sanctae scripturae," Written in Ireland in the Year 655', *Proceedings of the Royal Irish Academy*, XXXV: 189–207.

Fabricant, Carole (1982) *Swift's Landscape*, Baltimore: Johns Hopkins University Press.

—— (1995) 'History, Narrativity, and Swift's Project to "Mend the World"', in Christopher Fox (ed.) *Jonathan Swift: Gulliver's Travels*, New York: Macmillan.

Fennell, Desmond (1985) 'Irish Socialist Thought', in Richard Kearney (ed.) *The Irish Mind*, Dublin: Wolfhound Press.

Flanagan, Owen (1992) *Consciousness Reconsidered*, Cambridge, MA: MIT Press.

Flower, Robin (1947) *The Irish Tradition*, Oxford: Oxford University Press.

Foley, Tadhg and Ryder, Seán (eds) (1998) *Ideology and Ireland in the Nineteenth Century*, Dublin: Four Courts Press.

Foley, Timothy P. (1994) 'Thomas Maguire and the Parnell Forgeries', *Journal of the Galway Archaeological and Historical Society* 46: 173–96.

Foot, Michael (1966) *The Pen and the Sword: A Year in the Life of Jonathan Swift*, London: MacGibbon & Kee.

Ford, Alan (1986) 'The Protestant Reformation in Ireland', in Ciaran Brady and Reymond Gillespie (eds) *Natives and Newcomers*, Dublin: Irish Academic Press.

Foster, John W. (ed.) (1997) *Nature in Ireland: A Scientific and Cultural History*, Dublin: Lilliput.

—— (1997) 'Natural History in Modern Irish Culture', in Peter J. Bowler and Nicholas Whyte (eds) *Science and Society in Ireland, 1800–1950*, Belfast: Institute of Irish Studies.

Foster, R.F. (1988) *Modern Ireland 1600–1972*, London: Allen Lane.

—— (1989) 'Ascendancy and Union', in R.F. Foster (ed.) *The Oxford Illustrated History of Ireland*, Oxford: Oxford University Press.

Fox, Christopher (ed.) (1995) *Jonathan Swift: Gulliver's Travels*, New York: St. Martin's Press.

Fox, Christopher and Tooley, Brenda (eds) (1995) *Walking Naboth's Vineyard*, Notre Dame: University of Notre Dame Press.

Frame, Robin (1981) *Colonial Ireland, 1169–1369*, Dublin: Helicon.

Fraser, Ian (1968) 'Father and Son – A Tale of Two Cities', *Ulster Medical Journal* 37, 1: 1–39.

Freeman, Michael (1980) *Edmund Burke and the Critique of Political Radicalism*, Oxford: Blackwell.

Furlong, E.J. (1973) 'Philosophy in Trinity College 1866–', *Hermathena* 115: 98–115.

Gargett, Graham and Sheridan, Geraldine (eds) *Ireland and the French Enlightenment 1700–1800*, London: Macmillan.

Geoghegan, Vincent (1993) 'The Emergence and Submergence of Irish Socialism, 1821–51', in D.G. Boyce, R. Eccleshall, and V. Geoghegan (eds) *Political Thought in Ireland Since the Seventeenth Century*, London: Routledge.

Gerstenberger, Donna (1975) *Iris Murdoch*, London: Bucknell University Press.

Gibbons, Luke (1998) 'Alternative Enlightenments', in Mary Cullen (ed.) *1798: 200 Years of Resonance*, Dublin: Irish Reporter Publications.

Gillingham, John (1993) 'The English Invasion of Ireland', in B. Bradshaw, A. Hadfield, and W. Maley (eds) *Representing Ireland: Literature and the Origins of Conflict, 1534–1660*, Cambridge: Cambridge University Press.

Giraldus Cambrensis (1978) *Expugnatio Hibernica: The Conquest of Ireland*, ed. and trans. A.B. Scott and F.X. Martin, Dublin: Royal Irish Academy.

—— (1982) *The History and Topography of Ireland*, trans. John J. O'Meara, Dublin: Dolmen Press.

Graham, William (1872) *Idealism: An Essay, Metaphysical and Critical*, London: Longmans, Green.

Grattan, Henry (1874) *The Speeches of the Right Hon. Henry Grattan*, ed. Daniel Owen Madden, Dublin: James Duffy.

Graves, Robert Percival (1885) *Life of Sir William Rowan Hamilton*, 3 vols, Dublin: Hodges, Figgis, & Co.

Gravil, Richard (ed.) (1974) *Swift: Gulliver's Travels*, London: Macmillan.

Griffith, Gareth (1993) *Socialism and Superior Brains: The Political Thought of Bernard Shaw*, London: Routledge.

Grosjean, Paul (1955) 'Sur quelques exégètes irlandais du VIIe siècle', *Sacris Erudire*, VII: 67–98.

Gwynn, Aubrey (1933) 'Richard Fitzralph, Archbishop of Armagh', *Studies* 22: 389–405.

Hall, Marie Boas (1966) *Robert Boyle on Natural Philosophy*, Bloomington: Indiana University Press.

Hankins, Thomas L. (1980) *Sir William Rowan Hamilton*, Baltimore: Johns Hopkins University Press.

Harrison, Alan (1994) *Béal Eiriciúil as Inis Eoghain: John Toland (1670–1722)*, Dublin: Coscéim.

—— (1997) 'John Toland's Celtic Background', in P. McGuinness, A. Harrison, and R. Kearney (eds) *John Toland's Christianity not Mysterious*, Dublin: Lilliput Press.

Harth, Phillip (1961) *Swift and Anglican Rationalism: The Religious Background of 'A Tale of a Tub'*, Chicago: Chicago University Press.

Hayes, John (1996) 'Wittgenstein's "Pupil": The Writings of Maurice O'Connor Drury', in M. O'Connor Drury, *The Danger of Words and Writings on Wittgenstein*, ed. D. Berman, M. Fitzgerald, and J. Hayes, Bristol: Thoemmes Press.

Hederman, Mark Patrick (1985) 'The "Mind" of Joyce: From Paternalism to Paternity', in Richard Kearney (ed.) *The Irish Mind*, Dublin: Wolfhound Press.

Herren, Michael W. (1996) *Latin Letters in Early Christian Ireland*, Ashgate: Aldershot.

Herries Davies, Gordon L. (1985) 'Irish Thought in Science', in Richard Kearney (ed.) *The Irish Mind*, Dublin: Wolfhound Press.

Hill, Jacqueline (1995) 'Ireland without Union: Molyneux and his Legacy', in John Robertson (ed.) *A Union for Empire: Political Thought and British Union of 1707*, Cambridge: Cambridge University Press.

Hobbes, Thomas (1651) *Leviathan, or The Matter, Forme, & Power of a Common-Wealth, Ecclesiastical and Civill*, London.

Hoppen, K. Theodore (1970) *The Common Scientist in the Seventeenth Century*, Charlottesville: University Press of Virginia.

Houghton, Roy W., Berman, David and Lapan, Maureen T. (eds) *Images of Berkeley*, Dublin: Wolfhound Press.

Houston, Arthur (ed.) (1906) *Daniel O'Connell: His Early Life and Journal 1795–1802*, London: Sir Isaac Pitman & Sons.

Hume, David (1975) 'Of Miracles', in *Enquiries concerning Human Understanding and concerning the Principles of Morals*, ed. L.A. Selby-Bigge and P.H. Nidditch, Oxford: Clarendon Press.

Hunt, E.K. (1979) 'Utilitarianism and the Labor Theory of Value: A Critique of the Ideas of William Thompson', *History of Political Economy* 2, 4: 545–71.

Hunter, Michael (ed.) (1994) *Robert Boyle Reconsidered*, Cambridge: Cambridge University Press.

Hutcheson, Francis (1738) *An Inquiry into the Original of our Ideas of Beauty and Virtue*, 4th edn, London.

—— (1742) *An Essay on the Nature and Conduct of the Passions and Affections, with Illustrations on the Moral Sense*, 3rd edn, London.

—— (1747) *A Short Introduction to Moral Philosophy*, Glasgow.

—— (1755) *A System of Moral Philosophy*, Glasgow.

—— (1969–90) *Collected Works of Francis Hutcheson*, 7 vols, Hildesheim: Georg Olms.

—— (1994) *Philosophical Writings*, ed. R.S. Downie, London: J.M. Dent.

Ingram, John Kells (1864) 'Considerations on the State of Ireland,' *Journal of the Statistical and Social Inquiry Society of Ireland* 4: 13–26.

—— (1864) 'A Comparison between the English and Irish Poor Laws with Respect to the Conditions of Relief', *Journal of the Statistical and Social Inquiry Society of Ireland* 4: 43–61.

—— (1895) *A History of Slavery and Serfdom*, London: Adam & Charles Black.

—— (1901) *Human Nature and Morals*, London: Adam & Charles Black.

—— (1919) *A History of Political Economy*, London: Adam & Charles Black.

Jacob, Margaret C. (1976) *The Newtonians and the English Revolution 1689–1720*, Ithaca, NY: Cornell University Press.

—— (1981) *The Radical Enlightenment*, London: George Allen & Unwin.

Jeffares, A.N. (ed.) (1967) *Fair Liberty Was All His Cry*, London: Macmillan.

—— (ed.) (1969) *Swift: Modern Judgements*, London: Macmillan.

Johnston, Edith Mary (1974) *Ireland in the Eighteenth Century*, Dublin: Gill & Macmillan.

Johnston, Joseph (1970) *Berkeley's Querist in Historical Perspective*, Dundalk: Dundalgan Press.

Jones, R.F. (1961) *Ancients and Moderns*, 2nd. edn, Berkeley and Los Angeles: University of California Press.

Jordan, John (1985) 'Shaw, Wilde, Synge and Yeats: Ideas, Epigrams, Blackberries and Chassis', in Richard Kearney (ed.) *The Irish Mind*, Dublin: Wolfhound Press.

Kane, Robert (1845) *The Industrial Resources of Ireland*, 2nd edn, Dublin: Hodges & Smith.

Kearney, Hugh F. (1964) *Origins of the Scientific Revolution*, Longmans, Green, & Co.

Kearney, Richard (ed.) (1985a) *The Irish Mind*, Dublin: Wolfhound Press.

—— (1985b) 'Beckett: The Demythologising Intellect', in Richard Kearney (ed.) *The Irish Mind*, Dublin: Wolfhound Press.

—— (1997a) *Postnationalist Ireland*, London: Routledge.

—— (1997b) 'John Toland: An Irish Philosopher?' in P. McGuinness, A. Harrison, and R. Kearney (eds) *John Toland's Christianity not Mysterious: Text, Associated Works and Critical Essays*, Dublin: Lilliput Press.

Keating, Geoffrey (1902–14) *The History of Ireland*, 4 vols, ed. and trans. David Comyn and P.S. Dinneen, repr. with an introduction by Brendán Ó Buachalla (1987), London: Irish Texts Society.

Kelly, Patrick (1979) 'Locke and Molyneux: The Anatomy of a Friendship', *Hermathena* 126: 38–53.

—— (1988) 'William Molyneux and the Spirit of Liberty in Eighteenth-Century Ireland', *Eighteenth-Century Ireland* 3: 133–48.

—— (1998) '"Conclusions by no Means Calculated for the Circumstances and Conditions of Ireland": Swift, Berkeley and the Solution to Ireland's Economic Problems', in A. Douglas, P. Kelly, and I.C. Ross (eds) (1998) *Locating Swift*, Dublin: Four Courts Press.

—— (2000) 'Recasting a Tradition: William Molyneux and the Sources of *The Case of Ireland . . . Stated*', in Jane H. Ohlmeyer (ed.) *Political Thought in Seventeenth-Century Ireland*, Cambridge: Cambridge University Press.

Kenney, James F. (1993) *The Sources for the Early History of Ireland: Ecclesiastical*, 2nd edn, Dublin: Four Courts Press.

Keogh, Dáire (1993) *'The French Disease': The Catholic Church and Irish Radicalism 1790–1800*, Dublin: Four Courts Press.

Kiberd, Declan (1996) *Inventing Ireland: The Literature of the Modern Nation*, London: Vintage.

Kidd, Benjamin (1895) *Social Evolution*, 2nd edn, London: Macmillan & Co.

King, William (1702) *De origine mali*, Dublin.

—— (1709) *Sermon on Predestination and Foreknowledge*, Dublin.

—— (1732) *An Essay on the Origin of Evil*, trans. Edmund Law, 2nd edn, 2 vols, London.

Kivy, P. (1976) *The Seventh Sense: A Study of Francis Hutcheson's Aesthetics and its Influence in Eighteenth-Century Britain*, New York: B. Franklin.

Knox, R. Buick (1967) *James Ussher, Archbishop of Armagh*, Cardiff: University of Wales Press.

Kramnick, Isaac (1977) *The Rage of Edmund Burke*, New York: Basic Books.

Larkin, John (ed.) *The Trial of William Drennan*, Dublin: Irish Academic Press.

Larminie, William (1897) 'Joannes Scotus Erigena', *Contemporary Review* 71: 557–72.

Lecky, W.E.H. (1892) *History of England in the Eighteenth Century*, vol. III, London: Longmans, Green, & Co.

—— (1910) *History of the Rise and Influence of the Spirit of Rationalism in Europe*, 2 vols, London: Longmans, Green, & Co.

Lee, Joseph (1973) *The Modernisation of Irish Society 1848–1918*, Dublin: Gill & Macmillan.

—— (1984) 'The Social and Economic Ideas of O'Connell', in Kevin B. Nowlan and Maurice R. O'Connell (eds) *Daniel O'Connell: Portrait of a Radical*, Belfast: Appletree Press.

—— (1989) *Ireland 1912–1985*, Cambridge: Cambridge University Press.

Leerssen, Joep (1996) *Mere Irish and Fíor-Ghael*, Cork: Cork University Press.

Leibniz, G.W. (1996) *New Essays on Human Understanding*, ed. Peter Remnant and Jonathan Bennett, Cambridge: Cambridge University Press.

Lennon, Colm (1981) *Richard Stanihurst, The Dubliner*, Dublin: Irish Academic Press.

Leslie, T.E.C. (1870) *Land Systems and Industrial Economy*, London: Longmans, Green, & Co.

—— (1888) *Essays in Political Economy*, 2nd edn, Dublin: Hodges, Figgis, & Co.

Livesey, James (1998) Introduction to Arthur O'Connor, *The State of Ireland*, Dublin: Lilliput Press.

Livingstone, David N. (1997) 'Darwin in Belfast: The Evolution Debate', in J.W. Foster (ed.) *Nature in Ireland*, Dublin: Lilliput.

Lloyd, David (1993) *Anomalous States: Irish Writing and the Post-Colonial Moment*, Dublin: Lilliput Press.

—— (1999) *Ireland After History*, Notre Dame: University of Notre Dame Press.

Lock, F.P. (1998) *Edmund Burke: Vol. I, 1730–1784*, Oxford: Clarendon Press.

Locke, John (1708) *Some Familiar Letters between Mr. Locke and Several of his Friends*, London.

—— (1794) *The Works of John Locke*, 9th edn, vol. VIII, London.

—— (1975) *An Essay concerning Human Understanding*, ed. P.H. Nidditch, Oxford: Oxford University Press.

Louis, Frances D. (1981) *Swift's Anatomy of Misunderstanding*, Totawa, NJ: Barnes & Noble.

Lovejoy, Arthur O. (1960) *The Great Chain of Being*, New York: Harper & Brothers.

Luce, A.A. (1945) *Berkeley's Immaterialism*, London: Thomas Nelson & Sons.

—— (1949) *The Life of George Berkeley*, London: Thomas Nelson & Sons.

Luce, A.A. and Jessop, T.E. (eds) (1948–57) *The Works of George Berkeley*, 9 vols, London: Thomas Nelson & Sons.

Lurbe, Pierre (1999) 'John Toland and the Naturalization of the Jews', *Eighteenth-Century Ireland* 14: 37–48.

Lydon, James (1998) *The Making of Ireland*, London: Routledge.

Lyons, F.S.L. (1973) *Ireland Since the Famine*, London: Weidenfeld & Nicolson.

—— (1982) *Culture and Anarchy in Ireland 1890–1939*, Oxford: Oxford University Press.

McBride, Ian (1993a) 'The School of Virtue: Francis Hutcheson, Irish Presbyterians and the Scottish Enlightenment', in D.G. Boyce, R. Eccleshall, and V. Geoghegan (eds) *Political Thought in Ireland since the Seventeenth Century*, London: Routledge.

—— (1993b) 'William Drennan and the Dissenting Tradition', in D. Dickson, D. Keogh, and K. Whelan (eds) *The United Irishmen*, Dublin: Lilliput Press.

McCartney, Donal (1980) *The World of Daniel O'Connell*, Dublin and Cork: Mercier Press.

—— (1994) *W.E.H. Lecky: Historian and Politician 1838–1903*, Dublin: Lilliput Press.

MacCormac, Henry (1830) *A Plan for the Relief of the Unemployed Poor*, Belfast: Stuart & Gregg.

—— (1831) *An Appeal on Behalf of the Poor*, Belfast: S. Archer, J. Hodgson, and M. Jellett.

—— (1837) *The Philosophy of Human Nature*, London: Longman, Rees, Orme, Brown, Green, & Longman.

—— (1853) *Moral-Sanatory Economy*, Belfast.

—— (1877) *The Conversation of a Soul with God: A Theodicy*, London: Trübner & Co.

McCormack, W.J. (1994) *From Burke to Beckett*, Cork: Cork University Press.

MacCurtain, Margaret (1972) *Tudor and Stuart Ireland*, Dublin: Gill & Macmillan.

McDonnell, Thomas (1753) *An Essay towards an Answer to a Book, Entitled An Essay on Spirit*, Dublin.

—— (1754) *A Short Vindication of the Passages in the Essay towards an Answer to the Essay on Spirit, as Remarked on by the Author of that Essay*, Dublin.

McDonough, T., Slater, E., and Boylan, T.A. (2000) 'Political Economy before and after the Famine', unpub. paper, National University of Ireland, Galway.

McDowell, R.B. (1944) *Irish Public Opinion 1750–1800*, London: Faber & Faber.

McEvoy, J.J. (1987) 'Johannes Scottus Eriugena and Robert Grosseteste: An Ambiguous Influence', in W. Beierwaltes (ed.) *Eriugena Redivivus*, Heidelberg: Carl Winter Universitätsverlag.

McGinn, Colin (1991) *The Problem of Consciousness*, Oxford: Blackwell.

MacGinty, Francis P. (ed. and trans.) (1971) 'The Treatise *De Mirabilibus Sacrae Scripturae*: Critical Edition, with Introduction, English Translation of the Long Rescension and Some Notes', unpub. Ph.D. thesis, National University of Ireland, Dublin.

MacGinty, Gerard [Francis P.] (1985) 'The Irish Augustine: *De Mirabilibus Sacrae Scripturae*', in P. Ní Chatháin and M. Richter (eds) *Irland und die Christenheit: Bibelstudien und Mission/Ireland and Christendom: The Bible and the Missions*, Stuttgart: Klett-Cotta.

McGrath, P.J. (1995) *Believing in God: Reason and Religious Belief*, Dublin: Wolfhound Press.

McGuinness, P., Harrison, A., and Kearney, R. (eds) (1997) *John Toland's Christianity not Mysterious: Text, Associated Works and Critical Essays*, Dublin: Lilliput Press.

MacIntyre, Alasdair (1971) *Against the Self-Images of the Age: Essays on Ideology and Philosophy*, London: Duckworth.

Macintyre, Angus (1965) *The Liberator: Daniel O'Connell and the Irish Party 1830–1847*, London: Macmillan.

McKee, Francis (1988) 'Francis Hutcheson and Bernard Mandeville', *Eighteenth-Century Ireland* 3: 123–32.

MacKenna, Stephen (trans.) (1908) *Plotinus on the Beautiful*, Stratford-upon-Avon: The Shakespeare Head Press.

Mackintosh, R. (1899) *From Comte to Benjamin Kidd*, London: Macmillan & Co.

Macmillan, Gretchen M. (1993) *State, Society and Authority in Ireland*, Dublin: Gill & Macmillan.

McMinn, Joseph (ed.) (1991) *Swift's Irish Pamphlets*, Gerrards Cross: Colin Smythe.

McLoughlin, Thomas (1999) *Contesting Ireland: Irish Voices against England in the Eighteenth Century*, Dublin: Four Courts Press.

MacPherson, C.B. (1980) *Burke*, Oxford: Oxford University Press.

Maguire, Thomas (1866) *An Essay on the Platonic Idea*, London: Longmans, Green, Reader, & Dyer.

—— (1870) *Essays on the Platonic Ethics*, London: Rivingtons.

—— (1889) *Mr. Balfour on Kant and Transcendentalism*, Dublin: Hodges, Figgis, & Co.

Mahon, Joseph (1986) 'The Great Philosopher who Came to Ireland', *Irish Medical Times* 20: 7, 32.

Mahony, Robert (1995) *Jonathan Swift, The Irish Identity*, New Haven: Yale University Press.

Malthus, T.R. (1872) *An Essay on the Principle of Population*, 7th edn, London: John Murray.

Mandeville, Bernard (1970) *The Fable of the Bees*, ed. Philip Harth, Harmondsworth: Penguin.

Marenbon, John (1988) *Early Medieval Philosophy (480–1150)*, London: Routledge.

Meigs, Samantha A. (1997) *The Reformations in Ireland*, Dublin: Gill & Macmillan.

Menger, A. (1899) *The Right to the Whole Produce of Labour*, London: Macmillan & Co.

Mercer, Christian (1993) 'The Vitality and Importance of Early Modern Aristotelianism', in Tom Sorrel (ed.) *The Rise of Modern Philosophy*, Oxford: Clarendon.

Meredith, J.C. (1912) *Kant's Critique of Aesthetic Judgment*, Oxford: Clarendon Press.

Mezciems, Jenny (1995) 'The Unity of Swift's "Voyage to Laputa": Structure as Meaning in Utopian Fiction', in Claude Rawson (ed.) *Jonathan Swift: A Collection of Critical Essays*, Englewood Cliffs, NJ: Prentice Hall.

Micheli, Giuseppe (1993) *The Early Reception of Kant's Thought in England 1785–1805*, London: Routledge/Thoemmes Press.

Mill, John Stuart (1982) *Essays on England, Ireland, and the Empire*, ed. John M. Robson, London: Routledge & Kegan Paul.

Molesworth, Robert (1694) *An Account of Denmark as it was in the year 1692*, London.

Mollan, Charles (1997) 'The Tradition of Irish Chemistry 1660–1922', in J. Philip Ryan (ed.) *The Chemical Association of Ireland 1922–1936*, Dublin: Samton.

Molloy, Gerald (1873) *Geology and Revelation*, 2nd edn, London: Burns, Oates, & Co.

Molyneux, William (1692) *Dioptrica nova*, London.

—— (1698) *The Case of Ireland's being Bound by Acts of Parliament in England, Stated*, Dublin.

—— (1708) *Some Familiar Letters between Mr. Locke and Several of his Friends*, London.

Monck, W.H.S. (1872) *Space and Vision*, Dublin: William McGee.

—— (1874) *An Introduction to the Critical Philosophy*, Dublin: William McGee.

Moody, T.W. (1987) 'Fenianism, home rule, and the Land War (1850–91)', in T.W. Moody and F.X. Martin (eds) (1987) *The Course of Irish History*, Cork: Mercier Press.

Moore, James R. (1979) *The Post-Darwinian Controversies*, Cambridge: Cambridge University Press.

Moore, Michael (1692) *De existentia Dei et humanae mentis immortalitate secundum Cartesii et Aristotelis doctrinam disputatio*, Paris.

—— (1716) *Vera sciendi methodus*, Paris.

Moran, Dermot (1989) *The Philosophy of John Scottus Eriugena*, Cambridge: Cambridge University Press.

More, Louis Trenchard (1944) *The Life and Works of the Honourable Robert Boyle*, Oxford: Oxford University Press.

Morgan, Hiram (ed.) (1999) *Political Ideology in Ireland, 1541–1641*, Dublin: Four Courts Press.

Morgan, M.J. (1977) *Molyneux's Question*, Cambridge: Cambridge University Press.

Moriarty, Christopher (1997) 'The Early Naturalists', in J.W. Foster (ed.) *Nature in Ireland*, Dublin: Lilliput Press.

Moriarty, John (1994) *Dreamtime*, Dublin: Lilliput Press.

—— (1996; 1997; 1998) *Turtle Was Gone a Long Time*, 3 vols, Dublin: Lilliput Press.

Murdoch, Iris (1965) *The Red and the Green*, London: Chatto & Windus.

—— (1966) *The Time of the Angels*, London: Chatto & Windus.

—— (1970) *The Sovereignty of Good*, London: Routledge & Kegan Paul.

—— (1977) *The Fire and the Sun*, London: Penguin.

—— (1992) *Metaphysics as a Guide to Morals*, London: Chatto & Windus.

Murphy, J.J. (1869) *Habit and Intelligence*, London: Macmillan.

—— (1873) *The Scientific Bases of Faith*, London: Macmillan.

—— (1893) *Natural Selection and Spiritual Freedom*, London: Macmillan.

Murphy, John A. (1975) *Ireland in the Twentieth Century*, 2 vols, Dublin: Gill & Macmillan.

Nagel, Thomas (1986) *The View from Nowhere*, Oxford: Oxford University Press.

Nicolson, Marjorie and Mohler, Nora M. (1969) 'The Scientific Background of Swift's "Voyage to Laputa"', in A.N. Jeffares (ed.) *Swift: Modern Judgements*, London: Macmillan.

Nowlan, Kevin B. and O'Connell, Maurice R. (eds) *Daniel O'Connell: Portrait of a Radical*, Belfast: Appletree Press.

Nuttall, A.D. (1995) 'Gulliver Among the Horses', in Claude Rawson (ed.) *Jonathan Swift: A Collection of Critical Essays*, Englewood Cliffs, NJ: Prentice Hall.

O'Brien, Conor Cruise (ed.) (1968) *Edmund Burke: Reflections on the Revolution in France*, Harmondsworth: Pelican.

—— (1992) *The Great Melody*, London: Sinclair-Stevenson.

Ó Buachalla, Brendán (1992) 'Irish Jacobite Poetry', *Irish Review* 12: 40–9.

—— (1996) *Aisling Ghéar: Na Stíobhartaigh agus an tAos Léinn 1603–1788*, Dublin: An Clóchomhar Tta.

Ó Ceallaigh, Daltún (ed.) (1998) *New Perspectives on Ireland: Colonialism and Identity*, Dublin: Léirmheas.

O'Connell, Daniel (1980) *The Correspondence of Daniel O'Connell*, ed. Maurice R. O'Connell, vol. VIII, Dublin: Blackwater.

O'Connor, Arthur (1998) *The State of Ireland*, ed. James Livesey, Dublin: Lilliput Press.

O'Connor, Thomas (ed.) (2001) *The Irish in Europe 1580–1815*, Dublin: Four Courts Press.

Ó Cróinín, Dáibhí (1995) *Early Medieval Ireland 400–1200*, London: Longmans.

O'Donnell, Seán (1983) *William Rowan Hamilton: Portrait of a Prodigy*, Dublin: Boole Press.

O'Donoghue, John (1997) *Anam Chara*, New York: HarperCollins.

O'Dowd, Liam (ed.) (1996) *On Intellectuals and Intellectual Life in Ireland*, Belfast: Institute of Irish Studies.

O'Ferrall, Fergus (1981) *Daniel O'Connell*, Dublin: Gill & Macmillan.

O'Gorman, Frank (1973) *Edmund Burke: His Political Philosophy*, Bloomington: Indiana University Press.

Ó Gráda, Cormac (1983) 'Malthus and the Pre-Famine Economy', *Hermathena* 135: 75–95.

—— (1989) *The Great Irish Famine*, London: Macmillan.

Ohlmeyer, Jane H. (ed.) (2000) *Political Thought in Seventeenth-Century Ireland*, Cambridge: Cambridge University Press.

O'Keeffe, J.A. (1795) *An Essay on the Progress of Human Understanding*, London.

Ó Loinsigh, Pádraig (1977) *The Book of Cloyne/Leabhar Chluain Uamha*, Midleton, Co. Cork, n.p.

O'Meara, J.J. (1954) *The Young Augustine*, London: Longmans, Green & Co.

—— (1988) *Eriugena*, Oxford: Oxford University Press.

O'Meara, J.J. and Bieler, L. (eds) (1973) *The Mind of Eriugena*, Dublin: Royal Irish Academy.

Ó Tuathaigh, Gearóid (1972) *Ireland before the Famine 1797–1848*, London: Gill & Macmillan.

Pankhurst, Richard (1983) Introduction to William Thompson, *Appeal of One Half the Human Race*, London: Virago.

Parkin, C. (1967) *The Moral Basis of Burke's Political Thought*, Oxford: Oxford University Press.

Patey, Douglas Lane (1995) 'Swift's Satire on "Science" and the Structure of *Gulliver's Travels*', in Claude Rawson (ed.) *Jonathan Swift: A Collection of Critical Essays*, Englewood Cliffs, NJ: Prentice Hall.

Paulin, Tom (1998) *The Day-Star of Liberty: William Hazlitt's Radical Style*, London: Faber & Faber.

Paulson, Ronald (1972) *Theme and Structure in Swift's Tale of a Tub*, Hamden, CT: Archon.

Pearse, Padraic H. (Patrick) (1916) *Collected Works: Political Writings and Speeches*, Dublin: Phoenix Publishing.

Pettit, Philip (1993) *The Common Mind: Essays on Psychology, Society, and Politics*, Oxford: Oxford University Press.

—— (1997) *Republicanism: A Theory of Freedom and Government*, Oxford: Oxford University Press.

—— (2001) *A Theory of Freedom: From the Psychology to the Politics of Agency*, Oxford: Polity.

Pilkington, Roger (1959) *Robert Boyle: Father of Chemistry*, London: John Murray.

Pim, Henry Moore (1920) *A Short History of Celtic Philosophy*, Dundalk: Dundalgan Press.

Pitcher, George (1977) *Berkeley*, London: Routledge & Kegan Paul.

Plotinus (1908) *On the Beautiful*, trans. Stephen MacKenna, Stratford-upon-Avon: The Shakespeare Head Press.

Pocock, J.G.A. (1971) *Language, Politics and Time: Essays on Political Thought and History*, New York: Atheneum.

—— (1985) *Virtue, Commerce, and History*, Cambridge: Cambridge University Press.

Pope, Alexander (1963) *The Poems of Alexander Pope*, ed. John Butt, London: Methuen.

Principe, Lawrence M. (1998) *The Aspiring Adept*, Princeton: Princeton University Press.

Probyn, Clive T. (ed.) (1978) *The Art of Jonathan Swift*, London: Vision Press.

Przywara, P. Erich (1935) *Polarity*, London: Oxford University Press.

Pseudo-Dionysius (1987) *The Complete Works*, trans. Colm Luibhéid, New York: Paulist Press.

Putnam, Hilary (1981) *Reason, Truth and History*, Cambridge: Cambridge University Press.

Quintana, Ricardo (1955) *Swift: An Introduction*, Oxford: Oxford University Press.

—— (1965) *The Mind and Art of Jonathan Swift*, Oxford: Oxford University Press.

Raftery, Deirdre (1995) 'Frances Power Cobbe', in Mary Cullen and Maria Luddy (eds) *Women, Power and Consciousness*, Dublin: Attic Press.

Rankin, David (1996) *The Celts and the Classical World*, London: Routledge.

Rawson, C.J. (ed.) (1971) *Focus: Swift*, London: Sphere.

—— (1973) *Gulliver and the Gentle Reader*, London: Routledge.

—— (ed.) (1995) *Jonathan Swift: A Collection of Critical Essays*, Englewood Cliffs, NJ: Prentice Hall.

Redwood, John (1976) *Reason, Ridicule and Religion: The Age of Enlightenment in England 1660–1750*, London: Thames & Hudson.

Rees, B.R. (1988) *Pelagius: A Reluctant Heretic*, Woodbridge: The Boydell Press.

Reeves, W. (1861) 'On Augustin, an Irish Writer of the Seventh Century', *Proceedings of the Royal Irish Academy* 7: 516–19.

Reilly, S.M. Paraclita (1956) *Aubrey de Vere, Victorian Observer*, Dublin: Clonmore & Reynolds.

Richter, Michael (1988) *Medieval Ireland: The Enduring Tradition*, New York: St. Martin's Press.

—— (1995) *Studies in Medieval Language and Culture*, Dublin: Four Courts Press.

Robbins, Caroline (1968) *The Eighteenth-Century Commonwealthman*, New York: Atheneum.

Robertson, J.M. (1899) *A Short History of Freethought, Ancient and Modern*, London: Swan Sonnenschein & Co.

Rorty, Richard (1980) *Philosophy and the Mirror of Nature*, Oxford: Blackwell.

—— (1989) *Contingency, Irony, and Solidarity*, Cambridge: Cambridge University Press.

Ross, Angus (1978) 'The Hibernian Patriot's Apprenticeship', in Clive T. Probyn (ed.) *The Art of Jonathan Swift*, London: Vision Press.

Said, Edward W. (1991) *The World, the Text and the Critic*, London: Vintage.

—— (1993) *Culture and Imperialism*, London: Chatto & Windus.

Sargent, Rose-Mary (1995) *The Diffident Naturalist: Robert Boyle and the Philosophy of Experiment*, Chicago: University of Chicago Press.

Schwartz, Robert (1994) *Vision*, Oxford: Blackwell.

Scott, W.R. (1900) *Francis Hutcheson: His Life, Teaching and Position in the History of Philosophy*, Cambridge: Cambridge University Press.

Shaftesbury, Anthony Ashley Cooper, third earl of (1900) *Characteristics of Men, Manners, Opinions, Times, etc.*, 2 vols, ed. J.M. Robertson, Gloucester, MA: Peter Smith.

Shaw, George Bernard (1928) *The Intelligent Woman's Guide to Socialism and Capitalism*, London: Constable.

—— (1932) *Essays in Fabianism*, London: Constable.

—— (1944) *Everybody's Political What's What*, New York: Dodd, Mead & Co.

Sheldon-Williams, I.P. (1960) 'A Bibliography of the Works of Johannes Scottus Eriugena', *Journal of Ecclesiastical History* 10, 2: 198–224.

Simms, J.G. (1982) *William Molyneux of Dublin*, Dublin: Irish Academic Press.

342

Skelton, Philip (1749) *Ophiomaches: or Deism Revealed*, 2 vols, London.

Smyth, Marina (1996) *Understanding the Universe in Seventh-Century Ireland*, Woodbridge: Boydell Press.

Snukal, Robert (1973) *High Talk: The Philosophical Poetry of W.B. Yeats*, Cambridge: Cambridge University Press.

Speck, W.A. (1969) *Swift*, London: Evans Brothers.

Spenser, Edmund (1997) *A View of the State of Ireland*, ed. Andrew Hadfield and Willy Maley, Oxford: Blackwell.

Stanford, W.B. (1976) *Ireland and the Classical Tradition*, Dublin: Irish Academic Press.

Stanihurst, Richard (1979) 'A Treatise contayning a Playne and Perfect Description of Ireland', in Liam Miller and Eileen Power (eds) *Holinshed's Irish Chronicle*, Dublin: Dolmen Press.

—— (1981) 'On Ireland's Past: De Rebus in Hibernia Gestis', in Colm Lennon, *Richard Stanihurst, the Dubliner*, Dublin: Irish Academic Press.

Stanlis, Peter J. (1958) *Edmund Burke and the Natural Law*, Ann Arbor: University of Michigan Press.

Starkman, Miriam K. (1950) *Swift's Satire on Learning in A Tale of a Tub*, Princeton: Princeton University Press.

Stephen, Leslie (1962) *History of English Thought in the Eighteenth Century*, 2 vols, New York: Harcourt, Brace & World.

Stewart, A.T.Q. (1998) *A Deeper Silence: The Hidden Origins of the United Irishmen*, Belfast: Blackstaff Press.

Stewart, M.A. (ed.) (1991) *Selected Philosophical Papers of Robert Boyle*, Indianapolis: Hackett.

Stock, A.G. (1964) *W.B. Yeats: His Poetry and Thought*, Cambridge: Cambridge University Press.

Stokes, George Gabriel (1891; 1893) *Natural Theology: The Gifford Lectures*, 2 vols, London and Edinburgh: Adam & Charles Black.

Sullivan, Robert E. (1982) *John Toland and the Deist Controversy*, Cambridge, MA: Harvard University Press.

—— (1998) 'John Toland's Druids: A Mythopoeia of Celtic Identity', *Bullán: A Journal of Irish Studies* IV: 19–41.

Swift, Jonathan (1908) *The Battle of the Books, with Selections from the Literature of the Phalaris Controversy*, ed. A. Guthkelch, London: Chatto & Windus.

—— (1935) *The Drapier's Letters to the People of Ireland*, ed. Herbert Davis, Oxford: Clarendon Press.

—— (1948) *Irish Tracts and Sermons 1720–1723,* ed. Herbert Davis, Oxford: Basil Blackwell.

—— (1957) *Bickerstaff Papers and Pamphlets on the Church*, ed. Herbert Davis, Oxford: Basil Blackwell.

—— (1958) *A Tale of a Tub, to which is added the Battle of the Books and the Mechanical Operation of the Spirit*, ed. A.C. Guthkelch and D. Nichol Smith, 2nd edn, Oxford: Clarendon Press.

—— (1963) *The Correspondence of Jonathan Swift*, vol. III, ed. Harold Williams, Oxford: Clarendon Press.

—— (1963–72) *The Correspondence of Jonathan Swift*, 5 vols, ed. Harold Williams, Oxford: Clarendon.

—— (1995) *Gulliver's Travels*, ed. Christopher Fox, New York: St. Martin's Press.

Synge, Edward (1737a) *Free Thinking in Matters of Religion Stated and Recommended*, 2nd edn, London.

—— (1737b) *A Plain and Easy Method whereby a Man of Moderate Capacity may arrive at Full Satisfaction in All Things that Concern his Everlasting Salvation*, 2nd edn, London.

—— (1742) *Religion Tryed by the Test of Sober and Impartial Reason*, 2nd edn, London.

—— (1752) *A Gentleman's Religion*, 7th edn, London.

Temple, William (1705) 'An Essay upon the Ancient and Modern Learning', in *Miscellanea* II, 5th edn, London.

Thompson, D'Arcy Wentworth (1945) '*Sesquivolus*, a squirrel: and the *Liber de Mirabilibus S. Scripturae*', *Hermathena* 45: 1–7.

Thompson, William (1824) *An Inquiry into the Principles of the Distribution of Wealth*, London: Longman, Hurst Rees, Orme, Brown & Green.

—— (1827) *Labor Rewarded*, London.

—— (with Anna Doyle Wheeler) (1997) *An Appeal of One Half the Human Race, Women, against the Pretensions of the Other Half, Men*, ed. Dolores Dooley, Cork: Cork University Press.

Tinkler, John F. (1995) 'The Splitting of Humanism: Bentley, Swift, and the English Battle of the Books', in Claude Rawson (ed.) *Jonathan Swift: A Collection of Critical Essays*, Englewood Cliffs, NJ: Prentice Hall.

Tippett, Brian (1989) *Gulliver's Travels*, London: Macmillan.

Tipton, Ian C. (1974) *Berkeley: The Philosophy of Immaterialism*, London: Methuen.

Toland, John (1696) *Christianity not Mysterious*, 2nd edn, London.

—— (1701) *Anglia libera*, London.

—— (1702) *Vindicius liberius: Or, M. Toland's Defence of Himself*, London.

—— (1704) *Letters to Serena*, London.

—— (1718) *Nazarenus; or, Jewish, Gentile, and Mahometan Christianity*, London.

—— (1720) *Tetradymus*, London.

—— (1751) *Pantheisticon*, London.

—— (1997) *Vindicius Liberius*, in P. McGuinness, A. Harrison, and R. Kearney (eds) *John Toland's Christianity not Mysterious: Text, Associated Works and Critical Essays*, Dublin: Lilliput Press.

—— (1997) *John Toland's Christianity not Mysterious: Text, Associated Works and Critical Essays*, ed. P. McGuinness, A. Harrison and R. Kearney, Dublin: Lilliput Press.

—— (1999) *Nazerenus*, ed. Justin Champion, Oxford: Voltaire Foundation.

Tone, Theobald Wolfe (1998) 'An Argument on Behalf of the Catholics of Ireland', in Thomas Barlett (ed.) *Life of Theobald Wolfe Tone*, Dublin: Lilliput Press.

Torchiana, Donald T. (1966) *W.B. Yeats and Georgian Ireland*, Oxford: Oxford University Press.

Trevor-Roper, Hugh (1989) *Catholics, Anglicans and Puritans*, London: Fontana.

Tucker, Bernard (1983) *Jonathan Swift*, Dublin: Gill & Macmillan.

Tyndall, John (1865) *Heat considered as a Mode of Motion*, 2nd edn, London: Longman, Green, Longman, Roberts & Green.

—— (1872) *The Forms of Water*, New York: D. Appleton & Co.

—— (1874) *Address delivered before the British Association at Belfast*, London: Longman, Green, & Co.

—— (1875) *Sound*, 3rd edn, New York: A.L. Fowle.

—— (1895) *Essays on the Floating-Matter of the Air*, New York: D. Appleton & Co.

—— (1902) *Fragments of Science*, 2 vols, 6th edn, New York: Collier & Son.

Usher, James (1766) A *Free Examination of the Common Methods employed to prevent the Growth of Popery*, London.

—— (1771) *An Introduction to the Theory of the Human Mind*, London.

—— (1803) *Clio; or a Discourse on Taste*, ed. J. Mathew, London.

Ussher, James (1631) 'A Discourse of the Religion anciently professed by the Irish and British', in *The Whole Works of the Rev. James Ussher*, vol. IV, Dublin.

Vance, Norman (1999) *Irish Literature: A Social History*, Dublin: Four Courts Press.

Walsh, Katherine (1981) A *Fourteenth-Century Scholar and Primate: Richard Fitzralph in Oxford, Avignon and Armagh*, Oxford: Clarendon Press.

Warnock, G.J. (1953) *Berkeley*, London: Pelican.

Watts, Robert (1888) *The Reign of Causality*, Edinburgh: T. & T. Clark.

Webb, Thomas E. (1857) *The Intellectualism of Locke*, Dublin: William McGee & Co.

—— (1885) *The Veil of Isis*, Dublin: Hodges, Figgis, & Co.

Webster, Charles (1975) *The Great Instauration: Science, Medicine and Reform 1626–1660*, London: Duckworth.

Wedel, T.O. (1974) 'On the Philosophical Background of *Gulliver's Travels*', in Richard Gravil (ed.) *Swift: Gulliver's Travels*, London: Macmillan.

Wellek, René (1931) *Immanuel Kant in England 1793–1838*, Princeton: Princeton University Press.

Westfall, R.S. (1973) *Science and Religion in Seventeenth-Century England*, Ann Arbor: University of Michigan Press.

Wheeler, Anna Doyle (1830) 'Rights of Women', *British Co-operator*, April: 12–15.

—— (1830) 'Rights of Women', pt 2, *British Co-operator*, May: 33–6.

—— (1976) 'Letter from a Pioneer Feminist' (transcript of letter dated 15 November 1832, ed. Stephen Burke), *Studies in Labour History*, 1: 20–2.

—— (with William Thompson) (1997) *An Appeal of One Half the Human Race, Women, against the Pretensions of the Other Half, Men*, ed. Dolores Dooley, Cork: Cork University Press.

Whelan, Kevin (1996) *The Tree of Liberty*, Cork: Cork University Press.

Whyte, Nicholas (1999) *Science, Colonialism and Ireland*, Cork: Cork University Press.

Wilde, Oscar (1994) *Complete Works of Oscar Wilde*, ed. Merlin Holland, Glasgow: HarperCollins.

Wilkins, B.T. (1967) *The Problem of Burke's Political Philosophy*, Oxford: Clarendon Press.

Willey, Basil (1934) *The Seventeenth-Century Background*, London: Chatto & Windus.

—— (1940) *The Eighteenth-Century Background*, London: Chatto & Windus.

—— (1949) *Nineteenth-Century Studies: Coleridge to Matthew Arnold*, London: Chatto & Windus.

Williams, Kathleen (1967) *Jonathan Swift and the Age of Compromise*, Lawrence: University of Kansas Press.

Winnett, A.R. (1974) *Peter Browne: Provost, Bishop and Metaphysician*, London: SPCK.

Wisdom, J.O. (1946) *Causation and the Foundations of Science*, Paris: Hermann.

—— (1947) *The Metamorphosis of Philosophy*, Cairo: Al-Maaref Press.

—— (1952) *Foundations of Inference in Natural Science*, London: Methuen.

—— (1953) *The Unconscious Origin of Berkeley's Philosophy*, London: Hogarth Press.

—— (1975) *Philosophy and Its Place in Our Culture*, London: Gordon & Breach.

—— (1992) *Freud, Women, and Society*, New Brunswick: Transaction Publishers.

Wohlman, Avital (1998) Introduction to John Scottus Eriugena, *Treatise on Divine Predestination*, trans. Mary Brennan, Notre Dame: University of Notre Dame Press.

Wojcik, Jan W. (1997) *Robert Boyle and the Limits of Reason*, Cambridge: Cambridge University Press.

Wotton, William (1705) *Reflections upon Ancient and Modern Learning*, 3rd edn, London.

Wright, David G. (1988) *Yeats's Myth of Self*, Dublin: Gill & Macmillan.

Yeats, W.B. (1937) *A Vision*, London: Macmillan.

—— (1955) *Autobiographies*, London: Macmillan.

—— (1968) *Essays and Introductions*, New York: Collier.

—— (1972) *Memoirs*, ed. Denis Donoghue, Dublin: Gill & Macmillan.

—— (1994) *The Poems*, ed. D. Albright, London: J.M. Dent.

Yeomans, W.E. (1969) 'The Houyhnhnm as Menippean Horse', in A.N. Jeffares (ed.) *Swift: Modern Judgements*, London: Macmillan.

Yolton, John (1956) *John Locke and the Way of Ideas*, Oxford: Oxford University Press.

Young, B.W. (1998) *Religion and Enlightenment in Eighteenth-Century England: Theological Debate from Locke to Burke*, Oxford: Clarendon Press.

Zimmerman, Everett (1983) *Swift's Narrative Satires*, Ithaca and London: Cornell University Press.

INDEX